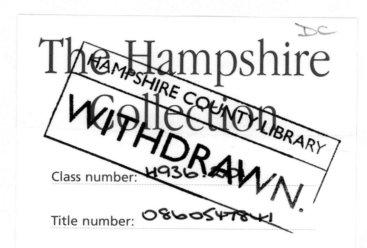

Ritual and Rubbish in the Iron Age of Wessex

A study on the formation of a specific archaeological record

J. D. Hill

TEMPVS REPARATVM

BAR British Series 242
1995

B.A.R.

All titles available from:
Hadrian Books Ltd, 122 Banbury Road, Oxford OX2 7BP, England

The current BAR catalogue, with details of all titles in print, post-free prices and means of payment, is available free from the above address.

All volumes are distributed by Hadrian Books Ltd.

BAR 242

Ritual and Rubbish in the Iron Age of Wessex: A study in the formation of a specific archaeological record

© J D Hill 1995

ISBN 0 86054 784 1

Tempvs Reparatvm Volume Editor: David P Davison

British Archaeological Reports are published by

TEMPVS REPARATVM
Archaeological and Historical Associates Limited

All enquiries regarding the submission of manuscripts for future publication should be addressed to:

David P Davison MA MPhil DPhil
General Editor BAR
Tempvs Reparatvm
29 Beaumont Street
Oxford OX1 2NP

Tel: 01865 311046
Fax: 01865 311047

Preface and Acknowledgements

"It is only a thesis" is a phrase that has been constantly said to me and by me over the last too many years. It is a phrase that can be used to mean a wide range of apparently contradictory things. This book is essentially only a thesis. Somewhat revised and, especially, made readable, but this book is basically the PhD thesis I submitted in 1994. As such, it suffers from many of the restrictions this form of writing necessarily brings with it. In particular, it is probably too narrowly focused. Cambridge University also has a strict 80,000 word limit, which means this study has too be extremely lean, and, at times, part of the argument may not be as fully presented as I would have liked. The first draft of the thesis was 120,000 words long. Even with cleaning up my English and hacking out most of the conditional phrases and sentences, still quite large chunks of the argument that were not totally necessary had to go. The great temptation in revising the thesis for publication was to simply put all these cuts back in, but I have resisted this. The main changes I have made compared to the thesis are as follows;

- The introduction has been lengthen to contain a broader background to the archaeology of Iron Age Wessex.
- Appendix 1 in this book is new, and hopes to fill a gap noted by my examiners.
- Parts of chapter 7 has been cut or changed.
- Appendix of the original thesis has gone and its contents put into chapter 9 where they originally belonged. They were only originally removed to make the main text fit into 80,000 words.
- Chapter 10 has been substantially revised and lengthen to clarify the basic argument. This was largely a result of presenting the contents as at recent meeting of the Osteoarchaeoloical Research Group in Cambridge.
- Chapter 12 has had a large section on the history of ritual practices in Wessex through the first millennium BC put back in and revised. This was not contained in the thesis.
- Chapter 13 has been revised and re-worded in places.

The figures for each chapter can be found at the end of that chapter, the tables are all put at the back of the volume, after the bibliography.

The biggest change has been to revise the English and spelling through the thesis. As a dyslexic, I hate writing and do not do it very well. My examiners may have thought the English in the submitted thesis was bad, but they did not see the original versions. This were only magically transformed into something submittable by the Herculean efforts of Lesley McFadyen- the best editor in the world. The text has been revised again in preparation of this book. I have revised all the chapters as best as I can, but Sue Thomas kindly went through chapters 1, 10, 11, 12 and 13.

The study would not have been possible but for access to unpublished site archives kindly allowed to me by David Allen (Hampshire County Museum Service), Mary Walkden (English Heritage), Frank Green (Test Valley Archaeological Trust), Sue Davies (Trust for Wessex Archaeology), and Elaine Morris (formerly of Trust for Wessex Archaeology) and, especially, Mark Maltby (Bournemouth University).

This study has grown through a mix of both private research, long discussions in pubs, outside TAG sessions etc. and through many presentations of the work in research seminars, conference papers, course lectures and written drafts etc. Very many people have been involved in this process, and I can only personally thank a few here.
Richard Bradley (Reading University), John Barrett (Glasgow University), Mark Bowden (RCHM(E)), Brian Boyd (Cambridge University), Andrea Bullock (Faunal Remains Unit, Southampton University), John Collis (Sheffield University), Chris Cumberpatch (formerly of Sheffield University), Mark Edmonds (Sheffield University), Chris Evans (Cambridge Archaeological Unit), Gill Ferrell (Durham County Council), Andrew Fitzpatrick (Trust for Wessex Archaeology), Annie Grant (Leicester University), Sam Lucy (Cambridge University), James McGlade (Cranfield), Dave McOmish (RCHM(E)), Mark Maltby (Bournemouth University), Simon Mays (AML- English Heritage), Martin Millett (Durham University), Koji Mizoguchi (Cambridge University), Elaine Morris (Trust for Wessex Archaeology), Al Oswald (RCHM(E)), Dale Serjeantson (Faunal Remains Unit, Southampton University), Marie-Louise Stig Sørensen (Cambridge University), Julian Thomas (Southampton University), Sander Van Der Leeuw (Cambridge University), Todd Whitelaw (Cambridge University), Bob Wilson (Abingdon), Ann Woodward (Birmingham University) and Peter Woodward (Dorset County Museum). Ian Hodder and Colin Haselgrove examined the thesis, and provided many useful comments and suggested changes.

Colin Haselgrove (Durham University), Richard Hingley (Historic Scotland), and Niall Sharples (Historic Scotland) has always been very generous with their time to comment and discuss all things pits and Iron Age.

In particular the inspiration (and Madagascan slide shows) of Mike Parker-Pearson (Sheffield University) must be acknowledged. Originally, I intended to 'Parker-Pearson' (cf.1984) Wessex, but the thesis turned out to prove that his forthcoming ideas on Later Prehistoric Settlements are basically right.

The research for the thesis was originally funded through a British Academy State studentship, but if were not for the assistance of the Department of Social Security, and then St Edmunds' College, Cambridge, this study would have never been completed.

My long suffering supervisor, Sander Van Der Leeuw, must also get the deep thanks he deserved for putting up with a rather trying research student. As must my partner, Wendy, who suffered even more than Sander during the research anf writing of this study.

Contents

RITUAL AND RUBBISH IN THE IRON AGE OF WESSEX:

A Study on the Formation of a Specific Archaeological Record

Chapter 1
Ritual and Rubbish in the Iron Age of Wessex: An Introduction

Pits are almost obligatory on Pre-Roman Iron Age (c.700 BC to c.AD 43) settlements excavated in southern England. They have provided an important focus for fundamental changing interpretations of the period since the beginnings of Iron Age excavations (see Cunliffe 1992, but esp. Evans 1989). Often up to several metres in depth and width, it is widely accepted that most were originally used as silos, as cereal storage pits. The subsequent fills of soil and chalk in these pits and the other features cut into the solid geology, 'natural', such as enclosure ditches, provide the major source for the finds recovered from these sites. These pot sherds, animal bones, carbonised plant remains, tools and other objects are the basic building blocks for understanding the economy, society and culture of the people living in southern England in the centuries before the Roman conquest.

What I want to do in this study is ask some detailed questions about how these basic building blocks actually got into the pits and ditches they were found in. Was this material *just* garbage casually thrown into conveniently empty pits or open ditches? Should we imagine, as is often implied, the Iron Age housewife (*sic*) using a disused storage pit as a convenient dustbin, or her husband (*sic*) needing to dispose quickly of the noxious remnants of butchering one of their herd by disposing it in the ditch surrounding their farmstead? Or should we imagine very different events leading up to and actually creating these deposits involving people who lived in worlds and households very different from our own? If the latter, how does that affect how we understand and analyse the finds, those basic building blocks, produced from settlement excavations, let alone the economy, society and culture of those Iron Age people we want to study?

The immediate origins of this thesis lie in a re-consideration of Iron Age social organisation and, particularly, the interpretation of hillforts. Iron Age hillforts have dominated our understandings of the period, and Professor Barry Cunliffe's key excavations at Danebury, Hampshire, have established the agenda for Iron Age studies in general. The need to develop a fuller understanding of the nature and origins of the archaeological record for the Wessex Iron Age became very apparent while testing one of Professor Cunliffe's interpretations of Danebury and other hillforts (Cunliffe 1984a& b). It was argued that Danebury was significantly different from other settlements, a claim I and others have assessed in a number of key areas by comparing data from hillforts and non-hillfort settlements (Hill 1988, 1995, forthcoming a; Marchant 1998; Morris 1994a&b; Stopford 1987).

In proposing this interpretation and in my own reassessment, Professor Cunliffe and I both used the archaeological record in similar ways. We both assumed that the range and quantities of finds more or less directly reflected the nature of the societies which produced or discarded them. As such, I assumed that the nature and scale of craft production and exchange activities in Iron Age Wessex were directly reflected in the quantities and relative proportions of finds excavated on Iron Age settlements. The broken objects and discarded waste from domestic, agrarian and craft activities were simply assumed to have been discarded, thrown away, into the pits and ditches from which they were eventually excavated. Such an assumption was supported by the very large assemblages of finds recovered from typical Iron Age settlement excavations. The many kilograms of pottery and thousands of animal bone fragments provide a statistical sense of security to inferences made from this data.

However, it soon became clear that you could not simply read off the social and economic organisation of past societies from an archaeological record, especially when the assumptions behind that reading saw the material evidence to be rubbish (Hill 1988:30-35).

The security of making straightforward interpretations of this evidence was questioned in two ways:

1.   That so little material is actually preserved.

2.   That much of this material comes from possible ritual, 'special', contexts.

1. Firstly, despite the very large quantities of finds of all kinds recovered from Later Prehistoric settlements, simple calculations suggest how much more has failed to be preserved. To demonstrate just how *small* the large quantities of data excavated from sites really are simply divide the number of finds deposited, or the number of pits on a site -- which are the main receptacles for finds on Wessex Iron Age sites -- by the probable length of time the site was in occupation.

For example, at Early Iron Age Winnall Down, an enclosed settlement near Winchester, there was only one pit filled for every seven to ten years, and only one *rim sherd* lost for every nine to twelve months of the site's assumed two centuries of occupation (Table 1.1.). Of course, Winnall may have only been occupied for comparatively short periods in the Early Iron Age, but even so very little material entered archaeologically recoverable features (Hill 1988:32-4). Given that an Iron Age pot weighed on average c.1kg, the 25.8kgs of Early Iron Age pottery from this site can be put in perspective. Even at Danebury, with its vast numbers of pits to trap finds, these calculations still show how small a sample our large assemblages of materials actually represent. Basic calculations suggest that about 4.5 pits per hectare per year were infilled in the Early Iron Age (cp1-5), and only 1 pit per hectare per year in the Middle Iron Age (cp6-8) (Table 1.1). Similar calculations suggest the 'loss' of only one loom weight or comb every two years, and approximately 100 identifiable bone fragments a year from a site with an assumed population of between 250-500 (Hill 1988:27, 32-34).

An alternative approach to demonstrate the smallness of these large databases is to 'guesstimate' the possible original quantities of broken pottery or animal bones that may have been discarded on a settlement. Using ethnoarchaeological studies, data for the maximum and minimum quantities of material possibly discarded by a household in a year or century can be worked out (See Appendix 2). This is not to infer any cross-cultural generalisation about ceramic discard rates etc. Rather, such figures provide some crude idea of what we are *probably* missing.

Using data summarised by Mills (1989), these games suggest the *mean* figures for a single household's pottery breakage and discard would be between 2.7 to 4.1 pots a year. That is 270 to 410 pots a century, each weighing an average of 1kg+ - 270-410kg+ of pottery a century compared to a total of 25.8kg from Early Iron Age Winnall Down (see Appendix 2). The *maximum* figures would be for 22 vessels a year (or 2200 a century). Similar calculations with similar results can be obtain for animal bones and other finds.

However, one exception to this pattern of extreme under-representation may be quern stones. It is possible that a very high proportion of all the querns used on a settlement are represented in fragments recovered during an excavation (see Appendix 2).

This realisation forces us to ask the question; *just how representative are these assemblages?* Do the proportions of different animal species really reflect the actual proportions and number consumed in the past? Does a high percentage of pottery from that site in a clearly non-local fabric actually reflect the real situation in which households depended on exchange to acquire pots in the past. Or is the recovered ceramic assemblage a product of chance and accident - or design - but not a good reflection of past activities or scale of exchange? Only animal bone studies have seriously addressed these issues (e.g. Maltby 1985a - see 3.7).

2. Secondly, other evidence suggested that the context of at least some of this small quantity of material was not incorporated into archaeological deposits by chance, or through the casual, daily, throwing out of the garbage. Human remains, ranging from mere fragments to complete corpses, and a series of possible ritual deposits of animal bone (see 2.2) have been found in approximately 25-33% of all pits, and also ditches and post-holes etc. on Wessex Iron Age sites. The interpretation and recognition of these deposits was and remains controversial, revealing the deeply-held assumptions that structure our interpretations of the past. I will briefly outline these controversies in chapter 2, and add considerable oil to the fire throughout this book.

While most human remains are interpreted as ritual deposits, many archaeologists have not extended this interpretation to 'special animal deposits'. Even when this was the case, both human and animal special deposits were often assumed to have been buried along with domestic rubbish, although there were hints that the rubbish with such odd deposits was different from the rubbish in other features (e.g. Grant 1984a:540). Attention was first drawn to the human deposits in the late 1970's by Whimster (1981) and C. Wilson (1981). Yet it has been essentially through the excavations at Danebury by Barry Cunliffe and his team that these 'special' deposits have continued to be the centre of debate (e.g. Cunliffe 1983, 1984, 1991, 1992; Grant 1984a; Walker 1984; Wait 1985 etc.). It is expected that the final Danebury volume (vol. 6) will considerably add to this discussion.

This study must be seen as inspired by and as a contribution to this debate. Initially, the research leading to this thesis intended to develop a new interpretation of Wessex Iron Age societies. However, such a social archaeology (then to be of a structural Marxist nature- c.f. Parker-Pearson 1984) clearly was hindered by the archaeological record which could not be securely or simply 'read'. Inspired by the taphonomic studies of animal bones by Mark Maltby and others (see 3.7), a detailed understanding of how all of that archaeological record was formed was required if I was to return to my initial goals. Was this material representative? Were special animal deposits the result of sacrifice? Were some humans social outcasts buried in domestic rubbish? Were the dumps of pot sherds, small finds, and animal bones the convenient disposal of the garbage created during the routine activities of farm and home, or material deposited with some deliberation as part of very occasional religious ceremonies? Was this rubbish or ritual?

	Probable Duration of Phase (years)	Total Number of Pits*	Probable Number of Pits filled per Year	Pits filled per Hectare per Year
DANEBURY	450	5000	11.1	2.1
GUSSAGE	650	381	0.6	
WINNALL	500	110	0.2	
Danebury cp1-3	100	2800	28.4	5.4
Danebury cp4-5	50	760	7.6	1.4
Danebury cp 6	100	540	5.4	1.0
Danebury cp7-8	200	850	4.2	0.8
Gussage EIA	200	128	0.6	
Gussage MIA	300	69	0.2	
Gussage LIA	150	184	1.2	
Winnall Down EIA	200	27	0.1	
Winnall Down MIA	300	80	0.3	

*Estimated total number of pits at Danebury
Both the Gussage and Winnall Down enclosures were approximately 1 hectare in area

The number of pits at Danebury, Gussage All Saints and Winnall Down divided by the probable length of occupation at these site, showing the small numbers of pits open at any one time to receive material (after Hill 1988)

1.2 Archaeological Formation Processes

These questions are essentially reducible to:

'How was the archaeological record formed'.

Unless we understand how the small quantities of material we recover came to be incorporated in archaeologically recoverable contexts and their possible subsequent transformation, how can we reliably understand the ways in which past societies were constituted through the activities which created, used and deposited those materials (Schiffer 1983:675; cf. Barrett 1991b:743)? However, many archaeologists still treat the archaeological record as an essentially direct record of past systems, as is exemplified in the widespread assumption that the spatial patterning of archaeological artefacts reflects the spatial patterning of past activities, an assumption which Schiffer (1972:156) and others have shown to be flawed. These assumptions may be more prevalent in British archaeology where, unlike North America, there have not been the debates concerning ethnoarchaeology and Middle Range Theory which placed formation processes as "the archaeological agenda for the 1980's" (Moore & Keene 1983:17).

The most comprehensive studies of formation processes have been by Schiffer (1972, 1976, 1983, 1987) who sought to create "a base of explicit, logically related credible laws about the formation processes of the archaeological record" (Schiffer 1972:163). This 'Behavioural Archaeology' considers the archaeological record as a "distorted reflection of a past behavioural system" (Schiffer 1976:12). By accounting for the effects of natural and cultural formation processes, distortions can be eliminated to reveal the past behavioural system. C-transforms predict what material would (or would not) be deposited by a social system, and therefore represent a set of relationships by which the nature of that system could be inferred. Most C-transforms are considered to be one type of *Refuse*; "the post-discard condition of an element, the condition no longer participating in a behavioural system" (Schiffer 1972:159). As the majority of material excavated on sites will be *Secondary Refuse* (see below) so there will be little correspondence between where the materials were made or used, and where they were ultimately discarded (Schiffer 1972:162; Murray 1980:490). This seriously questions the dominant concern with recognising *activity areas* in ethnoarchaeological and archaeological studies (e.g. papers in Kramer 1979; Kent 1987)

Ethnoarchaeological studies amongst sedentary, agrarian, societies has been little concerned with studying formation processes. The few studies of discard on sedentary sites are concerned with *Refuse Maintenance Strategies*, but not primarily with how the material entered the archaeological record (e.g. Arnold 1990; Deal 1985; Hayden & Cannon 1983). They consider the complex stages through

3

Schiffer's Basic Definitions
of Formation Processes and Refuse Types

Types of Formation Processes

Cultural Formation Processes
('C-Transforms') where the agency of transformation was human behaviour.

Natural Formation Processes
('N-Transforms') in which agencies stemmed from the processes of the natural environment.

Types of Refuse

Primary Refuse -
material discarded at its location of use.

Secondary Refuse -
material whose final location of discard was not the same as the location of use.

De Facto Refuse -
material not formally discarded, and so not *refuse* as such, but left at the place of use on site abandonment.

which material passed before its final destruction or deposition, stressing how much material was intentionally *Provisionally Discarded* for future disposal or re-use. One important conclusion can be drawn from these studies. Sedentary archaeological sites probably contain little primary refuse, indeed little refuse of any kind, as the vast majority was removed and destroyed, often by burning. A tiny proportion of almost all the types of material used on sites ends up scattered around the compound and so *may* become incorporated in archaeological deposits. However, there can be no security in using quantitative measures of relative abundance or proportions of objects (Hayden & Cannon 1983:159). *We should expect to find almost nothing excavating a rural settlement.* All finds should therefore be treated as 'special', since for some reason they have escaped the normal processes of dispersal and destruction. We should immediately ask how and why?

Answering these questions can never simply be a direct account of how materials were discarded and subsequently transformed by natural processes. Refuse is not a universal functional category (Hodder 1982a:24). Everything that has been discarded is not rubbish (Moore 1982:75; Welbourne 1984:22) and refuse must not be seen as a homogeneous category (Moore 1982, 1986) since it was structured according to cultural classifications and not simply according to what we consider to be artefact attributes (Bulmer 1976). Refuse is linked to culturally specific and highly charged notions of dirt and pollution (Douglas 1966; Hodder 1982a:155ff, 1982c:67; Moore 1982:76; Panoff 1970), so that the definition and disposal of refuse is structured by (and structures) a range of other relationships through which a society is daily reconstituted (e.g. Bulmer 1976; Moore 1986, Hodder 1982, 1987b). One result is that the deposition of rubbish can often be highly patterned, but it is important to recognise that such explicit symbolic behaviour is not ritual behaviour. Discovering significant degrees of structure and symbolism in archaeological deposits is not a secure basis for their

interpretation as ritual deposits (Richards & Thomas 1984:215; Barrett 1988:31; see 10.3), even if they include bits of humanity. To understand why, and the ways in which, certain materials were disposed of involves an understanding of the specific cultural context in which the activity took place. This cannot avoid spilling over to consider other questions: "If discard is to be understood within its own context, it becomes extremely difficult to write...about discard alone" (Hodder 1987b:424-5).

1.3. Rethinking the Iron Age.

It is important to see this study as part of a wider project of inter-meshed studies intent on re-thinking the Iron Age. In a real sense this research took place at the right time and should be set in a general sea-change within British Iron Age studies evident in recent meetings (e.g. New Approaches to the British Iron Age - Cambridge 1989, Edinburgh 1992 & Durham 1994) and publications (e.g. Barrett 1989; Bowden & McOmish 1987, 1989; Ferrell 1994; Foster 1989a&b; Fitzpatrick 1984, 1994a; Hill 1989, 1993, 1994a& 1995; Hingley 1984, 1990c, 1994; Parker-Pearson forthcoming; Sharples 1987; 1991a&c; Stopford 1987 etc.).

At the heart of my and other attempts to rethink the Iron Age, has been the desire to seize the possibility of a different Iron Age (Hill 1989). There is a major watershed in British Prehistory between the Neolithic and Early Bronze Age (an archaeological record dominated by communal and mortuary monuments), and the Later Bronze Age and Iron Age (an archaeology dominated by settlements), an apparent contrast between records dominated by ritual and domesticity, sacred and profane (Bradley 1991; Barrett 1989b; Barrett et al 1991). The archaeology of the Southern British Iron Age has always been considered familiar, lacking the overtly odd or ritual. Settlement evidence has always been interpreted in a straightforward manner (Champion 1987:106) as the product of common-sense reactions to functional needs.

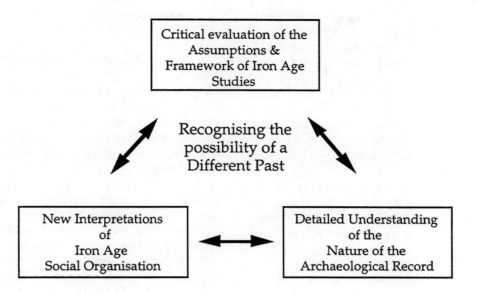

Rethinking the Iron Age

Such opinions are strengthened for the Iron Age by general assumptions of historical and racial continuities between modern northern Europeans and the first historical known northern Europeans (see Hill 1989; 1993; Champion 1987; Merriman 1987; Fitzpatrick 1991; Taylor 1991; Parker-Pearson forthcoming for elaborations on these arguments).

This desire for a different Iron Age has possibly two inter-linked strands. The first comes from a critique of the 'Celtic' centred nature of most Iron Age studies. This shackles archaeological studies of the period into a specific quasi-historical framework, and the assumption that social organisation, beliefs and racial characteristics are already known. The second strand has been the influence of Neolithic archaeology. Since Neolithic archaeologists have not had to operate on the threshold of history, they have been more free to exploit the archaeological record to the full in order to interpret social organisation and cultural structures. The difference in the Neolithic is clear, with the 'odd' nature of its archaeological record, and archaeologists have been open to the use of ethnography to understand this period (since archaeologically it is obvious they did things differently then). The success of these approaches, and the recognition that the Iron Age archaeological record contains equally 'odd' phenomena, has led to a 'Neolithicisation' of Iron Age studies (Hill 1989).

Central to such studies is the *demonstration* that the Iron Age was different from our expectations, through what can be termed a 'contrastive archaeology' (Thomas 1990a; Hill 1993). It is in this context that this study was originally

envisaged; as a study to attempt to demonstrate that a series of archaeological deposits which were thought to be understandable and straight-forward, were far from that. The evidence from these deposits revealed that people lived in very different, and perhaps ultimately unintelligible worlds, from our own. These arguments about the need for finding the difference of the past, how a contrastive or genealogical archaeological should work, and the ultimate political consequences of such an approach have been covered elsewhere (Hill 1989, 1993; Thomas 1990a). Although I will not address this issue again here, for want of space, they should be seen as one of the constantly present levels on which this study was meant to work.

The *difference* of the period is felt to lie in the everyday worlds of Iron Age people (Hill 1989; Parker-Pearson forthcoming, 1993). Normally this realm has been treated as unproblematic and straightforward in archaeological analyses. The organisation of settlements, the agricultural cycles, the daily routines of eating and sleeping, the disposal of rubbish have been seen as structured by universal functional concerns. However, developments in anthropology, geography, sociology and archaeology have increasing seen the everyday as *the* problem. Daily life is the arena through which society was continually constituted, and the evident differences in dress, settlement organisation, perceptions of identity, relationships to the natural world, notions of dirt, pollution and rubbish cannot be seen as colourful trimmings or merely 'symbolic'. These were the essential parts of culturally and historically specific different ways of thinking about and living in the world.

1.4. An Archaeology of Practice

An emphasis on the everyday has important archaeological implications, which can only be fully realised within a proper theoretical framework, a theoretical framework which seeks to understand how the easily demonstrable differences in Iron Age activities help to construct or challenge the larger traditional concerns of Social Archaeology; subsistence, economy and social organisation. As such this thesis not only takes for granted the arguments of 'post-processual' archaeologies (e.g. Barrett 1988a, 1993; Gero & Conkey 1991; Hodder 1982c, 1986, 1987; 1991a&b; Shanks & Tilley 1987a&b; Tilley 1991 etc.), but is specifically set in those studies exploring the contribution of 'Structuration Theories' to archaeology (e.g. Austin & Thomas 1990; Barrett 1988a, 1989, 1993; Barrett et. al. 1991:6-8; Gosden 1993).

Structuration Theory (see Johnson et al 1986:464-469) is a conceptual framework for how humans make history, through the understanding of how society is constantly produced, reproduced and changed (i.e. *constituted*) through human actions, especially daily routine practices (e.g. Bourdieu 1977; Giddens 1984; Cohen 1990; Pred 1986). Therefore, the larger concerns of social archaeology have no existence beyond the daily activities through which they were constructed. This questions the traditional gap, and division of labour, in archaeology between the excavation/study of the details of the archaeological record and grander syntheses and interpretations of economies and societies, writing history.

Theories of structuration are not a rigid program for research, rather they are a sensitising device providing a framework to inform and direct studies, particularly to ask new questions and provide fresh interpretations of mundane archaeological evidence. I do not intend to exhaustively discuss the nature of these theories, except to underline that society is at once the ever present *condition* and the continually reproduced *outcome* of human agency. All human actions, *practices*, draw on and reproduce rules and resources, *structures*, although often imperfectly due to differing circumstances and personal differences. Structures (human pre-dispositions, common senses and understandings of how the world is) are constantly and simultaneously reproduced through all human activities which are simultaneously the transformation and appropriation of nature, the socialisation of the individual, and the maintenance or challenging of relations of gender, power and authority (see below). As such, archaeological evidence for a specific activity such as crop processing is always evidence for far more than just the types of Iron Age crops, how they were processed, and where they were grown.

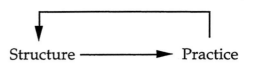

Structure ⟶ Practice

'The Duality of Structure'

This does not provide a universal model for how all human societies worked, rather a framework for understanding the different ways historically specific societies were constituted, which also recognises that societies are always messier than our abstractions expect. Space, time and the material world were not just the passive backdrops against which Iron Age history took place, but fundamentally implicated and integral to the constitution of Iron Age societies. Such an approach strongly emphasises the routine, daily practices in and through which social life is lived, against which can be contrasted the irregular practices of rituals such as seasonal festivals, funerals, weddings and initiations. This is to ask what is the place of ritual, and structure, in practice (Kelly & Kaplan 1990:141; cf. J.Turner 1991) (see 10.3, 12.3).

People produce history and places (and things) at the same time as people are produced by history and places (and things).

People do not produce history and places (and things) under conditions of their own choosing, but in the context of already existing and directly encountered social and spatial (and material) structures.

The practices through which social structure is both expressed and reproduced cannot be divorced from the structuring of space (and things) and the use of spatial (and material) structures. Previously structured space (and things) both contains and enables the reproduction of social practices and social structure.

(Pred 1986:198 as amended   by Koji Mizoguchi)

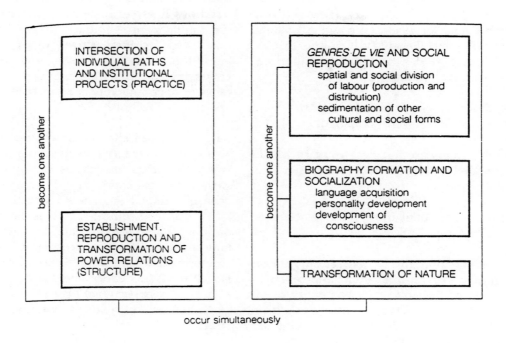

The simultaneous reproduction of society, individuals, and structure in practice :
Place as Historically Contingent Process (Pred 1986:10)

1.5. The Iron Age of Wessex

In essence, this thesis is about an arbitrary construct in a fictional county; The Iron Age in Wessex. The 'Iron Age' is only a natural unit because of our chronological division of prehistory in to three ages, which we have assumed correspond to real differences in technological, economic and social organisation/development. That is to assume there was a fundamental change occurred with the Bronze Age/Iron Age transition. 'Wessex' must always be recognised as a product of fiction and parable that became a geographical reality to visit, buy holidays homes in, and write prehistories about: Thomas Hardy's "a part real, part dream country" (Pelham 1964; Millgate 1989; Hynes 1987).

That a fiction has dominated British Prehistory may be thought particularly fitting. Although we use the term 'Wessex' as if it constituted a unified, or homogeneous, region in prehistory, this was probably not the case, and significant differences are now being recognised within the region (e.g. Sharples 1991c; Barrett et al 1991).

This thesis is foremost a contribution to a specific debate within British Iron Age studies, although through its detailed contextual argument it hopes to

contribute to more general archaeological issues. As such, I have not written a general background or literature review chapter of recent approaches to the British Iron Age, and will only provide here a brief introduction to the 'Iron Age' of 'Wessex'.

As the dominant regional focus for Iron Age studies in Britain, 'Wessex' is well served by a range of good, clear summaries and interpretations. Fitzpatrick and Morris (eds.) (1994) provide the fullest and most up-to-date review of recent research in the region. To this can be added the general chronological accounts offered by Cunliffe (1984b, 1993), Collis (1990) and Sharples (1990b, 1991a&b). Wessex's place within the broader context of the British Iron Age can be assessed through recent summaries contained in Hill (Forthcoming b), Cunliffe (1991), Haselgrove (1989) and a variety of papers in Champion and Collis (Forthcoming).

This study focuses only on 'Wessex', considering sites within the modern counties of Hampshire, Wiltshire, and Dorset. These counties have traditionally been the focus of prehistoric archaeological research in Britain. Research in these counties has been particularly important in the development of Iron Age studies. Particularly since the watershed in British archaeology during

7

the inter-war years, key excavations in the region have become the type sites for the British Iron Age as a whole, e.g. St Catherines Hill (Hawkes, Myres & Stevens 1929), Little Woodbury (Bersu 1940), Maiden Castle (Wheeler 1943), Gussage All Saints (Wainwright 1979) and Danebury (Cunliffe 1984b). The type site has played a particularly important role in British Iron Age studies in;

i. providing the analogies/parallels against which excavations in other areas were compared.

ii. providing the main chronological schemes which have been extended to the Southern British Iron Age generally.

iii. providing the dominant interpretative schemes for the British Iron Age.

In addition, the region has witnessed a greater concentration of Iron Age excavations and research than other parts of the country. The counties of Hampshire, Wiltshire, Dorset and Berkshire accounted for 25.9% of all the excavations in England that have encountered Iron Age material listed in the National Archaeological Record for England between 1770 and 1979 (Hill unpublished). This bias in research reinforces the dominance of Wessex which has only been challenged in recent years.

The benefits of this concentration of research are the quantity and quality of data to interpret the nature of economic, cultural and social organisation. Work on various aspects of craft production and exchange (e.g. Pottery -Morris 1994a; Metalwork -Ehrenreich 1994, Northover 1994; Salt -Morris 1994b; Querns - Peacock 1987) can be combined with studies of plant and animal husbandry (e.g. Jones 1984b, forthcoming; Grant 1984b; Maltby 1994) to establish the basis for reconstructing social organisation. However, this has been a controversial area of Iron Age research in recent years, especially when connected with the interpretation of the social role of hillforts. Interpretations drawn from traditional 'Celtic' models of Iron Age hierarchical chiefdoms (e.g. Cunliffe 1984a&b) have been challenged in recent years (e.g. Hill 1995; Sharples 1990c, 1991a&b). These debates are summarised by Haselgrove (1994a) and the questions about how representative the data excavated from sites is of past social and economic organisation form the starting point for this study.

The Wessex Iron Age conjures up images of massive hillforts such as Maiden Castle, Hodd Hill and Danebury. However, it is important to stress that the majority of the population lived on a range of small settlements and that many hillforts may have been only seasonally occupied. The Little Woodbury type enclosure remains the dominant form of settlement throughout the Iron Age in Wessex. Such enclosed sites vary considerably in size and shape (see Fig 1.2), but the bulk are surrounded by a ditch - for at least some part of their life - and contained round houses and a range of ancillary structures including 'four posters' - small raised buildings likely to have been granaries. The other ubiquitous features found on these sites are various pits. These are often of sizes up to 2-3m deep and 1-2m wide, and were also used to store grain. However, not all settlements were enclosed and a range of open settlements, some seasonally occupied, are known (McOmish 1989).

Larger enclosed sites, normally called hillforts, are also found unevenly spread across the region. The size of the banks and ditches around such enclosures varies and their primary defensive function has been questioned (Bowden & McOmish 1987, 1989; Hill 1995, forthcoming a). It is clear that hillforts are not a homogeneous category of sites, and there may be considerable differences between even contemporary sites such as Middle Iron Age Danebury, Winklebury and Maiden Castle. Where such sites were occupied they contain a similar range of structures and features as found on non-hillfort sites.

The chronology of the Wessex Iron Age is based on pottery and has been divided into three main blocks since the late 1920's. Hawkes' A B C chronology (Hawkes 1931) has essentially been re-labelled as Early, Middle and Late. A more refined ceramic chronology has been established through the Danebury research project (L. Brown 1984), divided into nine ceramic phases. However it is important to stress that chronology may wrongly assume a rapid, uniform adoption of new styles across a region.

The ceramic chronology questions whether a sharp distinction can be made between the Later Bronze Age and Early Iron Age in Wessex or Southern Britain as a whole. Previous interpretations have seen the transition as a major social and economic change, the end of the bronze exchange networks leading to a fundamental reorganisation of society (e.g. Cunliffe 1984a). However, continuity in ceramic styles and settlement forms from the 8th to 6th Centuries BC suggests a far more complex situation.

Possibly, the most important social, economic and social change took place during the Middle Bronze Age c.1400-1000BC (Bradley 1991). It was during this period that the long cultural traditions of monument construction and deposition that characterised the Neolithic and Early Bronze Age were transformed to produce landscapes now characterised by archaeologically visible settlements and field systems. This transformation can be understood in terms of a shift from a society in which the dead were the dominant cultural resource to one in which emphasis was shifted to the living (Barrett et al 1991). An archaeological record now dominated by enclosures containing evidence of domestic structures and activities was to be typical for the next millennia and beyond.

The transition from the Deverel-Rimbury ceramics to post-Deverel-Rimbury forms marks the beginnings of the Late Bronze Age proper (Barrett 1980). The basic forms of these ceramic forms continued across the end of the Bronze Age until the saucepan traditions and their contemporaries in the Middle Iron Age.

From the 11th to the 8th centuries (LBA 1-3) there was comparatively little acquisition and consumption of bronze objects - as evidenced through its ritual deposition in hoards etc. - in Wessex compared to the Thames Valley (Thomas 1989; Taylor 1993). The 8th and 7th centuries witnessed a major change in this situation, as the deposition of bronze hoards and use of bronze objects, and the social networks they sustained, came to end. This phenomenon, the Bronze Age/Iron Age transition, was not simultaneous across Southern Britain. Hoards essentially stopped being deposited in the Thames Valley by the end of LBA 3/Ewart Park - although some swords continued to be deposited in the Thames. However, as hoarding stopped in the Thames Valley, the deposition of hoards increased in Wessex through LBA4/Llyn Fawr phase.

Through the course of the LBA, but increasingly in the 8th to 7th centuries, the typical 'Little Woodbury/Old Down Farm' enclosures appeared across the Wessex chalkland. These enclosures contained large double or triple-post ring houses - as reconstructed at Butser, along with smaller ancillary circular structures. Such large houses are often associated with Barrett's (1980) decorated phase and both roughly coincide with the Llyn Fawr horizon of hoards in Wessex. Other characteristic features of the 8th/7th centuries were the construction of linear earthworks dividing up the Chalklands into large blocks of land and in north-west Wiltshire midden sites such as Potterne and East Chisenbury - large mounds of rubbish containing pottery, animal bone and some metalwork (Lawson 1994, G. Brown et al 1994).

A few large enclosed sites were constructed and used throughout the Later Bronze Age. Some, such as Balksbury, were of a considerable size, if lightly defended/enclosed - Cunliffe's 'Hilltop Enclosures' (1984a). Although palisaded enclosures from the 7/6th centuries are known on the sites of later hillforts, hillforts 'proper' appear largely to belong to the Early Iron Age 'proper' - 6/5th centuries. By this time the deposition of bronze hoards had ceased in Wessex, although iron objects were in use and manufacture from several centuries earlier. Enclosed 'Little Woodbury' type farmsteads continued across the region. In their midst hillforts, approximately 5-6ha in size were constructed. Sites such as Danebury and Maiden Castle contained large numbers of crop storage structures. However, it should be emphasised that the distribution of hillforts was always partial across 'Wessex', being concentrated in Wiltshire, East Dorset and West Hampshire.

A major ceramic transition can be seen between the Early and Middle Iron Age. While there is considerable continuity, it is increasingly seen by some that many of the deep transformations witnessed in the last two centuries of the Iron Age have their origins earlier in the Middle Iron Age. In several areas, many earlier hillforts fell into disuse, while a small number of 'developed hillforts' which continued in use witnessed considerable elaboration in their 'defences' and entrances. These include Danebury and Maiden Castle (Cunliffe 1984a; Sharples 1991a). Although at one level these sites are similar, it is important to recognise the considerable differences between Middle Iron Age hillforts in the region. It could be that Danebury is the mirror of Maiden Castle, an essentially non-permanently densely occupied enclosure within a densely occupied landscape, as opposed to a densely occupied enclosure in an unoccupied landscape. Not all hillforts were in constant use in the Middle Iron Age (e.g. Winklebury) and another was only built late in the period and appears not to contain any storage structures (Pilsdon Pen).

The exact function of such sites may have differed from hillfort to hillfort, but there is little to support the assumption that such sites played an important role in craft production or exchange. Nor is there much evidence for the existence of hierarchically organised societies or a class of warriors (Hill 1995, but see Cunliffe 1984a). In general, the Middle Iron Age was a period of important, if dimly seen and understood changes (Haselgrove 1989; Hill forthcoming b). Central to these changes were the expansion of permanent settlement and final clearance of scrub and woodland in many parts of lowland Britain. The chalk downlands would appear to have been a core area of settlement throughout the period, but occupation and exploitation of the coastal plain of Sussex and heath lands around Poole Harbour began in earnest during the later centuries of the Middle Iron Age.

It is in this context that the very evident changes in the archaeological record of the first centuries BC. and AD must be set. In Wiltshire and Hampshire hillforts appear to have been abandoned during the first century BC. This does not appear to have happened in Dorset and Somerset, where the function of such sites seems to have changed, although they remained central foci of some kind. In Hampshire and Wiltshire new ceramic forms and the potter's wheel were adopted, as in parts of south-east England. These innovations show the clear influence of northern Gaulish practices, as do the adoption of cremation burial, the use of shrines/temples and coinage (Cunliffe 1984b, 1993; Haselgrove 1989, 1995; Millett 1987; 1990).

The main focus of these changes was in West Sussex and East Hampshire. Here shrines such as Hayling Island (King & Soffe 1994), possible enclosed oppida - new low-lying hillfort-sized enclosed sites

(Whinney 1994; Hill forthcoming b) and the territorial oppida complex at Chichester were established during this period. The Chichester complex was located in the coastal plain which appears to have only come under intensive occupation in the MIA (Bedwin 1994; Fitzpatrick 1994b). This complex became the centre of an important Roman client kingdom after the conquest in 43 AD. (Cunliffe 1993). In terms of material culture this 'southern kingdom' or polity - which should be equated with the Atrebates - had much in common with developments in south-east England (Hertfordshire, Essex, Kent - the northern kingdom), as well as links across the channel.

However, to the east, in East Sussex/West Kent, local communities marked themselves as different and distinct from both the 'southern' and 'northern kingdoms', by not adopting the potter's wheel or new forms of pottery, or new mortuary rites, and with little use of coinage. Indeed, in this area hillforts continued in occupation or, built for the first time .

The west of Wessex also did not share fully in these supposedly 'mainstream' developments. Dorset hillforts, such as Maiden Castle, remained important foci, even if their use clearly changed. Sharples (1991a) has shown that this site was densely occupied in the MIA, but settlement shifted to small settlements in the surrounding area during the LIA. These changes are accompanied by the appearance of a mortuary rite for the first time in centuries. Small inhumation cemeteries, the bodies accompanied with grave goods, were associated with many settlements in South Dorset. Other changes at this time include the establishment and growth of the Poole Harbour pottery industry which came to dominate a very large area, replacing localised production. The production sites around Poole Harbour were also engaged in sea salt production, craft activities and cross-channel exchange (Hearne & Cox 1994). However, the most famous site engaged in the latter was Head (Cunliffe 1987). This site was clearly a major centre for long-distance exchange and craft production, receiving Gallic and Mediterranean objects up to fifty/sixty years before they became common in south-east England. The full nature of these contacts and their effects on local society are debatable (Cunliffe 1987, 1988, 1994; Sharples 1987, 1990b, 1991a&b).

1.6. Prelude

At its simplest this study asks whether the finds excavated from sub-soil features on Iron Age sites in Wessex were ritual deposits or daily rubbish. I have outlined above why this question is central, if we are specifically to use excavated material to understand the nature of Iron Age societies, and how it relates to more general archaeological questions about the nature of the archaeological record, and the need for a contrastive archaeology. The following chapters answer this question through a detailed study of how the material recovered from sub-soil features came to be there in the first place, suggesting that this was not accidental, and that the study of these processes can provide new ways of understanding the nature of Iron Age societies in the region.

The study begins with a detailed discussion of recent interpretations of so-called 'special deposits' from Iron Age sites, highlighting how our systems of classification have structured our understandings of prehistoric ritual. Following a detailed discussion of investigations and assumptions about how finds entered the archaeological record on Iron Age sites, particularly emphasising the important contribution of animal bone taphonomy, the aims of this study will be re-formulated and the approach to be taken outlined. Part two of the study considers the nature of pit fills, considering the nature of finds assemblages in individual layers, differences within different parts of the same pit, and the overall associations between all the material found in a single feature. The patterns which emerge will be shown to have existed in other features (especially enclosure ditches), and to have had an important spatial element. Part three provides a detailed discussion of the nature and interpretation of the patterns found in these feature fills. In particular it will ask whether 'special deposits' are special because they were the result of ritual activity; "formal procedure in a religious or other solemn observance" (OED definition). This section will also consider differences between sites and through time. Finally, I shall return to the question of how we can move from these archaeological deposits to consider questions of economic and social organisation.

Throughout, my study has two central questions (see below), and argues that the question of how we see the past in the way we do is neither incidental nor inconsequential. The thesis argues for a greater theoretical and practical concern with the formation of the archaeological record, necessary if we are to make valid interpretations about any aspect of the Iron Age, be it social organisation or simply chronology. I will suggest that the study of archaeological formation processes must always be more than simply accounting for the distortions and biases that supposedly intervene to screen a past and an archaeological record in the present. I will argue that the ways in which the archaeological record was created, the ways in which we see different periods in the past today, are intimately bound up with the specific ways different past societies were constituted.

Questions

1. Why is there an archaeological record?

2. How did past societies produce the specific archaeological evidences we recover today?

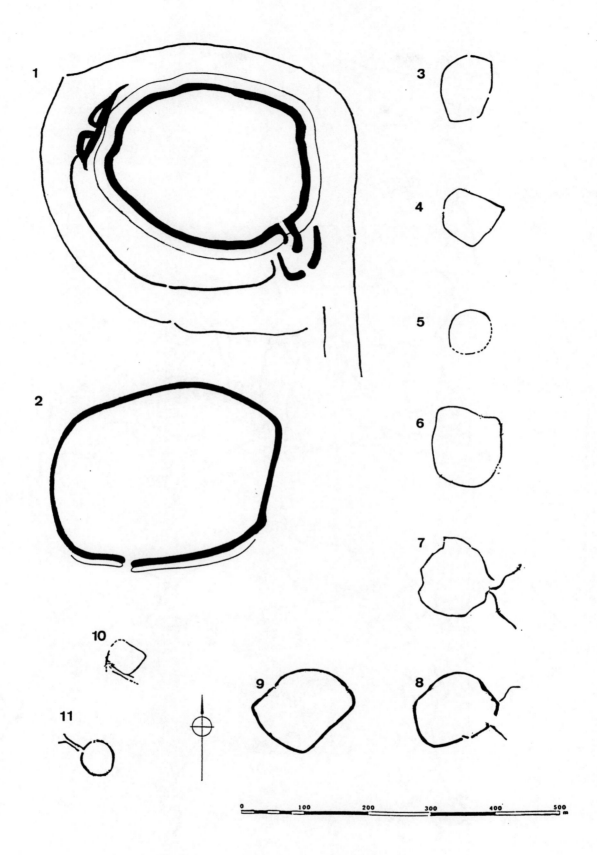

Fig. 1.2   Comparative plans of Early and Middle Iron Age enclosures (both hillforts and non-hillforts) from Wessex (after Cunlife 1984a & Fasham & Whinney 1991: Figs 67-9).   All the sites are in the county of Hampshire, except Little Woodbury (South-East Wiltshire), and Gussage All Saints (East Dorset).

1. Danebury   2. Winklebury
3. Ructshalls Hill   4. Winnall Down   5. Meon Hill   6. Little Somborne   7. Gussage All Saints
8. Little Woodbury   9. Old Down Farm   10. Viables Farm   11. Micheldever Wood

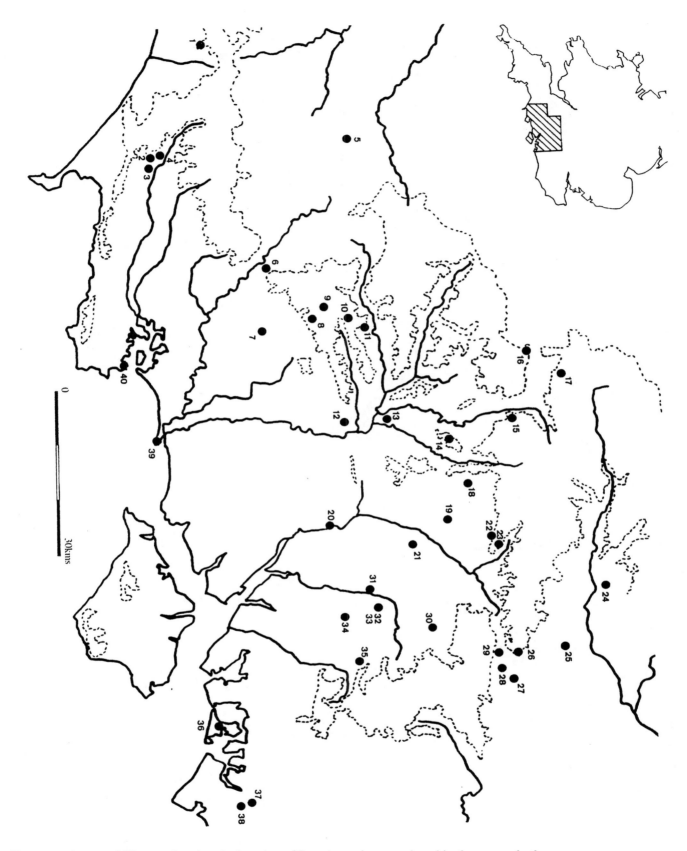

Fig. 1.1. A map of Wessex showing the location of Iron Ages sites mentioned in the text and others.

1. Pilsdon Pen	9. Woodcutts	17. All Cannings C.	25. Silchester	33. Easton Lane
2. Maiden Castle	10. Swallowcliffe D.	18. Lains Farm	26. Winklebury	34. Owslebury
3. Flagstones	11. Fyfield Down	19. Danebury	27. Ructshalls Hill	35. Bramdean
4. Poundbury	12. Little Woodbury	20. Romsey	28. Brighton Hill S.	36. Hayling Island
5. South Cadbury	13. Highfield	21. Little Somborne	29. Viables Farm	37. Westhampnett
6. Hod Hill	14. Boscombe Down	22. Balksbury	30. Micheldever Wood	38. Copse Farm
7. Gussage All Saints	15. East Chisenbury	23. Old Down Farm	31. Winchester	39. Hengistbury H.
8. Rotherley	16. Potterne	24. Dunston Park	32. Winnall Down	40. Cleavel Point

Chapter 2
"A Persistent and Interesting Feature": Previous Work on Ritual Deposits from Wessex Iron Age Sites

The presence of burials close to dwellings, often in pits not dug for the purpose, with evidence that the remains were deposited with little care..., as well as the frequent occurrence of detached and fragmentary human bones, is a persistent and interesting feature in connection with Iron Age sites
(Cunnington 1933:207).

2.1. Introduction

Formal ritual deposits have only recently been recognised from Later Prehistoric settlement evidence. Developed from Whimster's (1977) definition of the "pit burial tradition" the range of ritual deposits recognised has increased to cover all classes of material (though without consensus). This aim of this chapter is to summarise the interpretations of human remains and possible ritual animal deposits from southern English Iron Age sites at the beginning of my research in 1988-9. But more importantly, consider the general assumptions and underlying problems behind these interpretations and so provide the basis for some of the approaches taken in this study.

2.2. Human Remains

Humans remains have always been recognised during excavations of Later Prehistoric settlements, and provided the physical anthropological evidence to answer central questions of racial histories (e.g. Pitt-Rivers 1887, 1888; Boyd Dawkins 1917; Clay 1924; Morant & Goodman 1942). The occurrence of human remains on apparently domestic sites has continuously been considered odd and requiring explanation. Pitt-Rivers considered complete corpses in pits at Rotherley and Woodcutts as "burials", i.e. normal mortuary practice, deposited in pits because it was more convenient than digging a grave (1888:60). Partially articulated remains were seen as evidence for excarnation, deliberate dismemberment, or, less convincingly, cannibalism (Dunning 1976), while scattered human bones came from disturbed burials (1887:16).

Although Pitt-Rivers recognised complete corpses as burials, he also stressed the apparent "casual" nature of these practices, describing remains as "buried without care" or "thrown in (features) irregularly" (Pitt-Rivers 1887:11). This theme was common in the interpretation of human remains until recently; e.g. "not a burial in the proper sense...(the corpse) thrown into a convenient rubbish pit" (Richardson 1951:131), "casual treatment of dead bodies...disposed of with little ceremony" (Cunliffe 1974:316), "casual burials" (Fasham 1987:15) etc. This was particularly clear in discussions of human bone fragments "which turn up on quite an indiscriminate manner" (Liddell 1935:25) during excavations and have generally been regarded as

rubbish (e.g. Bersu 1940; Cunliffe 1991), all be it sometimes rubbish from massacres (e.g. Boyd Dawkins 1917; Clay 1924; Alcock 1972). This 'rubbish' interpretation was particularly evident in discussions of Early Iron Age layers behind ramparts or in hillfort ditches, where people 'apparently' lived amidst the filth of old animal bones, broken pottery and human bones (Cunnington and Cunnington 1917; Cunnington 1925; Hawkes 1939; Whitley 1943). Cunnington (1933:207 quoted above) summed up these 'casual' interpretations, and added a new twist:

> But a more interesting suggestion has been made...connected with the religious ideas of the people. The Druids taught that after death the soul passed from one body to another...A logical result of this teaching would be an indifference to what became of the body after death...it might to a great extent account for the remarkable rarity of rich and ceremonial burials of this period, and for the careless methods of burial within and about the settlements.

The few human deposits, with their apparent casual disposal and domestic context, drew little attention and so Hodson (1964:205 cf. Cunnington 1932:31) claimed that the absence of a burial tradition was the distinctive "negative fossil trait" of Early/Middle Iron Age culture in Southern Britain. However, Whimster (1977, 1981) re-examined this proposition and proposed that a coherent mortuary practice for a small proportion of the population could be recognised for Southern Britain prior to the Late Iron Age Aylesford cremation rite. This so-called "pit burial tradition" emphasised those complete human corpses deposited in disused storage pits over other similar corpses in other types of features such as enclosure ditches, or indeed other types of human deposits. These other locations and forms of human deposits were given equal attention in C. Wilson's (1981) study, although this important work has not perhaps been given the attention it deserves.

From these more recent discussions there appears to be a consensus about the major features of such EIA and MIA human deposits. Firstly, these remains represent only a tiny minority of the population of Iron Age Southern Britain, and it is generally agreed the majority of Iron Age people were excarnated on death, their bones subsequently disposed of in non-archaeologically traceable ways (Drewett & Ellison 1971; Whimster 1981; C.Wilson 1981). Secondly, it has been recognised (*contra* the Pitt-River's type interpretation) that this was a distinct tradition, with common elements across a wide area, and not the casual disposal of human remains (Whimster 1981:4-37; C. Wilson 1981; Walker 1984:442; Wait 1985:120-121). Yet something of the casual interpretation still at times surfaced when deposits were discussed in terms of "minimum expenditure of energy" (Walker 1984:443), especially in the use of an existing empty pit rather than going to the trouble to dig a grave (Whimster 1981:10). The importance of burial with apparently domestic detritus and garbage has been commonly stressed (e.g. Whimster 1981:10; Walker 1984:443). In addition, studies found no major difference in the treatment of remains according to gender (Whimster 1981:14-15; Wilson 1981:145; Wait 1985:92). Infants were generally more commonly deposited in the interior compared to the periphery of sites (Wilson 1981:143), and both infants and adult females were more common on non-hillfort compared to hillfort sites - especially in the Middle Iron Age (C. Wilson 1981:145; Wait 1985:90; Hill 1994b, forthcoming a). Therefore, human remains were not deposited randomly on sites. Deposits were often clustered and, especially in the case of 'burials' - i.e. complete human corpses -, tended to be made away from houses, often on the periphery of sites (C.Wilson 1981:141-4; Walker 1984:442-463; Wait 1985:99-100).

Despite the recognition of a range of different types of deposit of human remains, emphasis was placed on complete bodies - 'burials' - and their most common location -- the pit. Such deposits were generally found crouched or flexed, with the head often pointing between North and East (Whimster 1981:11-14; C. Wilson 1981:138-9) -- Danebury was exceptional with no preferred orientation (Walker 1984:450). Another important element stressed was the general absence of grave goods, or even items to suggest that corpses were clothed (e.g. Whimster 1981:16). Prime emphasis was given to the complete corpses, 'burials', even though they form a minority of the total number of human deposits (see Fig. 2.1 for examples). This is because 'burials' conform to our expectations of normal mortuary behaviour (Whimster characterised all other deposits as "non-orthodox burial techniques") and their primacy reaffirmed the expectation that, despite only representing a tiny proportion of the total Iron Age population, this was still mortuary practice. Therefore, such deposits have been described as; "burial ritual" (Cunliffe 1983:161), "inhumations" (Walker 1984:443ff), "burial" (Whimster 1981, C. Wilson 1981, etc.), "burial category" (Wait 1985:Chapter 4 to describe all types of human remains), "formal mortuary ritual" (Walker 1984:443, Wait 1985:Chapter 4). As mortuary practice, it can then be assumed that the treatment of the body related in some way to social status and so approached through the application of 'mortuary theory'. As such, in a chapter entitled 'The Social

Order' Cunliffe discussed human remains and how they introduced "us to some of the intricacies of social structure" (1983:165).

A range of other types of human remain deposits have been recognised (see later discussions). Walker, Wait and Cunliffe have all distinguished different categories, which they treat as both real and having originated from a distinctly different practices (Fig. 2.3.a summarises these differences).

"The distinct nature of the assemblage within each category would suggest that we are witnessing performances of a fundamentally different kind, but the main distinction appears to be the in the treatment of the body after death" (Walker 1984:442).

Since complete corpses represented burial, partial corpses and individual bone fragments were treated as evidence for the general excarnation of the majority of the population. Articulated limbs and "charnel pits" were evidence of "historical events" -- massacres. The depositional and historical contexts of complete skull remains were ignored, and interpretations were drawn from general 'Celtic' accounts of head hunting (cf. Cunnington 1933:207 quoted above). Infant remains are seen as the disposal of natural deaths. Individual bones were considered to have been selected and kept from exposed corpses, although discussion of their ultimate deposition suggested by this stage that they were just rubbish (e.g. Cunliffe & Poole 1991:418) However C. Wilson (1981:128) recognised that these categories were "fairly arbitrary", and hence did not necessarily reflect distinctly different practices.

Discussion became fixed on the pit as the prime context for 'complete' deposits. This was due to the ubiquitous nature of these features on sites, and their central focus in the discourse of such. However, it is also fair to say that the dominance of Danebury in more recent discussions has not helped, with its vast numbers of pits and comparative absence of other types of features such as working hollows, and especially, enclosure ditches. Whimster (1981:5) recognised that only half of all the human burials he had considered came from pits, although he still described this as a 'pit burial tradition', considering other locations as just an extension of this. Once again, C. Wilson (1981:143) was alone in *not* stressing the primacy of the pit. This study considered deposits of human remains within settlements as a whole and argued that the choice context depended on the preferred location for the deposition of the remains, not the type of context.

Grain storage pits, later used as rubbish pits, have been important in the interpretation of the nature of 'pit burials' (i.e.. complete corpse burials). It has been generally accepted that the majority of the population was excarnated, which raises the

Proposed Classifications of Types of Deposits of Human Remains

C.Wilson (1981:128)	Walker (1984:442)	Wait (1985:88)
1. Worked or utilised bone	A. Whole bodies	1. Single complete inhumations
2. Bone fragments	B. Incomplete skeletons	2. Single partial inhumations
3. 'Disarticulated' bones	C. Multiple, partial skeletons	3. Multiple partial inhumations
4. Articulated joints and limbs	D. Skulls and frontal bones	4. Articulated limbs
5. Partial burials	E. Pelvic girdles	5. Skulls
6. Complete burials	F. Individual bones and bone fragments	6. Individual bones

question of why a tiny minority were marked out for special treatment (*contra* Whimster). This discussion has often been confusing and inconclusive, invoking a range of ethnographic and 'Celtic' parallels.

Two basic distinctions in the evidence were recognised:

1. Burial in rubbish.

2. The importance of grain storage.

The first, 'burial in rubbish' has lead to arguments that this reflected those whose lifestyle or death had been abnormal (witches, criminals, suicides, death in child birth, etc.) (Harding 1974:113; Wait 1985:119-120; Walker 1984:461; Cunliffe 1983:164). This was a minority mortuary rite, but still understandable as *mortuary practice*. Wait, Walker and Cunliffe mentioned the same ethnographic parallel of the Ashante in support of this idea, who deny 'damaged' or 'incomplete' persons normal rites by burial in rubbish middens (MacLeod 1981:36-8).

Alternatively, 'the importance of grain storage' is employed to argue that 'pit burials' were offerings (Wait 1985:119; Walker 1984:461-2; Cunliffe 1983:166). For example, burials under ramparts -- often in pits -- have been interpreted as sacrifices. Although called foundation *burials* (Cunliffe 1983:164; Wait 1985:119), there has been a reluctance to extend this sacrificial explanation to other burials whose only difference is their location. Whimster (1981:31) was an exception, seeing these foundation burials as a bridge between "superficially normal and more esoteric series of deposits of human and animal remains". Wait (1985:119) has argued (from modern ethnographic evidence) that the majority of human deposits were not sacrifices, since;

(i) children are uncommon victims of sacrifice,
(ii) sacrifice should not be expected on small rural farmsteads.
Instead, he and Cunliffe saw neo-natal and infant remains as a reflection of natural infant mortality (Wait 1985:255; Cunliffe 1992:78). Cunliffe (1983:165, 1984a:560) generally accepted this view, and argued that complete burials represented the

unclean or inhuman, the skull remains were evidence for head hunting or a head cult, and fragmentary remains resulted from "a complex ritual involving excarnation followed by propitiatory burial". A link between fertility ritual, grain storage, and these remains which have been more strongly developed recently.

The range of individual complete and fragmentary human bones have been specifically considered by Woodward (1993), who argued that these represent a cult of relics in which the remains of ancestors or holy people were curated, concealed and venerated so that there powers might be conserved and tapped. This summary also reconsiders the choice of body part selected for deposition, showing a general emphasis on the skull and leg (see also C. Wilson 1981 & Walker 1984). The potential of detailed study of these remains is illustrated by Walker's (1984) study of the Danebury material, which showed a deliberate selection of bones from the right hand side of the body. Although, there was little agreement about whether such material was deliberately deposited or accidentally incorporated into archaeological deposits.

2.3. "Special Animal Deposits"

The second major class of possible ritual deposit found on Iron Age sites are the so-called "special animal deposits" (Wait 1985) (Fig. 2.2 for examples). Recently recognised, their interpretation as ritual deposits has not entirely been accepted by all animal bone specialists (Maltby 1985a; B.Wilson 1992) (see 3.7.7 for fuller discussion). These animal deposits consist of complete/partial skeletons, articulated limbs and complete skulls. Such deposits of bone have always been encountered on Iron Age sites, but they were rarely considered in need of explanation. This was partly because animal bones were, and still are, considered as essentially economic evidence and understandable in straight forward terms. Finds of complete skulls and associated bone, often in the same pits as human remains, might sometimes have been described, but they were rarely commented on (e.g. Pitt-Rivers 1888:108&198; Clay 1925:69). Articulated portions of bone were interpreted as "joints of meat gone bad" (Wheeler 1943:53), a complete sheep at Fifield Bavant "had all the appearance of having fallen and broken its neck" (Clay 1924:459). Similar functional, and often uncritical, explanations are still made (see 3.7.7 & 3.7.8).

Occasionally, ritual, non-functional explanations have been offered for animal deposits (although this is not always consistent). Thus, a complete dog buried in the south gateway of the eastern entrance at Maiden Castle may have been ritual, although, an equally carefully deposited dog in pit D4 drew no comment (Wheeler 1943:115 & 98). The concentration of cattle skull bones in the ditch at Harrow Hill, Sussex, led Holleyman (1937:250) to "theorise about sacrificial offering by mass slaughtering", and a cattle skull surrounded by flints at Findon Park, Sussex was considered to be an intentional deposit (Fox & Wolseley 1928:451). At South Cadbury similar remains were interpreted as ritual deposits on the basis of intentionality -- cattle skulls "not shot in" to pits -- and association with possible 'ritual' structures -- complete skeletons buried on their own in shallow pits around or aligned on the 'shrine' (Alcock 1969:36, 1970:16&25).

Complete/partially articulated groups of bones have been frequently recorded during the course of modern excavations in animal bone reports (e.g. Maltby 1985b, 1989; B.Wilson 1979), but only Grant (at Danebury) consistently argued that they represented a distinct category of ritual deposits (see 3.7.7 for further discussion). 'Special deposits' were singled out "either through their associations with other bones or by the manner and site of deposition" (Grant 1984a:533, also 542-3; Wait 1985:151 -- see 3.7.7). Grant distinguished three types of deposit -- animal burials, skulls, and articulated legs (cf. classification of human deposits). These were interpreted as having had a similar origin, unlike the more functional explanations which tended to separate these complete carcasses from smaller articulated units (see 3.7.7 - cf. explanations of different categories of human deposits). A terminology of "special" and "burial" separated complete carcasses from other bone deposits, which were alternatively described as the result of "dumping", or "butchery off-cuts". That is, Grant, followed by Wait (1985) and Cunliffe (1983:158-160) interpreted 'complete' deposits as the result of sacrifice and bracketed them off from other bone groups which, as rubbish, could be used to understand economic behaviour (e.g.. herd management).

Wait (1985:Chapter 5) extended Grant's study across Southern England, and demonstrated that the animals involved "were not those of most importance to the community" (Grant 1984a:543), i.e. sheep or cattle, but that horse and dog were more commonly represented in such deposits than in the overall percentages of bone recovered. The

implication was that these species were preferred for sacrifices (Grant 1984a:543; Wait 1985:152; Cunliffe 1983:159, 1992:77). 'Special animal deposits' were usually located close to houses or paddocks (Wait 1985:139) and Wait (1985:151) argued they were only deposited in disused storage pits. Cunliffe (1983:156-160) took this association with the pit further and argued, that the digging of a grain storage pit was to enter into the earth and entrust the grain to the gods of the underworld. Therefore, animal deposits represented thank offerings for storage, and were only one form of such "non-rubbish depositions" (Cunliffe 1983:159), others included layers of grain, groups of pots, tools etc. (see Fig. 2.3.b).

The procedure for how to identify such "non-rubbish depositions" was not discussed, and so the criteria for distinguishing 'special animal deposits' as 'special' has been questioned. Wait (1985:151) advocated five ways for in which such deposits were 'special':

1. They are animals or the parts of animals not exploited in the normal manner.

2. The number of species represented is not correlated with numbers of species present on sites.

3. There is consistency in the body parts of each species chosen, implying choice and deliberation.

4. There is evidence that care, if not ceremony, was taken in the placing of some remains,- bodies curled up, skulls consistently displaced or facing skywards, some burials accompanied by stones or chalk blocks (cf. Grant 1984a:542) -- also found with some humans (C.Wilson 1981:141).

5. Special deposits only occur in pits, not ditches which contain more general animal bone.

B.Wilson (1992) has raised important questions against these and other proposed criteria, which must be seriously addressed. The starting point for this study is neatly summarised by Wilson (1992:348);

> "...the arguments used by archaeologists to identify animal-bone-related ritual are, to date, mostly unsatisfactory".

Wilson has argued that quantities of articulated bone could be deposited as a result of normal carcass processing activities, and that such non-ritual processes on Medieval sites resulted in more articulated units of horse and dog in archaeological deposits than other species. Equally, he stresses that such 'special' deposits may only be special due to the fortunate circumstances of their survival (see 1.2). Maltby (1985a etc.) has made similar points, and has argued that many smaller articulated portions including skulls are simply butchery waste (see 3.7.7). This is to suggest that although to some extent such deposits might be regarded as 'special', it does not automatically equate with 'ritual'. Both B.Wilson and Maltby would agree that there is a need for a more rigorous evaluation of the evidence in the context of the full taphonomy of Iron Age bone assemblages, which would provide a baseline against which to judge the 'special' status of particular bone groups.

2.4. Recent Discussions: 'The Pit Belief System'

The previous sections have summarised the state of knowledge and interpretation about ritual practices at the start of my research. Since then discussion has laid even more of an emphasis on the pit as the location for ritual deposits.

This must be set in the growing emphasis on the symbolic aspects of daily activities and of space in recent Iron Age studies. Work has particularly concentrated on the enclosures that surrounded Iron Age settlements, which Hingley (1984) argued were not purely functional boundaries but marked more social and symbolic boundaries (see 7). These ideas were taken further by Bowden and McOmish (1987), who made a crucial link between this and depositional practices (see also Hingley 1990c). Parker-Pearson's (forthcoming) important paper on the symbolic nature of the spatial organisation of Later Prehistoric settlements, and made the link for the first time between space, human and special animal deposits, and daily practices. Sharples has integrated such ideas with the changing nature of social relations in the Wessex Iron Age, and stressed how excarnation and the deposition of some human remains "would limit the significance of the individual and symbolically tie them to the community" (Sharples 1991c:87).

Both Bradley (1981:234, 1984:159) and Cunliffe (1983:164) have recently argued that the deposition of human and other remains in grain storage pits was essentially a rite concerned with ensuring fertility. Both have recently elaborated this interpretation (Bradley 1990:163-5; Cunliffe 1991:518&536, 1992; Cunliffe & Poole 1991:162), going so far as to suggest that these deposits were evidence for a "Pit Belief System" (Cunliffe 1991:536, Cunliffe 1992). Bradley and Cunliffe appear to have recognised similarities between treatment of human on the one hand and that of other 'special' deposits on the other (i.e.. treated in the same way and deposited in the same contexts). This is a weakness of Wait's work (Fitzpatrick 1991:125). However, neither face the full implications of these similarities, since both still implicitly separate the treatment of humans from animals and other possible deposits. Thus, both interpret animal remains implicitly in terms of sacrifice -- although Cunliffe rarely uses those words explicitly -- yet do not extend such explanations to human remains. Bradley (1990:164)

is quite explicit in this; "This is not to suggest that the human remains have to be understood as 'offerings' ". However, Cunliffe has interpreted (some) human deposits as "propitiatory offerings", and once uses the word "sacrifices" for complete bodies in pits (1992:77).

Although, the basic division between humans and *other* deposits is still evident. For example, in Cunliffe (1991) human remains - labelled as "*pit burials*" - and special animal deposits from the similar, if not the same, features are discussed under separate sub-chapters; "Burial Customs" and "Religious and Ritual Locations". This situation is made more complex, since Cunliffe has interpreted different types of human deposits as distinctly different categories (Cunliffe 1991:507, Cunliffe 1992:76-77). Cunliffe has extended the range of possible ritual deposits beyond human and animal remains, suggesting "special deposits" for varying classes of artefact, including those archaeologically unpreservable on chalk sites e.g. wood, textiles, foodstuffs and drink (Cunliffe 1983:159-160, 1992:74-77). How such "non-rubbish" deposits (Cunliffe 1983:159) are defined is not considered in detail, although the completeness of the object and location on the pit base appear to be a common criterion (see Cunliffe 1992:75). This range of deposits is interpreted in terms of a "pit belief system", essentially a fertility cult, in which the very storage of grain in the ground is considered to have been a ritual activity. Cunliffe then argues that the chronological and geographic distributions of these beliefs, possibly a revival of Neolithic mortuary rites (1991:507), correspond to where and when pits were used to store grain (Cunliffe 1991:536, 1992:80-81).

2.5. Conclusions

This chapter has briefly outlined a history of the recognition and interpretation of human and other 'special deposits' from Later Prehistoric settlements in Southern England. A divide has been highlighted between the study of human remains and other categories of finds;

Human Remains
v
Animal and Other Finds

Ritual Explanations
v
Practical/Economic Explanations

Divisions which are essentially those western cultures make between;

Sacred
v
Profane

15

How these categories have been defined has created anomalies for archaeologists in terms of the explanations they use e.g. human remains amongst domestic detritus (explained as ritual), and the occurrence of skulls or complete carcasses of animal (explained as practical/economic). These views appear to have radically changed for some as can be seen by comparing the first editions of *Iron Age Communities in Britain* (Cunliffe 1974, 1978) with the most recent edition (Cunliffe 1991). Cunliffe's own interpretations appear to have completely turned around, from a position where all pit contents were explicable in straight forward terms, to one where the very digging of pits, if not all their subsequent deposits, was ritual. However, many animal bone specialists have questioned the criteria for identifying ritual/special deposits.

Critically approaching the recent discussions of these deposits suggests a series of inter-related issues and problems to be addressed by future work (in particular the criteria used to distinguish special deposits). On a more general level, the theoretical framework within which most discussions take place has to be revised, the implication being that there is the need for a more thorough and contextual approach to the material.

Furthermore, the archaeological identification of ritual is a thorny issue, made more difficult in a domestic context (Renfrew 1985), and no rigorous definition of special/ritual deposits have been made. As I have shown, human remains have usually been regarded as ritual, the opposite of animal and other deposits from the same contexts. Particular criticism has been levelled at the uncritical nature of Grant's and Wait's definition of *Special Animal Deposits* suggesting the need for a tighter analysis and testing of the evidence. This should be in the context of a fuller understanding of the processes that formed archaeological bone assemblages in pits and other features (B.Wilson 1992, Maltby 1985a). In this study I have called 'special animal deposits' *Articulated or Associated Animal Bone Groups (ABGs)* to avoid prejudging their 'special', i.e. 'ritual', status. Similar criticism can be made for other classes of special, "non-rubbish", deposits, which are distinguished on excavation through their "completeness" and location on pit bases (Cunliffe 1992:75). From a consideration of all types of special deposits, no account is taken of the site formation processes, which may explain such finds through factors of preservation (possibly a factor of feature depth- see 3.7.6). Archaeological patterns could have been created through daily carcass processing and refuse maintenance strategies. As all human behaviour is symbolically structured, especially daily attitudes to dirt and pollution, so associations not easily understood in functional terms should be expected in prehistoric rubbish deposits. Symbolic patterning in archaeological deposits need not be ritual (see 1.2, 10.2). Even if these Iron Age deposits are 'special', that is distinct from the other find assemblages,

they need not be ritual, rather a product of differently structured daily refuse maintenance strategies (different to our own) and/or taphonomic accidents.

This is to question the rigid distinction of ritual and rubbish, which is rooted in a basic opposition within our thought between Sacred and Profane, Symbol and Function etc. Anthropology suggests this is not a human universal as has been assumed, and perhaps archaeologists should investigate whether this also applies to the Iron Age before presuming its existence. This opposition results in a position where deposits or behaviour must be either/or. Thus, 'special animal deposits' are either ritual deposits or they are simply butchery waste, an argument which implies that the patterns generated from carcass processing and the disposal of waste from ritual consumption (feasting and sacrifice) will be different from those of non-ritual consumption. Once categorised as ritual, 'special animal deposits' are separated from other bone assemblages, which are usually interpreted directly as evidence of husbandry and subsistence (e.g. Grant 1984a). Such positions assume, that if an activity can be shown to have an (economic) function, then it cannot be ritual or symbolic. Thus, Cunliffe's categorisation of the "Pit Belief System" leads him to oppose below ground storage, which was ritually motivated, with above ground storage, which was practical and economic (Cunliffe 1992:78).

The above revision, leads to another series of questions which I feel need to be addressed. Are the apparent close links between the treatment of animals and humans in 'pit deposits' real, and what are the consequences of this? If animal ritual deposits exist, is it correct to maintain a distinction between rituals involving humans and those with animals (which are sometimes even found in the same pits)? For example, Cunliffe (1992) still uses a terminology of mortuary practice for human remains, implying the separation of human remains from practices which involve other types of finds (at the same time giving primacy to complete human carcasses). I have demonstrated how this divorce is enhanced by the classification of different types of human deposits into separate categories with different origins. I consider there to be similarities between the various types of human deposits and special animal deposits (compare classifications in 2.2 and 3.7.7). It is perhaps strange, that the archaeologists who propose different origins for varying types of human deposits, uncritically accept varying types of animal deposit to have the same origin.

The above issues raise the need for a thorough contextual study, bringing together all categories of finds normally considered in isolation, to understand more fully the processes which created the archaeological record. By comparing different categories of evidence, any similarities that exist between human remains, animal remains, and other small finds (possibly pottery), can be assessed. If similarities exist, then explanations must be made through a consideration of all the categories of material. Only through such a study, can the question of the identification of ritual deposits be approached, and the large quantities of data available allow for any major patterns to be demonstrated statistically (Cunliffe 1992:77). In studies where particular importance has been attached to the deposition of human remains (and other deposits) in household rubbish, a critical assessment of whether the material from these pits is similar to assemblages from other pits without 'special deposits' is needed (Walker 1984:443). This kind of approach could provide a more rigorous method of distinguishing special deposits, by considering if these assemblages are significantly different from the normal/average found in the majority of features. If such a 'signature' was observable, through a study combining different classes of material, this might provide a way of establishing if those pits without observable 'special deposits' contained any 'special deposits' of organic materials (as Cunliffe 1991:518, 1992:75-7 has suggested). In this way (even if a deposit were to leave no trace archaeologically), if it could be demonstrated that all 'special deposits' were accompanied by similar categories or quantities of pottery, bone, etc., or different types of soil matrices, their former presence could be inferred.

In addition, I would argue that although such a study may produce clear patterns between different classes of material, these must also be understood in terms of the cultural and natural formation processes at work on Iron Age sites. This is because archaeological patterns are as much produced by differential post-depositional preservation, and the varying processes by which assemblages entered different types of feature, as to how they relate to the activities and/or refuse maintenance strategies that created that material. Even when apparently odd patterns are found, these may have been due to cultural structures and norms, expressed through different attitudes and categorisations of dirt and garbage than our own. What archaeologists deem to be special deposits in the present (human, animal, pottery, etc.) may, therefore, not have been 'special' in the past i.e. ritual. They may have been the result of daily routine refuse maintenance strategies structured according to very different ways than our own, and we must recognise that it is possible that human remains could have been treated as 'refuse'. Equally, as B. Wilson (1992) has pointed out, such deposits may *only* be 'special' due to their chance incorporation in deep sub-soil features so that they escaped subsequent attrition, erosion, gnawing and scattering which destroyed the vast majority of all Iron Age rubbish (see 1.2.). It is possible that all this material, including the various categories of human remains, are simply rubbish that have for what ever reasons fortuitously survived.

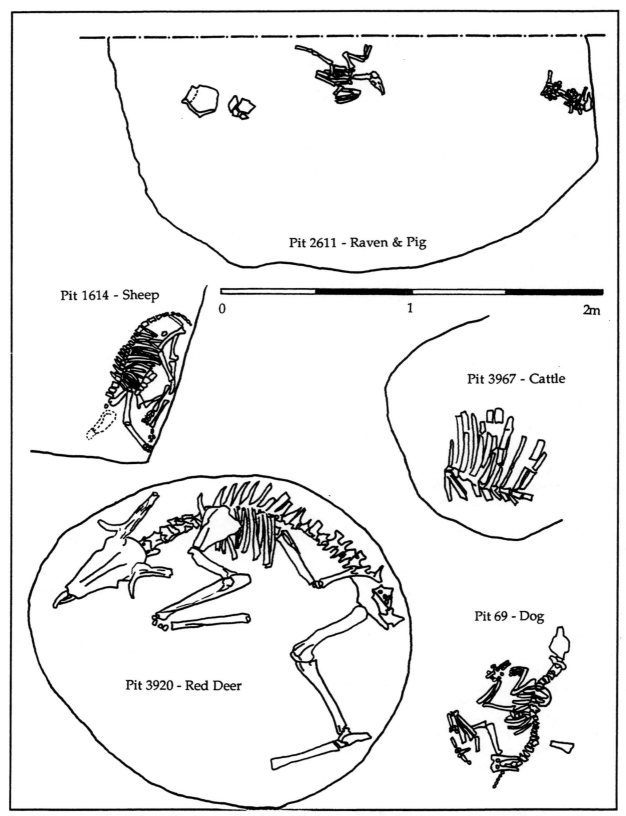

Pit 2611 - Raven & Pig

Pit 1614 - Sheep

0   1   2m

Pit 3967 - Cattle

Pit 3920 - Red Deer

Pit 69 - Dog

Fig. 2.1. Examples of deposits of large groups of articulated animal bone -- 'special animal deposits' -- from Iron Age pits at Winklebury (redrawn from microfiche in archive).

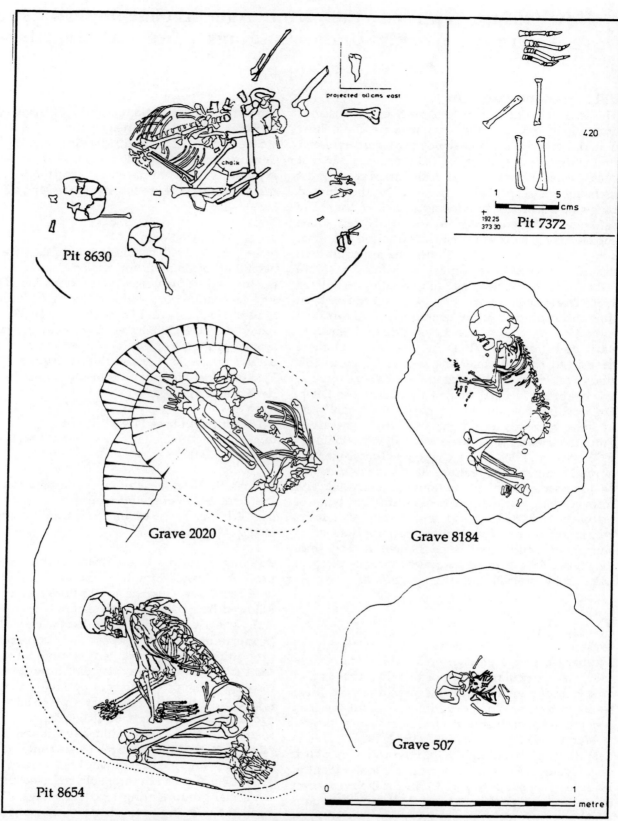

Pit 8630

Pit 7372

Grave 2020

Grave 8184

Pit 8654

Grave 507

Fig. 2.2. Examples of deposits of human remains from Iron Age pits at Winnall Down (after Fasham 1985:Fig, 21-3).

Chapter 3
How things entered the Iron Age Archaeological Record: Current Work, Understandings and Assumptions.

3.1. Introduction

This chapter will outline the previous discussions and, often unarticulated, assumptions about how material entered the archaeological record on Later Prehistoric British sites. It will become clear that such issues have been of little interest to most archaeologists, probably because of the limited range of questions previously asked of Iron Age settlement evidence, which are tacitly felt to be successfully answered. With the exception of animal bone studies (see 3.7), it will become apparent that, despite occasional references to Schiffer's (1976) "Behavioural Archaeology" (e.g. Bradley & Fulford 1980; Drewett 1982; M.Jones 1984), there has been little incorporation of the consequences of work on formation processes into Later British Prehistory until quite recently. It is in this area that there have been changes over the period in which this study was conducted which are not fully covered in this chapter. In particular, work at Mingies Ditch, Oxfordshire, has shown the considerable potential of detailed analysis on material from preserved ground surfaces, yard floors etc. (Allen & Robinson 1993; Wilson 1989). The chapter will consider the normal categories of features and finds, which will be discussed examining questions of preservation and recovery bias, variability between different types of feature and parts of a site, and vertical variability within features. The taphonomic approaches to animal bone studies will be considered in detail since they provide the fullest current understanding of Later Prehistoric site formation processes.

3. 2. Pits

A discourse on pits has been an essential feature of Southern British Iron Age archaeology (e.g. Evans 1989). A particular feature of this discourse is that of a lack of conviction in interpretations, for there seems to be a *need* for experimental proof the Iron Age pits were for below ground storage (e.g. Bowed & Wood 1968; Reynolds 1967; 1974; 1984). This is despite the considerable ethnographic evidence (e.g. Bersu 1940) and historical evidence (Fenton 1983, see Sheperd & Sheperd 1989 for the excavation of pre-improvement storage pit in Scotland) for crop storage in pits, which meant this never needed to be experimentally proved. This fixation with below ground storage is deep rooted in our culture. When Cunliffe (1992:78) says that "the concept of storing seed corn in underground silos, rather than in above-ground timber granaries requires consideration" and goes on to argue this was primarily for ritual reasons, he is simply echoing similar sentiments widely expressed since the enlightenment. Above ground crop storage, the main storage technique in Western Europe since the Middle Ages, has been seen as common-sensical, rational. Not so below ground storage. Like the 'need' for experiment in archaeology, agricultural texts since the Eighteenth Century have devoted far more discussion to explaining this apparently irrational practice compared to above ground storage techniques (Sigaut 1989).

3. 2. 1 Pit Form.

Since Bersu's (1940) conclusion that pits were not for habitation but mainly for storage, much discussion has focused on the variety of pit forms found on Iron Age sites and their possible differing functions. For example experimental work (Bowed & Wood 1968; Reynolds 1974, 1984) suggested that bell/beehive shaped pits were optimally shaped for grain storage because of the smaller mouth area requiring sealing. Two different types of classification schemes for pits have been employed:

1. Classification based on Pit Profile
(e.g. Bersu 1940; Jefferies 1979; Davies 1981; Rawlings 1991).

2. Classification based on a combination of the Profile and Plan of the pit mouth
(e.g. Whittle 1984; Fasham 1985; Cunliffe and Poole 1991).

Rawlings' simple classification (based on pit profile) allowed him to compare Maiden Castle with Danebury, Gussage and Little Woodbury, work followed here using a larger sample of sites (Fig. 3. 6.a). Clearly, different sites had widely differing proportions of pit shapes and volumes, with proportions having changed through time on the same site. Even if a few sites did show the expected increase in the proportions of optimally shaped pits (Fig. 3.5). I would argue that a pit's shape should probably not be equated to function, since all (regular?) shape-types could have stored grain (or other crops). While all sizes of pit could have been used for storage (Rawlings 1991 contra Whittle 1984:137). A pit's size probably reflected the size of the social group storing food (Rawlings 1991). As such, the differing proportions of different volumes of pits on different sites may have had wider social implications.

If different shapes or sizes of pit did have different functions, then we might expect possible differences in their fills and contents. No work has considered this, although it is clear that one rare pit form, the 'bathtub', was specifically associated with human remains at Danebury (Walker 1984:443). At Winklebury, a similarly shaped Early Iron Age pit contained a dense concentration of pot, bone and industrial refuse and so was felt to be a deliberately dug rubbish pit (Smith 1977:146).

3. 2. 2 Pit Fills

At a basic level, the fills of pits can be simply distinguished into natural or artificial, although detailed consideration of the origins and nature of artificial fills leads to complications, and combinations of natural and artificial deposition episodes are common. Whittle (1984) calculated the proportions of pits of natural, artificial, or with a combination of natural and artificial fills, for the first ten years of excavation at Danebury. The proportions were constant for the first three main phases of the site, with the proportion of natural infilled pits having dropped noticeably in the late phase (cp. 7-8) (see Fig. 3.6.b). Whittle (1984:145) suggested that the natural fills represented hiatuses in the occupation of Danebury (or at least of part of the fort), or alternatively, that the space inside the fort was closely organised into defined plots/enclosures so that open pits were not a danger to people or animals. However, I have shown that there is a greater proportion of natural pit fills at the Hampshire hillforts of Danebury and Winklebury (Smith 1977) compared to non-hillfort sites in Wessex (Fig. 3.6.b. - Hill 1994b; forthcoming a), and have interpreted this as an important difference between the permanence and/or density of the occupation at hillforts and non-hillfort sites (rather than hiatuses in occupation). Whether the greater numbers of natural silted pits on these hillforts related to differences in depositional practices, rather than a reflection on the nature of occupation, will be considered later in this thesis (see 7.9).

The most detailed consideration of pit fills is still Bersu's (1940:52-60), who distinguished seven classes of fill (the seventh further subdivided into different types of refuse). Bersu (1940:54) was the first to distinguish between 'primary' and 'secondary' fills of those pits; later layers were deposits collected in the hollow at the top of the settling pit (the contents of which should not, therefore, be used for dating the feature). At Danebury, an idealised notation has been proposed to classify pit fills concentrating on activity/inactivity sequences (Cunliffe and Poole 1991:162), which I take implies that the pits usually witnessed primary natural silting followed by artificial and natural fills.

Initial basal silts were very common in naturally or artificially filled pits, since they formed quickly from wind blown material, rain wash or leaf fall (Bersu 1940:53; Whittle 1984:145). At Danebury, a far greater proportion of natural fills were encountered, and Whittle (1984:145), following Shackley (1976), discussed the natural sequence of pit filling and how the initial forms of deposits differed with the profile of the pit. Overhanging profiles were particularly susceptible to erosion, and usually completely collapsed within the first year

(Fig. 3.4). Annual sequences of heavy winter erosion produced layers of chalk shatter from the sides, followed by summer lens of wash and soil. There were up to sixteen annual sequences visible in some of the pits at Danebury (Whittle 1984). The re-excavation of abandoned pits at Micheldever, left open for four years, did not confirm Whittle and Shackley's argument that natural silting was a rapid process. Here the depth of fill was fairly constant despite pit depth (Fasham 1987) (Fig. 3.4). The fragile nature of the overhanging neck of beehive shaped pits, so well preserved at Micheldever Wood, lead Fasham (1987:78) to propose that pits must have been deliberately infilled between use for crop storage in order to maintain the profile. The implications of this are far-reaching, for how many of the pits we excavate were originally only provisionally infilled, with the intention being for later reuse.

3. 3. Human Bone

The ways in which whole, or partial, human corpses entered the archaeological record has not been considered problematic, even when interpretations are confused (see 2). Whatever the cause of burial, it is recognised as the result of deliberate deposition. However, common 'stray' human bone fragments on Later Prehistoric sites are a conundrum (see 2.2&4), often interpreted as having come from disturbed burials or exposed corpses, through accidental loss or scavenging. However, Walker (1984) argued that human bone fragments were selected from excarnated corpses and then at a later stage deliberately or accidentally deposited. How this material actually became incorporated into archaeological deposits was only been briefly discussed, and it is disappointing that subsequent work at Danebury argued that stray bone fragments "need not result from a deliberate act of deposition" (Cunliffe & Poole 1991:418), despite significant associations with 'Special Animal Deposits' noted earlier (Grant 1984a:540). At Chanctonbury Ring, Sussex, human bone fragments recovered from the 'bath-tub' like Early Iron Age pit (see 3.2.1) packed with non-local red flint nodules and Cornish granite, pointing to other possible associations (Bedwin 1980:180).

3. 4. Small Finds

No excavation report of the Iron Age is complete without its carefully catalogued and drawn 'small finds' - objects made from metal, stone, worked bone/antler etc. Where used at all, small finds are generally employed as chronological indicators. Although they have been used to identify activity areas within settlements (Sharples 1991a:243-4), and reconstruct exchange and social systems (e.g. Cunliffe 1984a:544ff; Hill 1988 forthcoming a; Marchant 1989; Peacock 1987; Sharples 1991a:244). Yet, with the exception of important limited work on coinages (Haselgrove 1987) and at Maiden Castle (Sharples 1991a:153, 243-249), there is no consideration of the contexts of deposition. It has been simply assumed that the archaeological record was a more or less direct reflection of past activities.

If an explanation of the processes involved in precisely how these brooches, spindle whorls, combs and coins etc. entered the archaeological record is given, they are assumed to have been rubbish or casual losses. Why unbroken large objects, such as quern stones or latch lifters, were lost or discarded is not discussed. 'Unusual' circumstances of discovery have warranted more consideration, such as occasional pits containing large numbers of loom weights (interpreted as loom weight stores at Swallowcliffe Down -- Clay 1925:68-9, or rubbish at Little Woodbury -- Bersu 1940:52ff). At Old Down Farm a similar concentration of loom weights sealed an assortment of iron objects, including linch pins, which were interpreted as possibly an "attempt at concealment" of a "hoard" (Davies 1981:124).

Little attention has been paid to the biases in the recovery of small finds. Levitan (1982:27) suggested that colour, brightness, and the supposed academic value of the find were the greatest influence in manual recovery, with size and abundance playing secondary roles. Work at Maiden Castle (Sharples 1991a:153, Fig 128) has suggested that a greater proportion of clearly recognisable objects, regardless of size, will be recovered during excavation. Sites on chalk usually preserve metal, stone and bone objects well, although clay with flint cappings and other overlying drift deposits may affect this (Sharples 1991a:153).

The few studies which use small find distributions to infer the location of different activities, simply assume that the material was discarded as rubbish or casually lost close to the point of use. This assumption underlines Mytum's (1989) study of Walesland Rath, which quotes several studies to demonstrate that there probably has been little horizontal movement of objects since deposition. However, Mytum never explicitly discussed how and why materials were deposited in the first place. Two neighbouring pits at Winnall, with large deposits of loom weights, were used to infer a "high depositional rate of triangular loom weights", and therefore, weaving in that part of the settlement (Fasham 1985:130). If objects were deposited close to the point of their use, it is never asked why there is such apparent patterning in the Early Iron Age phase, when the "artefact distribution is not so revealing" in the following phase (Fasham 1985:131).

Small finds, particularly metalwork and coinage, deposited off-site have been increasingly interpreted from a 'ritual' perspective. Late Iron Age shrines have deposits of coinage and weaponry (Haselgrove 1989), and Late Iron Age gold coinages are almost exclusively known from off site contexts (Haselgrove 1987). The deposition of weaponry and cauldrons in watery contexts continued on from the Bronze Age (Bradley 1990, Fitzpatrick 1984), while similar fine objects and other classes of small find were occasionally deposited as grave goods in Middle-Late Iron Age East Yorkshire and Late Iron Age South East England (Whimster 1981). Wait (1985:47-49) noticed that the context of deposition of 'prestige' metalwork (weapons, vessels etc.) varied between different parts of Britain. In the Thames Valley and East Anglia 'prestige' items came from ritual deposits in rivers, while in Dorset and Somerset such objects were restricted to settlement sites, where they were *not* interpreted as ritual activity (Wait 1985:254). Hingley (1990c), suggested that in Central Southern England iron 'currency bars' were normally deposited at the margins of settlements, often in or close to the boundary earthworks, and were highly symbolic, if not ritual, deposits. Evidence for the selective deposition of small finds in boundary contexts is coming to light across Britain (e.g. Bowden & McOmish 1987; Ferrell forthcoming; Hingley 1990a) and "hoards" of iron objects have been 'recognised' at Danebury on the basis of the number of complete objects they contain (Cunliffe & Poole 1991:354). Such evidence suggests that the deposition of many of these objects was clearly structured, 'non-functional' (i.e. not our common sense expectations), if not ritual events.

3. 5. Pottery

Pottery has been considered the most important category of find from Iron Age excavations, and provides the major basis for establishing chronology (see 1.5). In addition, pottery is used to discuss exchange (e.g. L Brown 1984, 1987; Morris 1981, forthcoming; Peacock 1969), although social questions have been limited to the identification of 'tribal' affiliations (Cunliffe 1984b:32) through "style zones" (but see Blackmoor et al 1979 as an exception). There has been little consideration of how this pottery entered the archaeological record (exceptions Halstead et al 1978; Hamilton 1985; Lambrick 1984; Pierpoint nd..), although it has recently been recognised as one of the key academic questions in the study of pottery by the <u>Prehistoric Ceramics Research Group</u> (1991; 1992). Iron Age pottery reports are essentially concerned with form and fabric, chronology, and possibly exchange. The potential of pottery being used to address wider issues has been recognised, but not explored (exceptions e.g. Lock 1987, 1990; Lambrick 1984; Sharples 1991a:238-241). Yet, social and formation process questions have been addressed for Later Bronze Age ceramics (e.g. Barrett 1980; Barrett, Bradley & Green 1991; Barrett & Bond 1988; Bradley et al 1980; N. Brown 1988; Gingell & Lawson 1985; Needham & Sørensen 1988).

3.5.1. Preservation

There has been little concern with the bias produced by traditional recovery methods (but see L. Brown 1991:185, Fig 148; Lambrick 1984:162-4; Levitan 1982). In the absence of discussion, I assume that workers feel there is little deterioration of pottery after deposition, although shallowly buried pottery may be affected by trampling. However, Lambrick (1984) suggested that sherds may be affected by leaching on deposition, while Pierpoint's (nd..) study of pottery from Owlsebury (mainly Roman) showed that larger and less abraded sherds were recovered from the deeper features on the site (c.f. animal bone - see 3.7.6.). Pierpoint suggested this was partly due to the type of material entering features, but also that precipitation and weathering had an effect on shallowly buried sherds. Pottery is prone to weathering when exposed, but the effects vary considerably depending on the fabric and finish. The general absence of prehistoric pottery in most field walking collections suggests that it would not survive for many years if exposed on middens etc. Mechanical attrition, particularly trampling, is usually considered the main agent of destruction. In general, sherd size decreases logarithmically through time until halted on burial (Bradley & Fulford 1979:86). As such *Mean Sherd Weight* (*MSW*) can be used as a direct index of pre-depositional attrition (Bradley et al 1980:249), although recent work suggests *MSW* can be the same in different types of context but the degree of sherd abrasion significantly different (Sharples 1991a:239-242 Fig 191). Evans and Millett (1992:239) also suggest that *MSW* is "not necessarily a good discriminant of residual material", and a more detailed examination of these issues is a priority for future research.

3. 5. 2. Spatial Variability

Variations in *MSW* suggested a clear spatial patterning in the character of pottery deposition at the Late Bronze Age site of Aldermaston Wharf (Bradley et al 1980:248ff). From sub-soil features, sherd size was shown not to have any correlation with pot density, but did show a constant fall off away from the middle of the site. This was interpreted as a pattern consistent with the gradual clearance of refuse from the main settled area towards its periphery; the largest sherds tending to be buried closest to where they were last used or broken. Different pottery forms were deposited in different parts of the site, fine ware vessels (Barrett 1980 classes IV & II) concentrated around the houses, while certain large coarse jars (class I) had a peripheral distribution, possibly because they stood as the linings of shallow storage pits. Similarly during the Early Iron Age, at Little Woodbury, red coated fine wares were particular associated with the main house (Brailsford 1948), while at Early Iron Age Winklebury, large fineware sherds were associated with two porched houses (Fisher 1985:179). At Danebury (cp.. 6-8) a comparable pattern to Aldermaston may be seen in the fall-off of pot densities in pits away from the main concentration of houses in the lee of the rampart (L. Brown 1984:250).

3.5.3. Variation between Feature Types

Different types of feature may have different characteristic pottery assemblages because of the different taphonomic pathways through which their contents passed (c.f. animal bone see 3.7.). At Aldermaston the excavators envisaged that pit fills were homogeneous, whereas Pierpoint (nd..) noted considerable variation in the nature of Iron Age and Roman pit assemblages at Owslebury. There is a variation in artefact assemblages from different feature types. At Maiden Castle *MSW* and the proportion of fresh pottery recovered from pits, gullies, and different types of layers were similarly low, but pits contained less severely abraded sherds (Sharples 1991a:239-241 Fig 191).

It is clear that postholes have different artefact assemblages from pits (Fisher 1985:179, see 3.8.3), although how such material became incorporated into postholes is rarely discussed. The occurrence of pottery in postholes is surprising, unless it was used as a deliberate packing, or accidentally incorporated into voids after the destruction of a building. The latter assumes that there was material inside the structure on abandonment/destruction (e.g. Coe et al 1992) and given the small size of most postholes, the potential for this to occur might appear slight. Also the area in/around the structure may have been kept clean (c.f. ethnoarchaeological studies - e.g. Arnold 1990; Deal 1985; Hayden & Cannon 1983) as is suggested by well preserved Upper Thames Valley Iron Age house floors which were "almost entirely free of debris" (Hingley and Miles 1984:63). However, three eighth to sixth century sites in north Wessex have produced evidence for considerable quantities of pottery in the postholes from the south east quadrant of large circular structures. It is suggested such material was in this part of these buildings before they were destroyed by fire (Chadwick-Hawkes 1994; Coe et al 1992; Fitzpatrick 1994a). Although, the drainage gullies surrounding these houses often contain concentrations of material around the doorway, interpreted as the debris from sweeping out houses (Allen et al 1984; c.f. Hodder 1982d:57).

The distribution and origin, of the ubiquitous pottery in enclosure ditches around Later Prehistoric settlements are rarely discussed. Work from several Late Bronze Age sites has suggested that residual material that naturally eroded into fills may only account for a proportion of all pottery in ditches. Other material derived from deliberate dumping, sometimes of fresh material. Such concentrations were not haphazardly placed (see 8.5). At Lofts Farm, large pot sherds recovered from the outer ditch were interpreted as indicating external activities since it was assumed that fresh pottery would have been deposited close to where it was used/broken. Although, it was suggested that comparable dumps of plant material may have originated from inside the enclosure (see 3.6.2.). Ditches may have been regularly cleaned out and re-cut, constantly received large dumps of material which was later removed (Pierpoint nd.. - see 8.4). There are suggestions that deliberate deposits of pottery relate to the abandonment/closing of a site e.g. Late Bronze Age deposits at Lofts Farm (N. Brown 1988:271), the Late Iron Age site at Oving (Hamilton 1985).

3.5.4. Middens

It is often assumed that the majority of pottery was discarded onto middens, which are not preserved on most sites. Inferences about the nature and distributions of former middens have been made using *MSW* at Aldermaston (Bradley et al 1980), assuming midden contents were incorporated into subsoil features. Middens have survived on several unique Late Bronze Age sites such as Runnymede and Potterne. However, the extent to which these represent the general nature of other Later Prehistoric middens, or represent the refuse disposal practices unique to these sites, is debatable.

Studies on pottery from Runnymede (Needham & Sørensen 1988) and Potterne (Gingell & Lawson 1985) suggest very little post-depositional disturbance or movement within the middens (*contra* Bradley's observed patterning at Aldermaston, see 3.5.2). Sherd size appears to have changed little since deposition. Much of the pottery was deposited in distinct groups which represented particular depositional events. Needham and Sørensen (1988) have shown at Runnymede that these often sealed dumps of bone and burnt flint, and were comprised of either a few large sherds from a single vessel (but never representing the whole vessel), or large sherds from a range of vessels - 'primary deposits' (cf. assemblages in pit layers - see 5.2). Complete pots were rarely found in the midden, but were found at the base of the midden or in the river channel. In contrast, the Potterne midden contained secondary or even tertiary deposits of material, the pottery having been deposited somewhere else before being moved to the midden (E. Morris pers. com.). The fills of underlying sub-soil features at both do not appear to reflect the nature of the deposits in the middens that over-lay them. Although this is an important question for further investigation on those sites which both preserve sub-soil features and middens or other surfaces. Are the spatial distributions of material in surface layers and middens mirrored in the contents of sub-soil features - as Bradley argued/assumed at Aldermaston Wharf (see 3.5.2), or different? Even if there are apparent similarities, need these have the same causes? Distributions on surfaces and middens could reflect daily refuse maintenance strategies, those in sub-soil features from irregular ritual deposits.

3.5.5. How Pottery Entered the Archaeological Record

It is important to recognise that only a tiny proportion of the pottery used and broken on a site during its long use has been preserved in subsoil features -- Pierpoint (nd..) suggests between 10 and 1%, although I suggest this may be optimistic (see 1.1, Appendix 2)! There has been little explicit questioning about how pottery entered the archaeological record. What there has shows that assemblages are more complex than had previously been assumed (Lock 1989, 1991). Assemblages represent a combination of deliberate dumping (in some cases related to possible ritual or feasting events), erosion, and migration through natural and human agencies. As such, over-simplified models of deposition should be avoided (Lambrick 1984:167) especially since most assumptions have failed to consider the wider range of possibilities provided by ethnoarchaeology (e.g. careful management, curation and reuse of broken sherds).

Pottery recovered from sites is *secondary refuse* (see 1.2), and of little help in isolating activity areas. Despite the fact that Bradley's (et al 1980:249) study at Aldermaston recognised that pottery could only be used for spatial analysis when it could be demonstrated how it entered particular subsoil features, he moved *directly* on to a consideration of general refuse management strategies. Again, although Bradley acknowledged the nature of *secondary refuse*, he still assumed that large fresh sherds were deposited close to the location of the activity that had created them, reducing the many different origins of pottery assemblages to a single dimension (cf. N. Brown 1988:270). The possibility that this represented material carried some distance for disposal has not been considered, and it must be recognised the pottery we recovered might have been:

> rubbish from a specific operation deliberately discarded nearby; it could also be primary *in situ* rubbish cleared up and thrown out elsewhere; it could represent burial of rubbish which had accumulated on a midden having been generated by a variety of activities; or it may be scattered refuse accidentally incorporated in the backfills of pits, ditches and other holes in the ground (Lambrick 1984:167).

3. 6. Plant Remains

The study of the plant remains recovered from Iron Age sites has always been important. Early approaches concentrated on identifying crop seeds (e.g. Jessen and Helbaek 1944; Helbaek 1952), but in the 1970's it was recognised that weed seeds and other fragments in assemblages offered wider possibilities to understand past agricultural systems. Particular attention was paid to the recognition of 'signatures' in assemblages for different stages in crop processing (Dennel 1974; Hillman 1981; M. Jones 1985). A 'behavioural' approach (after Schiffer 1976), has made a significant impact on Iron Age studies, discussing crop processing activities, the ecology of plant communities, and the complex ways landscapes were articulated (e.g. M. Jones 1984a, 1984b, 1985, 1989).

3.6.1. Stratigraphic variability

The small number of samples usually taken for screening on sites has limited a detailed investigation of how carbonised material entered the archaeological record. Usually only single samples are taken from a few features, so it is difficult to explore any differences between contexts within single features. However, three pits from Danebury (M. Jones 1984a:489-450) and two from Micheldever Wood (Monk with Murphy 1987:55) were sampled in detail stratigraphically to investigate this question.

At Danebury clear changes were found, with the quantity of material and degree of preservation increasing with depth. Jones (1984a) considered three possible explanations for this:

> 1. Movement of material downwards through layers due to the effects of precipitation and faunal disturbance.

> 2. Greater susceptibility to post depositional attrition and destruction in upper layers.

> 3. Change in activities producing the refuse during the course of the pit being filled.

Of the above, the first was rejected since originally sterile layers were encountered within the profiles which showed no sign of collecting material as they may have moved down the fills. The second factor was considered the most important since observations had shown that carbonised material in the upper fills was generally less well preserved than from the lower fills. This suggested that material in the shallow layers was more susceptible to the actions of precipitation, freezing, and thawing, after burial. Jones felt that the third factor was more difficult to assess and that it had little concern with how material actually entered subsoil features. High densities of carbonised material in the basal layers of these pits represented, in at least one case, the burning of the partially germinated and fungus rich crust of a stored product around the pit-edge, as part of the pit cleansing process (M. Jones 1984a:492).

Different contexts within the same pits at Danebury showed considerable consistency in the ratios of grains:weed/seeds:chaff (Fig.3.7). The assemblages throughout a pit-fill had originated from the same particular processing activity, although, differences in the weed seeds between different layers demonstrated that the source material processed did not remain constant as the pit was filled (M. Jones 1984: 490). This is in contrast to the pits from Micheldever Wood where material in different layers clearly originated from different processing activities (Fig. 3.7.), and from the processing of different crops (wheat and barley). This may reflect the separate storage, use, and deposition of waste from processing different crops (Monk with Murphy 1987:55).

3.6.2. Spatial Variability

The spatial distribution of plant remains is important evidence for social and symbolic reconstruction (e.g. Hastorf 1991), but limited sampling on British sites restricts any detailed consideration of these issues (except M.Jones & Nye 1991). General spatial trends are discernible at Middle Iron Age Winnall Down, where wheat was concentrated in the west, especially in the house foundation gullies, and barley and weed seeds in the east of the site (Monk 1985:115 - see 9.5). Jones and Nye (1991:443) suggest that de-husking was a spatially distinct activity at Maiden Castle and Danebury. While at Danebury, clear spatial separation could be seen in cps 4-5, & 7 between high densities of weed seeds, grains and chaff (M.Jones & Nye 1991:444-5). The differences between Danebury and Micheldever Wood discussed above may have resulted from different processing activities spatially separated within Danebury's large interior, all confined within the narrow space of the Banjo Enclosure. At Ashville, Jones (1985:113-4) suggested that different crop processing activities took place in different parts of the settlement. Assemblages from the core of the settlement (from pits and house gullies) were particularly rich in grain, and those from the periphery (largely from ditches) were rich in weed seeds, suggesting that crop cleaning took place on the settlement peripheries.

But this variability at Ashville may reflect distinctions between the assemblages found in different types of subsoil feature, rather than any real spatial variability (c.f. 3.7.4.). Certainly, low density, wheat dominated, assemblages from house wall gullies probably represented casual loss and charring of cereals for dietary use (Monk 1985:112). However, wheat rich samples from pit fills at Ashville may have represented the cleansing of pits after use and not food preparation activities in the vicinity. This raises the need to consider how material actually entered the archaeological record, and how this may have varied between feature types. Identifying the location of activity areas, from plant or other remains, often assumes that the fills of sub-soil features simply reflected activities in their immediate environs. At Lofts Farm (N. Brown 1988), plant material was concentrated in the outer of the two ditches in discrete dumps, but it was suggested that this may not indicate crop processing outside the enclosure. Rather, it was proposed that the interior was kept very clean and the waste dumped outside (Murphy 1988).

3.6.3. How Plant Material Entered the Archaeological Record

There is little concern with how and why carbonised plant material entered the archaeological record, perhaps because of the success the 'behavioural' approach has had in interpreting plant assemblages. When 'formation processes' are discussed, this usually means the processes that created the *pre-carbonised* assemblage, not its subsequent carbonisation and incorporation into the record (e.g. Miksicek 1987). It is simply assumed that carbonised material became incorporated into middens/yard floors (dispersal, weathering, erosion, mixing of assemblages in middens etc. prior to deposition are not considered), and from there entered subsoil features (e.g. M. Jones 1978;107; but see Monk & Fasham 1980).

It must be recognised that plant material only became carbonised under extremely restricted circumstances (Miksicek 1987). The simple burning of crop waste, or a stored product, did not usually result in carbonisation. Moreover, only certain classes of plant product are likely to end up in hearths, ovens, and fires in the first place. Hillman (1981) suggested four main ways by which material can become carbonised, and I would add a fifth:

1. If a stage in crop processing involves drying or parching.

2. The destruction of a diseased crop product.

3. Burning waste as fuel.

4. Accidental carbonisation in food preparation.

5. Background material incorporated in fires etc.

Hillman (1981) suggested that the bulk of material on British sites were the result of the first process. However, the second is represented in sterilisation of pits, and the fourth possibly in the low density, grain rich, assemblages from house wall gullies at Winnall Down. Monk and Fasham (1980) suggested the third was the origin of the majority of carbonised material from pits at Micheldever Wood. Clearly, with the exception of the first and fourth processes, there need be no direct correlation between where (or when) any crop processing activity took place and where the product was burnt. Nor *for all situations* where the ash and cinders were eventually dumped. As such, crop cleaning could have taken place centrally on settlements, with the residues burnt at the periphery and/or ultimately dumped there. What matters is what happened to the material after carbonisation. *The archaeological record does not record the location of past activities but past disposal.*

3. 7. Animal Bones

Detailed examination of animal bones is today an important, if largely independent, feature of later prehistoric excavations. Bones have been collected and identified from the first excavations for species identification and metric analysis (e.g. Jackson 1927, 1943, 1948; Harcourt 1979). Although far greater time and effort is now invested in archaeozoological studies, Maltby (1985a:33) argues that these are still the main concerns in the majority of recent bone

reports, in order to establish the relative proportions of the different species, the age at death, and the identification of butchery mark, in an attempt to reconstruct meat diet and subsistence patterns. Mountenay (1981) argues that such work operates from three basic, questionable, assumptions:

1. An assemblage is derived in a straight forward manner from an animal population herded in the immediate area.

2. A bone assemblage from all types of features in any given site phase is homogeneous.

3. The bone assemblage more or less directly reflects the former living animal population.

These assumptions have been criticised (e.g. Mountenay 1981; Serjeantson 1991b; Wilson 1985, 1989; Coy 1987; Maltby 1979, 1985a) stressing the need to understand what happened to the animal bone between the death of the animal and its archaeozoological study -- taphonomy. Despite considerable work on taphonomic processes (e.g. Binford & Bertram 1977; Binford 1981; Gifford 1981), this has concentrated on gatherer-hunter groups, not sedentary agriculturists, whose bone assemblages have less straight forward taphonomies than those of temporary camps. Nonetheless, taphonomy provides general principles to understand later prehistoric bone assemblages and a combination of differential preservation, butchery, and disposal practices produced most of the observable variation in bone assemblages (Maltby 1985b:99, 1985a).

3.7.1. Retrieval Bias

Perhaps greater concern has been paid to retrieval bias in British archaeozoology than taphonomic questions (e.g. Barker 1975; Payne 1972), although almost all bones are still hand collected. Levitan (1982:27) suggested that bone is not ranked highly in the priorities of diggers compared to other finds, while factors such as fragment size, abundance and distribution are important in determining the degree of recovery. As such, it is important to recognise that *hand collections may severely distort the representability of any assemblage*, and are particularly biased towards larger bone fragments (see 6.3.3). Small bones (e.g. loose teeth, limb extremities, vertebrae), especially from smaller animals (sheep compared to cattle, new born and juveniles with unfused bones compared to adults), will be under represented with consequences for relative species abundance, assessments of the proportions of meat vs. waste bearing bone, and detailed taphonomic analyses using relative anatomical part frequencies (Maltby 1985a:36-40).

3.7.2. Preservation

Ethnoarchaeology has shown that bone in surface assemblages is easily destroyed through a variety of mechanical, chemical and biological agents. Dog gnawing has been particularly stressed (e.g. Binford & Bertram 1977; Legge 1991a; Kent 1981), along with trampling, weathering, and soil acidity (Serjeantson 1991b). The scattering of bones by dogs, and other natural and human activities, may move bones considerable distances from where first deposited. In general bone survival is directly related to density and robustness, a factor of animal size, age, and anatomy. Therefore, larger mammals such as cattle and horse have denser bones than sheep and pig, which are more prone to destruction. Size is related to age, but bones from younger animals are also more porous, and limbs are prone to fragmentation before the fusing of the epiphysis. Certain parts of the skeleton are denser or more robust than others, for example teeth are particular resistant and are the last part of the skeleton to survive after other bone has been destroyed.

Like retrieval bias, differential preservation challenges the basic assumptions behind most bone analyses. Poorly preserved assemblages severely under-represent the original proportions of smaller and younger animals, and different anatomical parts. Various measures have been proposed to assess the degree of preservation of bone assemblages such as the percentages of loose teeth, percentages of all anatomical parts, preserved articular surfaces, unidentifiable bone, eroded fragments, and gnawed fragments (Maltby 1985a:40-49). However, more spatial evidence than would at first appear likely can be obtained from poorly preserved bone material from preserved ground surfaces and yard floors (Allen & Robinson 1993; Wilson 1989). In general, ethnoarchaeology has suggested that the various destructive factors at work on bone assemblages, and the rarity of their deliberate or accidental burial on rural settlements (e.g. Hodder 1982a; Kramer 1982:44) would lead us to expect, especially where only sub-soil features are preserved, that *on later prehistoric sites only a tiny proportion of the bones originally discarded will be recovered, and they will be scattered, disturbed and badly preserved* (Maltby 1985a:55) (see 1.2).

3.7.3. Carcass Utilisation and Butchery

Another factor questioning an uncritical analysis of animal bone is the impact of differential disposal of parts of the carcass during butchery and subsequent consumption (Maltby 1985a:49-57). Halstead et al (1978) suggested that distinct proportions of meat bearing, skull:limb, bones in any assemblage reflected the different stages of carcass processing from butchery to consumption (c.f. the 'behavioural' approach in archaeobotany). Three types of waste were recognised, each with consequences for how bone entered the archaeological record and the species represented:

Slaughter & Butchery Waste	Kitchen Waste (food preparation)	Table Waste (food consumption)
Offensive waste		Inoffensive waste
Buried	<------------------ >	Discarded on ground
Cattle/Horse bone stripped of meat	<------------------>	Sheep/Pig meat cooked on the bone
Assemblages dominated by Cattle/Horse	<------------------->	Assemblages dominated by Sheep/Pig

The exact details of this work appear unrepeatable on other sites, and it can be criticised for not considering retrieval bias, overt presentism/functionalism, and, especially, a failure to consider taphonomic factors (see previous section). But other work does support these general distinctions e.g. at Micheldever Wood evidence suggested that sheep, but not cattle, were cooked on the bone (Coy 1987:46). At many sites a contrast can be made between assemblages dominated by bones from large species/adults and those dominated by bones from small species/young. This distinction is often expressed spatially (Maltby 1985a, 1985b; Wilson 1985).

3.7.4. Spatial Variability

At Wendens Ambo a clear contrast in the nature, quantity and quality of bone assemblages was evident between the centre and periphery of settlements. Bone densities decreased away from the focus of domestic activities, or at least the centre, at several sites (e.g. Coy 1987:49; B.Wilson 1985:88; Maltby 1985b:105). Greater proportions of large mammal bones were often found on the margins of sites compared to the core (e.g. Britnell 1989:116; Maltby 1985b:105), even in situations where very poor preservation greatly under represented the original abundance of sheep/pig bone (B.Wilson 1985:88-9). It was suggested that this implied that slaughter and butchery took place away from habitation areas, at Middle Iron Age Easton Lane this was possibly several 100m's from the settlement at Winnall Down (Maltby 1989:127). This pattern is explained by the functional needs of hygiene, that butchery waste, particularly from the larger species, would have been considered 'offensive' and so deposited on the margins of settlements.

Several qualifications must be raised against this interpretation, including its universalist/functionist premise (Moore 1982:75), and the basic assumption that refuse was deposited at or close to the location of the activity that produced it. As all bone assemblages from Wessex Iron Age sites are *secondary refuse*, they do not reflect the position of past activity areas but past depositional areas. It is possible to envisage slaughter of all animals in the centre of a site, but with the waste subsequently dumped on the margins. The periodic cleaning up of sites and the removal of large/coarse waste to middens, fires, or off site would effectively scramble any original discard patterns that related to activity areas (Serjeantson 1991 cf. Arnold 1990; Deal 1985; Hayden & Cannon 1983). Equally, the very notion of 'waste' in a subsistence economy can be questioned (Serjeantson pers. com.). It must be recognised that much of the apparent bias for dumping of butchery waste on the peripheries of Wessex sites comes from the occurrence of large exceptional dumps, often deliberately buried, of well preserved cattle/horse bone in these locations, distorting overall proportions of Cattle/Horse v Sheep/Pig. These need not necessarily represent daily practices (see 3.7.7.). Such gross spatial distinctions fail to account for the marked differences in the proportions of the principle species found between different types of archaeological feature. Ditches, usually by definition the periphery of an Iron Age site, have bone assemblages dominated by cattle and horse, but this may not be simply because of their location.

3.7.5. Variation between Feature Type

The differences in the bone assemblages recovered from enclosure ditches and pits are considerable (Maltby 1981, 1985a:41-8, 1985b:99ff), and largely due to differential preservation of bone between closed and open features. Bone in a closed feature (i.e. those infilled quickly) such as a pit, is largely protected from the effects of gnawing, trampling, weathering, compared to that in an open (i.e. slowly infilled feature) such as a ditch, house gully, or hollow. As such, assemblages from pits are better preserved than those from ditches. For any given species the less robust anatomical parts occur in greater proportions in pits. Similarly, smaller species such as sheep and pig will be better represented in pits than ditches. This would explain the high proportions of cattle bone in the gullies and occupation layers at Maiden Castle (Sharples 1991a:241 Table 93).

Close examination of the ditch fills at Winnall Down has shown that the high proportions of cattle and horse compared to the pit assemblages were not solely due to preservation, but also to the differential spatial deposition of the larger species. Sheep bone was very poorly preserved in the ditch, but most of the cattle/horse bone was deliberately buried in the ditch in a fresh state (Maltby 1985b:97). This would appear to be a general pattern for bone assemblages in ditches, a combination of poorly preserved 'background' material eroded into the ditch, with specific dumps of well preserved material, sometimes of a single species, rapidly buried. Equally, hut foundation gullies at Winnall Down have badly preserved assemblages but are still dominated by sheep bone - cooking/consumption waste (Maltby 1985b:104, in contrast to those at Maiden Castle Sharples 1991a:241). This suggested that no one factor can account for the variability seen in the archaeology, nor expressed by any one measure of bone preservation (Serjeantson 1991b:86). Different types of feature have distinctly different bone assemblages, largely due to the inter-relationship of *Preservation* and *Carcass Utilisation/Disposal* ;

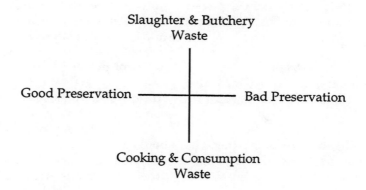

Slaughter & Butchery
Waste

Good Preservation ———————— Bad Preservation

Cooking & Consumption
Waste

The inter-relationship of these two factors has had important implications for attempts at subsistence reconstruction. The assumption (see 3.7.1.) is that all bone recovered from a single phase is homogeneous, and a direct reflection of the overall proportions of domestic animals and their age ranges in the herds kept by past settlements. Maltby (1985a) has pointed out, that since the greater proportion of an overall assemblage is provided from ditch fills compared to pits, so the overall proportions of cattle and horse will increase, and that this probably bore little relationship to their original abundance. As such the 'typical' Iron Age economy dominated by sheep needs careful re-evaluation. It may simply be a 'pit economy' (Maltby *per com.*). Equally, mortality profiles which are used to demonstrate culling regimes, and a concentration on wool and milk production in the period (e.g. Grant 1984:501ff, 1984b; Maltby 1985b:106), will be skewed by the better preservation of cooking/consumption waste and its higher than original proportions of younger animals in pits (it is further biased by the deliberate burial of considerable numbers of neo-natal animals, see below).

3.7.6. Stratigraphic Variation within Features

There can also be considerable variability between the contexts within a single feature type. Hodder (1982d:55) noted that the uppermost fills of pits at Wendens Ambo contained very different, high density, assemblages compared to the rest of the feature. Wilson (1985:89) showed that deeper features contained better preserved assemblages, hence pits and ditches contained better preserved bone than postholes, scoops, and yard floors. At Maiden Castle, shallow features contained higher percentages of root-etched bone than pit, although there was little difference in the proportions of medium and poorly preserved bone between different contexts (Sharples 1991a:240).

At Balksbury, Maltby (nd2) divided the pits into upper and lower halves to examine the above question, and showed that bones in the upper halves of pits were statistically significantly less well preserved than in the lower halves, with greater fragmentation, proportions of loose teeth, evidence of erosion, and under representation of the less robust elements of the skeleton. One consequence of this was that the proportions of cattle and horse were greater in the upper than lower halves. Maltby interpreted these differences as having indicated that bone in upper fills closer to the ground surface were susceptible to the effects of water percolation, freeze-thaw, root action, sediment compaction, and possibly trampling. Significantly, articulated/associated groups of bone were predominantly found in the lower halves, and this was possibly due to better preservation, or because of deliberate dumping in lower pit fills (the deeper burial of large parts of the carcass for reasons of hygiene (nd2:25)) (see 6.3 for further discussion).

3.7.7. Articulated/Associated Animal Remains & 'Animal Special Deposits'

The controversy over the identification and interpretation of 'ritual animal deposits' from Later Prehistoric settlement evidence has already been discussed (see 2.3). This 'ritual' class of animal remains must be considered within the overall context of the deposition of animal bone in general, if it is to understood at all (B.Wilson 1992). In order to be more critical of the term 'special', in this thesis I use the term *Articulated or Associated Animal Bone Group (ABG)*.

The definition of 'Special Animal Deposits' (Grant 1984a:533-546, 1984c) described a series of deposits encountered at Danebury, which were interpreted as a distinct ritual behaviour, distinguished "either through their associations with other bones or by the manner of their deposition" (Grant 1984a:533). The "manner of their deposition" included association of burials from more than one animal, major differences in the overall proportions of the different species represented compared to overall bone totals, and deliberate positioning which implied more than haphazard disposal (Grant 1984a:542). Grant (1984a:533), followed by Wait (1985:125), distinguished three types of Special Animal Deposit:

1. 'Animal Burials'

Fully or mainly articulated skeletons with *no signs of butchery*, not even skinning, often carefully placed in a pit. Sometimes the animal had been beheaded, and the skull displaced.

2. Skulls

Complete, or near complete, skulls. Grant also included complete horse mandibles in this group.

3. Articulated Limbs

Complete articulated limbs, or articulated portions of limbs. The occurrence of articulated groups of limb extremity may suggest the deposition of an animal skin.

Wait (1985:138-146) suggested that such deposits were placed in the interior of occupation sites, usually close to either houses or paddocks, in contrast to human remains which were deposited away from houses. It is also becoming clear that there are significant associations between the presence of 'special deposits' and human or bird bone, in pits during certain phases at Danebury (Grant 1984a:540-1). However, it is still assumed that the other contents of pits containing such deposits, are just rubbish similar to that in other features (Wait 1985:126).

Other archaeozoologists are more sceptical in describing such deposits as 'ritual' (see 2.3). At Maiden Castle only articulated/associated groups from partial carcasses were recovered. Although not considered as "usual domestic rubbish" they were felt unlikely to "represent ritual activity", although such "organised disposal of butchery waste" might be associated with "special meals" or a "celebratory event" (Armour Chelu 1991:146, 151). Maltby paid particular attention to identifying groups of associated bone from individual animals which may have represented the original articulated groups at deposition. But the language used to describe these is one of 'dumping' and 'discard', not 'placement' or 'offering'. At Winnall Down he distinguished three types of such groups (Maltby 1985b:103-4):

1. The burial of complete, or substantial parts of a, carcass with *little or no evidence of butchery*.

2. The burial of foetal or neo-natal carcasses.

3. Small groups of associated/articulated bone such as parts of limbs and vertebral columns.

Noticeably, Maltby only really discussed the last two. The second were taken to have represented some of the expected mortality of foetal and young animals. In particular, the large number of neo-natal dogs found at several sites were interpreted as the deliberate control over litter size (e.g. Maltby 1981:191; 1985b:107). However, Maltby never explained why any neo-natal fatalities should be dumped in pits at all, and not consumed or simply

disposed of above ground. The third type of deposit were simply regarded as the dumping of primary butchery waste (Maltby nd2;5). More or less complete skulls were not regarded as a distinct type of deposit, although these may have been specially treated, deliberately disposed of in the lowest layers of pits at Balksbury (Maltby nd2;10).

At Iron Age/Roman Owslebury it was suggested that some burials may also be of diseased animals (Maltby nd1). An extremely high proportion of dog bones from later prehistoric sites came from either complete carcasses, partial carcasses, or smaller articulated groups (Armour Chelu 1991; Maltby 1981, 1985b), and Maltby has suggested that the last two groups simply represented disturbed complete carcasses initially disposed of in rubbish heaps (Maltby nd1). However, if Runnymede is taken as *typical* of Later Prehistoric rubbish heaps it would suggest that such practices were not common. This midden contained very little articulated or associated bone, then usually of very small units, of any species (Serjeantson 1991b). Only once has Maltby argued that complete animal burials, a pig and dog in pit 6595 at Winnall Down, may have a "connection with some ritual or ceremonial event" (Maltby 1985a:56), and then not in the actual published report for the site (Maltby 1985b:25&103). In general Maltby felt that:

> although the slaughter of animals may often have been associated with ritual or ceremonial events...it is thought that the large proportion of articulated bones were not of any particular significance that cannot be explained *by the events normally associated with pastoral farming..* (Maltby nd1, my emphasis).

Maltby is open to the possible symbolic aspects of faunal remains (1985a:57). Equally, he, like Armour-Chelu 1991) has suggested certain deposits are evidence for feasting (1985a: 55-56,60-61). Note that both consider feasting as distinct from animal sacrifice (see 7.4 for further discussion). At several sites he has suggested that pits contained excellently preserved, high densities, of bone (usually cattle/horse) from a number of individuals (often with some small associated/articulated bone groups - see Fig 7.1), represented unusually large butchery events (e.g. Old Down Farm, Maltby 1981; Winnall Down, Maltby 1985b ; Lains Farm, Coy nd.; Winklebury, R. Jones 1977). The slaughter of animals in larger than daily/weekly required numbers, at the same time produced large quantities of obnoxious waste which made immediate burial desirable (after Kramer 1982:44). Although other ethnoarchaeology suggests burning as an alternative (Hodder 1987:426). It has been suggested that such exceptional events represented large inter-community feasting (c.f. Legge 1981; Mountenay 1981). These large deposits, "the most convincing examples of specific carcass utilisation events, are by their size, *unusual and atypical of the daily disposal of bone waste*" (Maltby 1985a:56, my emphasis). As such, their often marginal location on sites, contributing to the high proportions of cattle/horse at the periphery, may not have been typical of the location of daily animal butchery and/or the disposal of its waste (see 3.7.4.)- although work from Mingies Ditch may question this (Wilson 1989; Allen & Robinson 1993).

3.7.8. Wild Animal Bone

Non-domestic animals contribute only a tiny proportion of the bone recovered from Later Prehistoric sites in Southern Britain, and it is generally agreed that their exploitation was of little economic/calorific importance (Coy 1984a; Grant 1981, 1984a:546-7). Despite their rarity, there has been speculation about how wild animal and bird bone actually entered the archaeological record.

Rodent, insectivore, and amphibian bone often occur in great numbers in deep features, especially at or near the base (Armour Chelu 1991; R. Jones 1977b; Maltby 1989:126-7). These represented pit fall victims, small animals that have fallen into features and have been unable to climb/jump out. This was originally suggested by Bersu (1940:53), who even identified the marks on pits walls where the desperate animals tried to climb out! Alternatively, such bone could have come from the pellets or sprays of predators (Armour Chelu 1991; Coy 1984a:526). The remains of other smaller mammals are also usually interpreted as pit fall victims (Maltby 1989:126). Other suggested possibilities include natural deaths in burrows for fox or badger skeletons (R. Jones 1977a:65), or the deliberate killing of pests subsequently dumped in pits (Coy 1984a:526). At Winklebury, a red deer with twelve associated foxes in pit 3826 was difficult to explain. The only attempt suggested that "it is possible, but unlikely, that the animal (deer) fell in and was unable to extricate itself" (R. Jones 1977a:65).

The taphonomy of bird bones is poorly understood, and why bird bone is found on sites is rarely considered in detail (Livingstone 1989). It is simply assumed that the majority of bird bone came from food and, therefore, represented 'rubbish' -- Raven bones from two pits at Boscombe Down were interpreted as "perhaps the remains of raven stew" (Richardson 1951:129) -- although some might have by chance died naturally on site, or were brought on to the site by dogs or other animals/birds (Coy 1984b, Serjeantson 1991a:479). It has also been suggested that birds of prey were deliberately killed as pests (Harcourt 1979:155; Serjeantson 1991:481), or for their feathers (Serjeantson 1991a:481; Ericson 1987). Closer examination has suggested that the majority of bird bones recovered on Wessex sites are wing bones, and articulated/associated wing bones from individual birds are not uncommon (Coy 1984b:530; Serjeantson 1991:481) (Fig. 3.8.).

The few taphonomic studies of bird bone have commented on similar features in other assemblages.

Ericson (1987) argued that the proportion of posterior to anterior extremities (wing to leg bones) was an index of human utilisation. Heavy human exploitation of birds for food resulted in a high proportion of leg to wing bone. (1989) has shown that this approach takes no account of either preservation or differential recovery biases. Wing bones are the most robust part in most bird skeletons, although this differs between species. Waterfowl living in shallow water, and/or that take flight easily, have robust lower wing bones and such factors must be borne in mind considering Iron Age assemblages. However the recovery of complete articulated wings has suggested that some of the bias towards wing bones came from the removal of the wings from the main meat mass of the bird prior to cooking (Coy 1984b:530). This still does not explain why wing bones, sometimes articulated (and feathered), appear to have been selectively deposited in pits, and not the bone from the next stages of preparation and consumption.

Particularly for bird bones, symbolic and ritual motives behind their deposition have been suggested. At Danebury, Grant (1984a:540) discovered a significant relationship between the presence of 'animal special deposits' and bird bone in pits in certain phases, and argued that the deposition of (substantially) complete birds, particularly Ravens and other Corvids, might be a particular type of 'animal special deposit'. Such 'ritual' burials were quite common on other Iron Age sites in Wessex, and may include non-Corvid species, for example Buzzard (Serjeantson forthcoming). Several complete mammal carcasses may also have been ritual deposits (Winklebury pit 3825, Wait 1985:138). The occurrence of immature badger and fox skeletons in the same layer of the same pit at Danebury may have been "an unusual form of special deposit', although "this can only be a matter of speculation" Grant (1984a:526). However, these complete small mammal carcasses could have been skinned and the carcasses dumped (Serjeantson pers. com.; B.Wilson forthcoming).

3.7.9. How Animal Bones Entered the Archaeological Record

> Those who argue that the development of a more rigorous methodology involving the detailed recording of bone fragments and their context is of secondary importance to the traditional role of the faunal specialist (palaeoeconomic reconstruction) are suffering from the delusion that current methodologies are providing accurate 'answers'. Unless all causes of faunal variability have been considered, no claims about the pastoral economy can be regarded as reliable (Maltby 1985a:67).

Maltby and others have shown that the basic assumptions behind most previous archaeozoological work are wrong. They have stressed that bone assemblages are not a direct reflection of a past population, but represented only a tiny proportion of the carcasses processed/consumed on a site, and that this has been affected by a wide range of subsequent human and natural processes.

Bone ended up in the archaeological record in a variety of ways. Some bone was directly dumped into features, which Grant (1984a:496) and Armour Chelu (1991) have considered the origins of most bone assemblages. Maltby saw burial as the norm for large quantities of odorous waste from butchery, along with near birth fatalities and diseased animals. It was assumed that the majority of bone waste, especially less odorous material, was simply discarded on middens or yard floors (Halstead et al 1979:122-3; Maltby nd2:69). The material would then have been gradually scattered and destroyed through the actions of dogs, weathering, and trampling. The deliberate infilling of features with midden/yard floor material is not considered. The driving force behind such assumptions is a universalist, presentist/functional, notion of hygiene and abhorrence of obnoxious waste. As such faunal assemblages will be "scattered, badly disturbed, and poorly preserved" (Maltby 1985a:55).

3.8. How We Currently Understand How Things Entered the Iron Age Archaeological Record?

This chapter aimed to provide a thorough discussion of the assumptions about how the material we excavate from Later Prehistoric settlement evidence in Southern England became part of the archaeological record. In general, there has been little explicit concern with questions of archaeological formation processes with British archaeology. The detailed discussion of the few studies on Iron Age material that have sought to investigate these issues must be recognised as exceptional. When this research was begun there have been almost no attempts to systematically combine and compare different classes of finds, nor have there been attempts to investigate the possible associations between 'ritual' deposits and other material, although this may be a profitable line of enquiry (see 3.7.7). However, even the exceptional studies discussed above have usually failed to consider the basic question of how and why material became incorporated in subsoil features.

It is apparent that the general, usually unarticulated, assumption behind analyses of all types of find is that it was rubbish. This was a common premise about finds from settlement excavations generally, and as refuse (from household, agricultural, craft and exchange activities) the material was felt to directly and securely reflect past activities.

Maltby's pioneering work needs to be read by specialists on other classes of finds. Without considering the possible symbolic and ritual aspects

of deposition, the taphonomic investigation of bone assemblages questioned the basic equation of past living herd structure and present archaeological record. It must be recognised that this is equally the case for pottery assemblages, which will have no straightforward relationship to the original proportions of form and fabric, local or imported wares, used on a site.

Work on different classes of finds has demonstrated that there is considerable spatial variation in the composition and nature of assemblages on sites, particularly between settlement core and periphery (see 3.5.2.; 3.6.2.; 3.7.4). Considerable variation is also demonstrated between the nature of fills in different types of subsoil features (see 3.5.3.; 3.7.5.), and variability between vertical differences within the fills of single features (see 3.5.5.; 3.6.2.; 3.7.6.). This variability is the result of a complex interaction of factors which included the origins of the material, the state of preservation, and the time lapsed before final deposition. No single, simple reductionist explanation of formation processes is adequate (Lambrick 1984:167). We need to consider individual contexts and reconstruct their *taphonomic pathways, the 'life-histories' of features and assemblages*.

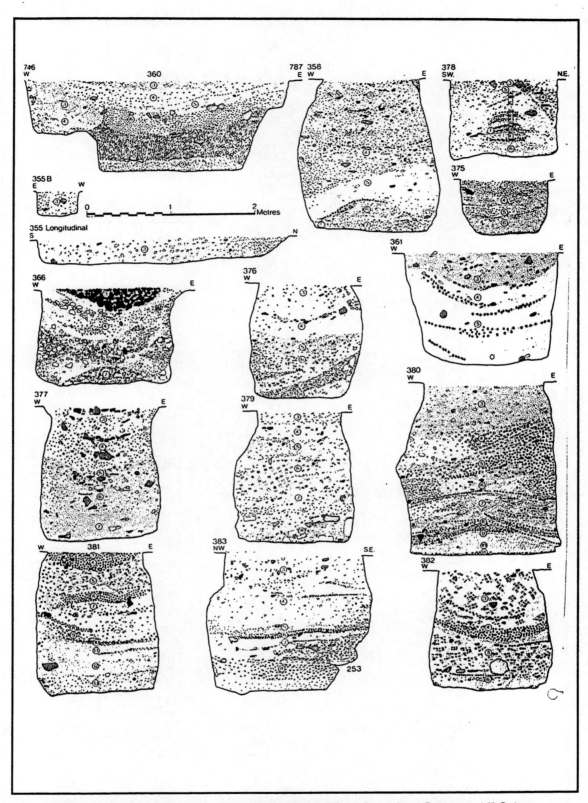

Fig. 3.1. Examples of pit sections: Early, Middle and Late Iron Age Gussage All Saints
(Wainwright 1979: Fig 14.)

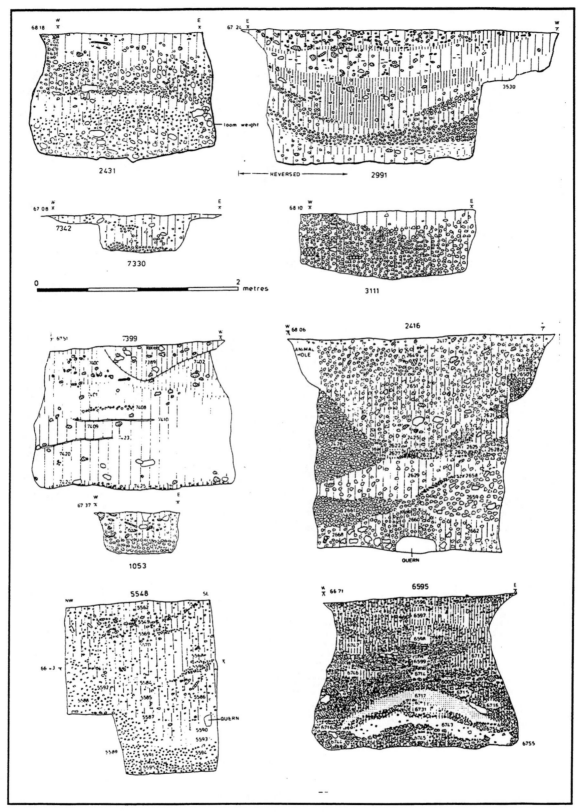

Fig. 3.2. Examples of pit sections: Early and Middle Iron Age Winnall Down
(Fasham 1985; Figs 14&19).

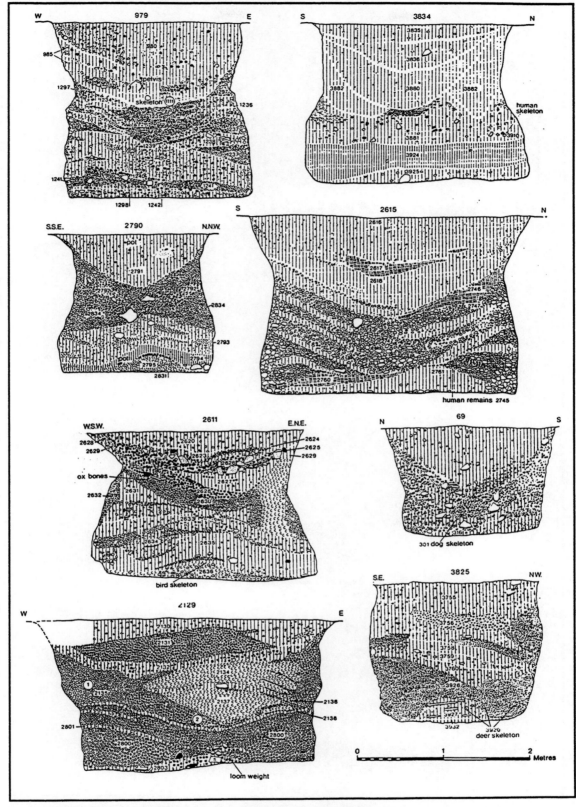

Fig. 3.3. Examples of pit sections: Middle Iron Age Winklebury
(Smith 1977; Figs 19, 20, 21).

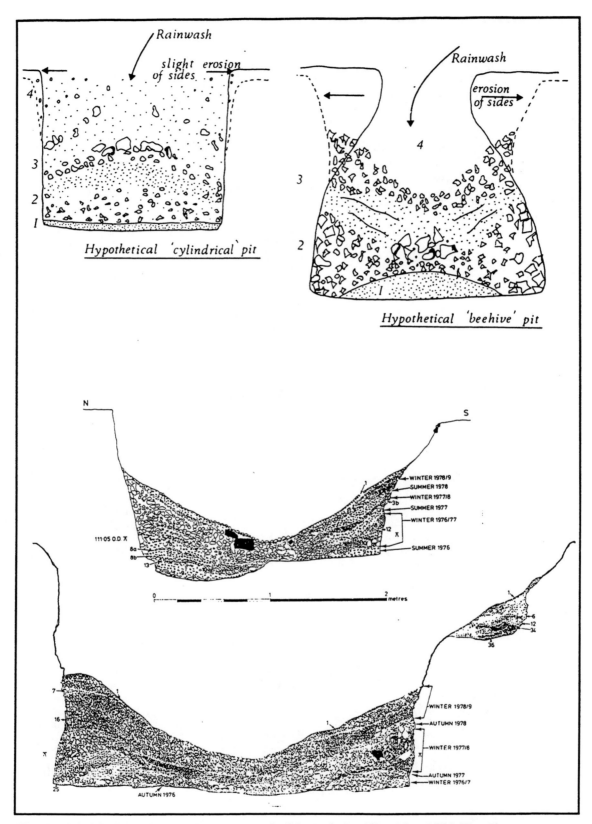

Fig. 3.4.(a). Models of natural erosion and silting of pits (Shackley 1976; Fig. 5).

Fig. 3.4. (b). Micheldever Wood. Sections through beehive shaped pits left open for three
years after they were originally excavated to study natural processes of erosion and
silting.

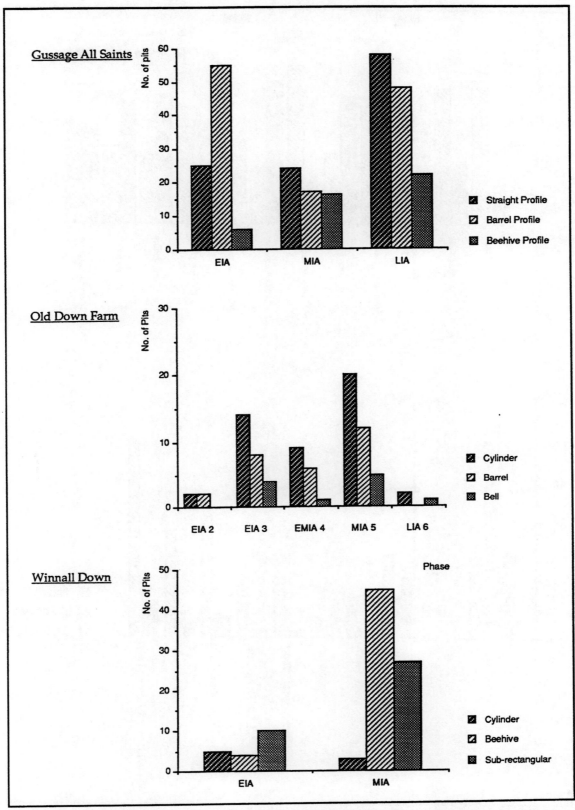

Fig. 3.5. Histogram of the change in proportions of different shapes of pit through time at Gussage, Old Down Farm and Winnall Down.

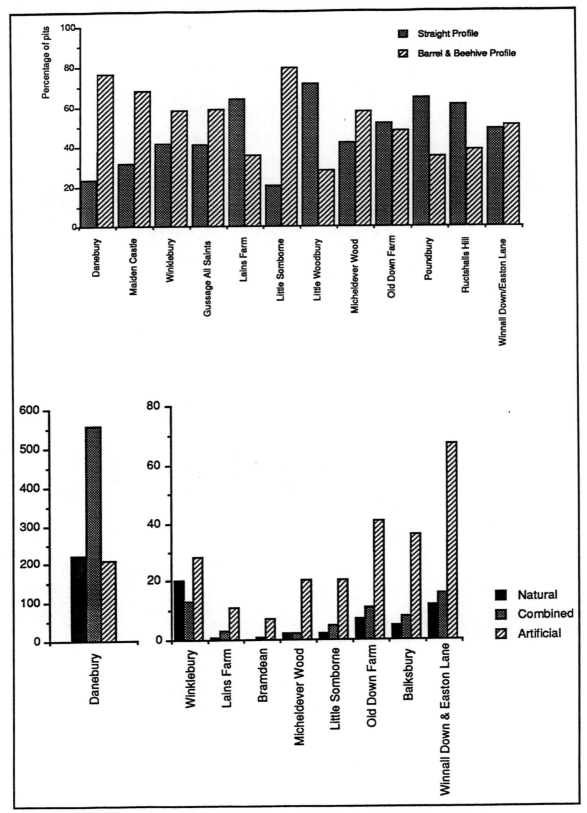

Fig. 3.6.(a). Histogram of the proportion of straight and barrel/beehive profiled pits at twelve sites in Wessex.

Fig. 3.6.(b). Histogram of the proportion of pits with natural, artificial, or combined fills at nine sites in Wessex.

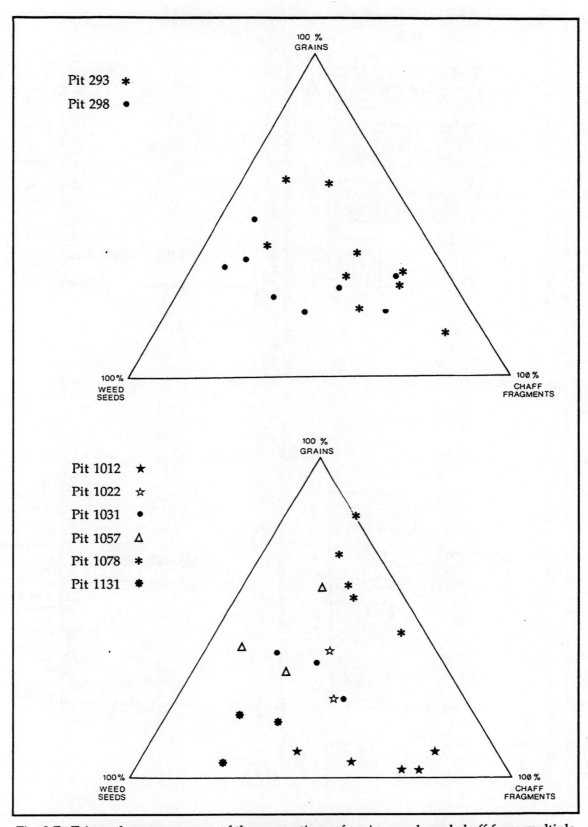

Fig. 3.7. Triangular scattergrams of the proportions of grain, weeds and chaff from multiple samples of carbonized plant remains taken from the single pits at Danebury and Micheldever Wood (after Jones 1984a: Fig 9.9. & Monk with Murphy 1987: Table 16).

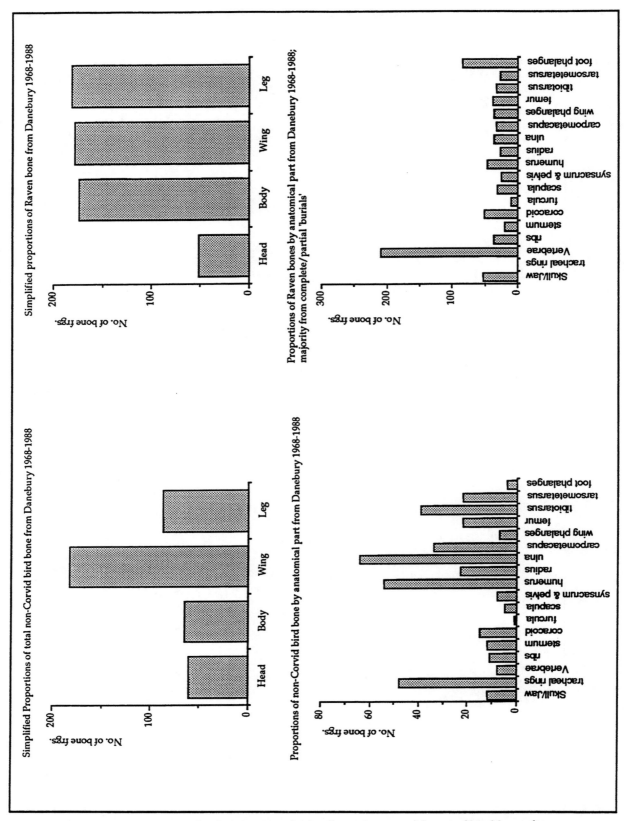

Fig. 3.8. Histograms showing the dominance of wing bone in assemblages of bird bone from Danebury. The Corivid bone at this site (Ravens, Crows etc.) predominantly came from finds of complete/partial skeletons, unlike all other bird bone.

Chapter 4
Questions, Methods & Data

4.1. Introduction

Previous chapters have summarised the current assumptions held about how the archaeological record on Iron Age settlements was formed. I have argued that there has been little concern until recently with questions of site formation processes in British Later Prehistoric archaeology, despite the demonstration by Schiffer and others that these *have to be central concerns for any archaeology*. Discussions of Later Prehistoric settlements are plagued by our oppositions between ritual and rubbish, sacred and profane, symbol and function. As such, despite the long recognition of 'odd' behaviour such as human burials on these sites, their consequences on the other contents of the same or other features have not been considered. This is still true when the common interpretation of all contents as 'rubbish' is inverted so they all become ritual. These discussions show the need to focus in greater detail on the archaeological record; recognising that apparent success in using archaeological data does not mean such uses are secure. This has been clearly shown by taphonomic studies of animal bone, an approach extended here to all categories of finds. From these previous discussions, six objectives for this study may be distilled, all related to the two basic questions asked at the end of chapter 1.

1. Why is there an archaeological record?

2. How did past societies produce the specific archaeological evidences we recover today?

To address these points I have attempted to understand the context of the material found on Iron Age sites through investigating the possible inter-relations between different classes of archaeological finds normally studied in isolation. As such, in this study I consider the possible relationships between the pottery, animal bone, small finds and human remains deposited in the same features and across a site. This is to concentrate on;

a) Which activities in the past may have produced the material we recovered.

b) What may have happened to that material before it entered the archaeological record.

c) Why it entered the record (was this accidental or deliberate?).

d) How that material may have been subsequently transformed after deposition.

Concentrating on pits, the analyses in the following chapters investigate the nature of their deposits, before considering spatial patterning within pit deposits and whether similar deposits are found in other types of feature. Throughout, the provisional nature of my conclusions must always be borne in mind. Particularly where I consider the vertical differences within feature fills, and, especially, the characteristics of individual feature fills/layers, there has been very little comparable work (except by some archaeozoologists - see 3.7.6). However, distinct patterns are observable in the data at these detailed levels of analyses which require further investigation before more solid interpretations can be made. The tentative conclusions I have made from these studies are supported by the more convincing conclusions that can be drawn from the investigation of associations within the overall contents of a pit. This is to stress that this study is not the final word, but only a beginning for further work on, the study of formation processes on Later Prehistoric settlements and the structuring of Iron Age societies.

Objectives

1. To recognise that only tiny amounts of the material used and created on Later Prehistoric sites entered the archaeological record, and that when ever material of any kind is recovered we should always first ask why this fortuitous event occurred if the material is to be interpreted correctly.

2. What are the consequences of the presence of human remains, ranging from complete 'carcasses' to individual fragments, on the other finds found in the same archaeological features? Are such assemblages of finds significantly different from those features without deposits of human remains?

3. The dichotomy in our thinking between rubbish and ritual is clearly seen over the interpretation of so called 'Animal Special Deposits'; are they sacred deposits or butchery waste - or both? Can a rigorous approach be developed to assess whether deposits of any material were rubbish or ritual, if not something else?

4. In answering such questions, it is necessary to develop a detailed understanding of the nature and formation of archaeological deposits on Iron Age sites in Wessex, their transformation by natural processes, and, especially, the culturally/ historically specific social practices which produced them.

5. It can be demonstrated that excavated settlement evidence, and the associated artefacts and ecofacts, could have been structured according to symbolic schemes, rationalities and common senses very different to our own. This suggests that the

recognition of such differences has wide implications for our understanding of European societies in the past and raises new questions to ask of our data.

6. Finally, we need to recognise that considerations of site formation processes seriously challenge our reconstructions of prehistoric economies and social organisations. A concentration on the detail of the archaeological record must inevitably lead to archaeological focus on human practice/praxis, which ought to lead to a reformulation of Social Archaeology.

4.2. The Selection and Nature of the Data

From the outset of this study, I chose to investigate a number of sites. It is possible that a single well excavated site, such as Winnall Down, would have provided ample data for a thesis, but the result would have been narrowly focused. As this study initially arose from a comparison of hillforts and non-hillforts sites in an attempt to understand something of Iron Age social organisation, it was natural to extend such a comparative approach to a consideration of deposition. Were there differences in the depositional practices on different types of sites? A large number of sites also allowed possible variations between the same type of site to be examined.

The majority of the sites studied were from Hampshire, the result of the focus of rescue work in the county over the last twenty years. This emphasis on Hampshire has two advantages. Firstly, it allows a consideration of similarities and differences between sites relatively close to each other. A study encompassing the whole of Wessex would have to confront the differences in both depositional practices and social organisation that are becoming apparent within what was assumed to be a homogeneous region (e.g. Sharples 1991c). Secondly, these sites can be directly compared with the work at Danebury, the site that dominates the Wessex Iron Age, and several sites considered here are within ten kilometres of this hillfort. The only exception to this concentration was Gussage All Saints, included as it is a type site for Downland Iron Age settlements. All the sites in this study were located on the chalk of the Downlands and so similar processes of natural erosion, infilling and post-depositional transformation can be assumed to have operated on all the sites. They were all excavated in a similar manner, with machine stripping of the topsoil and then hand excavation of the features cut into the chalk. In all cases this involved the sectioning of such features, and usually only one half of a pit fill was excavated.

Ultimately, the selection of the sites was determined by the state and the availability of their archives. This is one of the first studies in British archaeology that have attempted to use site archives from rescue projects in a detailed way. As a result, I have found that many archives do not contain adequate information to allow a full, detailed, 're-excavation' of the site on paper. Equally, archives are often not as well curated as the finds from the same sites. Access to the site archives was difficult for both Danebury (because of work in progress) and Gussage, where investigations for this study relied solely on information in the published reports. It was only after the completion of the thesis that I looked at the Gussage archive in detail, and some of the results from this later study have been added here. For the other sites it was possible to consult the archives, although the degree of detail recorded varied considerably (see Table 4.1 for a summary).

Ultimately only Winnall Down provided full enough information about all classes of material at the level of individual feature fills/layers I required. On other sites such information might be available for the animal bone, with data on species and anatomical identifications for each layer (especially if the bone was studied by Mark Maltby and his colleagues), but quantitative information on the number and weight of pottery sherds might only be available in the form of overall feature totals -- if available at all. How the material was recorded in the archives varied considerably. For Winnall and Winklebury each context/layer was described along with quantitative information about the finds it contained (not bone at Winnall which was contained in a separate archive). However, for other sites such information would be only available in the form of separate archives for different categories of material, and then not always complete. A problem encountered on some sites was that articulated groups of animal bone were not recorded either during excavation or later identification (e.g. Gussage, Micheldever Wood). Differences over the identification of such deposits makes a direct comparison of bone assemblages studied by different specialists difficult. Equally, differences in the level of recovery must considered between different sites. Where recovery was poor, notably Central Excavation Unit compared to M3/TWA excavations, the material recorded in the archives will be biased towards larger pot sherds, finds and animal bones, making direct comparisons between sites difficult. Because of all these differences, no two sites provided the same range of information at the same level of detail.

Ideally, all quantitative information should be recorded with the basic context descriptions, as at Winnall and Winklebury, as this minimises the possible risk of mislabelling etc. In several instances at Winnall, pits with considerable quantities of pottery contained no bone and vice versa. This could be due to real depositional practices (see 7.8&7.9), but in some instances were the result of transcription errors e.g. 6595 written down as 6565 etc. Such errors are unavoidable -- I am sure I made some transferring data to my proforma sheets etc. -- but are more difficult to trace in transcribing layer numbers than for features etc. They are of no importance when specialist reports simply provide total figures for each phase etc., but are damaging when attempting detailed contextual analyses. I would estimate such transcription errors could effect at least 5%, if not more, of the data, and this should always be borne in mind in any study. Other mistakes found just at Winnall include micro-fiching section drawings out of focus and the probably loss of several separately bagged animal special deposits between the excavations and the bone specialist.

It is important to stress the incomplete and often poorly excavated data on which this thesis is based. It could be argued this makes any attempt to 'put these sites back together' impossible, and any conclusions suspect. However, if the considerable effort and resources invested in excavations, especially rescue archaeology, are not to be wasted, we can not dismiss the potential of even pre-1939 excavations to provide useful data for new approaches and questions before we have tried to use them. This study shows, when approached critically and in conjunction with other sites, we can squeeze useful information from the most poorly recorded archives or reports.

4.3. Methodology
The next chapters summarise the results of a detailed study and interpretation of the deposits found in pits and other features cutting the chalk on these Downland Iron Age sites. The study begins with the nature of finds assemblages in individual feature fills - layers-, building up to consider the overall contents of pits, before considering the spatial distributions of deposits across sites. These detailed chapters summaries the results of analyses are somewhat dense at times! Finally, I offer an interpretation of these deposits, suggesting many were the result of a distinct human activity which happened very infrequently, and arguing that the associations between different classes of material can be understood as manifesting and reproducing the dominant structuring principles, predispositions, which were drawn upon in human activities.

It was considered that the order of the first three chapters should be reversed, starting with an analysis of the overall contents of pits and working backwards to finally considering individual layers. This was because it felt the associations between different factors were more convincingly demonstrable when considering overall contents of pits, than the finer analyses which are necessarily weaker as they try detailed investigations little attempted before in British archaeology with possibly unreliable data. The results of these studies on the characteristics of finds assemblages in individual layers and vertical differences within fills must be considered provisional, but they do show the potential future work has in this field. However, the order of starting with the individual layers and working upwards was kept, as it appeared a more logical way to both structure the actual research and the writing. The result is, hopefully, a kind of 'thick description' in which the links between the associations found at each level of analysis should become apparent.

The methodology of this study is simple, and in essence attempts to put the contents of pits and ditches back together, to investigate the possible relationships between different classes of material and the processes through which they passed to enter and survive in the archaeological record (c.f. Barrett, Bradley & Green 1991). This is a contextual approach, emphasising the problems caused by traditional methods which divide the different types of material found in the same locations to be studied and published in isolation from each other in different parts of a report, with the implication they provide evidence for different distinct areas of prehistoric life.

The analyses of feature fills was carried out on three levels, using the same two basic approaches. Studies began by considering the nature of finds assemblages from individual layers/contexts isolated in the excavation of different pits. Quantitative information on the different types of finds (e.g. number, weight, and mean sherd weight of pottery; total number of bone fragments, and for each species; number of small finds; presence of human bone or articulated units of animal bone etc.) and the matrix (chalk, loam, clay) was recorded and analysed in two ways. Firstly, the relationships between all different numerical variables were investigated graphical. Scatter plots for every possible combination of variables were drawn after Lambrick (1984:168) had shown the potential of such an approach. Lambrick's plots of different refuse-characteristics against each other revealed that the contents of most features at Mount Farm, Oxfordshire, shared similar average characteristics; assemblages were more or less the same in each case. However, a small number of contexts clearly did not share these average characteristics, suggesting the input of material from distinct activities. I followed a similar approach here, although considering individual layer as well as total feature contents, to test Lambrick's conclusions. This found a similar pattern on all sites; an average 'signature' for the mass of samples, but a few clearly non-average assemblages.

As well as plotting each variable against each other, the possible associations between different variables in terms of presence/absence were considered. Such an approach might be considered more valid than quantitative measures if poor recovery of finds was felt to seriously bias assemblages. Hayden & Cannon (1983:159) argued that despite the processes which meant the vast majority of material originally used or discarded on a rural site will not enter the archaeological record, some always will but not necessarily reflect the original quantities of proportions. Such processes make any quantitative measures suspect, but do suggest the value of presence/absence analyses (Fisher 1985:172-3). As such correlation matrices for all the different variables available at the level of layers/contexts on a site were constructed.

In addition to the simple presence of any variable, the presence of a variable in clearly non-average abundance was also considered. Despite Hayden and Cannon's suggestions, the graphical plots of different variables did suggest a few layers contained clearly exceptional quantities or weights of material. It seemed important to investigate whether layers containing very large quantities of animal bone (often identified as 'specific carcass utilisation events' - see 3.7.7) or large sherds of pottery (possibly freshly broken) were associated with human remains or, especially, 'special animal deposits'. To isolate these 'non-average' assemblages, I calculated the mean value and standard deviation for all variables with quantitative data. The presence of layers with values of more than one standard deviation greater than mean (+ Std Dev) were distinguished in this way, incorporated into the correlation matrices. The correlations between different variables were then statistically tested using the Chi Square test, as calculated using the *Statview* statistical package. This package calculates the probability of the correlation. The conventional probability of 0.05 was used to reject the null hypotheses. That is I have taken situations where there is less than a 1 in 20 chance that correlation could be random as a statistically significant relationship.

At the next level of analysis, pits were divided into lower, middle and upper thirds to consider possible vertical variations within pit fills and associations between material in neighbouring layers. Again, graphs were drawn to show the relationships between all variables at all the sites considered, along with constructing correlation matrices and conducting statistical tests. In addition, the distribution of material through the pit profile was considered, and detailed studies of the preservation of different anatomical elements of the main domestic species at Winnall conducted.

At the third level of analysis, the same procedures were followed for the overall contents of pits on all the study sites. Here, additional information, such as pit shape and size could also be considered. For both pit totals and thirds, calculations of the density of animal bone and pottery were made to make the comparison of thirds/pits more systematic. Here one potential problem arises in comparing the deposition of bone and pot. Animal bone is usually only recorded as fragment counts, while the number and weight of pottery is usually available. This means comparisons of pot and bone density are not comparing like with like (fragments per m3 cf. weight per m3). Future studies could also dry weigh animal bones to provide information on fragment size to compare with mean sherd weight.

For Danebury, information was only available at this level from the published report of the first ten years work, and then only for human remains, special animal deposits and small finds. For Gussage, such information was only available for human remains and small finds in the published report. Later work on the archive has added to this information, providing detailed data on the location of human remains and small finds by layer and feature number, and quantitative information for the number (but not weight) of pot sherds at this level. However, the large numbers of small finds (any find which was not pottery, carbonised plant material or unworked animal bone) at both these sites meant that possible associations with objects made of different material (iron, bronze, stone, bone etc.) could be considered from just the published reports.

The same procedure was carried out to investigate the nature of deposits in the enclosure ditch at Winnall (see 8.3). The work was supplemented by a consideration of the spatial distributions of finds in the ditch at Gussage and other Later Prehistoric enclosures. I have attempted no systematic study of the assemblages from other subsoil features such as post holes or working hollow because of lack of time. However, human remains and possible special animal deposits are known from these features and some of the results of this research suggest greater attention should be paid in the future to these features and also occupation layers where they are occasionally preserved on sites (c.f. Allen & Robinson 1993). Finally, the spatial distributions of material found in pits were considered (see 9). For all sites, the distribution of all possible variables (e.g. pit shape, bone density, pot mean sherd weight, decorated pottery, human remains, different types of small finds) were plotted, and possible patterns investigated. In addition, individual pits were investigated in detail at Little Somborne, Micheldever, Winnall, MIA Gussage, and Winklebury, to reconstructing their sequences of fills and deposits (see 7.9).

Clearly, these levels of analysis have provided a vast quantity of basic information in the form of graphs, correlation matrices, raw statistical scores and site distribution plans - and only a representative selection are illustrated.

This methodology and its use of statistics are open to criticism because of their comparative lack of sophistication compared to analyses in other parts of the discipline. The simple reliance on Chi Square tests only came after applying a range of analyses available on computer statistics packages on sample data sets. These included multivariate approaches such as factor analysis, but the results were not easy to interpret and the main axes of variation found in the data were those already clearly shown using simpler bivariate approaches. This might be expected if most of the patterning in the data was symbolic, a product of humanly structured deposition, and not natural processes, as it could be argued that human classifications are not multidimensional.

This is not to argue that I have exhausted all the possible statistical examinations of such data. There is considerable scope for all forms of future work on the issues and data discussed in this study, including the use of more sophisticated statistical techniques. One particular problem Chi Square encountered was with the small samples available for some analyses. Alternatives more suited to small samples, such as Confidence Intervals (Kent 1984:166-7) were considered, but I felt it important to use the same tests for all my analyses on all my study sites.

Ultimately, these simple approaches were adopted for several reasons. Notably, the large quantities of data this study used meant a straightforward approach was a necessity. Had I concentrated on investigating a single site, such as Winnall Down, detailed and sophisticated analyses would have been appropriate (cf., Rodgers 1987, 1988), but I felt it important to establish that the possible associations within deposits reflected a widespread social practice, and so were less likely to be the product of possibly site specific natural processes. Equally, it is important that the types of analyses conducted here are easily repeatable. If more considerations of site formation processes and the relationships between different classes of objects are to become as common place as they deserve, then straightforward and repeatable methods are required. Just as importantly, the quality of the data from many of the sites probably could not stand more sophisticated treatment.

New excavations and more detailed analyses of the questions raised in this thesis are required. The basic aim of this study is to demonstrate that there are a series of dimensions to our data from Iron Age settlements that we have not previously recognised, and point to the directions in which they may be realised. This does not require a sophisticated treatment, nor complex statistical methods. Ultimately, the most complex analyses will not produce results unless they are used to ask the appropriate questions.

4.4. The Study Sites

Winnall Down /Easton Lane, Winchester
The Winnall Down and Easton Lane (Fasham 1985, Fasham et al 1989) complex of archaeological sites are two kilometres north-east of Winchester (SU 49 30). A D-shaped enclosure known from aerial photographs was totally excavated in 1976-9 to reveal a multi-phase site with activities from the Neolithic to the Early Roman period. The excavations aimed to provide a detailed study of a complete Iron Age settlement comparable to work at Little Woodbury (Bersu 1940), Gussage All Saints (Wainwright 1979) and Bishopstone (Bell 1977). They were also one of the first to be completely computerised, so that the archive should be instantly accessible to future scholars. In the end, due to repeated changes in technology, this was not a success (Rodgers 1987), and I worked from the full print out of the archive fortunately stored by Hampshire County Museum Service. Construction immediately west of the Winnall Down site lead to the sampling of 15 hectares in 1982-1983. This provided fuller evidence for the long term use and settlement of this area throughout prehistory, including the unexpected discovery of a new unenclosed Iron Age settlement. Information was not as available in the archives for this site as for Winnall. In particular data only on the pottery, and not the animal bone or small finds, was available for individual layers/contexts. The development of this settlement complex is considered in some detail in chapter 9.

4.4.2. Micheldever Wood
Located approximately half way between Winchester and Basingstoke along the M3 (SU 527 370), this is one of two published excavations of a Banjo enclosure in the area, a particular form of enclosure which appeared during the Middle Iron Age (Fasham 1987). Usually round, with a long funnel entrance flanked by earthworks, their function is debated (Perry 1969; Hingley 1984; Bradley in Fasham 1987; Corney 1989; Barrett et al 1991). Located in dense woodland on clay with flints overlying the upper chalk, the site is one of a complex of banjos and interconnecting earthworks in the area. About 60% of the interior, and most of the entrance was excavated in 1976-1977. The quality of the excavation and level of recovery of finds at this, and other M3 sites, was of the highest standards. The enclosure was first built and pits dug in the Middle Iron Age, although considerable quantities of Late Iron Age and Early Roman material were found in the upper fills of the ditch and internal features.

4.4.3. Old Down Farm, Andover
The importance of the excavations at Old Down Farm (Davies 1980) must not be underestimated. The publication of total excavation of this sub-oval enclosure set new standards for both the study of animal bone and pottery, especially when compared to the Gussage report published only a year earlier. Situated on the Northern outskirts of Andover (SU 356 465), it was ten kilometres north-east of Danebury and two kilometres north of Balksbury (see below). The site was largely excavated by amateurs in very difficult circumstances from 1975 to 1977, and levels of recovery and recording were high as on full time, professional excavations under good circumstances. The published report provides the fullest account of the site. The archive is

incomplete, lacking organised animal bones data per feature/layer, while quantitative pottery information was only available for selected features. The site had a long history (five Iron Age phases), starting with three pits dated to the Late Bronze Age, before the site was enclosed in the early part of the Early Iron Age. The site was used throughout the period, and re-organised in the Late Iron Age.

4.4.4. Little Somborne, Near Romsey

This site was between the villages of Upper and Little Somborne (SU 389 328), ten kilometres south-east of Danebury (Neal 1980). This oval enclosure was partially excavated by the Central Excavation Unit in advance of a gas pipeline in January-February 1977. The rescue conditions and bad weather probably affected levels of recovery. A 15m strip was diagonally excavated across the site, revealing two houses and thirty pits. The report suggests two distinct periods of occupation, but I would argue for a continuous occupation running from the end of the Early Iron Age, through the proto-saucepan phase, and stopping early in the Middle Iron Age. Every pit found is illustrated and described in the published report, and information on pottery was available in the archive at layer/context level. Unfortunately no detailed quantitative information is available for the animal bone, and the assemblages were heavily biased towards the larger species by the poor recovery and poor level of identification.

4.4.5. Balksbury Camp, Andover

Balksbury (Donaldson forthcoming) is the largest 'hillfort' in Hampshire, lying on the southern outskirts of Andover (SU 354 448). The site was investigated when crossed by a new road in 1967 (Wainwright 1969), but approximately half of the interior was investigated during the building of a housing estate in 1973 and 1981. The slight bank and ditch around the site were found to date from the Late Bronze Age, and a scatter of related four posters and some small pits were found near the southern rampart. Occupation from the Early Iron to Roman period concentrated in the centre of the enclosure and probably represent a typical farmstead. The excavations are not yet published, but the animal bone from the excavations have been studied in extreme detail by Mark Maltby (nd2). Quantitative data was available for animal bones and small finds at the level of individual layers. However, there was no usable quantitative data for the pottery.

4.4.6. Winklebury, Basingstoke

This site, again on upper chalk, was excavated before the construction of housing and a school. On the north-west outskirts of the town centre of Basingstoke (SU 613 529), this is the other recent major hillfort excavation in Hampshire. Excavated by the Central Excavation Unit over the winter of 1975-1976, two hectares of the interior were investigated. This represents approximately the north-west corner of the interior. Recovery were poor compared to M3 or recent TWA standards, probably because of the rapid rescue excavation in the winter. Only a limited sample of all the features found were excavated. Like Little Somborne, the identified bone assemblage was biased towards horse and cattle. The well prepared archive provides detailed information about the finds in each layer/fill, although it only gives the weight and not the number of pot sherds. This information was used by Fisher (1985) to investigate the spatial patterning within the excavated area. The site had two main phases of occupation. The ramparts were constructed in the 7th Century BC, and a number of porched houses and four posters belong to this phase. The site was re-defended and occupied in the Middle Iron Age. The majority of the pits on the site, and a large rectangular enclosure date to this later period.

4.4.7. Danebury, near Andover

Excavations at this hillfort (SU 324 377) have dominated Southern British Iron Age studies, both by providing the key finds assemblages etc. to compare with other sites, and the interpretative framework proposed to explain the evidence (Cunliffe 1984a; Cunliffe & Poole 1991). Little work has so far been published on the nature of deposition at the site, or the spatial distribution of material within the interior. I had hoped to include a detailed study of the Danebury material in this study, but ultimately I have simply used the data published about the first tens years excavations (Cunliffe 1984a vols 1 & 2) to supplement my analyses. These provide information on the context of human remains, articulated animal deposits and all classes of small finds. I have no information on the location of each pit, so spatial studies were impossible. Excavations at the site provide the basis for the ceramic phasing used for the Hampshire Iron Age, and use of the site spans the whole period.

4.4.8. Gussage All Saints, Dorset

Like Danebury, my work on Gussage (Wainwright 1979) was initially been limited to the information published in the site report. After completing the thesis I did follow up analyses using the excavation archive. This provided fuller information on the human remains and small finds, and numbers of pot sherds in features. It was considered because of its central importance as a type site for non-hillfort settlements. Located on Cranborne Chase in Dorset (ST 998 101), the wider context of this site has recently been addressed (Barrett et al 1991). Information in the published report was limited to the location of human remains and small finds to the level of feature and layer/context. Full site plans have allowed work on the distribution of different types of material. The site was excavated by the Central Excavation Unit in 1972 to re-assess Bersu's Little Woodbury. Three main phases were distinguished, dating to the Early, Middle and Late Iron Ages

Chapter 5
Investigations of Pits: Level 1 - Individual Layers

5.1. Introduction

The reasons why pits are sectioned, stratigraphy recorded, and finds attributed to individual layers is today simply how things have been habitually done on excavations since the 1940's. Except on rare occasions, little use is made of this detailed level of recording and for most purposes the effort and expense of recording and identifying material at the level of individual layers and contexts is largely redundant. The potential which this considerable effort has for investigating the characteristics of individual layer/context assemblages is the subject of this chapter. It considers the individual layers/contents as the basic building blocks on which rest all other aspects of the study of feature fills. To my knowledge there have been few other attempts in British archaeology - outside Palaeolithic/Mesolithic studies - to considered assemblages at this level of detail, and, because of this, my conclusions can only be considered as provisional. However, the results discussed in this chapter hint at patterns and associations that can be more convincingly shown to exist when considering the overall contents of pits (see 7). But above they all demonstrate that there is considerable patterning of interest to be found in the detailed investigation of individual layers/contexts. A level of analysis which could be fruitfully investigated on other sites of all periods.

Information on the finds recovered from individual pit fills/contexts was only available for six sites and this data allowed three areas of investigation;

Relationships with the matrix of fills (i.e. chalk, loam, clay etc.),

Graphic plotting of numerical data for different classes of finds,

Statistical analyses of presence/absence data for different classes of finds.

Rather than exhaustively consider each site in detail, the discussion will summarise the general patterns revealed. Table 5.1. summarises the basic information on the number of layers with different classes of finds, with calculations of the means and standard deviation for the number/weight of pot sherds, number of bone fragments and Mean Sherd Weight's (MSW's) for the study sites. Comparisons of the numbers of pot sherds or animal bone fragments between different layers make no account for possible differences in the size of layers. Clearly, there could be considerable differences between a thin lens of burnt stone, and a tip of loam filling half the feature. Initially, I did attempt to calculate the volume of each layer/context to use measures of the density of finds. However, in many case this proved to be extremely difficult, and time consuming. It was also found that the exceptional large quantities of finds found in some layers were not simply a product of the size of that layer/context.

Iron Age pit fills usually contain many different layers, demonstrating their complex depositional histories. The number of layers distinguished in excavated features is partially dependent on the care of excavation and recording. Pit fills were more coarsely distinguished, with corresponding fewer layers per pit, on older Central Excavation Unit excavations, when compared to M3 Excavation Committee/Trust for Wessex Archaeology excavations (see table below).

The coarseness of distinguishing context units will affect direct comparisons between sites. For example, coarse recording may fail to distinguish between discrete layers with different assemblages, such as one with just animal bone and one with just pottery. This probably happened at Winklebury and Balksbury. The proportions of layers containing finds will be similarly affected, and will vary between sites.

CEU sites	M3/TWA sites	Other sites
Balksbury = 5.8 Little Somborne = 4.8* Gussage = 5.9* Winklebury = 5.6	EIA Winnall = 7.1 MIA Winnall = 10.5 Micheldever = 16.5 Easton Lane = 12.3 Maiden Castle = 7.7*	Danebury = 5.6*

* calculated only from published sections in reports

CEU = Central Excavation Unit; TWA = Trust for Wessex Archaeology

The average number of layers/fills distinguished per pit on a selection of excavations

The distribution of number/weight of pottery, number of animal bone fragments and MSW recovered in each layer with pottery and bone were similar for all the sites considered here (e.g. Fig. 5.1.&2.). *The majority of layers contained no or very material.* Approximately half of the layers with pottery or animal bone at Middle Iron Age Winnall contained five or less, or no, sherds of pottery or bone fragments. Layers at Micheldever were richer (mean pot no. 18.8 c.f. 10.4, mean bone no. 26 c.f. 15), a result of better preservation, better recovery and/or real differences in the original densities of material deposited (is the small constrained space of the enclosure at Micheldever compared to the open settlement at Winnall an important factor?). At all sites, there are a small number of layers with exceptionally large quantities of pottery or bone.

The distribution of sherd size follows a positively skewed distribution on all sites, again with a few layers with very large sherds. Comparing the graphs for Winnall and Micheldever, shows that the distribution is more skewed to the right for the former and that, overall, Winnall has slightly higher MSW's than Micheldever. Fig. 5.3. shows the distribution of the number of identifiable bone fragments per layer for the five main domestic species at Middle Iron Age Winnall.

5.2. Matrix

Where possible, the relationship between the matrix of individual layers -- e.g. loam ('soil'), shattered chalk, burnt flint -- and the finds they contained were investigated. These relationships may relate to the origins of the fills, although with exceptions. For example chalk fills may come from the natural chalk shatter of the sides or from deliberate excavations. This analysis was hampered by a lack of information about layer matrix for most sites. This was usually taken from section drawings, as time prevented looking at original context descriptions where these were preserved in site archives. Complete sets of section drawings were often not available, and expense prohibited photo-copying all original drawings. All pit sections for Winnall Down were available on fiche cards, but many were fiched out of focus, so that matrix information was only available for 14 EIA and 49 MIA pits. Full information for all pits was available at Little Somborne (28 pits) and Winklebury (72 pits). To simplify analysis, layers were distinguished into four broad categories;

Loam ('soil'),
Loam & Chalk,
Chalk
Other (burnt flint, daub, charcoal etc.).

Table 5.2. shows the results of this study. As expected, the largest assemblages of pottery, bone and other material came from loam matrices, although these may have had diverse origins. Some might represent dumps of soil containing finds, others dumps of finds immediately covered with layers of soil, others midden/'occupation soils' whose high organic content has been subsequently heavily leeched. Chalk fills, natural or deliberately created, at Winklebury, Early Iron Age Winnall and Little Somborne less frequently contained finds than loam layers, but where they did, they did so in numbers comparable to loam layers. A greater proportion of those chalk shatter layers, at Middle Iron Age Winnall contained finds of all kinds and might represent 'dirty' surface dumps of chalk. Although, the statistically significant association of large pot sherds with these layers suggests careful sealing of freshly broken pottery with chalk from digging pits and other sub-soil excavation. At other sites/phases, where pottery was present in chalk layers, mean sherd weight (*MSW*) was comparable to loam layers. This points to the need for greater care in recording layers/fills to distinguish whether finds were evenly distributed within layers -- hence originally from middens, or yard soils etc.-- or lay at the interface between layers to which they have been attributed.

5.3. Graphical Analyses.

Lambrick (1984:168) showed the value of scatter plots to investigate the characteristics and origins of material from different contexts. This approach has been followed here, although quantitative data was only available to study individual pit layers from six sites (Table 5.1.). As the selected examples show (Figs. 5.4-8.), the relationship between almost any two variables is remarkably similar. The majority of all layers contain no finds, the bulk of the rest small quantities of material and so cluster in the lower left hand corner of the graph. Very high values of any one variable generally correspond to very low values of any other, and vice versa.

5.3.1. Pottery

This relationship is particularly clear when considering Mean Sherd Weight (MSW), one index of pre-depositional ceramic attrition (see 3.5.1.). Large sherd size has been used to suggest deposition of pottery shortly after initial breakage and not left for subsequent degradation through sweeping, trampling, erosion etc. This assumption does not consider the possible protection offered against further breakage through incorporation of pot sherds in midden deposits, nor careful curation and provisional discard of broken pottery, as noted in several ethnoarchaeologies (e.g. Deal 1985; Hayden & Cannon 1983). On all the sites where it has been possible to calculate MSW for individual layers, except Early Middle Iron Age Easton Lane, an essentially logarithmic relationship is apparent between MSW and the number of sherds per layer (Fig. 5.4.). The majority of layers cluster in the lower left hand corner of the graphs with small numbers of small sherds, but it is clear that the higher MSW's tend to come from smaller assemblages (less than 10 & esp. 5 sherds) and vice versa. There are very few layers which contain large or very large numbers of large or very large pot sherds.

Without similar work on assemblages from other periods and regions it is impossible to argue conclusively this is not a general characteristic of ceramic assemblages. However, personal observations and information gleaned from pot reports suggest it does represent a specific Iron Age cultural practice. Pierpoint's (nd:20) work at Owslebury indicates that a possible recurrent feature of Romano-British assemblages is the occurrence of major primary dumps of large sherds from a number of vessels. Such deposits, containing considerable numbers of big sherds and significant proportions of fine wares, probably represent the periodic clearance of large provisionally discarded sherds from many vessels on the site. Deposits representing large sherds from a number of individual vessels (3 or more), similar to Pierpoint's Roman assemblages, would appear to be rare on the Iron Age sites I have investigated suggesting the observable patterns are the results of particular social practices which might be separated into three distinct types of pottery assemblages;

    i.)   Low densities of small-medium sized sherds - the bulk of layer assemblages.

    ii.)   Large assemblages of medium-small sherds.

    iii.)   Deposits of small numbers of large-very large 'freshly' broken, or at least carefully curated, sherds.

This continuum needs to be confirmed through further work paying closer attention to the different fabrics present and the actual material. Indications suggest the third type of deposit usually represent portions of single pots, some of the larger deposits of large sherds coming from just one or two vessels, but rarely more (see 8.3.1).

5.3.2. Animal Bone

Further graphs suggest that these exceptional types of pottery deposit are distinct from exceptional deposits of animal bone. Graphs plotting the number of animal bone fragments against the number of pot sherds, but especially the weight of pottery or MSW in different layers for all the sites studied show, again, that the majority of all layers would appear to have no or low numbers of bone fragments (c. less than 10) and no or low numbers of small to medium sized pot sherds (Fig. 5.6.). Large bone deposits do not generally appear to occur in the same layers as large numbers of pot sherds or high MSW, although there are exceptions. Plotting the relationships between different species is also basically logarithmic (Fig. 5.7.). Such relationships between

cattle and sheep are predicted by the distinction between butchery and kitchen/table waste (see 3.7.3.). But this can not account for similar patterns for horse, pig, and dog. Rather, large assemblages of bone (articulated or otherwise) from one species often did not occur with large number of bone fragments from other species.

5.3.3. Small Finds

The numbers of small finds (metal, stone, worked bone/antler objects etc.) in individual layers shows similar coarse relationships to those outlined above. Where two or more small finds occur together in any layer they are generally associated with low number/weights of pottery, small to medium size sherds and low numbers of animal bone fragments, although there are exceptions (Fig. 5.8.). The relationship with human bone and other material is more variable.

5.3.4. Conclusions

It has been suggested that the essentially logarithmic relationship observed between any two variables in individual layers is evidence for a distinct Iron Age cultural depositional practice.

The majority of contexts in Iron Age pits contained no or small quantities of material of all kinds. This 'background' is often material unintentionally incorporated as part of soil, midden material etc. deliberately deposited or naturally eroded into pits.

Against this background layers dominated by medium to very high values of any one given variable stand out. These assemblages do not represent deposits of thoroughly mixed material as might be expected if fresh midden material was dumped in pits. Although often accompanied by other classes of finds, it is clear, especially in the extreme cases, that these are intentional deposits of single classes of material. The other material in these layers may have been accidentally incorporated, as found in the majority of layers described above. Although, some accompanying material was also probably deliberately chosen to be part of these deposits (see 5.4. re. dog bone).

I would distinguish four categories of such exceptional deposits (see below).

Category Ia represent a few (less than 5-10) large sherds apparently from just one or two vessels. At times it would appear complete vessels are represented, but rarely are found unbroken, and sometimes were careful placed and covered. Although often regarded as 'fresh' sherds, and so implying deposition soon after breakage, provisional discard and careful curation of sherds could protect many sherds from subsequent attrition. This might explain why only a proportion of a vessel often seems to be represented in these deposits, as was also true of the well preserved potsherd groups in the midden at Runnymede which rarely represent complete vessels (see 3.5.4). In the

	Ia.	Small Numbers of Large to Very Large Sized Pot Sherds
I. POTTERY	Ib.	Large Numbers of Small to Medium Sized Pot Sherds

II. ANIMAL BONE — Large Numbers of Bone Fragments, the majority often from a single species, and often including articulated/associated groups of bone

III. SMALL FINDS — Two or more Small Finds

IV. HUMAN REMAINS

<u>Four categories of exceptional deposits from individual layers/contexts</u>

main, Ia deposits represent only a proportion of a vessel which was deliberately deposited (cf. Beaker Pottery in non-funerary contexts - K. Mizoguchi pers. com.).

Category Ib deposits of more than 20 to 30+ of small to medium sized sherds imply some pre-depositional attrition. They might represent deposits similar to category Ia, but with a longer or less 'safe' time span between initial provisional discard and deposition. These deposits might appear to originate from dumps of pottery, discrete from similar dumps of animal bone or small finds. This separation of discarded pottery from bone would question distinctions of butchery, kitchen and table waste which applied to both pottery and bone (Halstead et al 1978 - see 3.7.3.). Pottery may have been broken at the same time as animal carcass processing and consumption occurred, but the refuse was possibly initially discarded in a different place and/or manner. This basic distinction, and the refusal to mix, these two common classes of archaeological finds is very important.

Category II deposits of more than 30-40 of animal bone fragments are often dominated by bones from one species. For some layers, this is because many come from articulated/associated groups of bone which range from groups of metapodial bones to complete skeletons (see 7.3.3). But the presence of articulated bone does not account for all these exceptional assemblages. Obviously where assemblages contain articulated bone groups, this implies swift deposition of freshly butchered/consumed animals. But deposition need not have been *that* immediate. Articulated limbs at Flagstones, Dorchester, were deposited after dogs had time (hours?) to gnaw their extremities (Bullock nd.), while cattle skulls from Easton Lane pit 329 were buried a considerable time after butchery (Maltby 1989:125). Most of the non-articulated bone in these layers might similarly have been deposited soon after butchery/consumption, although this requires further examination of the state of the bone to assess erosion and fragmentation etc. Certainly, many of

the large deposits represent the specific carcass utilisation events Maltby (1985a:56) has distinguished (see 3.7.7), bones that would not survive unmixed or scavenged on the ground surface unprotected for long.

Although generally large pottery deposits do not occur with those of animal bone, it is important to recognise the existence of layers with large quantities of both materials. These rarely contain extreme values of either (Fig. 5.3.) and might represent a fifth possible group of exceptional pot/bone layer assemblages (V). Those examples of very high values of both pottery and bone in the same layers at Winklebury (Fig. 5.6.) may be a product of the coarser division of contexts/layers at the site compared to Winnall (see 5.1.). But this does not appear to be the case for Middle Iron Age Winnall and closer examination of the six layers with both above one standard deviation above mean quantities (+ Std Dev) of pot and bone suggests these are not simply larger than normal deposits of mixed bone and pottery. Four of these six layers have +Std Dev MSW's, four also contained small finds and all came from pits whose other contents mark them out as distinct in some way through the presence of articulated animal remains and/or human burials and/or large quantities of small finds -- Pits 1095, 1941, 4475, 6595, 7257, 7372.

Category III represents deposits of small finds from individual layers. The small finds are usually broken, although come complete metal objects are found. Many single small finds may represent stray discarded or lost material that became incorporated in deposits fortuitously. However, these layers were often significantly associated with other exceptional layer deposits of human remains, *ABG's*, pottery etc. when the overall contents of pits are examined (see 7). Where several small finds were recovered, particularly three or more, it is clear these were not simply accidentally 'lost' or 'broken' and so thrown away, but deliberately deposited, probably after curation/provisional discard.

Category IV are those deposits of human remains. Especially where these remains are complete or partial bodies ('carcasses'), these were often deposited in layers containing little or no other material.

5.4. Presence/Absence Analyses

Presence/absence of different variables in layers was investigated to reveal possible associations through correlation matrices for factors such as presence of pottery, small finds, articulated animal bones, bone from different animal species, etc. In addition, calculations of standard deviation were used to isolate layers containing exceptionally large quantities of finds and correlations between these layers and other factors investigated.

5.4.1. Relationships between mean sherd weight, number, weight of pottery and number of bone

A consistent set of statistically significant relationships was observed on all studied sites. These were between layers with above one standard deviation above mean of the (abbreviated as +Std Dev.) numbers of pot sherds and one standard deviation above mean of the (+Std Dev.) weight of pottery, and also between layers with +Std Dev. MSW and +Std Dev. weight of pottery. Inevitably the larger the number of small sherds, or the larger the size of sherds, so the overall weight of pottery in any layer will increase. Unexpected, given the relationship between pottery and bone discussed above, is the third consistent association between +Std Dev. numbers of bone fragments and +Std Dev. numbers/weight of pottery in a layer. Observed on all sites where possible to do so, this relationship does not contradict the general pattern where by single layers tend to be dominated by a single category of finds. Further investigation showed they represent those few layers tentatively suggested as a fourth category of exceptional deposit above (see 5.3.4).

5.4.2. Relationships between the different domesticated animal species

If most bone came from either scattered, badly preserved assemblages or general mixed midden deposits onto which all bone was originally dumped, I would expect the majority of layers to contain thoroughly homogeneous deposits. However, patterning between large and small species which resulted from differential carcass utilisation and disposal has been identified on several sites (see 3.7.3). As such I would expect to find in bone assemblages associations between the presence of cattle and horse bone (butchery waste) on the one hand, and sheep and pig bone (kitchen/table waste) on the other. Winnall Down, Micheldever Wood and Balksbury provided suitable data to investigate these relationships. Statistically significant correlations between the presence of sheep and pig bone were found on all sites as expected (Table 5.3.). While at no site was the presence of sheep and cattle bone significantly associated again as expected, although only at Balksbury was horse significantly associated with cattle. Other associations with horse and pig complicate this picture. On all four sites, horse bone was significantly associated with the presence of bone from one of the smaller main domesticates, and on all four sites pig was significantly associated with cattle (Table 5.3.).

These, associations can not be interpreted as a straight forward distinction on body size would expect. Some of these associations are in assemblages which were deposited directly, or soon, after the activities which produced them and provide direct evidence for specific processing/consumption events. But this can not account for all assemblages, many of which must represent the deliberate or accidental incorporation of older bone. If carcass size was the determining factor in bone treatment and discard, I should not expect consistent associations between cattle and pig bone, nor those between horse and pig, or horse and sheep, particularly when bone was deposited soon after butchery. It seems straight forward to suggest that these associations relate, in some manner, to specific processing/consumption activities. The least common major domestic species, pig and horse, might have been consumed (or butchered) generally in the company of the others - or deposited together. This is not to deny the basic distinction made between butchery and later stages of processing the carcass, but the refuse from the same overall event was deposited together(?). Where horse was consumed with sheep or cattle with pig, horse/cattle meat probably was stripped from the bone and sheep/pig cooked on the bone, possibly different parts of the site or landscape (see 3.7.3). It is clear that horse and pig are more likely than cattle and sheep to come from layers with three or more species represented in them (Table 5.4.).

Dog bones show a series of relationships with other species on some of the sites considered here (Table 5.4.). Unlike other species, individual dog bones are usually extremely well preserved, and complete or substantially complete, compared to other species (e.g. Maltby nd1, nd2:40 - see 6.3.2). Horse comes the closest to dog in this respect, as more horse long bones are recovered substantially complete and unprocessed for marrow than cattle bones of a similar size (see 6.3.2). A far higher proportion of all dog bone come from complete or partial carcasses, or smaller associated/articulated groups of bone, than for other species. Explanations for the burial of dogs are generally common sensical, such as the large number of neo-natal/young animals found on many sites suggesting deliberate control of litter sizes (see 3.7.7.). Maltby has even suggested that the large number of partial carcasses and smaller articulated groups of dog bone come from disturbed complete burials in middens subsequently incorporated into pit fills etc.

If this was the case, then the associations shown in Table 5.3. are hard to understand. It is clear that if any dog bone is recovered from a pit layer, then so usually will bones from three or four other domesticated species (Fig. 5.9.). This is not a random distribution, nor restricted to the presence of articulated groups of dog bone, but also individual bone fragments. At Middle Iron Age Winnall Down articulated groups or burials represent 60-70% of the total dog bone for the phase (and were associated with very large sherds of pottery -- MSW 31.3±25.6 compared to an overall MSW of 17.9±17.4). These *ABG's* came from six layers, another twenty-two layers with four or more species including dog contained only one or two dog bones. Unarticulated dog bone is also correlated with the presence of articulated/associated bone groups from other species (prob. 0.0023 at Middle Iron Age Winnall). At both Middle Iron Age Balksbury and Winnall many were skull or mandible fragments. The well preserved, unfragmented nature of most 'stray' dog bones suggests that disturbed burials were not the major source for such bone.

The simplest interpretation would be to suggest, even more than pig and horse, that dog was generally only eaten (or at least the carcass dismembered) in the company of other species and, more so than other species, the resulting waste was deposited soon afterwards (unless carefully curated so they were not subsequently gnawed etc.). Often only one or two dog bones seem to have been deliberately selected for deposition, and often in contexts marked out in other ways. For example, was it purely fortuitous that the only other identifiable bone in the same layer as the near complete horse skeleton from Middle Iron Age Winnall (context 10164, pit 10161) was a dog rib, in a peripheral pit containing only a few other sheep bones, a hare skeleton and a few scraps of badly eroded pottery? If deliberate selection is a possibility, might this also explain some finds of horse bone, whose bones are often well preserved, and even some bones of other species? These provisional conclusions require following up with more detailed studies.

5.4.3. Relationships with small finds, presence of human bone and articulated/associated animal bone

Where possible the relationships between other categories of finds were examined, although only at Winklebury and Winnall was information available at the level of individual layers for the presence of small finds, human remains and articulated/associated animal bone groups. Significant associations were hardly found between the presence of any of the variables considered at any site. Those that were found at both Winklebury and Middle Iron Age Winnall are shown below, two were not strictly statistically significant (see 4.4). This lack of significant associations within layers, particularly compared to those evident within adjacent groups of layers (see 6.2) or using overall pit

totals (see 7), confirms the discrete treatment of separate types of material deposited so that it would appear normal for large quantities of any one class of material to be deposited essentially on its own.

	Winklebury	MIA Winnall
Presence of human bone and bird bone in the same layer		prob. 0.0634
Presence of +Std Dev. numbers of pottery and articulated bone groups in the same layer		prob. 0.0084
Presence of articulated bone groups and human bone in the same layer	prob. 0.0642	

5.5. Conclusions

This chapter has studied the characteristics of the finds assemblages found in individual layers within Iron Age pit fills. This level of detailed investigation, combining different classes of finds for a large sample of features, has rarely been attempted before in British archaeology (but see Maltby nd1 for just animal bones). I have shown there is considerable potential in such studies, although they produce no simple answers and I could be accused of over-forcing the data in an attempt to generate general statements about the nature and origins of these assemblages. Such work for sites of all periods has the potential to understand more fully the basic constitution, the building blocks, of our sites. Through such understanding we can interpret past refuse maintenance and depositional practices, and hence the cultural norms they manifested and reproduced.

The detailed study outlined here is limited by the poor data set, but has demonstrated that considerable patterning does exist within individual layers/contexts with considerable potential to provide information on both natural and cultural formation processes. The provisional conclusions I have made should form the basis for similar work in future. Some clear results have emerged, such as the association between all classes of finds and loam matrices. The graphical analyses show that the majority of all layers have an 'average signature' of mixed, medium to poorly preserved small quantities of material of all kinds - or no material at all. It has been suggested these average layer assemblages represent background or mixed 'old' midden/surface material. Their finds were accidentally incorporated with the soil, chalk, midden, hearth ash etc. artificially dumped or naturally eroding into the pit. Far fewer layers were distinguished by 'non-average signatures', the majority deliberate deposits of finds which were often dominated by a single category of material.

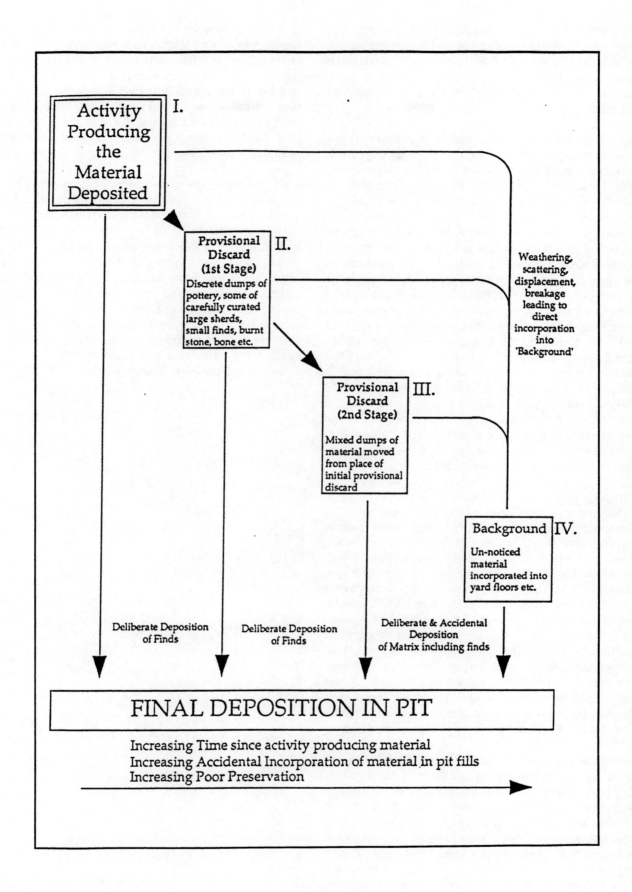

I.
Activity Producing the Material Deposited

II.
Provisional Discard (1st Stage)
Discrete dumps of pottery, some of carefully curated large sherds, small finds, burnt stone, bone etc.

III.
Provisional Discard (2nd Stage)
Mixed dumps of material moved from place of initial provisional discard

IV.
Background
Un-noticed material incorporated into yard floors etc.

Weathering, scattering, displacement, breakage leading to direct incorporation into 'Background'

Deliberate Deposition of Finds

Deliberate Deposition of Finds

Deliberate & Accidental Deposition of Matrix including finds

FINAL DEPOSITION IN PIT

Increasing Time since activity producing material
Increasing Accidental Incorporation of material in pit fills
Increasing Poor Preservation

A provisional model drawn from the results of ethnoarchaeology and taphonomic studies of the stages through which material may have passed before final deposition or incorporation in the fills of pits, ditches and other sub-soil features.

Further studies of the overall contents of pits fills (see 9) and detailed studies of the sequences of fills in individual features (see 9.9), show that these exceptional layers tend to cluster in the same small number of pits which also contain human remains and *ABG's*.

I have suggested a classification of four basic groups of such exceptional deposits. Using ethnographic models of refuse maintenance strategies (e.g. Arnold 1990; Deal 1985; Hayden & Cannon 1983) and the characteristics of layer assemblages outlined above, a general model for understanding the stages/condition of material entering pit fills can be suggested (see below). This suggests a broad division of four possible stages through which to <u>think</u> about the paths through which material may have passed before incorporation within a pit fill. I would suggest the majority of 'average' layer assemblages entered pit fills only after stages III and IV, those exceptional assemblages either directly after the activity producing them or after the first stage of provisional discard, stages I and II. *It must be remembered that the vast majority of all material was never finally deposited/discarded in pits* (see 1.1 & 1.2), and evidence presented in the rest of this study suggests that much which did, particularly the non-average layer assemblages, were not accidental incorporations.

Although requiring further work, I would suggest these 'non-average' layer assemblages can provide important information about Iron Age classifications of refuse and relate to the initial, final or provision, discard of material from distinct activities which are often felt to have been lost by the assumed subsequent mixing, poor preservation and chance survival of material (e.g. MacDonald 1991:64-5). They show that for Early/Middle Iron Age Wessex there existed no single, general, category of rubbish/refuse. It was not the case that all discarded material was simply treated in the same way and dumped in the same place (see 8&9). Nor was it that refuse produced in the same stages and places of food processing/cooking/consumption were discarded in the same place, time (?) and manner.

Important here is the *basic distinction between the deposition of pottery and animal bone,* both in terms of final discard immediately after breakage /butchery-consumption, and those deposits, of pottery in particular, that appear to have entered pits some time after breakage. As work at Runnymede suggests (Serjeantson 1991b - see 3.7.9), it may be wrong to envisage pottery and bone as having been treated in the same ways, or having passed through the same chain of events from initial refuse creating activity to final deposition. Bone and pottery were dealt with separately, and may imply initial distinct 'dumps' of provisionally discarded pottery and bone. The practice of treating separate categories of material as distinct entities, at least in the initial stages of discard, probably also extended to other groups of material not considered above. Distinct layers of burnt flint/stone, daub/clay and charcoal in pit fills represent a similar pattern. Again, these were not dumped onto a single initial midden and so are not found as homogeneous fills, but were treated separately. Not all these layers probably relate to initial final discard. Rather, like pottery, they probably represent discrete entities of provisionally discarded material.

Is it possible, then, to envisage these sites with discrete dumps of pottery, small finds, ash, burnt stone, old daub, and, possibly, bone in and around dwelling structures, along with more general, 'older', and, possibly more mixed, middens and yard floors, toft areas etc. ? This archaeologically attestable practice has important consequences. Such practices manifested and reproduced specific conceptions and perceptions. Further work is needed to consider whether a propensity to divide and treat this one aspect of the material world into discrete entities was restricted to refuse, or reflected a more wide spread predisposition (see 11).

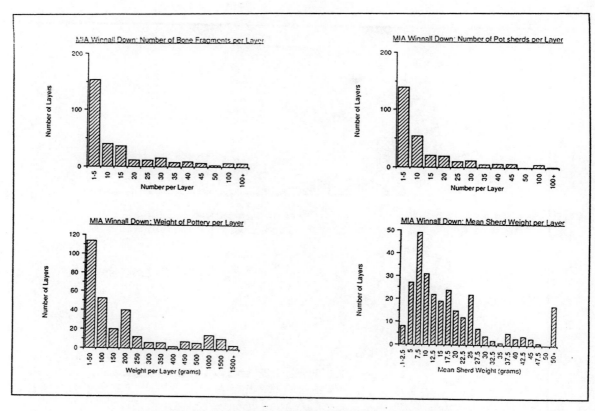

Fig. 5.1. Middle Iron Age Winnall Down: Histograms of the frequency distribution of the number of pot sherds, weight of pottery, number of animal bones and mean sherd weight per layer.

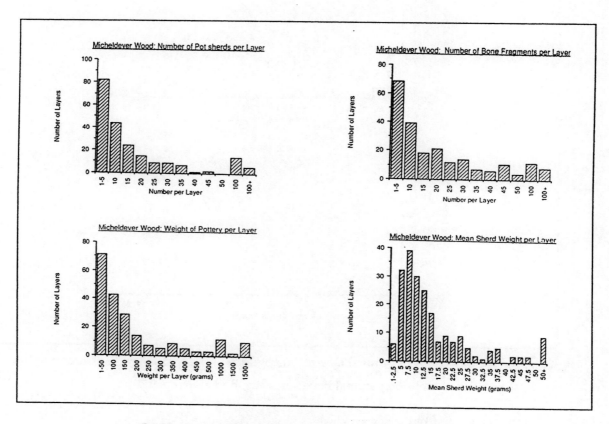

Fig. 5.2. Micheldever Wood: Histograms of the frequency distribution of the number of pot sherds, weight of pottery, number of animal bones and mean sherd weight per layer.

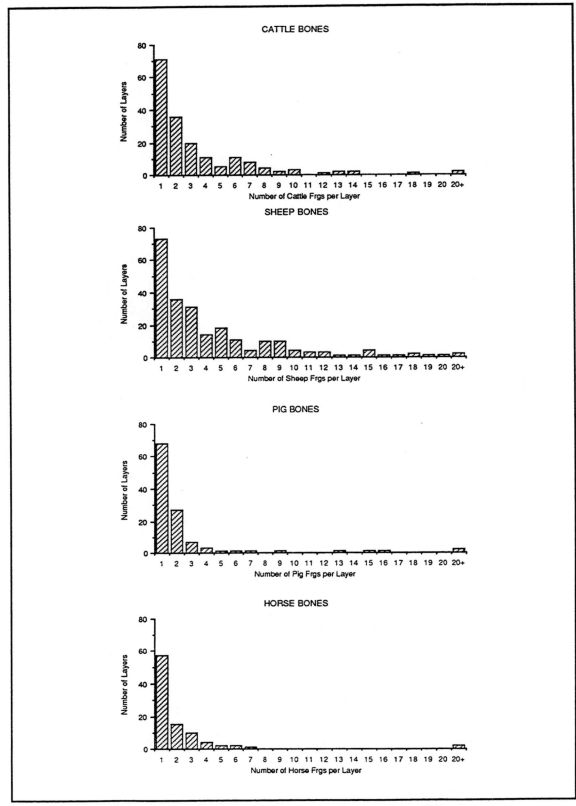

Fig. 5.3. Middle Iron Age Winnall Down: Histograms of the frequency distribution of the number of identified animal bones of cattle, horse, sheep and pig.

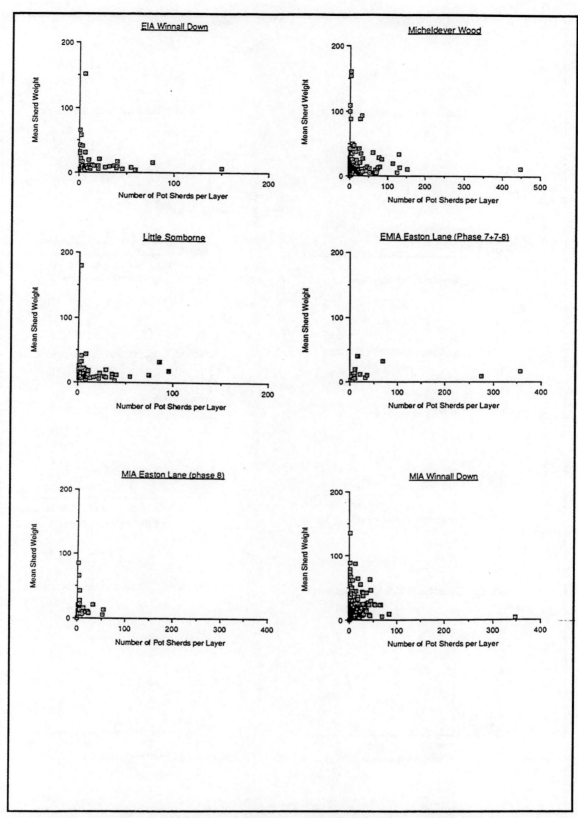

Fig. 5.4. Graphs showing the relationship between Mean Sherd Weight and the Number of Pot Sherds recovered per layer at selected sites.

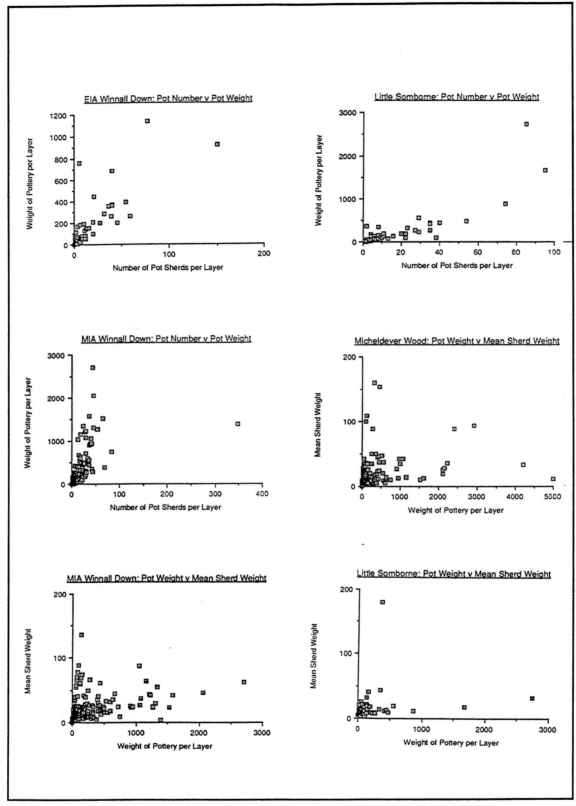

Fig. 5.5. Graphs showing the relationship between Mean Sherd Weight and the Weight of Pottery recovered per layer at selected sites.

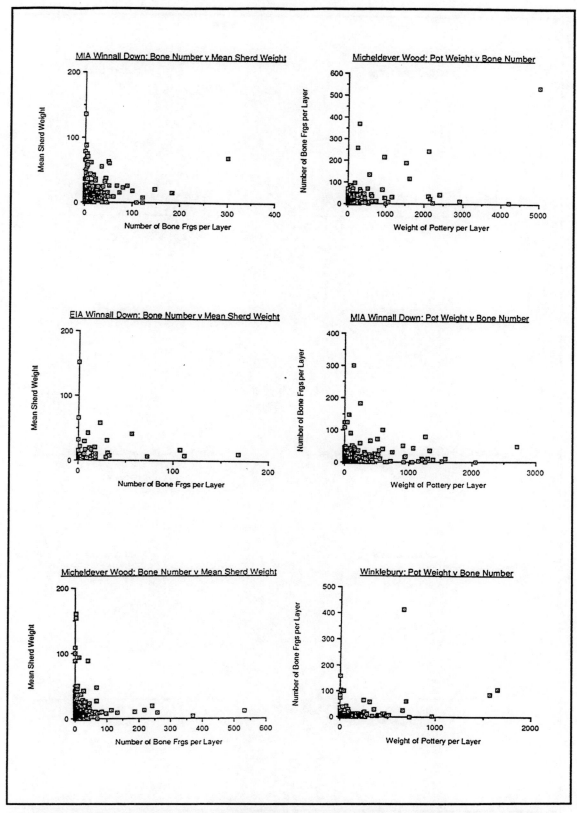

Fig. 5.6. Graphs showing the relationship between the Number of Bone Fragments and the Mean Sherd Weight and the Weight of Pottery recovered per layer at selected sites.

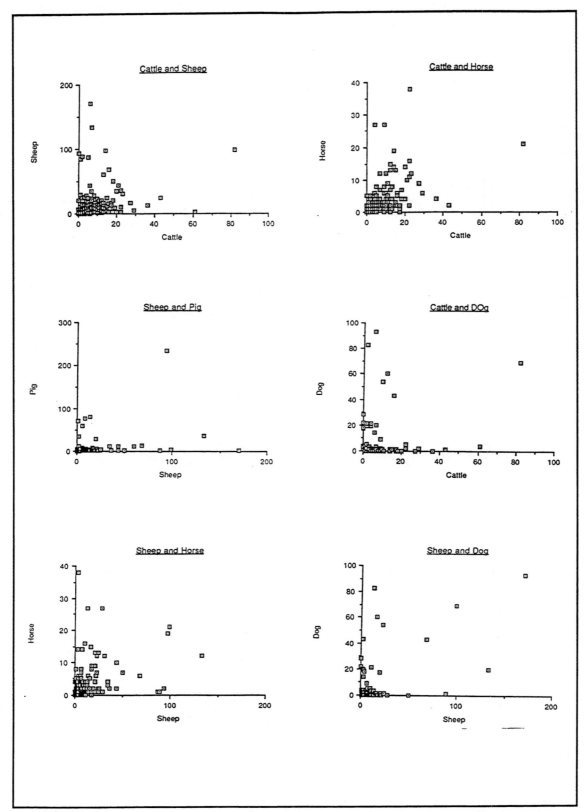

Fig. 5.7. Graphs showing the relationship between the Number of Bone Fragments from different species of domestic animals recovered per layer at Balksbury.

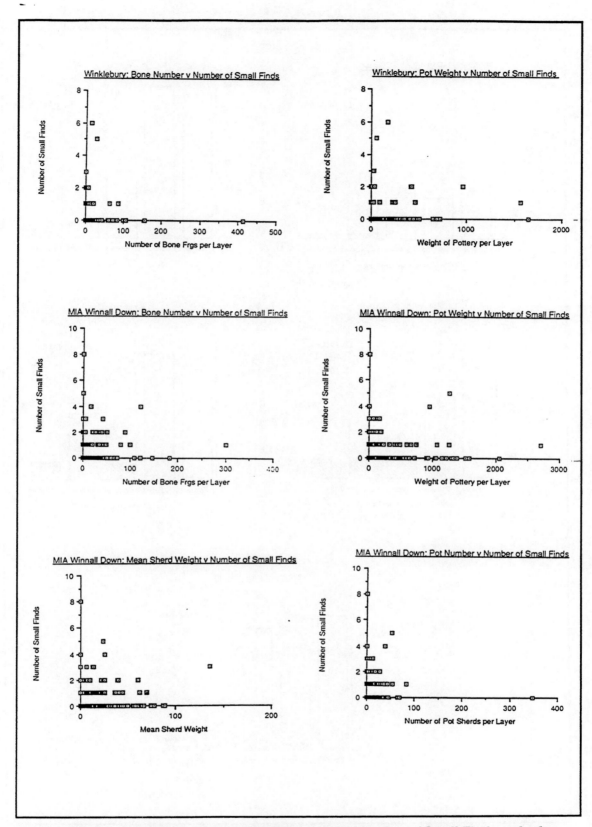

Fig. 5.8. Graphs showing the relationship between the Number of Small Finds and other classes of finds recovered per layer at Middle Iron Age Winnall Down and Winklebury.

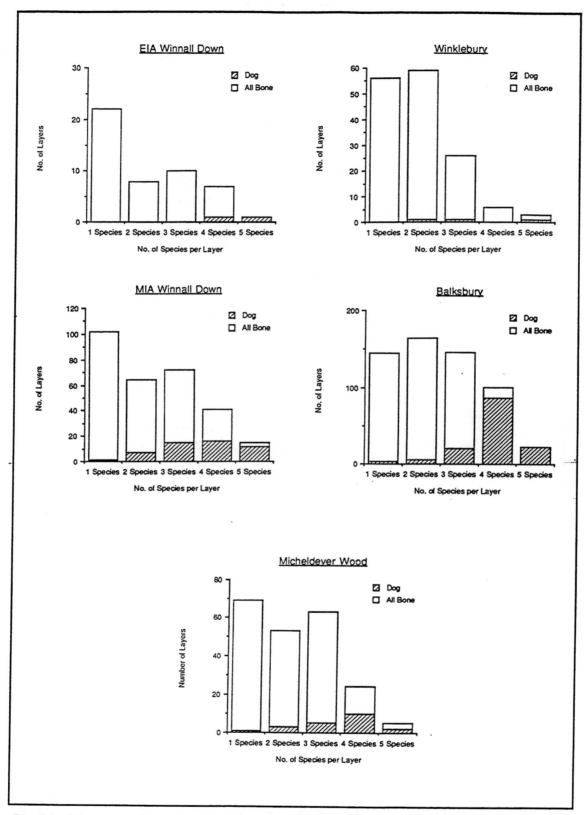

Fig. 5.9. Histograms showing the relationship between the presence of dog and the number of different species present in different layers from selected sites.

Chapter 6
Investigations of Pits: Level 2 - Pit Thirds

6.1. Introduction

This chapter investigates in more detail the vertical differences in the finds assemblages throughout the fill of a pit. It follows up the vertical differences suggested by previous studies of seeds (see 3.6.1) and animal bone (see 3.7.6). Like the study of individual layer/context assemblages in the previous chapter, it must be recognised that there has been very little work on this question, with the notable exception of Maltby's (nd2) innovative study at Balksbury. However provisional the conclusions made in this chapter, I do show the need to consider this question and that the vertical differences in assemblages of finds from features are not solely caused by natural factors. Again, many of the associations between different classes of material I describe below will be more strongly shown when I consider the overall contents of pits in the next chapter.

At Balksbury, Maltby divided pits into upper and lower halves to investigate differences in the preservation of animal bone related to the depth of their burial. I followed this approach, particularly as I wished to directly compare results from Balksbury and Winnall, but with the refinement of dividing pit fills into upper, middle, and lower thirds. Coarsely dividing pits into thirds may be crude, but it was simple to use, an important factor with the number of pits to analyse, and will be shown to produce significant results. For calculating the volumes of each pit third it was simpler to treat all pits as cylindrical in shape. Clearly, for those well preserved beehive pits, each third will not have equal volumes, but many beehive pits often had severely eroded mouths, and, more importantly, section drawings to calculate precise volumes for pit thirds were not always available for all pits on all sites. Future work on these aspects must test this approach against considering the actual depth of burial of deposits (i.e. divided pit fills into equal units of depth e.g. 25 or 50cm). It could be argued, especially if differences within fills were largely the result of post-deposition natural transformations, that this would be a constant function of actual depth. However, observations suggest that the differences I note below may relate more to the sequence of infilling a pit, which was similar regardless of the actual depth of a pit. As such a crude division into pit thirds or halves does produce valid results. although this needs to be tested in future studies.

6.2. Presence/Absence Analyses

Correlation matrices were drawn up for all sites to investigate possible relationships between different factors within the same third of a pit fill. Although the crudity of the division of pit fills into three parts must always be borne in mind, the aim was to investigate possible associations between the contents of neighbouring individual layers. The presence of pottery and bone in the same thirds was significant on all sites and suggests a distinction can be made between those thirds with or with out material. While statistically significant associations between the presence of human bone, articulated/associated animal bone groups (*ABG's*), small finds, +Std Dev. pot and bone densities, and MSW's are evident at this level of analysis at Middle Iron Age Winnall and Winklebury (Table 6.1.). These relationships between these classes of material were also found when considering the overall contents of pits at these and other sites (see 7). None of these relationships were seen considering individual layer assemblages, where I suggested different classes of material were often deposited on their own (see 5.4.3.). This suggests that although individual layers may contain exceptional deposits of largely discrete categories of material, such exceptional layers were often deposited in close proximity to each in the same part of a pit fill. Closer study of individual pits confirms this, and suggests there was an order in which layers containing different types of material had to be deposited in the pit (see 7.9). It also suggests that in most pits, these clusters of exceptional layer assemblages (stages I and II in the model proposed in chapter 5.) were deposited over a short period of time, with no evidence for natural erosion or silting separating them.

Intriguingly, Early Iron Age Winnall did not reveal the range of associations visible in the site's later phase. This might be due to the smaller sample size, but also suggests changes in depositional practice on the same site through time (see 9). The details of the associations between factors differ between Winklebury and Middle Iron Age Winnall, which might be a due to different excavation strategies and recovery. But it is important to stress that they are similar variables which are associated in different ways at both sites and they both share three important statistically significant associations (see 12.2.1);

The presence of *ABG's* with +Std Dev. densities of pottery,

The presence of human remains with small finds,

The presence of human remains with wild animal /bird bone,

Two sites do not provide strong enough results to provide water tight conclusions, but these relationships were also found when considered the overall contents of pits as these and other sites (see 7). At Winklebury and Middle Iron Age Winnall it is clear that the deposition of exceptionally large quantities of pottery or bone and/or large pot sherds, often took place in layers deposited in close in space and time to those containing small finds, human remains, *ABG's*, bone of non-domestic species etc. I will return to these associations and their interpretation later in the thesis (see 10 & 11). But, at least this work confirms previous suggestions that the presence of human bone fragments, amongst other items, did result from deliberate acts of deposition (contra Cunliffe & Poole 1991:418). These clusters of associations plainly demonstrate that the deposition of human remains or *ABG's* were not accompanied by 'just rubbish'. The contents of other layers in and around such possible 'ritual' deposits might be rubbish, but it was evidently different from other rubbish in other pits or other parts of the same pit.

6.3. Vertical Differences

6.3.1. Introduction;
General Differences in pottery and bone density and presence

Vertical differences, particularly in the preservation of material, within the fills of features have been suggested in previous studies of carbonised plant material, pottery and animal bone (see 3.5.1, 3.6.1, 3.7.6). In particular, Maltby's work at Balksbury shows significantly poorer preservation of animal bone in the upper than in the lower portions of pit fills (see 3.7.6 and below). These differences have been interpreted as a result of differential preservation after deposition, which assumes that all pit fills were basically homogeneous. Here, I have followed Maltby's approach, although considering all categories of finds and not just animal bones. Although recognising the problems a crude division into thirds and imperfect database provide, the work does show the potential of future, more detailed, studies on these questions.

Investigating this issue is not made easy by the observable variations between the different sites investigated. No consistent patterns were found, but how much this is a factor of different excavation strategies and levels of artefact recovery is hard to assess. Table 6.7. and figures 6.1-6 show the differences in the presence, densities and *MSW's* of pottery, animal bone, small finds, human remains and *ABG's* in different thirds of pits on a number of sites. At Little Somborne, Winnall and Winklebury, but not Micheldever Wood, it is clear that pottery was more frequently present in the upper thirds of pits than in the middle and lower thirds (Table 6.7.). A similar pattern for the presence of animal bone can be seen at Winnall (Table 6.7.). Calculations of the density of pottery and bone show no consistent patterns (Table 6.7; Fig. 6.2&3.). Pot densities showed a marked increase in the upper

thirds of fills at Winklebury and Little Somborne. High bone densities were present in the lower thirds of pits at Balksbury, Early Iron Age Winnall and Winklebury. At Middle Iron Age Winnall they remain the same through pit profiles, and at Micheldever were similar in lower and upper thirds.

Bone density measures the number of bone fragments per cubic meter, and is not directly comparable to pottery density, a measure of pot weight per cubic meter. Ideally, densities of the weight of animal bone would give a more direct comparison, as the density of bone fragments makes no allowance for differences in the size of bone fragments. Maltby's (nd2) analysis of the bone from Balksbury demonstrates that the bones in upper pits fills are smaller and more fragmented than those in lower fills (see below). This implies that densities of bone fragments from upper pit fills over estimate the actual weight, and original number of whole bones represented by these assemblages. It may be that the real abundance of animal bone may generally decrease from bottom to top of most pits.

The majority of *ABG's* were generally only found in lower/middle pit fills (Fig. 6.4. & 6.5). There were no vertical differences in the distribution of different types or species of *ABG's* (Table 6.2.). At Winnall and Winklebury, human remains reverse this pattern, increasing in frequency in the middle and upper thirds of pits (Fig. 6.4&6.5). These relationships are summarised below;

	Human Remains	*ABG's*
Upper	+	−
Middle	+	+
Lower	−	+

At Winnall the majority of complete or fragmented human skeletons and individual bone fragments were found in middle and upper fills (see 7.9 - Figs. 7.9&10). At Winklebury, all the complete or fragmentary skeletons came from the middle fills, which are predominantly natural in origin and clearly separate the main deposits of animal bone in the lower thirds (see 7.9). This preference for middle/upper positions within pit fills for human bone groups is not universal. While found at Viables Farm and Micheldever Wood (and a suggested common pattern East Hampshire generally?), for Wessex as a whole more burials have been recovered from lower fills (Hill unpublished; Whimster 1981). At Danebury human remains are evenly distributed throughout fills, but with particularly complete skeletons in lower thirds (Cunliffe 1992:75) and a large proportion of individual bone fragments coming from the topmost layers of pits (Table 6.2.). At MIA Gussage All Saints human remains were evenly distributed throughout the fills. But in the LIA phase, the majority of all human deposits were placed in the lower fills of pits.

	Complete Adult Body	Infant Bodies	Human Bone Frags
Upper	-	1	-
Middle	1	-	3
Lower	-	2	1

Middle Iron Age Gussage

	Complete Adult Body	Infant Bodies	Human Bone Frags
Upper	2	6	1
Middle	4	5	1
Lower	3	13	-

Late Iron Age Gussage

The three human bone fragments found in middle fills in the MIA phase were all deposited after larger deliberately deposits of pottery and either quern stone fragments or bronze working moulds. This raises the important issue of sequence in which materials were deposited in the pit. This will be discussed later in this study, but lays behind all the vertical distributions discussed in this chapter. Thus for example, at LIA Gussage All Saints where adult and infant human bodies were deposited in the same pit, the adult bodies were always placed in the feature after the infants.

The distribution of small finds at Winnall and Winklebury showed the number of thirds yielding small finds changed little. But other vertical differences are apparent at both sites. For example, layers with two or more finds tended to be in the middle/lower thirds. At both Winnall and Winklebury, loom weights were more common in lower and middle thirds, but iron objects and all brooches (see 7.6) in upper thirds. 'Unusual' items such as near complete quern stones, decorated weights and chalk moulds tend to occur in lower or middle thirds (see 7.6).

These relationships shown at Winnall and Winklebury are summarised below, and must be understood in terms of the ordered sequences of pit fills shown in the studies of individual pits (see 7.9).

Similar patterns can be seen in the evidence from Gussage. In all phases at this site quern stones were more likely to be recovered from the middle and lower fills of pits. This was especially true of the few complete quern stones and those substantial fragments which were large enough to have their weight recorded in the feature cards in the archive. Loom weights in all phases were also mainly recovered from lower and middle fills. Other types of small finds show a more varied picture. Worked bone and antler objects were recovered from middle and lower fills from all phase pits. In the MIA phase, as at Winklebury and Winnall, what might be classed 'unusual' finds all came from the lower fills - here the famous massive deposit of bronze working debris in pit 205 and the scrap iron deposit in its 'twin' 437 (see Appendix 1).

	Small Finds	Loom Weights	Iron Objects	Unusual Objects	Brooches
Upper	+	-	+	-	+
Middle	+	+	+	+	-
Lower	+	+	-	+	-

The vertical distribution of different types of small finds in pit fills at Winnall and Winklebury

Gussage All Saints: Querns and Bone/Antler objects

	Total Querns	Quern Frgs	Large Quern Frgs	Complete Querns
Upper Fills	8	7	1	-
Middle Fills	12	11	1	-
Lower Fills	25	15	6	2

The vertical distribution of Quern finds from EIA pits at Gussage

	Total Querns	Quern Frgs	Large Quern Frgs	Complete Querns
Upper Fills	1	1	-	-
Middle Fills	1	1	-	-
Lower Fills	3	2	1	-

The vertical distribution of Quern finds from MIA pits at Gussage

	Total Querns	Quern Frgs	Large Quern Frgs	Complete Querns
Upper Fills	7	7	-	-
Middle Fills	15	11	3	1
Lower Fills	37	18	11	1

The vertical distribution of Quern finds from LIA pits at Gussage

	EIA	MIA	LIA
Upper Fills	4	5	2
Middle Fills	13	5	10
Lower Fills	19	3+8 frgs	12

The changing distribution of antler and bone tools from pits at Gussage

6.3.2. Bone Preservation and bone Fragmentation

Vertical differences within pit fills are apparent for all classes of material. The central question is whether these represent changes after deposition, or relate to the condition of the material put into the pit. If the latter, this would imply different types of material, from different sources, where placed/dumped into the pits at different stages of their filling (see 7.9). However, where these differences have been considered before, differential *in situ* preservation has been suggested (see 3.6.1 & 3.7.6).

Maltby's analysis of pits at Middle Iron Age Balksbury (nd. 2 - see 3.7.6) demonstrated that upper halves of pits contained poorer preserved and more fragmented bone than lower halves. Maltby's data on the number of modern breakages and the degree of fragmentation for different anatomical elements of cattle, horse and sheep are summarised in table 6.3. These figures suggest that cattle and horse bone are particularly prone to modern breakages in the upper halves of pit fills. I would suggest this is probably caused by heavy machinery. From figures showing the completeness of the non-modern broken fragments for each element, I have calculated an index of fragmentation (after Maltby nd1);

For each bone fragment is assigned a value

1 for a complete bone,

0.75 for a three-quarter complete bone,

0.5 for a half complete bone,

0.25 for a quarter or less complete bone,

The sum of these values is divided by the total number of bone fragments to give a mean value of fragmentation;

Maximum possible score = 1

Minimum possible score = 0.25

The degree of bone fragmentation is a factor of animal size, the anatomical element involved and of carcass utilisation, particularly the effort spent splitting bone for marrow extraction (Maltby nd. 2). The results from Middle Iron Age Balksbury are probably applicable for other Downland Wessex Iron Age sites and do show that bone, particularly from sheep, is generally more fragmented in upper, compared to lower, layers (Table 6.3). The less fragmented lower assemblages of cattle and sheep were not simply because of the higher proportion of articulated bone from lower fills. At Middle Iron Age Balksbury, a comparatively small proportion of cattle and sheep bone was articulated in lower fills (Table 6.7.).

Average Indices for all elements considered;

	Cattle	Sheep
Upper	0.336	0.371
Lower	0.417	0.579

6.3.3. Preservation of different skeletal elements

At Balksbury, Maltby investigated bone preservation through considering the different skeletal elements for the five main domestic species between upper and lower pit halves (Table 6.4.; Fig. 6.8.). While not considering information on the fragmentation of individual bone elements, I have attempted to repeat this work for Middle Iron Age

Winnall as a comparison, but using upper, middle and lower pit divisions (Table 6.5.; Fig. 6.8.). Any direct comparison could be complicated by possible differences in the sampling strategies for bone at both sites. If more care in the retrieval of bone took place at one of one, proportionally more of the smaller bones may have been collected, affecting overall percentages of the different anatomical elements. However, as Fig. 6.7. suggests although it could be argued that the greater proportions of smaller elements such as loose teeth, tarsals, carpels and phalanges point to a better of degree of recovery at Winnall, there are no gross differences between the sites (Fig. 6.9.).

Cattle and Horse
At Balksbury, cattle and horse skull bones were more abundant and better preserved in the lower halves of pits. Relatively high numbers of complete skulls of both species lead Maltby to suggest deliberate deposition of skulls in the very lowest layers of pits (Maltby nd2:10). This was not found for cattle skulls at Winnall, but horse skull fragments did make up a substantial proportion of the total horse bone from lower thirds. Horse mandibles were also more abundant than expected in lower thirds at Winnall, but not so at Balksbury. Cattle mandibles were more abundant in lower layers at both sites.

The vertical differences in the proportions of other skeletal elements are not identical for both sites. This is partly a factor of the presence of articulated bone groups from both species which may distort overall patterning. This can be seen particularly for the middle fills at Winnall where 68% of the horse assemblage came from a single near complete skeleton. Sample size may be also important. Differences for any element are largely a factor of differential preservation. Cattle femurs at Balksbury and Winnall, and horse femurs at Balksbury make up slightly higher proportions of assemblages in lower fills because this is relatively slender bone is prone to breakage and difficult to identify once fragmented (Maltby nd2:13). Equally, the high percentage of cattle tibia fragments in middle and upper thirds at Winnall, may relate to the robust nature of tibia shaft fragments compared to other elements, so that they make up a higher proportion of badly preserved assemblages.

All the smaller skeletal elements -- carpals and tarsals, metapodia, sesamoids and phalanges -- are grossly under represented at both sites, as is to be expected in hand collected samples (see 3.7.1). These elements represent approximately 80% of complete fresh cattle and horse skeletons, but at Middle Iron Age Winnall represent only 21% of the retrieved cattle and 18% of the horse assemblages. High proportions of cattle phalanges and sesamoids in the lower fills at Balksbury came from articulated groups of lower limb bones (30 out of 39 bones), and similarly unrecognised *ABG's* might account for high percentages at Winnall. Such extremities may remain attached to the skin after

skinning and it is possible that this waste, if not the skins themselves, was selectively deposited in lower fills (see 7.3.2). Vertebrae are often hard to identify to species, but this is made easier where articulated groups of vertebrae are recovered. At Balksbury 'stray' vertebrae, particularly in upper fills, were poorly preserved as their spongy structure is particularly susceptible to canid gnawing (Maltby nd2).

Sheep and Pig
At both sites the overall low numbers and high proportion of articulated groups for pig bone hampered detailed discussion of differences in preservation throughout pit fills. Sheep bones at Balksbury were less fragmented in lower compared to upper halves (Table 6.3.). Like cattle and horse, sheep skull at Balksbury was found in significantly large proportions in lower fills, even after taking into account bone from articulated groups (Maltby nd2:25). This was not the case at Winnall, even though post-depositional transformation processes were probably similar on both sites. Mandible fragments were more abundant in upper compared to lower fills at both sites. This may be a factor of poorer preservation. Although generally more fragmented in upper fills, I would suggest that mandibles are robust elements, certainly more resistant to dog gnawing (Legge 1991b:79), while their size and distinctive shape may mean a greater proportion of mandible fragments will be hand collected compared to other poorly preserved fragments. Of the limb bones, sheep tibia, like cattle and horse tibia, formed a higher proportion of upper assemblages. Oddly at Winnall sheep femur fragments were more abundant in middle and upper thirds, even though this is generally a fragile bone. The proportions of the smaller bone increase with depth, reflecting both better overall preservation and the larger proportion of *ABG's*.

Loose Teeth
As the most robust element of the skeleton, the proportion of loose teeth in any assemblage is a good index for the overall preservation of animal bone. At both sites for all species except dog, significantly higher percentages of loose teeth were found in upper layers indicating the poor preservation of bone assemblages (Fig. 6.6.). At Balksbury, Maltby also showed that the percentage of loose teeth was even higher in the top most layers of pits (e.g. Sheep 31.3% n125 top most layers c.f. 21.4% n1115 for all upper layers). For the other sites examined, the difference in the overall percentage of loose teeth in the topmost layers compared to all upper fills was not so great

Micheldever		10.0% in topmost layer
	c.f.	7.5% all upper layers,
EIA Winnall		9.3% in topmost layer
	c.f.	4.9% all upper layers,
MIA Winnall		11.4% in topmost layer
	c.f.	10.4% all upper layers.

There are several possible explanations for this discrepancy, including the effects of comparing Maltby's figures which divided pit fills into two halves, and my approach using three divisions. Secondly, it is possible that a cruder distinction was made of the upper layers at Balksbury compared to Winnall. Observation from the sections in the archive suggests, as at Gussage, that the uppermost distinguished layer at the former site was often quite deep and at other sites, such as Winnall, would have been further sub-divided into several contexts (see 5.1.).

6.3.4. Conclusions

The detailed study for Middle Iron Age Winnall confirmed the general conclusions from Maltby's Balksbury study, although there are detailed differences for various skeletal elements. These are partly due to discrepancies in recovery, and show variations in specific depositional practices between sites (see 12.2.1). It is clear at Balksbury that skull bone was selectively deposited on or near the base of pits. Some or all of these may represent the careful deposition of complete skulls which Grant and Wait classify as special deposits (see 3.7.7.). Complete or partially complete skulls may have been crushed from the weight of overlying fills. If so, then it is probable that the identification of these special skull deposits significantly under represent their original abundance. The work confirms that animal bone in upper layers of pit fills is generally less well preserved than that in lower fills. Data from several sites confirm (see 3.7.6) an important consequence is that the larger species' bone will be more abundant in upper fills because they are more robust than those of smaller species.

6.3.5. Vertical Differences in Bone Assemblages: A Pre- or Post-Depositional Explanation?

Assemblages in upper fills are less well preserved, but why? Maltby, B. Wilson and others have argued that this is largely due to the penetration of weathering and root action into upper pit fills. Using my crude division into pit thirds this would often have to be to a considerable depth, up to 0.5m+ in many cases. This explanation assumes that the assemblages entering pits were basically similar regardless of their final position within the pit fill. Alternatively the differences could have been caused by depositing originally better preserved material into the lower parts of pits, and poorly preserved material in the upper. That is the differences in preservation occurred before the material entered the pit. This is not to deny that *in situ* weathering is an important factor, but I would suggest its penetration into fills is limited and particularly only heavily felt in the very top most layers of pits. Two characteristics of the bone assemblages support this alternative explanation.

First, are the causes of bone fragmentation demonstrable in upper fills? It has been shown that bone is generally more fragmented in upper than in

to lower fills. However, this does not apply to all species equally. It has already been noted that dog bones are generally recovered well preserved and substantially complete (see 3.7.7, 5.4). This applies to both those from articulated groups and individual bones which are recovered from upper fills. Equally, horse bones from upper fills are less fragmented than cattle bones of a similar size (Table 6.3). If the poorer bone preservation in upper fills was post-depositional why do dog, and to some extent horse, bones escape theses processes? This suggests that most bone fragmentation occurred before deposition, caused by deliberate smashing of bone for marrow extraction and attrition, weathering, and, particularly, gnawing before burial. Dog and, to a lesser extent, horse bone may be better preserved because these bones were less frequently smashed during carcass processing, and/or were deliberately deposited substantially complete into pit fills.

Further, evidence points to different types of bone assemblages being deposited in different parts of pit fills. At Balksbury preferential disposal, if not deliberate placing, is evident for skulls in pit bottoms. The presence of ABG's in lower fills was due to selective disposal. Although Maltby (nd2) still implies poor preservation is the major factor for their absence in upper fills. I would suggest that this over estimates the effects of post-depositional weathering and attrition, and that articulated and other well preserved bone were in the main deliberately deposited in the lower and middle thirds of pits. ABG's could survive even if only shallowly buried on chalk sites, as examples from all the sites studied here show (Fig. 6.5., Table 6.2.). Some of the articulated groups in upper fills are from limb extremities, which might not be expected to survive well in conditions of poor in situ preservation due to their fragile natural. The same would apply to the preservation of a hare skeleton in upper fills of Middle Iron Age Winnall pit 1061 - c.f. the hare skeleton in the upper fills of Winklebury pit 3825. Although no information is given in the report on the position of 'animal special deposits' at Danebury, it is clear from the illustrations that at least one well preserved burial was found in the top of a pit (Grant 1984a:fig. 9.32). Shallowly buried, but well preserved, complete carcasses were excavated at South Cadbury (Alcock 1969:36; 1970:16&25; Jane Downs pers com.).

Shallow cattle burials were also found at the Middle Bronze Age sites of Itford Hill (Burstow & Holleyman 1957:188) and South Lodge (Barrett, Bradley & Green 1991:157ff). Legge's (Legge 1991a:90-91; Barrett, Bradley & Green 1991:167) discussion of the latter is important here. The bone of this burial, which consisted of only the left side of the carcass lying on its side, was "rather poorly preserved", suggesting that shallow burial does have some effects. But despite this, all skeletal elements originally present seem to be well represented and both articulation surfaces at either end of the long bones survive. Such articulations are fragile and quickly lost with poor preservation (particularly caused by gnawing and attrition as opposed to weathering?). That this originally represented the burial of a complete carcass, but the upper, more exposed, right side was "severely eroded to the point of dissolution" was considered but discounted. Rather, only the left side of the carcass was originally buried.

Finally it should be added that human skeletons were frequently deposited in the upper fills of pits at Winklebury and Winnall. Although preservation and the state of the bone is rarely commented on in human bone reports, illustrations suggest that such adult skeletons are complete and well preserved e.g. the adult burial in the upper fill of Winnall pit 4475. I would argue if complete or large portions of animal skeletons were regularly deposited in upper pit fills they would also be generally well preserved.

6.3.6. Pottery

It has been suggested above that the animal bones entering upper pit fills were already more fragmented and poorly preserved than those deposited in lower and middle fills which also contain a large proportion of well preserved articulated/associated bone material. Pottery need not follow this pattern because of different patterns of disposal and different reaction to weathering and attrition. As attrition is usually suggested to be the main cause of pot deterioration, it could be that pottery would be less effected than bone by *in situ* erosion.

On all sites to a greater or lesser extent, pottery appears to be more abundant in upper thirds of pits, compared to the lower/middle thirds. Pottery appears to be more abundant in upper thirds than animal bone. At Winklebury a clear bone/pot opposition can be seen, with high densities of bone in lower thirds, separated by largely natural chalk shatter middle fills from high densities of pottery in upper fills (Fig. 6.2&3.). I have already shown that bone in upper fills is poorly preserved and more fragmented than bone lower in pit fills. This greater bone fragmentation makes comparisons of changing animal bone densities vertically through pit fills difficult. There may be more, or similar, densities of bone in upper thirds compared to lower/middle thirds, but the size of these fragments could be much smaller. Here, dry weights of animal bone, to calculate densities by weight and mean bone fragment weight are urgently required to make secure comparisons with pottery.

Pottery is probably more abundant and better preserved in upper pit fills than bone. This could be a result of differential preservation. Originally pottery and bone were probably equally abundant, but as bone is probably more susceptible to weathering than pot, a far greater proportion of pottery has survived. This requires further study. Using Mean Sherd Weight as an indicator of

preservation, showed that MSW's were lower in the upper thirds compared to lower/middle fills. This is shown at Middle Iron Age Winnall, Middle Iron Age Easton Lane and Micheldever (Fig. 6.1.) and in the distribution of layers with above one standard deviation above average MSW's (Table 6.7.). MSW's fell consistently in the topmost most layers in pits compared to other layers in the upper thirds (see below).

	MSW in Topmost Layer	MSW in all Upper Layers
Little Somborne	8.8g	11.5g
Micheldever Wood EIA	5.5g	8.7g
Winnall Down MIA	6.0g	9.8g
Winnall Down	8.8g	12.5g

Comparison of MSW's in the topmost and all layers in upper thirds of pits

As the case with animal bone, it is clear that some large pot sherds can be found in upper fills, suggesting where large sherds were deposited they have survived with little subsequent attrition. I would suggest that poor pottery preservation in upper fills is largely not a result of post-deposition factors. Sherd size would seem to be most affected by attrition and breakage, while large sherds may be broken when deposited into a pit, or when covered by heavy fills, etc., little further breakage would occur, except perhaps from trampling in the top most layers of pits. As such, smaller MSW's in upper thirds are an indicator of the different nature and origins of these fills.

In her study of material at Winklebury, Fisher (1985) pointed out the large amount of Early Iron Age pottery found in Middle Iron Age pits. Much of this residual material comes from the upper fills with their dense concentrations of pottery. This is obviously not freshly broken material, and Fisher (1985:177) suggests spatial concentrations of this residual material mark the presence of former Early Iron Age middens/pottery dumps. The mixed pot assemblages in these upper fills probably derive from mixed, 'general' middens and from background material in the soil.

At Micheldever, the pottery from upper thirds is also obviously different from that of the lower thirds in pit fills. Here two distinct pottery phases can be identified, Middle Iron Age 'Saucepan' assemblages and Late Iron Age/Early Roman assemblages with wheel made pottery. It is apparent that the Late Iron Age/Early Roman assemblages come only from the upper thirds of pits and are largely unmixed with the Middle Iron Age material lower down (Table 6.5.). The Late Iron Age/Early Roman pottery is far smaller, with much lower *MSW*'s than the Middle Iron Age pottery (7.4

±4.9g c.f. overall layer *MSW* for all layers including Middle Iron Age 15.1±16.4g), and compared to the over all *MSW* for upper thirds (8.7±4.5g). This could be a factor of the different forms and fabrics between the two assemblages, and further work is needed to assess if Late Iron Age/Early Roman pottery to is more robust, and so had larger *MSW's.*, than Middle Iron Age pottery. The different date of the material in the upper thirds at Micheldever strongly confirms that pit fills and assemblages are not homogeneous, and that vertical differences relate mainly to pre-deposition preservation.

6.3.7. Conclusions

This section has shown that there are considerable vertical differences in finds assemblages within pit fills, that pit fills are not uniform and that such variations are not primarily a factor of differential post-depositional preservation. One important difference that has been identified at Winnall and Winklebury is the preference for depositing articulated animal bone groups in lower and middle fills. Loom weights and 'unusual' small finds also seem to have been usually deposited in lower and middle fills. The poor preservation of bone and pottery, its different origins and even date, in upper fills suggests in general this material had a different immediate origin from that first deposited in pits. As has been stressed, there are problems using the crude division of pits into thirds, rather than using units of depth, and the nature of the available data. However, there is considerable potential for further work on these questions.

Deliberate deposits of all kinds of material, not just possible 'special animal deposits', were concentrated in lower and middle fills. Much of this material was deposited soon after the activity created them, or represents provisionally discarded/curated material, stages I and II in the provisional model outlined above in chapter 5 e.g. large assemblages of animal bone, collections of small finds, small groups of large pot sherds etc. This does not account for all the material in these fills. Assemblages in most layers are the small numbers of unintentionally incorporated finds within the soil, midden material, ash and burnt stone fills equating to stages III and IV in the model outlined in chapter 5

In one sense, the general characteristic of upper fills is largely the absence of this 'fresh' or curated material. Although, there were deliberate deposits of stage I and II material, they were rarer than in the lower/middle fills. This explains the poorer preservation of the material, which should be seen as coming from stages III and IV, old middens and the background of material in the soil within and surrounding the settlement. This material had been exposed to a variety of destructive agencies for some time before incorporation in pit fills, including the effects of weathering, trampling, scattering and scavenging. Pottery may be more resistant to such processes than bone, and so be more abundant in such layers. This material entered the upper portions of pits in a variety of ways. It is important to realise that pit fills do settle with time, and this might be particularly pronounced where large quantities of organic material have decomposed in lower fills e.g. a large layer of 'green' midden material or crop processing residue, or a large portion/complete human/animal carcass. The proportions of some of the Micheldever pits with Late Iron Age/Early Roman layers show how much pits could settle with time. The hollows created by settling pits were recognised at the time. In some case they were deliberately infilled and levelled, where they were seen as a nuisance, with a variety of material, including soil/middens material or burnt stone and compact chalk. As such the upper fills combine a mix of layers deliberately deposited soil etc. to originally infill the pit, followed by both natural and deliberate infills as the pit settled. Weathering and trampling did have some impact on material in these upper fills, but I would argue their effect was limited. As such, it would be an important transformative factor on those layers exposed for some time in the slow process of settling and final natural infilling, generally only those at the very top of the pit - as shown by there extremely high percentage of loose teeth and low *MSW's* (see above).

The high densities of pottery, in particular, found in these upper layers may have a range of origins. At Winklebury, such concentrations are partly due to the presence of older pottery dumps/middens in the area of pit digging. The high concentration of pottery was a 'background' in the soil in this area, or, if the pot dump/midden survived as a coherent and recognisable feature, the deliberate use of this material as a convenient infilling. This deliberate use of midden material as a convenient infilling might explain the pottery concentrations at other sites. Another cause for such concentrations is the way the hollows in the tops of infilled pits might have acted as traps collecting and concentrating a range of background material -- pottery, loose teeth etc. -- scattered around the area (Bersu 1940:54; Hodder 1982c:52).

The distinction between the deposition of loom weights and iron objects seen at Winnall and Winklebury partly relates to the factors discussed above. Loom weights were mainly deposited in lower and middle fills, unlike iron objects. This would seem to be a factor of size. Large objects were probably not common in stage III middens and stage IV background material around the site. They seemed to have been provisionally discarded/curated separately, and some were finally discarded in lower/middle fills. In contrast, most of the iron finds from both sites are comparatively small, and many may have been an unnoticed component of middens and the finds' background. However, this is not to suggest convenience was the only factor influencing the initial discard and final deposition of these finds.

Iron objects may also have been selectively treated in a different way than loom weights for other cultural reasons and deposited differently.

The differences between upper and middle/lower fills have important consequences for the phasing of pits. As the situation at Micheldever clearly demonstrates, there could be a considerable time gap between the deposition of material in lower/middle thirds and that in the top of the pit. This can also be seen at several pits at Winnall where upper, particularly top, layers contain Late Iron Age or Roman material. The ceramic phasing of pits should only rely on that material which can be argued to have been contemporary with the initial infilling. In most cases this will be the 'freshest' material in lower/middle layers of the pit. Simply using the latest occurring material anywhere within the pit fills or overall pit total assemblages is insecure. This may seem an obvious observation, and has been stated on several previous occasions (see 3.2 -- Bersu 1940:54; Hodder 1982c:52).

This is a general model for pit fills, obviously there will be exceptions. The two Hampshire hillforts whose pits fills have a far higher proportion of natural episodes of filling, may be significantly different (see 7.9). At Winklebury the majority of pits show a clear middle fill of naturally eroding in chalk shatter lens. Work on the Winklebury pits suggests this only makes the general distinction between lower and upper fills more pronounced and evidently separated by the episodes of natural silting. Nor must it be assumed that there can not be deliberate depositions in upper fills of the kinds that typify middle/lower fills. There can be deposits of 'fresh' animal bone, large pot sherds, collections of small finds, and, particularly, articulated human bone groups in upper fills, although usually in low numbers. T these deposits of such pottery, small finds or human bone groups in upper pit fills at Winnall and Winklebury were not later insertions dug into the tops of pits. None of the section drawings at these two sites show this; rather the human deposits were part of the overall sequence of depositional episodes, and, as will be shown in the next sub-chapter, often show a knowledge of the previous material deposited in the pits.

6.4. Conclusions

This chapter set out to investigate the vertical differences that exist within pits fills and to look for possible associations between various factors within neighbouring layers in the same part of pit fills. Dividing pit fills into three equal parts, it has taken Maltby's work on animal bone and combined it with studies of other materials to build a fuller understanding of the processes that lead to the filling of a pit, the origins of the various fills and the nature of post-depositional modifications. The use of a division of all pits, regardless of depth, into upper, middle and lower thirds, as opposed to dividing pit fills into equal units of depth (e.g. 50cm units), has not been found to seriously effect the results. While very shallow pits may have poorer preservation throughout their fills, results here suggest that the basic sequence of fills outline of above is found in pits of all depths; that the division into thirds corresponds to a real division in the nature of the fills themselves and reflects the sequence in which material was deposited, placed, in the pit. This is an issue for further investigation. It has been shown that vertical differences do exist both in the distribution and the state of preservation of different classes of material within pit fills. In particular, the bone and pottery in upper pit fills is generally less well preserved than that found in lower parts of the pit. It has been suggested that this can not be caused by just *in situ* post-depositional factors, but actually demonstrates the different origins of these upper fills. It has been suggested that an 'average' pit saw more and fresher material directly deposited in the lower and middle fills, with the upper fills derived largely from old midden material, yard floors, soil etc.

This work confirms previous suggestions that pit fills should not be considered as self contained wholes, as homogeneous in origins and contents. Differences in the survival of different skeletal elements and different species in different parts of the same pit fill do seriously effect attempts to use overall bone totals to draw general conclusions about subsistence economies etc. (see 3.7). It also has important implications for the phasing of pits. As has been pointed out before, the use of material from the upper fills of pits can not securely be used to phase such features. Although residue material will be present throughout pit fills, simply using the latest pottery anywhere within a pit fill to provide a *terminus post quem* must be rejected. Overall pit assemblages should be treated with caution. Rather attempts to isolate the freshest material in the main body of the pit should be used to phase features.

The demonstration that a cluster of statistically significant associations are evident within pit thirds must be emphasised. Similar associations were absent within individual layers, where studies showed that exceptional assemblages within single layers tended to concentrate on a single category of material. What is clear is that such exceptional layers were often combined in a sequence as part of the same overall depositional event. It is this combination of different deposits, each individually of one main class of material, that explains the associations found when using the thirds of pits as the level of analysis, or the whole pit contents, as in the next chapter. This is best demonstrated in the detailed studies of individual pits (see 7.9). The nature and implications of these inter-relationships are the main subject of the next chapter, where they will be shown to exist when using overall pit totals on a larger sample of sites.

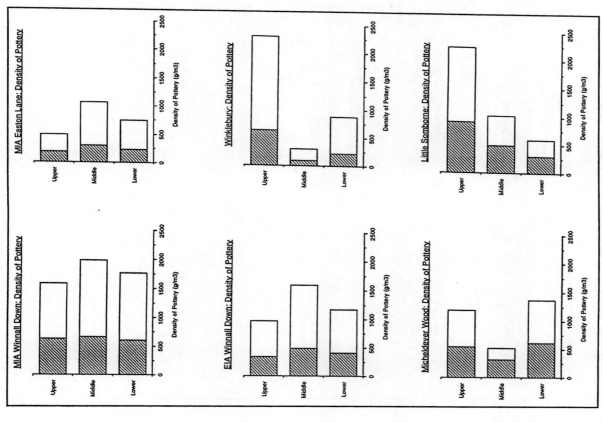

Fig. 6.2. Histograms of showing the changes in Density of pottery with depth in pit fills at six sites/phases (shaded area = Mean Sherd Weight, clear area = +1 std. dev).

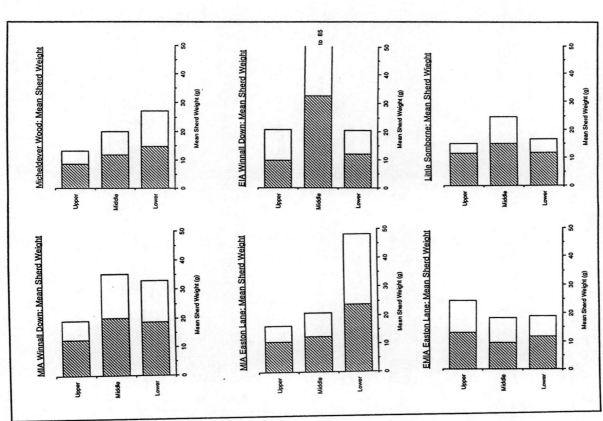

Fig. 6.1. Histograms of showing the changes in Mean Sherd Weight with depth in pit fills at six sites/phases (shaded area = Mean Sherd Weight, clear area = +1 std. dev).

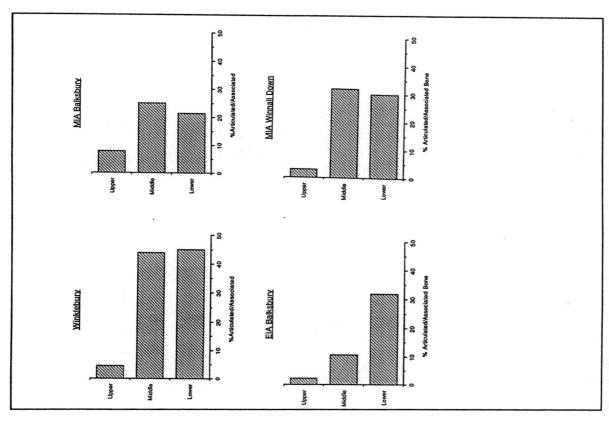

Fig. 6.4. Histograms showing the changing proportion of bone coming from articulated/associated animal bone with depth in pit fills at four sites/phases.

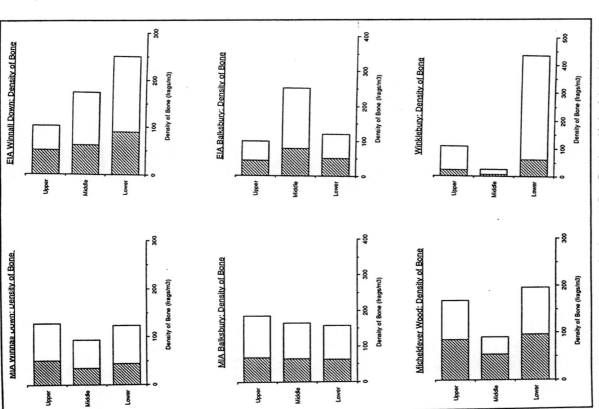

Fig. 6.3. Histograms of showing the changes in Bone Density with depth in pit fills at six sites/phases (shaded area = Mean Sherd Weight, clear area = +1 std. dev).

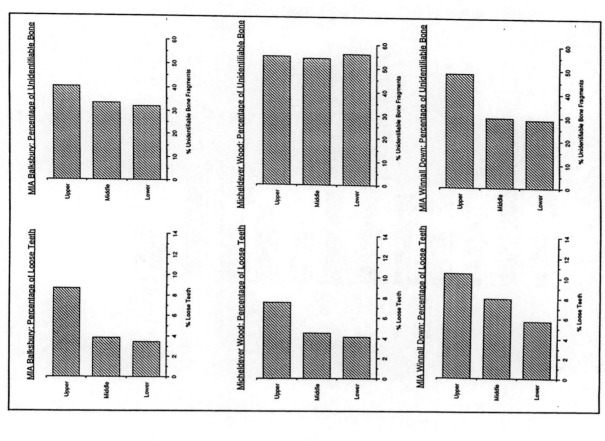

Fig. 6.6. Histograms showing the changes in measures of poor bone preservation with depth in pit fills at Middle Iron Age Winnall Down, Micheldever Wood and Balksbury.

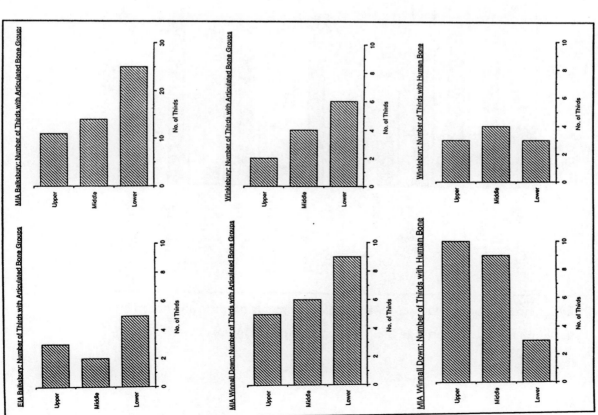

Fig. 6.5. Histograms showing the distribution of Articulated/Associated Animal Groups and Human Remains at three sites.

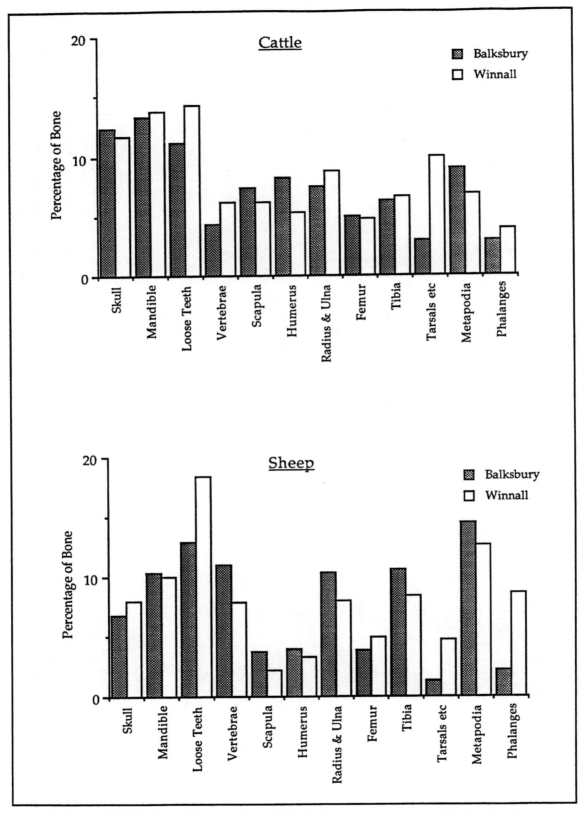

Fig. 6.7. Differences in the proportions of anatomical elements of cattle and sheep bone recovered at Middle Iron Age Balksbury and Winnall Down.

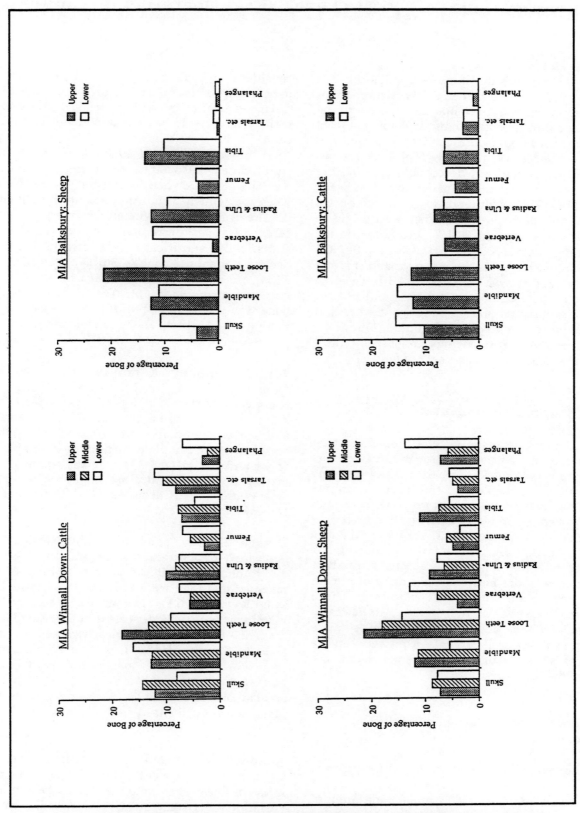

Fig. 6.8. Changes in bone preservation with depth: Histograms showing the changing proportions of different anatomical elements of cattle and sheep bone with depth within pit fills at Middle Iron Age Winnall Down and Balksbury.

Chapter 7
Investigations of Pits: Level 3 - Overall Pit Contents

7. 1.   Introduction

This chapter completes the study of pit fills through considering their overall contents. The patterns that have emerged in the previous analyses will be amplified, and new factors such as pit shape, pot form and pot fabric considered. The chapter is broken down into ten sections covering such topics as human remains, pit shape and pot decoration, etc. offering detailed discussions of relationships found between various factors. The result tends to overwhelm in its particulars, and perhaps is not what Geertz had in mind when he advocated *'Thick Description'* in the understanding of other societies and cultures. But it is necessary both to show the general associations found between the factors *and* the detailed differences in these patterns between particular sites and phases. These general patterns and associations are brought back to the individual events of people infilling pits at the end of the chapter, which concludes with a resume of the analyses and argument so far.

7.2.   Human Remains
7.2.1.   Introduction

Previous chapters have shown that human remains were not randomly distributed through homogeneous 'rubbish' deposits in pit fills (see 6.2). These patterns are the result of people placing human remains in pits according to 'rules' which meant on some sites they could only deposit human remains after or before placing other items in the pit. These individual acts working within, unintentionally changing or challenging these 'rules' (see 12.1&2) acted to produce a range of associations between the putting of human remains and other materials in pits. These associations can be shown to be statistically significant. Such positive relationships were discovered in the overall contents of pit between the presence of all sorts of human remains and the presence of the following;

Above Standard Deviation Densities of Pottery

Above Standard Deviation Densities of Bone

Articulated/Associated Animal Bone Groups

Small Finds, especially in numbers

These are not a universal set of rigid co-presences. Rather some associations are found at one site, or phase, but not others. This variation is common across all the range of material deposited in pits. There are broad general patterns in the types of material people were depositing in pits, but

considerable local variations in how these broad patterns were manifest. This important issue is discussed later in this study (see 12). An example of such variability can be seen at Winnall Down/Easton Lane. In the pits at Easton Lane (Early Middle Iron Age) human remains of all kinds were statistically significantly associated with high densities of pottery (+ Std Dev densities) (prob. .0453). However, when the settlement moved back up the hill slope to the site of the former Winnall Down enclosure in the MIA, all types of human remains now show a statistically significant relationship with high densities of animal bone (+ Std Dev densities) (prob. .0353), but not pottery. A similar association between human remains and + Std Dev densities of animal bone was also found at Middle Iron Age Old Down Farm (phase 3) (prob. .0039 respectively).

7.2.2.   Human Remains and Articulated /Associated Animal Bone Groups

It is clear that people were very often placing human remains in the same pits as *ABG's* at several sites/phases studied here. All types of human remains (from complete corpses to individual bone fragments) and *ABG's* in the same pit were statistically significantly associated at Middle Iron Age Winnall, Early Iron Age Old Down Farm and Danebury cp7-8.

I have already suggested that where people deposited, if not carefully placed in some cases, ABG's and human burials in the same pit, care was usually taken so that they were very rarely deposited in the same layer (see 6.1). In one case where an human infant was unusually deposited in the same layer as a mass of *ABG's* they were clearly placed on different sides of the pit, Middle Iron Age Winnall pit 4006 (Fig. 7.1). No single species nor type (complete carcass, skull, limb etc.) of *ABG's* was specifically singled out to be put in the same pits as human remains across all sites.

Although *ABG's* and human remains were often significantly associated, the species or types of *ABG* is one of those areas were there could be considerable variations between sites. At Middle Iron Age Winnall groups of dog bones were commonly found in the same pits as human bone, yet only one of three pits with complete adult human skeletons and *ABG's* contained a dog *ABG* (Pit 8564 - neo-natal fatality). Results for the first 10 years excavations at Danebury show that, in all phases, when *complete* adult human skeletons were found with *ABG's* these were either of cattle or horse. However, only sheep or pig *ABG's* came from pits containing *partial* adult human burials .

7.2.3. Human Remains and Small Finds

On several study sites the results show that when people were depositing human remains in pits these were also often the same pits in which people had or would put small finds. Such actions produced statistically significant relations between human remains and the presence of small finds (objects of metal, worked bone, clay, stone etc.) in the same feature.

Any sort of small finds and human remains in the same pit were significantly associated at;

> Danebury cp1-3 (prob .0027),
> Winklebury (prob .0015),
> Early Iron Age Winnall (prob .0001),
> Gussage All Saints phase 3 (LIA) (prob .0306)

but not Easton Lane nor Middle Iron Age Winnall.

At several sites/phases it was apparent that human remains were clearly deposited in the same pits that people had also placed several or more small finds. Human remains were associated with larger than average numbers of small finds at Middle Iron Age Gussage (1+ small finds - prob .0364) and Danebury cp7-8 (9+ small finds - prob .0239). However, a reverse situation occurred in Danebury cp 4-5. Of this phase's 142 pits, 9 contained human bone, 42 small finds, but none contained both (prob .0507) suggesting that people deposited of these materials so that they deliberately would not occur in the same pits.

These small finds in the same pits as human remains can not be described as 'grave goods'. This is even applies to the few cases where small finds were unbroken and obviously placed, e.g. at Viables Farm pit 5, which contained *paired* decorated combs, undecorated combs; toggles, terrets in a small cist in the pit's base. The fill sealing this cist contained *pairs* of sheep, cattle and horse *ABG's* and adult female human corpses (Millett & Russell 1982).

Although significant relationships were found with clay objects at Danebury cp7-8 (prob. .0001) and with bronze objects at Middle Iron Age Winnall (prob. 0009), three groups of finds seem to have been particularly put in the same pits as human remains on all sites;

Quern Stones, Iron Objects, Worked Bone/Antler,

Putting querns stone fragments and human remains in the same pits seems to have been a particularly important association to make. In particularly, at both Middle Iron Age Winnall and Gussage querns were deposited in the same pits which later received infant human remains (Winnall prob. .0047; Gussage phases 2 - complete querns prob. .0008 -- phase 3 - quern fragments prob. .0547). In one Winnall and three Gussage pits complete or near complete quern stones were placed on/or near the pit's base before placing neo-natal/infant corpses later in the sequence of fills (e.g. Gussage pit 604 [Wainwright 1979:Plate xxxi] and Winnall Down pit 2416 - see Fig. 3.3). This situation was also found in pit 7 at Bramdean (Perry 1982:62). At LIA Gussage a total of six pits contained human infant burials deposited after quern stones (complete or fragments) had been placed in the pit. While another complete quern was placed on the base of one of the only three pits in which *ABG's* were recognised at this site (Pit 61 which contained articulated cow and calf skeletons in the same layer).

Iron objects and human remains were related at three sites; Winklebury (prob. .0346), Late Iron Age Gussage (prob .0023), and at Danebury -- phases cp7-8 (prob .0279 -- cp 1-3 prob .0615).

Worked bone and antler were associated with human remains in the same features at Danebury, Gussage and Winnall; Middle Iron Age Gussage (prob .0290 & .0290 respectively), Late Iron Age Gussage worked antler in the same pits as infant burials (prob .0100). At Middle Iron Age Winnall only worked bone, not antler, objects were recovered from the same pits as human remains (with adult human burials prob .0190), while no worked bone came from pits that contained *ABG's*. Similarly, worked bone and antler were related with human remains at Danebury cp7-8 (prob .0096 & .0242 respectively), but not *ABG's*. Of the 15 pits with bone/antler combs from this phase, 8 came from pits in which human bone had also been placed (prob .0022). Although more antler combs at Danebury, in all phases, were decorated compared to bone (11 out of 15 combs in cp7-8), those antler combs from the same pits as the complete human burials were all undecorated.

	Decorated Combs (9 pits)	Undecorated combs (6 pits)
Pits with *ABG's*	5	2
Pits with Human bone	4	5
	3 with human bone fragments	3 with complete human burials,
	1 from a charnel pit,	0 with human bone fragments,
	(1 decorated comb)	1 from a charnel pit,
		(2 undecorated combs)
		1 with a pelvic girdle

Associations between decorated and undecorated bone and antler combs and human remains and/or *ABG's* from the some pits at Danebury

7.2.4. Age and Gender of Human Depositions

Gender distinctions are evident in burials across Iron Age Europe, but were generally absent in these depositional practices. Neither the type of *ABG's* nor small finds found in the same pits as human remains show a connection with the biological sex of those human deposits. An exception is Late Iron Age Gussage where a spatial separation of male and female complete corpses, 'burials', was made - males in the north east half of the site, females in the south west half, and where spindle whorls occurred in the same pits as male inhumations. These gender distinctions are related to similar gender differences in the Late Iron Age 'Durotrigean' burial tradition (see 12.2.2.4). It could be that the absence of clear associations with different biologically sexed human remains is a product of small sample size, but such associations were not noted in earlier, larger, studies of these practices (C. Wilson 1981; Whimster 1981; Wait 1985). Equally, the variability witnessed between sites and within different phases of the same site, could mean that such strong associations existed at some sites and times. However, I would suggest that gender was not an important element physically articulated in these deposits. Age was more important, on some sites at least, with associations between neo-natal/infant depositions and quern stones (see 7.2.3.), and differences in where infant and adult remains were deposited (see 9.4).

7. 2.5. Summary

These associations with other factors were not restricted to complete or partial human skeletons. They also importantly include the presence of fragments of human bone. Indeed on some sites/phases it is with these remains and not 'burials' that the bulk of the associations occur. It is probable that differences in the associations with different types of human deposits are more important than those between age and sex. This study has shown a difference in the treatment of complete and partial/disarticulated adult deposits at Danebury and other sites. Partial burials were at Winklebury and Winnall placed in the lower fills of pits, in contrast to complete burials in the middle/upper fills. A situation reversed at Danebury (Cunliffe 1992:75). The partial burial from Winnall was the one human deposit associated with a large number of small finds of different types, high *MSW*, wild animal bone, but no decorated pottery (see 7.5 & 7.8.3). The differences in associations with a variety of factors across various types of human deposit at Winnall are summarised in Table 7.6.

An initial question at the beginning of this thesis was whether the presence of human remains had any impact on the other contents of the sub-soil features they were found on. This study has shown that they clearly do, and that it is incorrect to perceive all finds assemblages from features as an undifferentiated whole. The presence of human remains has been shown to be statistically significantly associated with the presence of *ABG's* and small finds in several sites/phases. People particularly placed certain types of small finds, such as querns and worked bone/antler, in the same pits where they placed human remains. While no obvious gender differences appear to have been made by the people conducting these deposits, there were differences in the associated material deposited with infants and adults.

7.3. Articulate/Associated Animal Bone Groups

7.3.1. Species of Animal

As with human remains, Iron Age people appear to have deposited articulated/associated groups of animal bone (*ABG's*) in a limited number of pits in which they also deposited other material (and so producing statistically significant relations in the excavated data) including the presence of human bone, small finds and wild animals/birds. However, it is important to re-emphasise the difficulties in directly comparing sites studied by different archaeozoologists.

ABG's of all the major domesticated species and various wild species have been found deposited Wessex Downland sites. Grant (1984a:542-3) and Wait (1985:129) both noted that horse and dog *ABG's* are more common than should be expected compared to their overall abundance in bone assemblages. Meanwhile sheep are under represented. What could be taken as an essentially cultural-materialist argument (c.f. Harris 1974) was used by both Grant and Wait to explain the preference for horse and dog in ritual deposits because, as they provided little traction, food, milk, clothing etc., their use would "minimise the real loss" to the community (Grant 1984a:543). As well as discussing the role of horse and dog in 'Celtic' religion/myth, they both assumed that horse and dog were particularly favoured animals in sacrifices in Iron Age Wessex.

Here the abundance of different species *ABG's* has been compared to the overall percentages of bone recovered for each species (Tables 7.2). This approach also allows both the calculation of the percentages of the total bone for each species that came from *ABG* deposits as compared to non-articulated/associated bone (Tables 7.2; Figs. 7.2) and also the calculation of the total of all articulated/associated bone from all species. Neither calculation was applicable for Danebury where no figures for the quantities of articulated/associated bone are reported. These calculations confirm Grant's and Wait's general conclusions. Of the total of all bone fragments, the smaller the percentage coming from one species the greater the proportion of that species' bone came from *ABG's*. The rarer the species, the more likely the bone came from *ABG's* (Figs. 7.2).

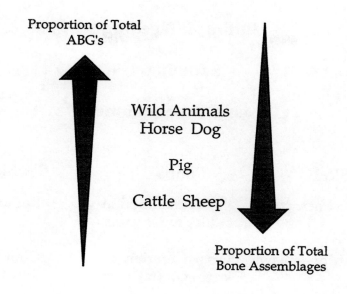

Proportion of Total
ABG's

Wild Animals
Horse Dog

Pig

Cattle Sheep

Proportion of Total
Bone Assemblages

A Hierarchy of Animal Species in Iron Age Wessex?

This general pattern should not mask important differences between sites and within the phases of individual sites. The proportions of different species represented as *ABG's* vary considerably. Sheep and cattle were the most *ABG* abundant deposits at Danebury, but this is not the case at Middle Iron Age Winnall (where horse & dog *ABG's* were most common) or Middle Iron Age Balksbury (pig & dog). The proportion of dog deposits varied widely and any dog bone was uncommon at both excavated Hampshire hillforts, and also at Early Iron Age Balksbury and Winnall. Dog bone became commoner at Middle Iron Age Balksbury and Winnall, contributing 30-40% of the ABG's (Table 7.2), this might reflect changes in where and/or how dog bone was deposited on sites, not the overall abundance of these animals on sites (see 9.5).

Different methods of calculating the abundance of *ABG's* may also produce different results. For example, pig at Middle Iron Age Winnall may contribute only 5.6% of the overall number of deposits of *ABG's*. Yet because one was a complete carcass, pig contributes 21% of the total articulated/associated bone from all species. Similar discrepancies occur where there may be a large number of deposits of a single species, but each only of a small group of bones (e.g. sheep at Middle Iron Age Winnall). Different species *ABG* at Middle Iron Age Winnall have different associated *MSW's*, pot and bone densities etc. (Table 7.6).

7.3.3. Type of Deposit

Grant and Maltby distinguish different types of *ABG's* (see 3.7.7). As with species choice, Grant interprets skull and limb deposits in terms of

"minimising real loss to the community", suggesting that losing only a portion of a sacrificed animal left the rest of the carcass to be utilised. Combining the two classifications and with an understanding of carcass processing for the period, four groups of *ABG's* have been distinguished here.

A   Complete/Partial Carcasses

B   Skulls

C   Complete/Portions of Articulated Limbs

D   Portions of Vertebral Columns and/or Ribs

A Classification of Articulated/ Associated Bone Groups

Similar patterns observed across different sites of the location and frequency of butchery marks from filleting, skinning and marrow processing allow a basic model for Southern British Iron Age butchery practice to be proposed (esp. Maltby 1981: 150-151 and B. Smith 1978:119-122; also Armour-Chelu 1991:150; Grant 1984a:542; Maltby 1985b:101,106-7, Maltby nd2:66). All species were treated in similar ways, with most dismemberment marks found around the base of the skull and the major limb joints - shoulder and cubital, hip and knee. Fewer marks are recorded on sheep/pig compared to horse/cattle, and these are confined to larger/older specimens. The basic stages of carcass processing can be simplified as;

Slaughter

Gutting & Bleeding

Skinning

Carcass Dismemberment

Skull	Limbs	Trunk
Removal of horn cores	Disarticulation at ankle/wrist joint	Removal of flanks
Removal of lower jaw	Disarticulation at knee/cubital joint	Chopping ribs to set size
Lateral splitting of skull to extract brain		Marrow extraction from long bones

<u>The stages of carcass reduction and butchery in Iron Age southern-Britain</u>

No visible marks from the cause of death have been noted on southern English animals (unlike Gournay, France -- Meniel 1985:140-141) and it is likely that animals were killed by throat slitting and/or suffocation. Gutting, bleeding and skinning would have followed. Skinning marks are found on complete/partial skeletons, *ABG's*. Animal hides can be removed with the lower limb extremities, and sometimes the skull, attached (e.g. Beaker 'head and hoofs' burials - Robertson-Mackay 1980) and this has been suggested for Iron Age Wessex (e.g. Maltby nd2:16; Wait 1985:125). However, finds of complete limbs from the humerus/femur or tibia/radius downwards suggests this was not a universal practice. The next stages involved initial carcass dismemberment, detaching the head and limbs. Further reduction and processing followed, the trunk 'flanked', removing of the complete rib cage.

ABG's were deposited after all these stages of carcass processing, and the four main types distinguished here are based on this carcass reduction process;

A
Complete/Partial Carcass

B	C	D
Skull	Articulated/Associated Group of Limb Bones	Articulated/Associated Group of Vertebrae/Ribs

<u>The four groups of Articulated and/or Associated Animal Bone Groups distinguished in this study related to the process of butchery and carcass reduction</u>

Complete deposition (Type A deposits) of the carcass was rare (e.g. dog in pit 6595 Winnall Down - Fig. 7.9). More common are partial skeletons (Type Ap deposits) representing deposition part way through the basic dismemberment. In these the head was often removed or displaced, as might some or all the limbs (e.g. Winnall pit 7257, a sheep lacking head and both fore limbs, or pit 6595, a pig missing the lower right fore leg - Fig. 7.9, or pit 10161. a horse lacking hind limbs - Fig. 7.1). There appears to be no general preference for removing hind or fore limbs, left or right.

In at least one instance, a complete articulated sheep with a displaced skull appeared to have the skull from a different individual (Winklebury pit 1614 - R. Jones 1977:62 - Fig. 2.1). In another case, a headless sheep was represented by the vertebrae and ribs, both fore limbs, and both upper hind limbs. However the pair of lower hind limbs from the same layer that make up this carcass came from a different individual (Balksbury pit 494 - Maltby nd2:24). These are both examples of complete bodies that were reconstituted from different individuals. Other similar deposits may have not been recognised and a partial carcass of back, ribs and hind limbs, is very similar to a deposit of the back and ribs of one individual and hind limbs of another. I have not investigated whether this propensity to reconstitute a complete skeleton, so to speak, was also accomplished by mixed remains from different species e.g. front limbs and back of a sheep occurring with hind limbs of a pig. Quite what lies behind these practices is not clear. However, it does stress the continuum within types of *ABG's*.; Some carcasses lacked limbs or skulls, other deposits contained just skulls or limbs (see 7.4).

Other types of deposit represent the deposition of various parts of the dismembered carcass. Although there is evidence that some sheep skulls, at least, were split laterally to remove the brain (Grant 1984a), *recognised* skull deposits are usually complete skulls (Type B) (e.g. the three horse skulls found in Old Down Farm pit 2778). There are exceptions. Half skulls accompanied partial sheep skeletons at Maiden Castle (Armour-Chelu 1991:146-147) while Winklebury pit 616 contained eleven half cattle crania (R.Jones 1977:60-1). Articulated/associated limbs (Type C) were not just the convenient disposal of 'off-cuts'. Although lower limbs and extremities are common, deposits of upper limbs, the main meat bearing bones, and complete limbs are also found (e.g. Grant 1984a:fig.9:35) (e.g. Balksbury pit 36, complete horse right fore and hind limbs or Winnall pit 7257, cattle humerus, radius and ulna -- see also pit 4006 Fig. 7.1). Portions of backbone (Type D) represent the disposal of remains after flanking (e.g. fifteen thoracic and lumbar vertebrae from a sheep in Winnall pit 1941). At Winklebury rib cages and vertebrae were recorded together (see Fig.2.1), but the problems of identifying rib to species hinder the recognition of articulated/associated groups of ribs, explaining the lack of deposits representing one side of the rib cage after flanking.

Throughout this thesis I have referred to such groups as articulated/associated bone groups (*ABG's*). This is important because the majority of such groups were *only* recognised after excavation, so that it is impossible to be sure if they were fully articulated on deposition. They could have been disarticulated in the pit due to a time lag between dismemberment and burial (left in an open pit, or between butchery and deposition), or because the bones were fully processed/consumed but still deposited as a group. The latter was the case with an unique deposit from the Hebrides where cattle and sheep bones were collected together after consumption and deposited in discrete groups, as were a collection of human infant bones (Barber et al 1989). Even where such bones were recorded as apparently articulated groups, the bones could have been placed in the roughly correct position after defleshing, as was the case with the head transplanted sheep in Winklebury 1614 (Fig. 2.1) or with the pig remains in East Yorkshire Iron Age 'Arras rite' graves (Legge 1991b:144).

It is unlikely that *ABG's* were not butchered differently than animals not destined to be *ABG's*. The different type of *ABG's* relate to all the stages of carcasses processing, suggesting it is wrong to attribute different origins to different types of *ABG's*, e.g. separating skulls and limbs as butchery waste from complete carcasses as the disposal of diseased animals. Interpreting type A deposits as diseased animals does not account for the many partial carcasses; why remove (for consumption?) limbs or skulls from a diseased animal? Nor do the proportions of those buried 'diseased' animals reflect the general proportions of species found on Iron Age sites, as might be expected (Wait 1985:129). Rather, the similar context of all types of deposit implies similar origins. Importantly, little attempt was made to distinguish different types of deposit. Although at some sites, particular types of deposit have strong relationships with other factors; at Danebury the presence of small finds was particularly associated with skull deposits (see 7.3.5.), at other sites the associations were with any type of *ABG* (A to D deposits).

People across Iron Age Wessex did not always deposit the same type of *ABG* in pits. The type of deposit, part of carcass, chosen for deposition varied from site to site and through the centuries. At Danebury, skull deposits are the most common recognised *ABG's*. Although acknowledging the low recognition of type C, the proportions of A to B deposits varies across Danebury's phases (Fig. 7.3) with a higher proportion of complete/partial carcasses in the middle phases (these are possibly contemporary distinct depositional practices, not chronological phases -- see 7.8.4). This is a site specific pattern which is not a product of how the bones were recorded and analysed (Table 7.2&3; Figs. 7.2&3). At Winklebury no type C deposits were recognised, and at Old Down Farm, Balksbury and Winnall there are higher ratios of type A to B deposits, probably because fewer skulls were recognised. Different types of deposit may have particular associations with the other pit contents. Calculations for Middle Iron Age Winnall showed differences in overall *MSW*, pot and bone fragment densities between different types of *ABG's* (Table 7.6).

7.3.4. Do different species occur more frequently as one type of deposit?

Where two or more deposits occur in the same pit, they were rarely of the same species (Fig. 7.4). Often more than one *ABG* were placed in the same pit or layer, with a clear relationship on all sites. This applies where deposits clearly belonged to the same depositional episode, or where separated in depth and time implying knowledge of the species of the initial deposit was important for deciding which species to subsequently deposit. Where deposited together, different species were probably deliberately slaughtered (almost) simultaneously. This represents a specific custom, and not just a reflection that a mix of species were herded kept at the time.

The mixing of components may have been an important principle structuring these deposits. This applied both to reconstituting single carcasses from different individuals and the mixing of different species of animal together in deposits. At Middle Iron Age Winnall single *ABG's* in a pit were either sheep or dog. While, cattle, horse, pig and wild species were only found in multiple deposits. Complete skulls were confined to multiple deposits and never on their own. In contrast, at Danebury, 74 % of the pits with skulls contained just skulls. Is this possibly due to differences in how *ABG's* were identified? A far greater proportion of pits with multiple deposits than those with single deposits also contained small finds.

The proportion of different types of *ABG's* is not consistent for all the species on the same sites (Table 7.3). Wait (1985:134-7) concluded that sheep occur usually as complete/partial carcasses, cattle predominantly as skulls and horse as skulls or articulated limbs. This general pattern is confirmed here, and would appear to be a factor of body size. Smaller animals -- sheep, pig and dog -- occur more frequently as complete/partial carcasses, rather than the larger species -- cattle and horse (Table 7.3; Fig. 7.3). At Danebury a higher proportion of cattle were type A deposits, particularly in cp1-3, compared to other sites distorting the general expectation. However, if body size is an important factor, 7 out of these 11 cattle deposits were of immature/neo-natal animals.

On other sites there were fewer complete cattle deposits made, but again they were often of immature animals (e.g. Winklebury pit 260; Old Down Farm phase 6 pit 966). Deposits of horse carcasses, *all partial* and Middle Iron Age in date, were even less common (e.g. Winnall pit 10161 - Fig. 7.1, Winklebury thorax and hind limbs in circular structure gully 2253, Viables Farm pit 5 - Fig. 12.2). Horses more frequently occur as type B or C deposits but rarely as type D, particularly in comparison to cattle. The smaller sized species more commonly occurred as complete/partial species. The large number of pigs deposited as *ABG's* at Middle Iron Age Balksbury were all type A/Ap, as were sheep on most sites. Middle Iron Age Winnall was exceptional as only a single mature sheep Ap was placed in all the pits on the site. Dogs were particularly deposited as complete carcasses (type A deposits), but rarely as individual dog skulls (heads) placed in deposits, on all sites (Table 7.3).

Although neo-natal and young cattle complete/partial carcasses were deposited, comparatively fewer neo-natal or young sheep, pig and dog *ABG's* were placed in pits, although young animals still represent a major proportion of the total. This does not seem to be the case with horses, possibly because of the small number of type A horse deposits, but also because horses were not bred on Downland sites (Harcourt 1979:158; Grant 1984a:521-22). Discussions of the high numbers of immature animal burials usually concentrate on individual species, stressing the high infant mortality in sheep or control of litter size in dogs (see 3.7.7). These fail to ask the fundamental question why, even if there was high infant mortality or deliberate culling, a tiny proportion of the resulting carcasses of immature animals of all species should have been deliberately put in pits or ditches etc. and not either consumed, burnt or discarded on the surface. Nor do they consider why the deposits of immature animals can be accompanied by other *ABG's* of older individuals of the same or other species (e.g. Old Down phase 5 pit 593 1 adult, 4 immature and 2 neonatal sheep accompanied by a partial dog carcass). Rather than discussing individual species, these deposits should be interpreted in the context of *ABG's* as a whole.

The choice of how much of an animal was deposited as an *ABG* was a factor of body size. Such differences are not comfortably interpreted as 'simply' butchery waste. Why discard more smaller than larger sized animals at an earlier stage in carcass processing? Firth's (1963) discussion of *reservation* in animal sacrifice is useful in understanding these deposits. Partial carcasses, skulls, limbs etc. represent the reserved portion of the animal specifically not eaten and deliberately deposited, while the rest of the carcass was consumed. Small animals, with less meat on the carcass, were more frequently deposited (near) complete, than the larger animals. The very high proportion of dog type A/Ap *ABG's* perhaps reflects the rarity of eating dog (see 3.7.7).

Those instances where complete bodies were apparently reconstituted from two individuals, allowed the consumption of a whole animal and the reservation of another. That parts of both were reserved suggests it was important that parts of both individuals were consumed and deposited. A similar logic may explain the importance of mixing different species represented in multiple *ABG* deposits.

This should not be seen as minimising some gross measure of calorific loss, but in terms of loss of potential social relations created and sustained through sharing the meat. The unusual deposition of a complete cow or horse might be interpreted as a particularly grand gesture, and it is worth noting that sheep, pig and dog occur far more frequently in multiple type A deposits than the larger species.

7.3.5. Relationships with Small Finds

As has been shown when human remains were deposited in pits (see 7.2.4), when people put *ABG's* in some pits, this was likely to have been pits in which they had, or would, deposit small finds. This lead to statistically significant relationships between the presence of *ABG's* and any type of small find in the same pit;

Danebury cp3   (prob. .0001)
Danebury cp7-8 (with 1+ small finds prob .0257)
Middle Iron Age Winnall (prob. .0423)
but not quite at Winklebury (prob. .0671).

No constant overall associations existed between the presence of any individual species, type of deposit or small find put in the same pit. At Danebury there is a clear relationship between skull and small finds placed in the same features. However, the actually type of small finds put in these pits varied through time:

cp1-3   with worked bone, worked stone, loom
        weights;
cp6   with iron objects;
cp7-8   with bronze, iron, worked bone, clay objects
        and worked stone;

Querns were the only type of small find significantly associated with all types of *ABG's* in cp7-8 (prob .0434) (cf. 7.2.4).

A general association found at Danebury was between the presence of small finds and the cattle and/or horse *ABG's* in the same pit. In cp 1-3,4-5, and 6 more pits containing cattle and horse *ABG's* than expected contained small finds (cf. 7.3.2). All Middle Iron Age (cp6, 7-8) pits with dog *ABG's* contained small finds. Table 7.4 shows the significant associations between different species (including humans) and types of small finds in cp7-8 pits. Is it important that horse, unlike cattle, shares many of the same relationships with types of small finds as human bone?

As should now be expected, other sites do not share the same detailed relationships. At neither Winklebury, Balksbury nor Winnall were any individual species statistically associated with small finds generally or in particular. At Middle Iron Age Winnall pits with *ABG's* were usually those in which high numbers of small finds (>2) were also put. In this phase quern fragments occurred in all pits containing dog *ABG's* (c.f. the relationships between quern and human bone -- see 7.2.3). The reverse was found at Middle Iron Age Balksbury where only one pit containing quern fragments and dog *ABG's* was found (expected number 2.2), despite the fact that dogs were the most common *ABG's* in this phase of the sites occupation. Quern fragments occurred in more pits with horse and sheep *ABG's* than expected if randomly distributed. At Early Iron Age Balksbury, the only type C and D *ABG's* occurred with small finds. In the Middle Iron Age small finds occurred in the same features as all *ABG's*, types (A to D); skulls (3 out of 6 pits with finds), complete carcasses (11 out of 23), limbs (9 out of 25).

7.3.6.   Summary

Finding an *ABG* in a pit implies it is likely that human remains and/or small finds will be found in the same feature. Although the nature of these associations varies between sites and phases, the presence of all types of *ABG's* was statistically significantly related with the presence of human remains and small finds. All *ABG's* had similar origins. The proportion of the carcass deposited was dependent on body size and, importantly, the minority species were accorded special treatment.

7.4. Animal Bones Generally
7.4.1. Individual Species

As well as considering possible associations with *ABG's*, those possible associations between unarticulated animal bone and other factors have been examined. Statistically significant correlations were found between the presence of bone from different individual species and other factors at Winklebury and Winnall.

At Early Iron Age Winnall, some of the associations between species shown within individual layers (see 5.4.2) were still evident using pit totals. Within these pits bone from the different domestic species were preferentially deposited with particular types of material (e.g. sheep with pottery, horse with *ABG's* - in this phase all *ABG's* were of sheep or pig.) These relationships show that animal bone in this phase did not enter pit fills through random processes;

	Pottery	Small Finds	ABG's	+Std Dev Dens of Bone
Sheep	.0471	-	-	-
Cattle	.0351	-	-	-
Pig	-	.0143	-	-
Horse	-	-	.0277	-
Dog	-	-	-	.0027

The Statistically Significant Correlations between the Presence of Different Species and Other Factors at Early Iron Age Winnall Down

In the Middle Iron Age phase at Winnall these specific patterns were not repeated. The presence of all species was significantly associated with the presence of human bone and, except dog, small finds. High densities (+Std Dev) of bone from different species in pits showed more variation. Only high densities of cattle and sheep bone were (almost) significantly associated with the presence of human bone (prob. .0544 & .0547). These can not be explained by an association between *ABG's* of these species and humans which may inflate bone fragment totals. Although one type A sheep deposit was found in the same pit as human bone, this is not enough to explain the overall pattern and cattle were only represented as skulls or groups of vertebrae. If large bone assemblages were the results of specific butchery events/meals this might suggest consumption (but not reservation) of cattle and sheep as part of the practices that accompanied the deposition of human remains. Alternatively, fresh sheep and cattle bones were deliberately selected from middens for these deposits. Similar arguments relate to the relationship of high densities of cattle bone and the presence of small finds. High densities of unarticulated sheep and cattle bone were also significantly associated with the presence of the following at MIA Winnall;

	1std+ Sheep Bone	1std+ Cattle Bone
Horse	(prob. .0028)	(prob .0213)
Dog		(prob. .0179)
Pig	(prob. .0122)	(prob. .0339)
Bird	(prob. .0501)	(prob. .0001),

1std+ = One Standard Deviation above Mean Densities of Bone

This fits the pattern that minority species were deposited along with other species found in individual layers (see 5.4.2). Although, the association with bird bone may be indirect, a product of the association between bird and human bone in this phase (see 7.5). At Winklebury, dog bones were especially put in those pits with +Std Dev densities of bones, particularly of cattle and horse (prob. .0015 & .0098). Dog bone was found only in three pits (one a type A *ABG*, the others 'stray' bone). Horse was also comparatively uncommon (put in 22 out of 70 pits) making the association between the two species more marked. Horse bone was also particularly put in those pits also containing human bone (prob. .0407). As at Early Iron Age Winnall, pig was also significantly associated with the presence of small finds (prob. .0215).

These associations further demonstrate that dog and horse were accorded special treatment in their deposition and perception (cf. 7.3.1, 5.4.2). These minority species were possibly specially eaten/deposited on rare occasions, and then usually with other species. This suggests feasting, or at least non daily consumption of meat. If we envisage the deposition of most of this bone as the result of

consumption, and not simply the selection of bones discarded on the surface or on middens (cf. Firtree Field Grooved Ware pits -- Barrett et al 1991:75-81), then such consumption was often associated with the deposition of human remains and small finds.

7.4.2. High Densities of all Animal Bone Fragments

Here, overall high densities of all bone will be considered. Maltby interpreted *specific carcass utilisation events* (see 3.7.7) as the result of feasting. There is no *a priori* reason why such waste need be buried (see 3.7.9). This *deposition* of large quantities of fresh waste must be set within the context of other materials deposited in the same features. High densities of bone fragments were associated with the presence of human bone and small finds, which can be interpreted as the product from the slaughter/consumption/deposition of unusually large quantities of meat (Maltby 1985a:56- see 3.7.7). Such high bone densities were not all the result of the presence of *ABG's* inflating bone totals for pits e.g. of the 21 layers with +Std Dev densities of bone fragments at Middle Iron Age Winnall, only 11 contained *ABG's*; while a further 15 layers with less than +Std Dev densities of bone contained *ABG's*.

Calculations of overall bone density for pits at Winnall and Winklebury suggest high densities of all bone share the cluster of associations already outlined in this chapter. At both Early Iron Age Winnall and Winklebury +Std Dev densities of bone were significantly associated with +Std Dev densities of pottery. The unusual occurrence of dog and wild animal bone at Early Iron Age Winnall was significantly associated with those pits with +Std Dev bone densities. At Middle Iron Age Winnall +Std Dev bone densities were significantly associated with the presence of +Std Dev *MSW*, human remains, bird bone, and *ABG's*. Although not investigated in detail, the bone in these large assemblages often seems to be well preserved bone deposited after butchery/consumption or carefully curated (cf. Easton Lane pit 329 - Fig. 9.11). This is supported by the roughly inverse relationship between indices of bone preservation and density of bone fragments from pits (Fig. 7.4).

It is important to establish the relationship between large concentrations of unarticulated animal bone and articulated/associated animal bone groups (*ABG's*). As has been stressed, many *ABG's* may *not* have been articulated groups, but collections of unarticulated bone from the same individual. This stresses that the division between *ABG's* and other bone is very blurred. This should be further emphasised by considering the processes of butchery/carcass reduction (see 7.3.3). All animal bone should be seen as part of the same sequence of carcass reduction processing and disposal. The bone from *ABG's* was treated no differently from any other bone. In discussing the types of *ABG*, I used Firth's notion of *reservation* in sacrifice, suggesting *ABG's* were the reserved portion of the carcass, the rest consumed. But how was the unreserved portion of the carcass which provided an *ABG* treated and disposed? Would these unreserved remains be disposed of after consumption differently than other bone? Where the reserved portion would be undetectable by archaeological techniques (e.g. flesh, offal, blood, chyme or the spirit -- as in the majority of ethnographic examples of sacrifice) these questions apply to all the animal's bone.

This is to recognise that there is no neat separation between feasting and sacrifice (Hill 1992). In most ethnographic examples feasting is integral to sacrifice and most feasts have a ritual, if not a sacrificial element. As such, ABG's belong in a continuum of deposits including large deposits of fresh unarticulated bone. The distinction is inevitably blurred. Further blurring arises where many *ABG's*, especially small portions of the carcass, are found associated with large deposits of unarticulated fresh bone, Maltby's specific butchery events (e.g. Winnall 6595). As such 'specific carcass utilisation' events may be essentially similar to much articulated bone, the large densities of unarticulated animal bone sharing similar associations with different types of small finds and human remains shown to exist with *ABG's* . One immediate consequence of recognising this continuum of types of bone deposits is that it is invalid to distinguish between unarticulated and articulated bone made in many bone reports, assuming the former more directly reflects the assumed 'real' proportions between numbers of living animals.

7.5. Wild Animals

Wild mammals and birds are usually treated separately from domestic species in bone reports and it is suggested the exploitation of wild resources played a very minor role in Iron Age diets (see 3.7.8). Wild animal remains must be set within the broader context of the deposition and the treatment of wild animals fits into a continuum with other domestic species, where the smaller the contribution to the overall bone assemblage, the more marked out is the deposition of that species in terms of associations with other species and treatment. Like horse, pig, and dog, a very high proportion of wild animal bone came from articulated/associated groups (see 7.2). Explanations of wild *ABG's* usually fail to place them in the context of similar domestic *ABG's* (see 3.7.8), and again there is no universal determinate factor why wild *ABG's* should be deposited in subsoil features at all.

There are few statistically significant associations between the presence of wild bone and other factors. This is partly due to the limited number of sites with suitable data, but also because the broad category 'wild animal bone' may dilute more specific relations with different species. For example, at Middle Iron Age Winnall Down, although the presence of wild animal bone and small finds was significantly associated (prob.0404), the more specific category of bird bone was not. This association was between deer

antler and other small finds. At Winklebury significant associations within individual layers between wild animal remains and high densities of horse bone were not apparent using overall totals. At this site no individual bird bones were recovered, probably reflecting the conditions of the excavations (see 4.4.6.). A complete raven was deposited spread eagled on the base of pit 2611 associated with a complete carcass of an immature pig and several large sherds from one or more complete vessels (see Fig.2.1, Fig. 3.3). The upper fills of this pit included associated cattle vertebrae and ribs. The other wild *ABG's* were concentrated in two pits. Pit 240 contained six or more badgers, an immature cattle partial carcass, a carved chalk object, but no other bone fragments and only 1g of pottery. Pit 3825 contained 35 unarticulated/associated bone fragments (only cattle and horse), 620g of pottery, a hare, twelve foxes and a red deer (Fig. 2.1., Fig. 3.3).

At Middle Iron Age Winnall hare bone was also deposited in the same pits as other *ABG's*. A whole hare was found in pit 10161 along with the unusual deposit of a substantially complete horse. This pit contained virtually no other bone or pottery. Hare bone was also recovered from pit 6595 which contained type A dog and pig deposits and from one other pit. In this phase bird bone was deposited in particular contexts and was statistically significantly associated with +Std Dev densities of animal bone, small finds and, especially, human bone (prob .0027), found in five out of the eight pits with bird bone (see 5.4.7). This distribution was not the random result of natural fatalities and haphazard dispersal of refuse. The two pits with bird *ABG's* also contained domestic species *ABG's* (prob .0436 for overall presence of wild animal remains and *ABG's*). Pit 4006 contained a Heron's wing, along with much fresh unarticulated cattle/horse bone, *ABG's* (DogA, CattleB, 2xHorseC, 2xHorseD , 4xCattleC), a human infant corpse and adult human femur (Fig. 7.1). Pit 4475 contained the carcass of a *Turdus* (Thrush or Golden Oriole?) species with a PigD *ABG* and a human adolescent corpse and human bone fragments (see 7.9, Fig.7.10). This special status was present in the preceding phases of the site. At Easton Lane bird bone was significantly associated with the +Std Dev bone densities and *ABG's*. and at the Early Iron Age enclosure it was deliberately excluded from interior features (see 9.3).

However, these associations were not universal on all sites. Given problems of recovery, it is impossible to determine the role of bird bone at Winklebury or Old Down Farm, but this is not the case at Balksbury. A large number of pits contained bird bones, and several *ABG's* were identified: mallard wings and several complete ravens. However, no significant associations were found between bird bone and other factors. Danebury had many bird *ABG's*, especially *Corvids* but also waterfowl and two Kittiwakes. The feature numbers of those pits with articulated wings of non-*Corvid* species and all Kittiwake finds are given (Coy 1984b). All were associated with the presence of *ABG's*, human remains, or small finds;

Species		Pit	Phase	Small Finds	ABG's	Human Remains
Goose	wing	63A	1-3	13		
Duck	wing	264	7-8	5		
Buzzard	wing	949	1-3	0	SheepA, PigB	Frag
Goose	wing	1135	1-3	0	Sheep Bx2	Frag
Buzzard	wing	1149	4-5	0	DogA, SheepB, PigB	Frag
Kittiwake	mand.	22	4-5	1	PigA	
Kittiwake	wing	23	7-8	4	SheepB, HorseB+C, PigC	Fragx2
Kittiwake	wing	620	7-8	1	HorseB	Inhumation
Kittiwake	hum.	658	1-3	7*includes amber bead		

* beads were rarely deposited in pit fills (see 7.6.4.)

The relationships between the deposition of bird bone and other finds at Danebury:
Those finds found in the same pits as those in which the site report (Cunliffe 1984) lists specific bird bone as coming from.

Kittiwake and one cormorant bone (Serjeantson 1991) are the only sea birds recorded on Downland Iron Age sites (cf. Harcourt 1979:155) and must have been deliberately brought to Danebury. As none were recorded in the final ten years' excavations (Serjeantson 1991), Kittiwakes were possibly deposited in specific parts of the site, as suggested by the close feature numbers containing this species (22 and 23, 620 and 658). Why Kittiwakes, and not similar species, were treated in this way is unclear (Serjeantson pers com.). Without further contextual information it is impossible to investigate further possible relationships with other bird remains, but in all phases, except cp6, bird bone was significantly associated with the presence of ABG's , but not with human bone (Grant 1984a:540-1).

Confirming previous suggestions (Grant 1984a:526; Wait 1985:138), many wild animal remains recovered from Downland sites were 'Special Deposits'. While some wild mammal and bird ABG's probably result from natural causes, this can not explain the majority of remains and the statistically significant relationships they have with other material deposited in pits. This is not to suggest many rodents and amphibians found in some features were deliberate deposits (see 3.7.8). These were clearly pit fall victims, but this may not necessarily explain other smaller species such as weasels and martins (see 9.4). The special treatment of wild animal remains questions the limited functional/economic approaches that dominate archaeozoology and raises the possibility of investigating past emic ethnobiological classifications (see 11.2.2). Hunting and fishing apparently played a minor role in the overall composition of bone assemblages and, by inference, Iron Age diets in Southern England. But on the rare occasions when wild animal remains were deposited on sites, they were usually treated distinctly to the majority of other recovered bone. If this is the case, the choice of species hunted probably was not directly related to their abundance or economic value, but probably reflects cultural and symbolic concerns (see

11.2.2.). While of little calorific importance, wild animals were probably of considerable social/symbolic value.

7.6. Small Finds
7.6.1. Introduction
In the previous chapters it has been shown that the deposition of small finds, usually (unintentionally) broken objects, was clearly not random, that groups of finds were intentionally deposited on their own in layers (see 5.3), often as part of depositional episodes clearly associated with layers with either pot, bone, human bone and ABG's.. That is to say, that people were deliberately choosing to put small finds, often of specific types and usually already broken, in the same pits as they put human remains and ABG's. These practices have been outlined (see 7.2.3, 7.3.5, 7.4.1, 7.5) and this section will only examine those aspects of small find deposition not already discussed in this chapter.

7.6 2. Number of Small Finds per Pit
The majority of pits contained none or only one small find. But a small proportion of pits contained finds in larger numbers (Tables 7.5; Figs.7.5) with which other materials were especially deposited e.g. human bone fragments, multiple ABG's (see 7.2.3, 7.3.5). However, not all pits with large numbers of finds also contained human remains or ABG's, and such concentrations relate to the deposition of discrete finds groups as a particular type of 'exceptional layer deposit' (see 5.3.4). It was suggested that these usually represented curated material -- which may also account for many single finds. It must be stressed that this material was usually broken. 'Hoarding' might explain the rare deposits of complete objects or reusable broken material such as metal scrap. But, these few collections of metalwork must be set within the context of the deposition of broken small finds, and other material in general.

7.6.3. Associations between Small Finds

Associations between different types of object, for example the functional categories used for Roman finds (Crummy 1983) applied at Poundbury (Ellison 1987) and Maiden Castle (Sharples 1991:243), have not been investigated in detail. Analyses have only investigated different materials from which (iron, bone etc.) objects were made from. An exception was to distinguish loom weights and spindle whorls, and also quern stones. Results from the large assemblages from Gussage and Danebury further highlight the importance of iron objects, worked bone and antler and querns (see 7.2.3 & 7.3.5). These three finds types were not only significantly associated with each other in certain phases but with other classes of small finds (see Table 7.10).

Complete, or substantially complete, querns were often deposited in pits. This might be regarded as the convenient disposal of an inconvenient object. However, the demonstrable associations with other material (see 7.2.3 & 7.3.5) argue that this was not just dumping of discarded or broken querns. Neither both upper *and* lower rotary quern stones, nor saddle querns and rubbers were deposited together. Like the fragments of querns, even where whole stones were deposited they are still incomplete.

The deposition of worked bone and antler have been discussed above (see 7.2.3 & 7.3.5). The unusual patterning of bone/antler combs at Danebury may be compared with the unusual deposition behaviour at Early Iron Age Gussage, where bone 'socketed knives'/ 'gouges', appear to have been deposited in pairs. These objects were recovered from 20 pits, in 10 cases two gouges were found, in no pits more than two. In six of the pits with two gouges both came from the same layer, in two more from adjacent layers. This practice was unique to this phase and site.

At Winnall bronze objects and those unusual finds such as the decorated measuring weight and chalk mould also appear to have been deposited in 'unusual' contexts. A proportion of the small number of pits with such finds also contained human remains, high *MSW*'s, and large pot and bone densities (Table 7.6). For example three stone measuring weights were recovered at Easton Lane and Winnall, one uniquely decorated in the La Tene style. All three came from pits which also contained *ABG's*.

Another example of this pattern is the (in)famous pit 209 from Middle Iron Age Gussage All Saints. Pit 209 is well known for its concentration of metalworking moulds, hearth material, crucibles and bone tools (Spratling 1979). The implications of this deposit for Later Prehistoric metalworking technology and organisation have been widely discussed (e.g. Spratling 1972, 1979; Foster 1980; Northover 1984; Fell 1988; Henderson 1991), as have the social ramifications of the manufacture of c.50 sets 'chariot' fittings (e.g. Wainwright 1979; Ashbee 1978; Cunliffe 1984a, 1991). However, the *deposition* of this material has not been considered. Spratling (1979:141) recognised that "the bulk of (metalworking) debris... does not normally survive the vicissitudes of time" but concluded that;

> "the practice of disposing rubbish in empty pits in later prehistoric settlements in Britain and elsewhere ought to lead sooner or later to the discovery of other deposits of such an informative kind as this one."

This sees this deposit as fortuitous, but I would not see this as an accident. This pit also contained a human skull fragment in the upper fills, along with other small finds and large sherds of pottery -- 15 large enough to be illustrated in the report (all saucepans or bowls, not jar, sherds and only one small decorated sherd - Wainwright 1979:Figs 61-2). This pit contained the largest number of pot sherds of any pit in this phase by a considerable margin. Finds of metalworking debris and associated objects were particularly concentrated near the entrance of this enclosure in all phases (Spratling 1979) and linked to the values and meanings associated with crossing the thresholds of Later Prehistoric enclosures (see 8.6). This waste from this transforming technology was intentionally deposited along with other material in a particular part of the enclosure. This accident may not have been that exceptional, pit 437 to the north of the entrance could be considered its parallel, also containing debris from metalworking and a large accumulation of scrap iron.

7.6.4. What Small Finds are absent?

It has been shown that the incorporation of small finds in pit fills was not a random process, nor explainable in simple utilitarian terms. Certain objects were deposited in certain ways, so it can not be assumed that the range and quantities of small finds recovered from excavations are a direct reflection of their original abundance. Certain groups of small finds might have been present on sites but were not considered appropriate to deposit in pits. One large group of objects rare or absent from Wessex Iron Age sites were weaponry, fine metalwork and objects of personal adornment (see 3.4). The absence of these classes of finds has been used as one piece of evidence to suggest an essentially egalitarian social structure for Early Middle Iron Age Wessex (Hill 1995).

The Danebury data was examined to investigate possible differences in the contexts from which different types of finds were recovered. The majority of finds came from pits (e.g. 78% of the total animal bone for the first ten years excavations - Grant 1984a:Table 61), others came from gullies and post holes, layers in the quarry hollows behind the ramparts, in the ramparts and in the entrance area. Different groups and types of small finds were deposited in different proportions in different contexts (Table 7.6). Some differences could be due to poorer preservation in more exposed contexts such as quarry hollow layers. This might explain why higher percentages of metal compared to bone/antler came from layers or trenches. However, poor preservation would not explain the small proportions of stone objects and quern fragments that came from these contexts, nor the comparatively higher percentage of clay objects, which would appear particularly vulnerable to weathering. This suggests differential deposition was a more important factor.

This is reinforced considering specific types of finds which show considerable differences in the distribution of objects made from the same material (Fig. 7.6). Of the clay objects, all spindle whorls and 83% of the loom weights were found in pit fills, but 80% of the perforated clay balls (function unknown) came from layers. Of bone/antler objects, a quarter of the needles were recovered from layers, the rest from pit fills, while a higher proportion of bone gouges and awls, than of combs (objects of comparable sizes) were recovered from non-pit contexts. Both combs found outside pits were undecorated, even though overall there were slightly more decorated combs recovered from the site (18 to 14) (cf. 7.2.3). Similar patterns can be seen within the metal objects which can not simply be understood in terms of object size.

It appears that the 'finer' objects were rarely deposited in pit fills and were more common in layers and trenches.

Object	Pit Contexts	Non-Pit Contexts
Bronze Fibula	0	5
Bronze Terret	0	1
Bronze Terminal	0	2
Iron Spearhead	2	3
Chape/Scabbard	1	1
Beads	3	5
Shale Bracelet Frags	2	1

From the first ten years excavations at Danebury the few finds of weaponry, and fine metal objects mainly came from non-pit contexts, as did the brooches. This was also true for non-metal objects of a personal nature, such as beads and shale bracelets. Beads may be easily overlooked and it is likely many beads were not recovered during excavations. However, I would not expect the recovery of beads to be any better during the excavation of the quarry hollow and other layers at Danebury, compared to pits. As such the high proportion of beads from non-pit contexts reflects a real pattern.

Even if the brooches are considered as stray losses, a higher number would be expected to have accidentally ended up in pit fills than did as part of stage III and IV types of deposits (see Fig 5.10). Where 'finer' objects came from pit fills, study shows most came from the topmost layer, not the main body, of the pit e.g. one complete and one fragmentary bronze bracelet/armlets and the one bronze loop fastner. As the illustrated Danebury pits contained on average 5.6 layers (see 5.1), this is not a random distribution of finds throughout the fills. I suggested these uppermost layers of pits relate to the material

on the surrounding surface, and were often not deliberate pit fills (see 6.3). 'Fine' objects from the second ten years excavations show a continuation of the same pattern. Only two brooches were found, one came from a pit (layer 2), one from the ground surface. Of the four terrets, three came from pits. However, other objects such as the bronze ornamental disc and finger ring, iron cauldron hooks, four bridles (three from the same post hole), two harness rings, iron penannular brooch and fibulae pin all came from either top pit layers or non-pit contexts. Coins share this distribution, the two coins found at Danebury came from layers in the eastern entrance.

A similar situation occurred at Gussage. Considering just the 24 Late Iron Age fibulae and pennanular brooches, four came from ditch segments, four more from a large working hollow (F2). Of the remainder, half were recovered from the uppermost layer of a pit. As the illustrated pits have an average of 5.9 layers this, again, is not a random distribution of brooch finds. The only fibula from Early or Middle Iron Age Winnall was again recovered from the top layer of pit 7257. This could be considered as causal loss, but was it an accident that this LT I/II brooch came from the pit with the largest number of small finds from this phase along with the neo-natal burial of a dog, the associated vertebrae of another adult dog, skull of a third, a partial sheep carcass and lower limb of cattle?

These examples indicate that the absence of fibulae from the main body of pit fills is not simply the result of their exclusion from deliberate deposition in pits, so that they alone were subject to 'normal' random, utilitarian processes of entering the record. Rather, their deposition was structured too. This has chronological implications as fibulae are often used as dating evidence and it raises questions about the 'flourish' of fibulae in the archaeological record of Late Iron Age and Early Roman sites (see 12.2.4). Does the greater 'loss' of brooches per decade/year, indicate an increasing abundance of fibulae, or a change in the cultural processes that lead to the formation of the archaeological record?

7.6.5. Unphased Features

The differential deposition of types of small finds would also seem to have influenced whether objects were deposited in phaseable features. Why unphaseable features occur is rarely discussed, the assumption appears to be that they were a misfortunate product of the haphazard processes through which features were filled. However, it must be recognised that the absence of pottery from a pit may have been intentional (see 7.9). At Danebury 106 pits (10.2 percent of the total for the first ten years) were unphased, probably because they contained little or no pottery. However, half of all the Iron 'pruning hooks'/hook-shaped cutting tools' were deposited in these unphased features suggesting they were selectively deposited in features without pottery. Of the seven such objects found in cp7-8 phased pits, all came from features also containing *ABG's* -- found in 36% of pits in this phase.

7.6.6. Summary

This analysis shows that the deposition of small finds was clearly structured. The majority of finds from pits were not casual losses nor simply the convenient disposal of any/all discarded objects, even though most finds can be considered as 'rubbish', broken or discarded after use and not deliberated damaged. Small finds were associated with the presence of *ABG's* and human remains, but may often occur in some numbers on their own, suggesting these be considered as a third kind of 'special deposit'.

Although the details of the associations vary across sites and phases, three groups of small finds (iron objects, worked bone/antler and querns) have been highlighted as being particularly important. The latter two would appear to be closely connected with the transformation of agricultural/natural resources (see 11.4), while at least one iron type agricultural implement at Danebury appears to have been singled out for special treatment. Further work is necessary on the context of specific types of iron objects. A number of iron plough bars have been found on many sites, while other tools include knifes and wood working objects. The deposition of such iron objects must also be related to the probable ritual deposition of iron currency bars on site margins (Hingley 1990c). Equally, less frequently demonstrated associations with loom weights and spindle whorls on some of the sites can be approached in terms of the transformation of agricultural/natural products. Much of this material appears to have been purposefully deposited in pits. It would seem that 'fine' metal objects such as ornaments and fittings in particular were deliberated excluded from these deposits.

7.7. Pit Shape

An unexpected result of this research is to suggest that the shape of pits is an important factor in the nature of the material subsequently deposited in them (see 3.2.1). At Winklebury and Winnall it is clear that pit shape was important. Bee-hive shaped pits contained a far higher proportion of all categories of finds than would be expected from a haphazard distribution of material (Table 7.7; Fig. 7.7). At both sites pits were divided into three broad groups; straight sided, bee-hived/overhanging sides and other profiles. At both sites animal bone was particularly associated with bee-hive pits, an association specifically marked for horse and pig bone at Winklebury (prob .0087 & .0007 respectively). At both, more than expected bee-hive shaped pits contained small finds, but this was only statistically significant at Winnall (prob .0115). All human remains were significantly associated with bee-hive pits at both sites (prob .0005 & .0357).

How this relates to discussions of pit shape and function is not clear (see 3.2). It has been argued that

bee-hive shaped pits were especially suited to cereal storage, even to the point that other shaped pits must have had a different function. *If* this one shape was particularly associated with storage, the connection with human remains in the context of notions of fertility etc. would appear to be particularly important (see 2.4, 11.7). However, what must be emphasised is that at neither site did *ABG's* share these associations, and that these types of deposits were not just restricted to pits (see 11.7).

7.8. Pot Fabric, Form and Decoration

Iron Age pottery was usually only studied for constructing chronology, although production and exchange are increasingly emphasised (see 3.5). This contrasts with recent discussions of earlier pottery which have concentrated on form, decoration and deposition to consider the active social role of ceramics (e.g. Barrett 1991b; Richards and Thomas 1984; Shanks & Tilley 1987a:155-171; Thomas 1991a:79-102). It could be that pottery was more common in the Iron Age and so considered merely a commodity, but pottery's symbolic and social roles are not diminished with large scale pottery use (e.g. Miller 1985) and the abundance of pottery in Iron Age Southern England must be set in the wider largely aceramic British context.

7.8.1. Pot Fabric

The identification of fabric has become central to Later Prehistoric pot studies for chronology and, especially, exchange. Fabric was only considered here at Winnall, the report's 35 Later Prehistoric fabrics simplified into nine groups. There were a wide range of Early Iron Age fabrics compared to the Middle Iron Age, when the bulk of pottery were fine/medium flint tempered wares. Whether this narrowing range relates to a decreasing proportions of non-locally produced pottery on the site and/or a decrease in the number of sources needs consideration.

Perhaps even more than pot form, our categories of fabric type are taken as an objective description of real attributes. It is assumed that our fabric groupings were similarly recognised in the past (Barrett 1991b). But can we be secure in this assumption? Do the various distinctions we make to discern different fabric types and their larger groupings actually match those of the producers and users of the pottery we study? One way to investigate this is to examine if different fabrics were deposited or treated differently.

A wide range of fabrics were used at Early Iron Age Winnall, but they were not found evenly across this phase's pits. Minor fabric groups were deposited in particular parts of the enclosure (see 9.2.2). This spatial distribution partially explains the significant associations between the presence of different groups such as that between flint/organic and shell and the disassociation between coarse and fine/medium flint tempered wares. Associations between specific fabric groups and other factors were not numerous. Fine wares and flint/organic wares were statistically significantly associated with the presence of bone (prob .0049 & .0027), while other fabrics had associations with some minority species e.g. organic and pig (prob .0317), organic and deer antler (prob .0084), sand and deer antler (prob .0084), shell and dog (prob .0039).

In the Middle Iron Age the ubiquitous fine/medium flint tempered wares were found in all pits. The presence of this fabric group in very high percentages was disassociated with the presence of sandy wares (prob .0080) as expected as one replaced the other as the dominant fabric here and elsewhere in Hampshire (Cunliffe 1984a:236-240; J.Hawkes 1989:94). The minor fabric groups, such as coarse flint and flint/grog, were associated with the presence of human remains (CF prob .0398, F/G prob .0073 esp. with bones fragments), +Std Dev. bone densities (F/G prob .0003) and ABG's (F/G prob .0031).

Interpreting these associations is difficult without further consideration of the relationship between fabric and form, function, or origin, or closer attention to individual assemblages. For example, are the Middle Iron Age coarse flint and flint/grog tempers particularly associated with jars not saucepans, particularly in those pits with human remains or ABG's ? Given the relationships described below, are these fabrics more likely to be decorated? However, consideration of form and fabric at Winnall show that there is no simple correlation of distinct forms and fabric types (J.Hawkes 1985:Tables6 & 8). Thus, while Early Iron Age fine ware fabrics were most commonly found in bowl forms, fine ware jars also occur. Only Early Iron Age sandy wares were predominantly associated with a single form (6 jars 1 bowl).

What is clear from Winnall is that the less common fabric groups do appear to be distinguished in their deposition through associations with deposits already marked out as distinct in this study. These issues require further study, but it would suggest that our categories of fabric groups might correspond in some way to the past realities we try to understand.

7.8.2. Decoration and Burnishing
Considerable importance has been attached to vessel decoration for delimiting 'styles zones', production sources and as 'art'. For this study contextual information on the location of decorated pottery was available for only Winklebury and Easton Lane -- in terms of simple presence -- and at Winnall -- where quantitative data for both the weights of decorated and burnished, but undecorated, pottery per pit was available. Using this information, it is clear that the deposition of decorated pottery was as structured as other materials.

At Winklebury the presence of animal bone was significantly associated with decorated pottery in the same pits (prob .0499) along with cattle and sheep (prob .0307 & .0371) and +Std Dev densities of horse bone (prob .0295). Decorated pottery was particularly deposited in the same pits as small finds (prob .0001). At Easton Lane decorated sherds were recovered from three of 29 pits, including the only pit with human remains (prob .0455).

At Middle Iron Age Winnall, this association of decorated pottery and human bone was continued, although not as strongly as the relationship between burnished pottery and human remains. In terms of the significant relationships between the presence of decorated or burnished pot and other factors in pits, decorated and burnished sherds had an antipathetic relationship. Decorated pottery was deposited with +Std Dev densities of pottery and bone, but only the smaller domestic species when in high numbers/densities. Burnished, undecorated sherds were deposited with the larger domestic species and small finds (see Table 7.11). This relationship, particularly the possible opposition in the deposition of decorated and undecorated pottery, suggests the surface treatment of Middle Iron Age pottery needs greater consideration. Decoration and surface treatment were not simply the reflection of technological achievement nor a casual afterthought in production, nor can they just be considered in gross terms of the manifestation of ethnicity/tribal affiliation. Decoration and surface treatment were not incidental to the deposition, nor, by implication, the use, exchange and manufacture of Iron Age pottery.

7.8.3. Decoration and chronology
Whether deliberate or a by-product of other factors, the patterning evident in the deposition of decorated pottery has important consequences. For example, it raises the need to consider in more detail the contexts in which the small quantities of 'South-Western'/'Glastonbury Wares' were deposited in Wessex. Considerable attention is paid to this pottery with its distinctive decoration as evidence of long distance exchange and it occurs in very small numbers on a range of MIA sites. Similar questions could also be raised about the depositional context of other exotic pottery, especially Late Iron Age imports. It has been argued that imported pottery was not deposited in contexts distinct from local wares on Late Iron Age settlements. Although requiring further investigation, this may not be true. Sharples' (1987) reassessment of the amphorae at Hengistbury Head suggest they were deposited in distinct contexts, with distinct associated material. Work here shows that imported pottery at Late Iron Age Gussage was deposited in discrete parts of the site and was associated with the presence of +Std Dev numbers of small finds (n. >=3) (prob .0001) (see 9). If LIA imported pottery was being discretely deposited in set ways, this may have important chronological implications, as the presence of imported pottery is often used to date sites/activities.

The clearly patterned deposition of decorated pottery at Middle Iron Age Winklebury and Winnall also has implications for the internal chronology of the Middle Iron Age. The current Wessex ceramic chronology is based on excavations at Danebury combined with older excavations and envisages the possible existence of nine *ceramic phases* (Cunliffe 1984a:233-4). Since publication, this chronology has been refined and tested as excavations at Danebury and other sites in the environs have continued. In particular, considerable attention has been paid to the various phases within the Middle Iron Age. The discussion of this Middle Iron Age phasing discussed here is based on the material presented in the first ten year's report of the Danebury excavations (Cunliffe 1984), and does not take into account Lisa Brown's more recent work on the problems. It is presented here to explore the possibilities that decorated pottery was deposited in certain pits along with particular material, as the same time as undecorated pottery was deposited in other pits containing other material.

The Middle Iron Age, defined by fully developed 'saucepan' pots, has been distinguished into an earlier, *plain*, and later, *decorated*, phase (cp6 & 7). This phasing schema is a "hybrid" of objective observation in a " matrix of subjectivity" and as Cunliffe admits;

> "It has strengths and weaknesses; in parts it is clear cut, in others obscure. For example, ceramic phases 9, 8, and 7 are clear and unshakeable, but cp 6 is far less certain; stratified groups were found without the decorated vessels typical of cp 7 but *the absence of decorated types need not be of chronological significance. In other words cp 6 may not exist,* but since it could theoretically exist it has to be allowed for" (Cunliffe 1984a:233-4 *my emphasis*).

A layer or pit appears to have been assigned to cp 7 on the presence of decorated Middle Iron Age material in the first ten year's Danebury report (see 6.3), as such cp 6 is in some ways a 'negative' phase. Support for the overall ceramic sequence came from a range of tests and radio carbon dating (Cunliffe 1984a:234-43). These include investigation of the quarry hollow stratigraphy. Here only one stratigraphic level - 1977/8 Ah - was archaeologically 'preferred' to belong to cp 6, even though at least one layer in this level was assigned to cp 7 - presumably on the presence of decorated Middle Iron Age pottery. In all those levels held to date to cp7, or 7-8, a considerable proportion of layers were assigned to cp 6, presumably because they contained only undecorated Middle Iron Age pottery (Cunliffe 1984a:235). Seriation and investigation of fabric change both support the broad chronology but do not provide definite evidence for the chronological existence of cp 6. Certainly there is a change from sandy to fine flint gritted wares, but this appears to be a gradual, not a sudden shift.

The radio carbon chronology is equally diffident. Although a large number of dates were taken, their subsequent manipulation to produce a neat chronology may be something of a statistical slight of hand.

Haselgrove (1986:364) stressed the weaknesses of the radiocarbon chronology, particularly that the "excellent statistical work... is not balanced by a more comprehensive archaeological discussion of what it is that is being dated". As a consequence the relationship between the large sample of dates and the opening and closing of the ceramic phases it tries to establish "is thus indirect and anything but straightforward". For cp 6 it is noticeable that there are two clusters of dates. The earlier appears to support the existence of cp 6, the later is in the middle of cp 7. The statistical manipulation suggests "there is no need to suppose that the later group of dates in cp 6 really belongs to cp 7, *although,,, archaeologically this may be likely*" (Cunliffe & Orton 1984:195 my emphasis).

The seriation of pit assemblages suggests a distinction between those Middle Iron Age features with and those without decorated pottery, but as Lock recognises "variables other than time, for example social class or function, may be responsible for differences recognised within a seriated sequence" (1984:237). I would suggest that these differences could account for the differential deposition of plain and decorated Middle Iron Age pottery on the other sites considered in this study. Some decorated pottery was recorded amongst assemblages from Early/Middle Iron Age Easton Lane (cf. Danebury cp4-5). This suggests that decorated saucepans and jars were present from the beginning of the Middle Iron Age in some parts of Hampshire, although it is possible that the proportions increased through the period. This would account for the first cluster of Danebury C14 dates, but also imply that the earlier cp 7 dates are also 'correct'. Equally the later cluster of plain Middle Iron Age assemblage (cp6) dates need not be considered anomalous. Rather, I would suggest that decorated pottery might have been selectively deposited in certain features, at the same time as plain pottery was deposited in others throughout the Middle Iron Age at Danebury, as seems to have been the case at Winnall and Winklebury.

This suggests that a finer division of the Middle Iron Age on any site will be difficult, particularly in conjunction may the problems of feature phasing, and residuality that have already arisen in this study (see 7.6.5). The implication is that the spatial and depositional patterning that distinguish cp 6 and 7 might not have been a product of changes in the locations of activities, nor depositional practices through time. Rather, at any one time throughout the Middle Iron Age plain pottery was deposited in different locations and with different associated deposits than decorated pottery. In terms of the human and animal deposits, if the 'phases' were not chronological, it would appear that certain types of deposits were associated with decorated pottery, others with plain wares. More pits contained small finds and decorated pottery (cp7). There were also differences in the range of human deposits associated with decorated and undecorated pottery (e.g. cp 6 pits contain no partial inhumations, charnel deposits or pelvic girdles and only fragments from the skull and lower part of the body) and the only inhumations were confined to the northern part of the excavations (Walker 1984:443-450,457).

	cp 6 plain pottery	cp 7 decorated pottery
Complete Corpses	4 (all male)	6 (2 male, 4 female)
Partial Corpses	0	3
'Charnel' Deposits	0	2
Pelvic Girdles	0	1
Skulls	1	5
Bone Fragments	Head and Leg only	All parts of body

It would appear that skull *ABG's* were generally not deposited with undecorated pottery (Table 7.3). Clearly, there are important differences between the range of deposits associated with those pits determined to belong to cp 6 and those of cp7-8.

At Danebury it has been suggested that the number of burials of humans and animal special deposits increases towards the end of the Middle Iron Age. This has been interpreted in terms of a reaction to the increasing social stress before the transformation of the Early-Middle Iron Ages social system (Cunliffe 1984b:31). However, this argument rests on the assumption of the later decorated saucepan phase questioned here. So too do claims that the rate of deposition of all artefact classes at the site dramatically increases in the last century of the Middle Iron Age, interpreted as indicating greater economic activity or general site use (Salter & Ehrenreich 1984; Grant 1984a:497). As Table 7.8 and Fig. 7.8 suggests, if pits at Winklebury and Winnall are divided on the basis of the presence of decorated pottery, because of the demonstrated associations between different factors and decorated pottery, those 'later' pits with decorated pottery show a similar pattern to Danebury with a higher proportion of pits with humans remains, *ABG's* , high densities of bone, high average numbers of small finds per pits etc. Certainly, both these sites have a smaller proportion of pits with decorated Middle Iron Age pottery than Danebury, but this may relate to local site specific practices, not to a general chronological trend. To summarise, if the differential deposition of plain and decorated Middle Iron Age pottery at Danebury might have been a contemporary practice. If this turns out to be the case with further work on the Danebury material, it has wide implications for the understanding of the possible social and economic changes in the period.

7.9. A Closer Look at Individual Pits

It is important in the discussion of the overall associations found within the contents of pits on different sites not to lose sight of the fact that these resulted from a series of individual tips and placements. Nor that they do not represent some generalised pattern of behaviour, but were individual performances, all drawing from a similar tradition but in individually different ways. Perhaps I should have written the whole thesis differently, concentrating on individual pits and drawing out the generalities through their discussion, rather than the traditional approach taken here. Such a way of writing would have made the connections between overall associations found in pits and the individual layers they were constructed from stronger, and would also have stressed the importance of the set sequences in how different materials entered a pit shown at Winnall and other sites (Detailed studies on many pits were produced in the coarse of this study - Hill Unpublished). It is such a necessary ordering, the importance of *sequence* within pit fills, that explains many of the vertical differences in the location of human remains, *ABG's* and other deposits shown in chapter 6. This importance of *sequence* and how the overall associations shown in this chapter came in to being, can be shown by discussing a few pits in detail.

Pit 6595   Winnall Down

TOP

6.   Largely deliberate fills with few finds.

5.   Covered by layers of chalk/loam and burnt flint with some bone, pot and half an upper rotary quern stone.

4.   Sealed by a dome of compacted chalk.

3.   A female pig laid on its left side in the centre of the pit, a probably female dog laid on its right side in the south of the pit.

2.   Levelled layer of daub with a very large assemblage of cattle/horse bone, large pot sherds, and half a chalk mould.

1.   Initial Fills of chalk, loam and burnt flint with large sherds, cattle/horse bone, a hare bone and a loom weight.

<u>Sequence of fills in Pit 6595 (cf. Fig. 7.9)</u>

Middle Iron Age Winnall pit 6595 (Fig. 7.9) is a rare example of a pit and its contents discussed in detail in a published site report (Maltby in Fasham 1985:25 & Winnall archive). It was chosen for discussion because it was found to contain two complete animal carcasses (type A *ABG's*) in the same layer. As is common on the sites discussed in this study, both carcasses were of the smaller domesticated species. Equally, as now can be expected the deposit contained carcasses of *different* species -- a dog and pig (see 7.3.1, 7.3.4). The larger domestic species were also present in this pit, represented as fresh substantially complete disarticulated bones of cattle and horse (skull and upper limb bone) found in the layers beneath the main deposit. This bone was deposited fresh and suggests that at least twelve cattle, and several horses were slaughtered and consumed as part of the practices that accompanied this deposit. These layers also contained hare bone (see 7.5) and a very large assemblage of very large sherds of pottery, much of it decorated (see 7.8). This pottery can be compared to the freshly 'broken' animal bone and was deposited fresh. It probably represents several individual vessels. Finally there were also four

70

small finds, an example of the common pattern of finding small finds, often in numbers, in the same pit in which were also put *ABG's*. These finds, all broken, were two loom weights, a substantial part of a quern stone and an 'unusual' find; half of a chalk mould (see 7.6). As is typical of the small finds from these contexts, the mould is incomplete and broken. Again, as is typical at Winnall, these small finds were deposited early on in the sequence of filling this pit.

6595 contained many associations outlined in this thesis -- *ABG's*, + Std Dev. densities of pottery and bone, + Std Dev. *MSW*, presence of wild animal, unusual small finds etc. But it is important to remember that this is evidence of not just a particular cultural and historically *specific social practice*, but a evidence for specific, *particular*, social practice, a single event or performance. That is to say that we lose sight of something significant about understanding this deposit if we just see it as a representative of a general pattern, rather than the product of a group of people at a particular time and place in the Iron Age.

This pit's contents were not dumped haphazardly, nor does the material represent a homogeneous mixed fill. Rather the events the lead to the filling of this pit were the product of a clear ordering of the sequence in which the various material entered the pit. Nor was this material simple dumped into the pit. For example, we must envisage the filling of this pit as part of a range of activities which involved the bringing together and slaughter of an unusually large number of animals - 12+ mature cattle, several horses, an adult pig and adult dog. Slaughter of this number of animals would not have been a common event, indeed that number of mature cattle may not have belonged to same settlements' herds. The two complete carcasses deposited in the pit must have been passed down by people at the top of feature to several(?) people standing in the pit 1.5m deep. The dead-weight of a complete Iron Age pig, even if smaller than present day varieties, would have been considerable. After being passed down, both carcasses were carefully laid out on the, by now, compacted fill.

But this only took place after the bulk of the bone, pottery and small finds had been deposited in three layers, the last a thick deposit of daub that was possibly levelled to take the carcasses. Then this episode was sealed by a layer of deliberately rammed chalk -- we must envisage people again in the pit stamping/using implements to ram the chalk -- followed by the remainder of the pottery and bone, before the upper half of the pit was infilled with relatively sterile dumps of soil and chalk. If we assume that neither the unarticulated animal bone, nor the pottery, was carefully curated, but were created by activities which took place at the same time as the deposits were made, then it is clear the placing (and killing?) of the pig and dog were the end(?) of the series of events they provide evidence for. We must envisage activities involving the

slaughter and consumption of at least sixteen or more animals of four different species, not including hunting and eating the hare, the possible deliberate breaking of several vessels, and the planned deposition of some of this material in a pit. But not just any pit. This was a beehive shaped pit (see 7.7) and in a particular location on the site (see 9.5). The sequence of these fills was not haphazard and was similar to other pits in this phase with *ABG's*. Rarely were the *ABG's* initial deposit in a pit, there is usually at least one layer on the pit base before the placing of the articulated carcasses. This would seem to particularly apply to complete carcasses (type A deposits), and only small portions of articulated/associated limb bone were found directly on a pit's base.

However in other ways the pig and dog in 6595 could be seen as more similar to human deposits on this site. Other *ABG's* were usually not, but humans often were, deposited after exceptionally large deposits of (fresh) animal bone and decorated pottery. Like all the complete adult human depositions in the phase, this pit was dug just beyond the course of the former Early Iron Age enclosure ditch (see 9.5).

Pit 7372   Winnall Down
Middle Iron Age Winnall pit 7372 (Fig. 7.10) is similar to 6595 except with remains of two human infant, rather than two animal, 'carcasses'. Sequence was again important in this pit and these human deposits, like others at Winnall, only followed after people had deposited a range of other material and finds. Because of this need to follow such sequences, in this and other pits, human remains were found in the middle/upper fills of the Winnall Down pits (see 6.3). Here the sequence was as follows;

TOP

9. Final fills, largely natural, settling in the top of the pit, but including one mallard bone (fortuitous?).

8. A sealing layer including sheep bone and one bird bone

7. The placing of the infant bodies.

6. Dumps containing a fragment of a human adult femur, a large number of sheep bones and large pot sherds.

5. The remains of two more complete pots carefully placed on the west side on the chalk layers, followed further fills containing sherds from another vessel.

4. After two layers of chalk very large sherds from at least one complete pot and an *ABG* (associated dog vertebrae).

3. Bone, pot and four small finds including two unique objects, part of a speculum/'collar' and the only decorated measuring weight known.

2. Sealed by dome shaped thick dump of chalk .

1. Initial large deposit of medium sized sherds.

Sequence of fills in Pit 7372 (cf. Fig. 7.10)

71

As with 6595, people started to filling this pit with a series of fills containing large quantities of freshly broken pottery, although with fewer bone fragments. Like 6595, these initially layers contained a number of large small finds, including loom weights, and 'unusual' finds. In the case of 6595 this was an unusual mould, in this case, the two unusual finds were a bronze collar fragment and a decorate stone measuring weight. These finds were placed/dumped after a domed shaped dump of chalk rubble. This rubble dome had a depression made at the point of the dome. It would be tempting, but it is impossible to prove, that the collection of small finds were placed in this depression. The next stage in the filling sequence involved the deposition of large quantities of large, freshly broken, pottery. These would appear to represent three complete vessels, and two of these appear from the original section drawing, to have been carefully placed by people (whole/or in large pieces) in the side of the pit under the over hang c.1m down. This pottery was accompanied by a group of dog vertebrae (and ribs?) (Type D *ABG*).

It was only after this activity that the human remains were put in the pit, after it had been half infilled. Again more large (freshly broken) pottery was deposited in two layers. The last included the largest assemblage of animal bone fragments and a fragment of a human adult fragment. After another mall dump, the two infant human bodies were placed in the pit. These bodies were placed directly over the layer containing the two complete/substantially complete pots in the surviving overhang. They were covered with soil tipped in from the same side of the pit in which the bodies and pots were put. This rapid sequence of fills continued with fills containing more large quantities of large pot sherds and three fragments of quern stones.

In this pit, the emphasis was placed on pottery, rather than animal remains as in 6595. Here, again, a pit was rapidly infilled. Whether this event took place on the death of the two human infants, or their deaths were deliberately caused as part of the events leading to the filling activities, is impossible to establish. However, again a similar sequence to that in 6595 can be seen. Again unusual broken objects were placed in the lower fills of a pit, rapidly infilled (in hours/days), leading up to the burial of the two infants and further fills. All these fills contain a very large quantity of freshly broken (or carefully curated) pottery. In total, some 8.25 kg of pottery were recovered from this one pit; this represents 8.5% of the total Middle Iron Age pottery recovered the site. This pottery represents at least three, if not more vessels. Were these deliberately broken (in an analogous manner to the slaughter of animals) as part of the events that involved/lead to the formation of this pit fill?

Pit 4475 Winnall Down
A similar pattern is visible in Winnall pit 4475 (Fig. 7.10), which cut through the Early Iron Age enclosure ditch and contained the only human body at the site

with 'grave goods' (see 9.5). The adolescent body was deposited in the top of the fills, but only after a complex sequence of fills and deliberate levelling which very simplified was as follows;

TOP

7.	Human Burial
6.	Pottery
5.	Most of a complete vessel placed in the scoops.
4.	Deliberate levelling with scoops then dug at the sides of the levelled fill.
3.	Loom Weight, Pottery, Sheep bone.
2.	Animal Bone - PigD *ABG* Bird (Thrush?)A *ABG* Cattle bone.
1.	Pottery.

Sequence of fills in Pit 4575 (cf. Fig. 7.10)

This pit showed a similar sequence of deposits as those found in 7372, with human remains placed in the upper fills of the pit only after people had deposited and carefully created a range of deposits to fill in the first two thirds of the pit. Here an initial deposit of large pot sherds was sealed with a thick layer of daub - building material. Then followed a series of fills which included placing the associated vertebrae of a pig, and the skeleton of a thrush or related species in the pit. These were followed with fills were more large pot sherds before a pause in the sequence. after a large deposit of over 1 kg of pottery. The section drawing clearly shows that the fill at this point is level, implying people carefully tipping, or more likely working in the pit, to level the current 'floor'. Then at both sides of the pit, material was dug away from this levelled fill by people obviously in standing/kneeing in the pit. Into these cuts was then placed at least three quarters of a single pottery vessel.

Further fills were then made before they were levelled off near the top before the complete body of an adolescent male (oddly wearing a shale bracelet) was carefully arranged on one side of the pit. Further deposits collected in the hollow that formed in the top of the pit, before a person or people dug into the top of the pit (co-incidently?) above where the body had been placed earlier placed. Again, especially given the rapidity of the filling sequence, the care and clear action of people placing material and doing things in this pit, shows that the other contents of this feature were not coincidental with the final placing of the adolescent's corpse. As such, it was not fortuitous that a bird was hunted and then placed in this pit. Given such associations, was the location of this pit, in the south of the site and cutting through the old enclosure ditch also co-incidental? (see 9)

Pit 10161 Winnall Down
Not all pits distinguished as different show all the associations proposed here. Winnall pit 10161,

contained a partial horse and a complete hare skeletons, but I would suggest deliberately contained little else (Fig. 7.1.). The absence of pottery *or* bone is common in a pit, mirroring the oppositional relationship between pot and bone found in individual layers (cf. layers - see 5.3.4 & ditch terminals - see 8.4). As has been shown above, choosing not to put pottery in a pit could have been a deliberate choice taken by the people filling these features. At Danebury, during the first ten years' excavations, it would appear that a pit chosen not to place pottery in was often the same pit in which an iron reaping hook was deposited (see 7.6.5).

Pit 6038 Winnall Down
Very little pottery was deposited in this Winnall pit 6038, even though section drawings show that this pit was subject to a complex sequence of rapid despite a complex fills. These fills included the deliberate infilling of this pit with a mass of small flint noodles (4,042) and several thousand fragments of burnt flint (3,821 burnt flints). As well as these unusual fills, this pit as contained animal bone (including a Dog A *ABG*). It was also unusual in that this pit appears to have been dug in the middle of a circular structure, N.

Pit 7257 Winnall Down
This pit, which contained four *ABG's* , yielded the largest number of small finds from any pit at the site. These thirteen small finds come from a pit unlike those discussed so far, which appear to have an unbroken sequence of fills. This pit would appear to more closely follow the pattern proposed for Danebury with marked phases of activity and inactivity (see 3.2.2). Two phases of deposition took place, both including a pair of spindle whorls. Only the lower episode involved *ABG's,* all dog. The uppermost layer of this pit contained the only fibulae for either the Early Iron Age or Middle Iron Age at Winnall (see 7.6.3).

Pit 2416 Winnall Down
The only other pit with a broken sequence of filling was 2416. Like 6038, this was in the centre of circular structure, T, and was the largest pit of this phase (see 9.5). It also contained an infant burial, placed after other deposits, but was unusual as this pit was left open for some time during its infilling. After a *complete* upper rotary quern stone (of considerable weight) had been passed down into the deepest pit on the site - 2.3m deep - and placed in the centre, material, including some human bone, sheep bone and probable horse skull, were dumped/placed into the pit. There then followed a phase of natural erosion, with the formation of classic chalk shatter lens, suggesting several months over a winter (?) - if not longer - before placing the infant and subsequent mix of natural and artificial fills. If this pit was left open, over winter, it would imply that either structure T was infrequently in use at the time, or the structure was demolished(?) before the pit dug.

Conclusions
This latter pattern was common at Winklebury, where initial deliberate fills were usually followed by a period of inactivity and natural silting, before renewed deliberate deposits in the upper fills. For example in 2611 a complete raven and young pig laid out on an initial tip of chalk, before a substantial deposit of pottery. After a period of natural silting, a loom weight and rib cage of an ox were then placed in a charcoal rich matrix. The pit was then deliberately infilled and capped with a layer of flint and stone which contained a large assemblage of cattle bone. In 979, initial deposits included bones from a human hand and foot before an episode of natural silting, followed by a complete human corpse. In these examples, and others at this site a deliberate decision was taken suspend infilling the pits for some time. How long this interval lasted is difficult to assess. The classic middle fill chalk lens in this pit is generally a product of winter erosion, but as the re-excavated pits at Micheldever Wood show (Fasham 1987), they may take several winters to accumulate. I have suggested elsewhere (Hill forthcoming a), that both Danebury and Winklebury are different from non-hillfort settlements in Wessex because far greater proportions of their pits were left to partially or completely naturally infill. This, I suggested, might indicate seasonal use/occupation or low density permanent occupation. At Winklebury at least, this related to a practice of leaving a considerable interval between initial deposits and their completion which is probably another key difference between hillforts and non-hillfort sites in Hampshire.

Individual pits show how the general associations found between different factors were created through people deliberately creating a complex sequence of deposits. In these sequences general patterns are discernible. It is clear the *ABG's* had to be placed early in the sequence of fills, while human remains had to be placed much later, and often only after several 'exceptional' deposits of bone, pot and small finds. This pattern of humans on top is also found in the complex First Century BC pit deposit from Viables Farm (Millett & Russell 1982), where human burials followed ABG's. However, there were differences between sites. At Winnall, *ABG's* were almost never placed in the initial pit fills, unlike at Winklebury, while at other sites human remains were often placed in the lower fills of pits (see 6.3). This is particularly so at Danebury, where complete human corpses seem only to have been deposited in the initial stages of pit fills (Cunliffe 1992:75).

7.10. The Analysis of Pit Fills: Some Conclusions
A cluster of associations has been found in a limited number of pits that demonstrate that the deposition of human remains or animal carcasses/articulated limbs etc. were indeed 'special'. These associations were created as people chose to place certain types of

Categories of Plant Assemblage	Total	Pits with Small Finds	Pits with Human Bone	Pits with ABG's
Group 1 (low densities gain,chaff,weeds)	5	2	-	-
Group 2 (High Density grain rich)	4	1	1	1
Visible concentrations of Grain	2	2	1	1
Group 3 (High barley, mixed weeds)	7	4	-	-

<u>The associations between different types of plant assemblages at Danebury and other types of finds</u>

material together with others, according to a sequence, in pits. Not all these associations are always found together, and there are differences between sites, and phases on the same site. On some sites/phases not all these elements are associated, but the same basic elements were involved but combined and expressed in different ways (see 12.2.1). This group of associated elements was identified through a contextual analysis that investigated possible patterning between groups of finds traditionally studied in isolation. It is the associations and similarities across these groups that are an essential element in identifying structured deposition. Arguments for the intentional deposition of ABG's are considerably strengthened by the similar treatment of pottery, small finds and human remains. Equally, contextual approaches break down the different interpretations made for different types and species of ABG's. The associations found between ABG's and other factors were not restricted to any species/type of ABG and a neat division between ABG's and deposits of freshly unarticulated or clearly associated bone should be rejected.

An important result was the distinct treatment of bones from the minority species; pig, but especially horse, dog and wild animals. The details of these treatments could differ between sites and phases, and are manifest both in ABG's but also 'background' deposits suggesting these structures were present in both daily practices and rarer practices resulting in exceptional pit deposits. When considered 'internally' from just the perspective of animal remains, such treatment might be explicable from a functional perspective (B.Wilson 1992), but this is difficult to sustain in the wider context of the associations discussed here.

This wider context is also essential against over emphasising the important division between different types of human deposit. The associations discovered here apply as much, in some cases more, to individual fragments of bone as they do to complete human carcasses. Studies on pottery suggest an analogous treatment to animal bone, with a continuum of deposits ranging from;

Deposits of distinct individual vessels, either complete or (more commonly?) broken,

Deposits of only part of an individual vessels, often 'freshly broken' (sometimes curated?)

Deposits of large assemblages and/or large 'freshly broken' sherds (sometimes curated?)

Deposits of mixed, often worn, sherds

Deposits of soil etc. containing small assemblages of worn sherds

The absence from pits of the 'finer' (museum/'Celt' friendly) metal objects and personal ornaments such as brooches or beads, was a deliberate exclusion. Certain types of objects, usually broken, were deposited in pits and querns, iron objects and worked bone/antler were accorded special treatment.

One important class of evidence that has not been considered in this study is plant remains, because limited sampling meant evidence is only available for a small proportion of features (see 3.6.3). However, it is clear that in certain cases carbonised plant remains, often deliberately burnt (and presumably uncarbonised remains) were deposited in pits. Of the limited number of pit assemblages discussed by Jones (1984a:493-4) at Danebury, only his Group 2 (Grain rich, end product of cereal cleaning) had any associations with human remains or ABG's; one out of four pits was one of the two 'charnel' pits. Of the two pits with visible concentrations of grain, one contained a human bone fragment, the other ABG's. The other two groups of plant assemblages had more associations with small finds. Clearly, there are patterns here for further investigation and plant remains must be set within the broader context of deposition discussed here.

Clearly the contents of those pits in which people chose to place human remains and articulated groups of animal bone differed from the larger number without 'special deposits'. This can be shown by dividing those pits which contained human remains or ABG's from those without at Middle Iron Age

74

Winnall and Winklebury. From the characteristics of the finds in both groups, those pits with humans and/or *ABG's* are clearly distinguished (Table 7.9 and Fig. 7.11). At both sites the proportion of pits with small finds and the average number of small finds per pit were far higher for pits containing humans/*ABG's*. There are differences in the distribution of different types of small find. At Winnall a greater proportion of pits in which were put humans/*ABG's*. were also those in which were placed querns. But this was opposite at Winklebury. This pattern was reversed for loom weights. Animal bone densities are higher, but only at Winnall are pot densities greater. At both sites a greater proportion of the minor species and decorated pottery came from pits with humans/*ABG's*.

This intentional deposition of material in pits, and other features, was not a daily, or often even annual, occurrence on sites. Human remains or *ABG's* have been found in approximately 15-30% of all pits on most Wessex sites. Estimating the number of pits filled per year or decade, and assuming these deposits were made at regular intervals throughout a site's life, would suggest these deposits were distinctly irregular (Hill 1988). That is we must not envisage people filling these pits on a daily, monthly, or even annual event. If Winnall is typical of Middle Iron Age non-hillfort settlements then such deposits were, perhaps, only made once every ten to twenty years, or more (cf. Table 1.1). Playing these games would suggest Danebury is distinctive, having perhaps one to three human and/or *ABG* depositions each year throughout all its phases. These games assume only that one pit was infilled with a 'special deposit' at any one time. It is entirely possible that several pits received deposits simultaneously. This would particularly make sense of many of the spatial patterns shown in latter chapters. If so, that even longer periods of time separating these episodes must be envisaged.

The implications of this work are much wider than just chronology. Maltby's work on the formation processes of animal bone assemblages have been consistently arguing that there is no direct relationship between the original composition of past herds associated with, or dead stock slaughtered on/brought to, a site. These arguments are greatly strengthened by the recognition of the structured deposition outlined here. Equally, there may be no direct relationship between the age profiles from mandibles recovered and the actual population structures within past animal herds they are often used to reconstruct. Similar arguments also relate to inferring from the proportions of local and non-local pottery the exact details of production and exchange, or use of small finds to infer site status or scale of production.

To conclude, the previous chapters tried to begin a detailed, contextual understanding of the cultural formation processes (the ways people acted to create an archaeological record), and natural formation processes that led to the creation of a specific archaeological record which we know as that of Iron Age settlements in Wessex. They showed how the small proportion of all the material used and discarded on Later Prehistoric sites entered sub-soil features through a non-random process, and one not adequately explained (away) by functional interpretations. The bulk of the material excavated in pits on the sites studied resulted from *a distinct, irregular, social practice* involving the deliberate deposition of human and animal remains, pottery, and a specific range of broken small finds combined together according to site specific rules and sequences.

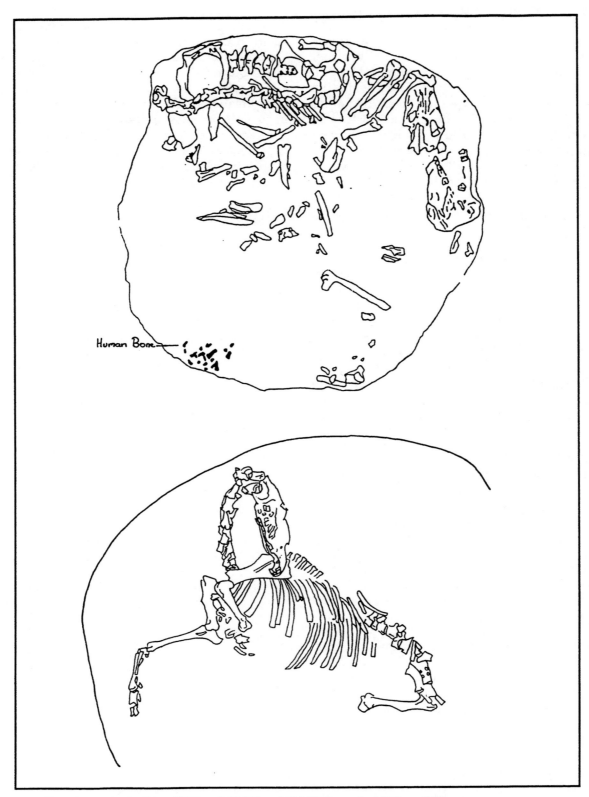

Human Bone

Fig. 7.1. Deposits in Pits 4006 and 10612 at Middle Iron Age Winnall Down.

Pit 4006 Context 4028:- Human Infant Bones and a mass of Animal Bones including small groups of associated/articulated Cattle and Horse limbs, Horse vertebrae and the wing of a Heron.

Pit 10161:- Partial Horse Carcass

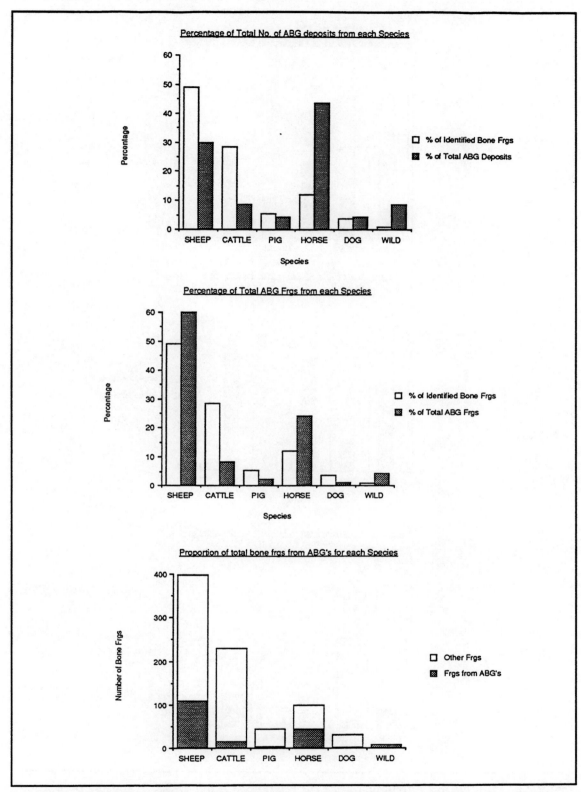

Fig. 7.2.a. **Early Iron Age Balksbury:** The relationships the *ABG's* and the proportions of bone from the different species in the overall bone assemblage.

    i.   Percentages of the total number of *ABG* deposits and overall bone

    ii. Percentages of the total number of bone from all *ABG's* and overall bone

    iii. Proportions of bone from each species recovered from *ABG's*

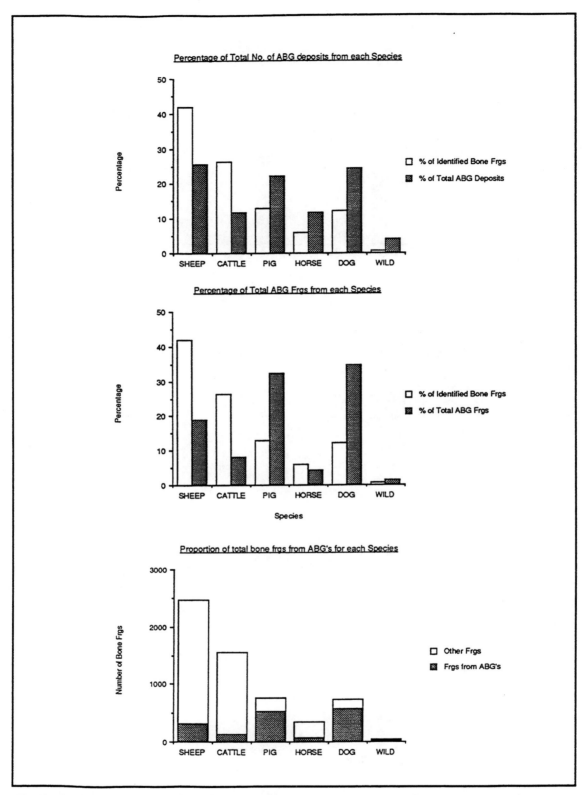

Fig. 7.2.b. **Middle Iron Age Balksbury:** The relationships the *ABG's* and the proportions of bone from the different species in the overall bone assemblage.

      i.   Percentages of the total number of *ABG* deposits and overall bone

     ii. Percentages of the total number of bone from all *ABG's* and overall bone

   iii. Proportions of bone from each species recovered from *ABG's*

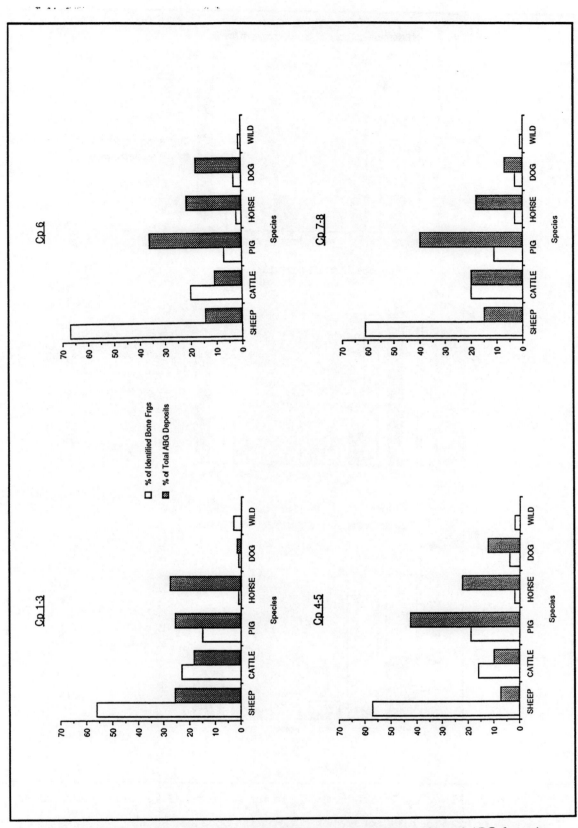

Fig. 7.2.c. **Danebury:** The relationships percentages of the total number of *ABG* deposits and the proportions of bone from the different species in the overall bone assemblage.

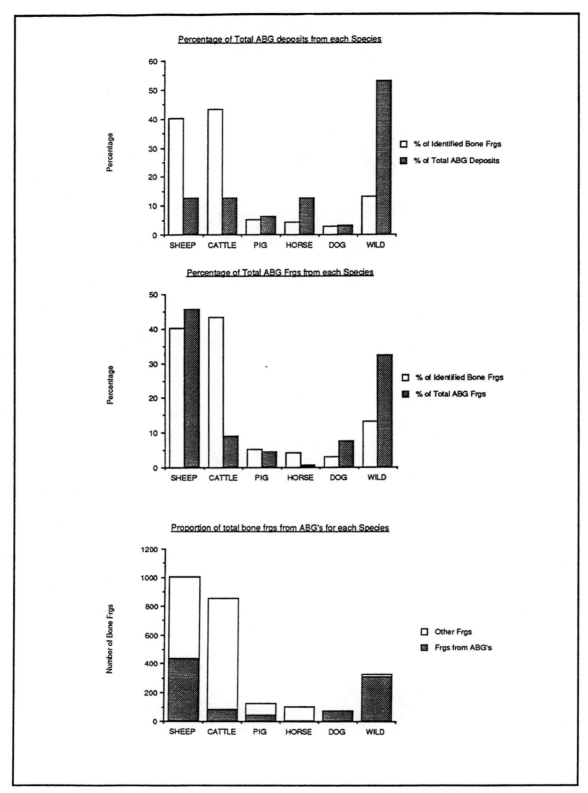

Fig. 7.2.d **Middle Iron Age Winklebury:** The relationships the *ABG's* and the proportions of bone from the different species in the overall bone assemblage.

    i.   Percentages of the total number of *ABG* deposits and overall bone

    ii. Percentages of the total number of bone from all *ABG's* and overall bone

    iii.Proportions of bone from each species recovered from *ABG's*

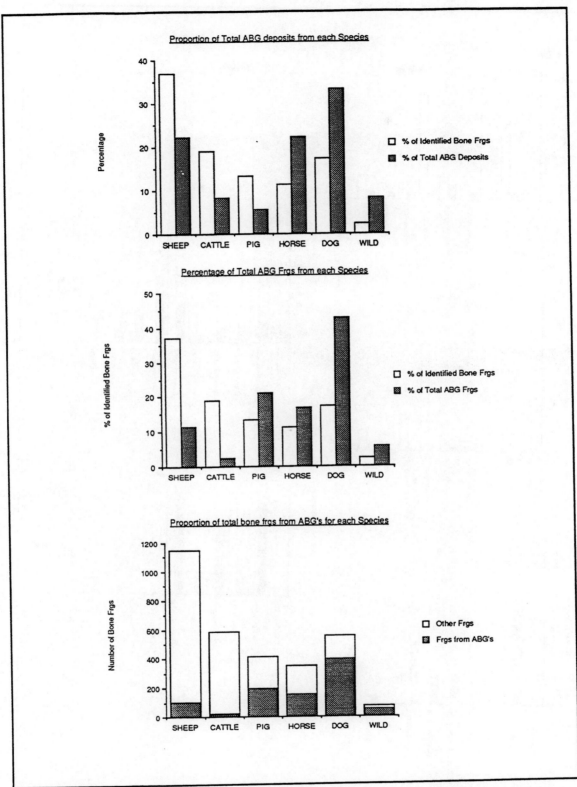

Fig. 7.2.e **Middle Iron Age Winnall Down:** The relationships the *ABG's* and the
proportions of bone from the different species in the overall bone assemblage.

    i. Percentages of the total number of *ABG* deposits and overall bone

    ii. Percentages of the total number of bone from all *ABG's* and overall bone

    iii.Proportions of bone from each species recovered from *ABG's*

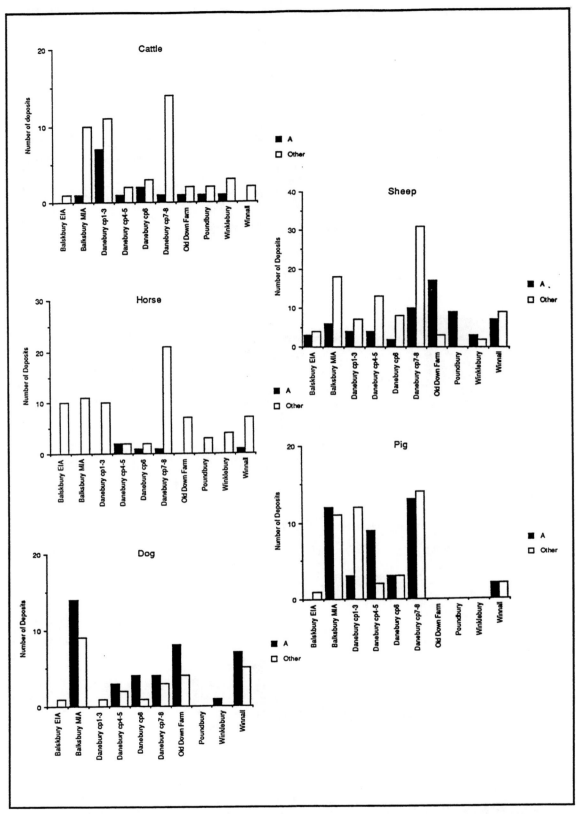

Fig. 7.3. The proportions of type A and all other types of *ABG's* of the main domestic
species on six sites, showing the rarity of complete/partial carcass Cattle and
Horse deposits.

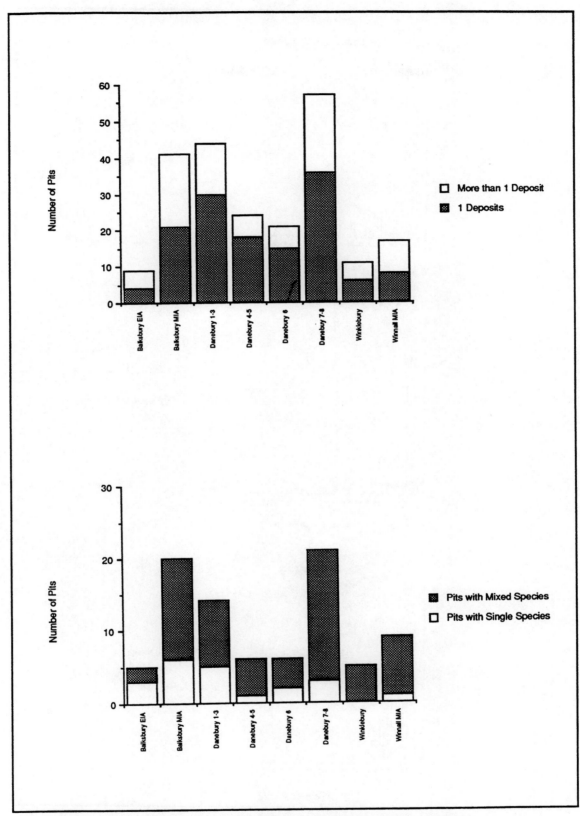

Fig. 7.4.a The proportions of pits with one or more *ABG* deposits at six sites.

Fig. 7.4.b The proportions of pits with one or more species of *ABG* deposits at six sites.

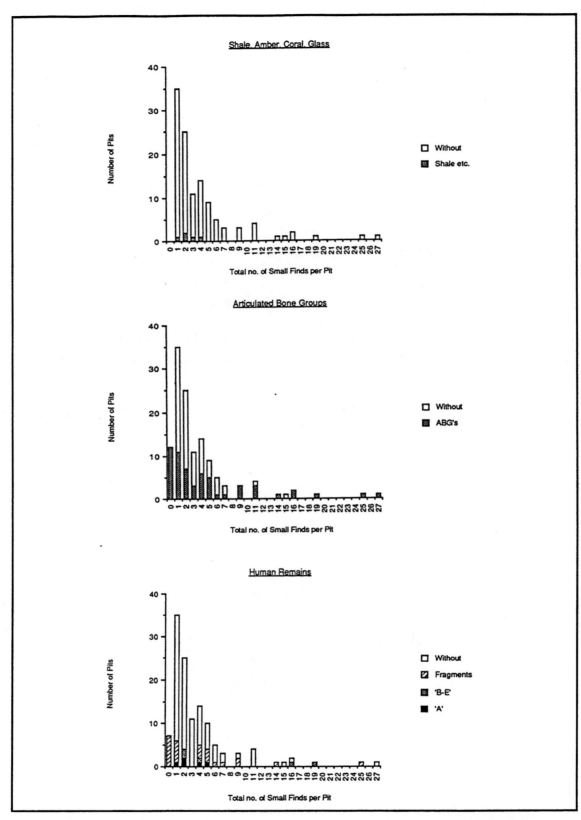

Fig. 7.5.a **Danebury**: The number of small finds in a pit and the presence of different types of find, articulated/associated animal bone groups and human remains.

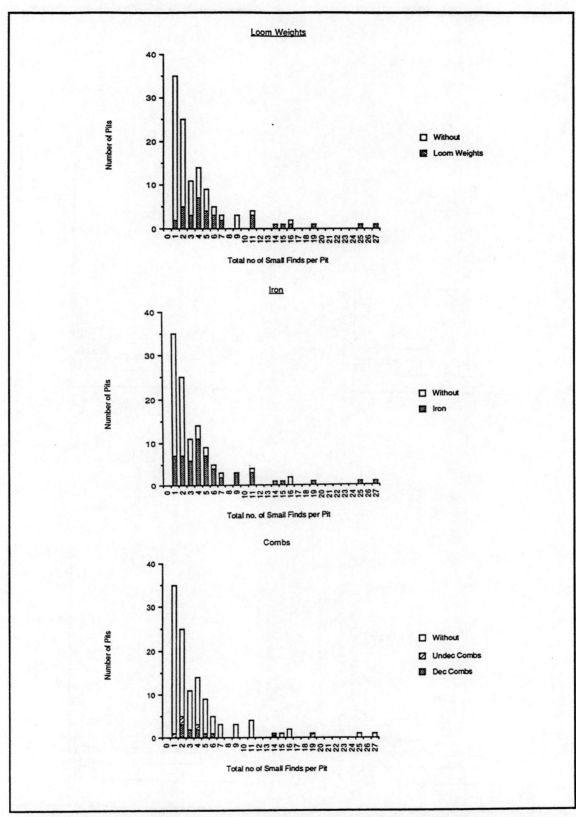

Fig. 7.5.b **Danebury**: The number of small finds in a pit and the presence of different types of finds.

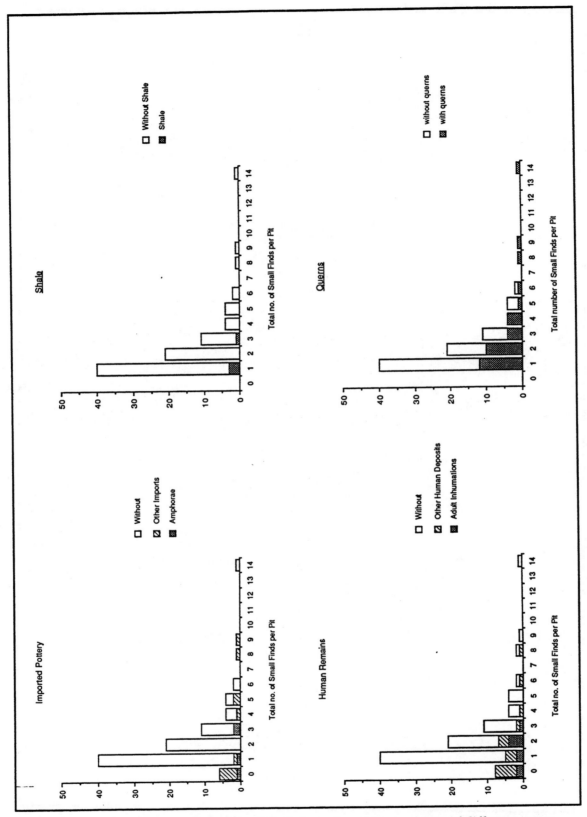

Fig. 7.5.c **Gussage:** The number of small finds in a pit and the presence of different types

of finds and human remains.

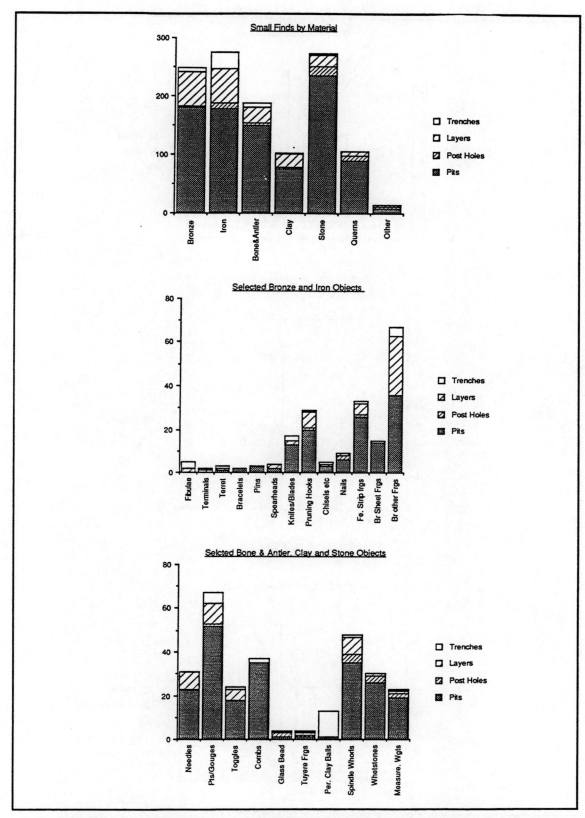

Fig. 7.6. **Danebury**: The distribution of different types of Small Finds recovered from Pits, Post Holes and Layers in the Quarry Hollows and Entrance.

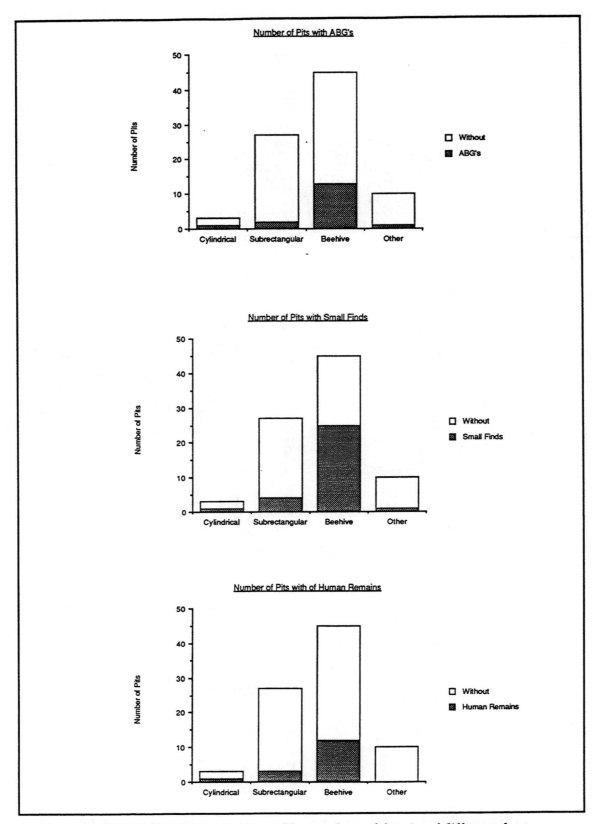

Fig. 7.7. **Middle Iron Age Winnall Down:** The numbers of the pits of different shapes with *ABG's*, Small Finds and Human Remains.

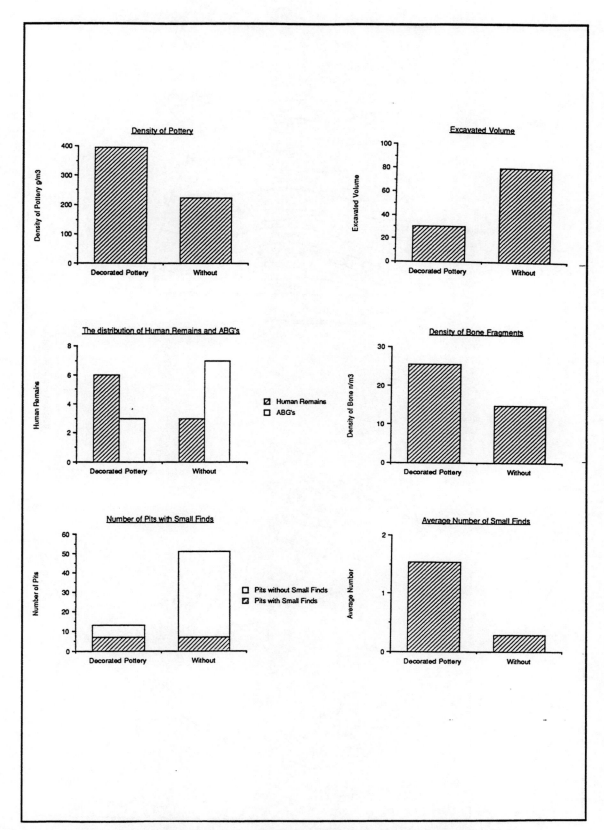

Fig. 7.8. **Middle Iron Age Winnall Down:** The different characteristics of the find assemblages recovered from pits containing decorated compared to those without decorated pottery.

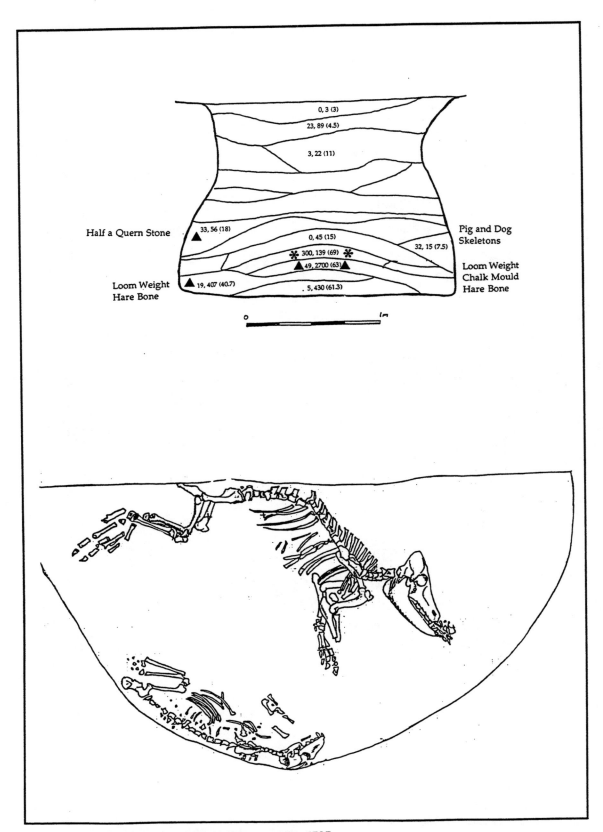

Half a Quern Stone

Pig and Dog
Skeletons

Loom Weight
Hare Bone

Loom Weight
Chalk Mould
Hare Bone

Fig. 7.9. **Middle Iron Age Winnall Down: Pit 6595**

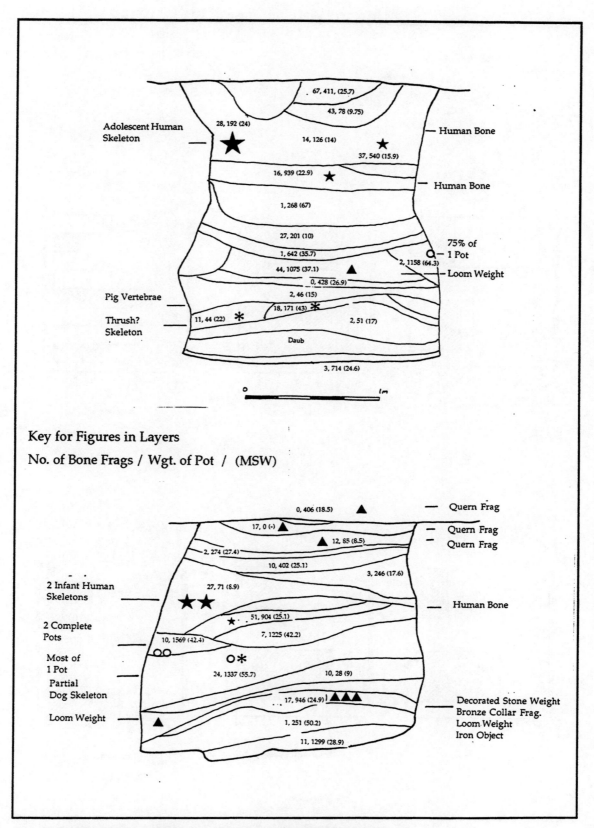

Key for Figures in Layers

No. of Bone Frags / Wgt. of Pot / (MSW)

Fig. 7.10. **Middle Iron Age Winnall Down: Pits 4575 and 7372**

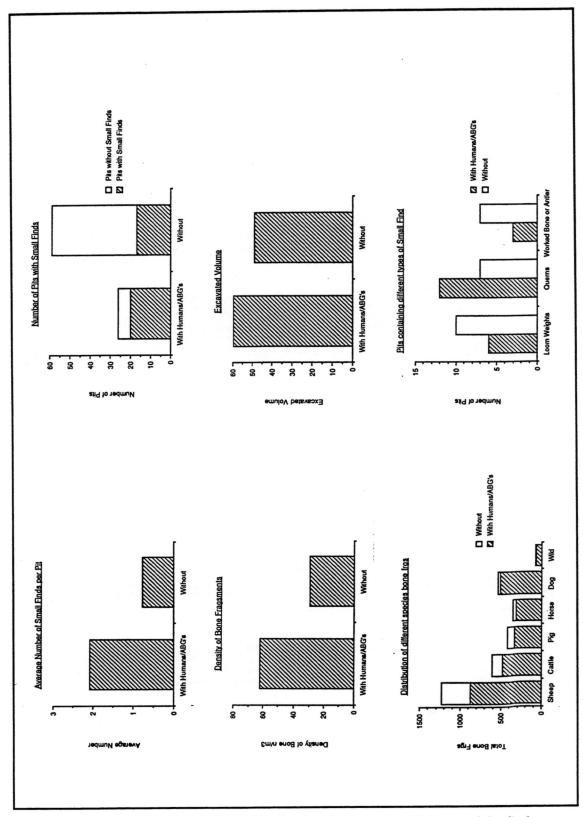

Fig. 7.11.a **Middle Iron Age Winnall Down:** The different characteristics of the find assemblages recovered from pits containing *ABG's* and/or Human Remains and those without.

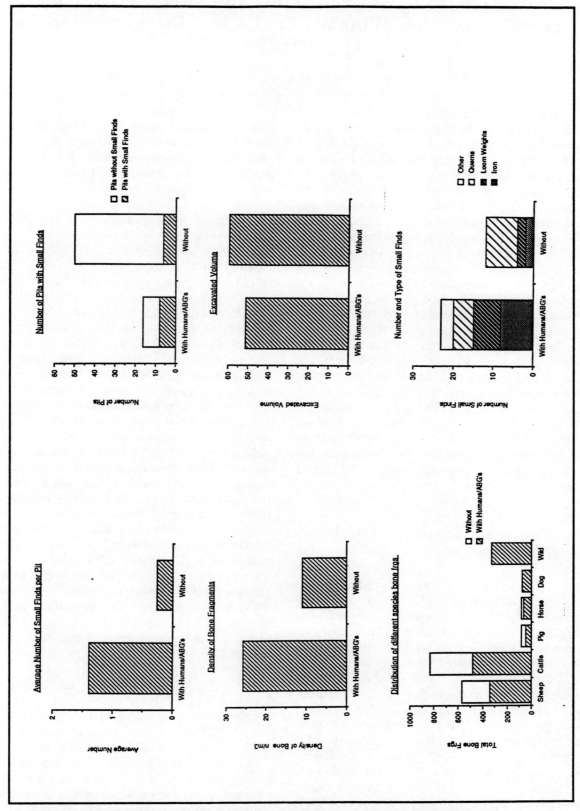

Fig. 7.11.b **Middle Iron Age Winklebury:** The different characteristics of the find assemblages recovered from pits containing *ABG's* and/or Human Remains and those without.

Chapter 8
The Required Barrier and the Required Threshold:
Are deposits in the Winnall Enclosure Ditch similar to that in Pits?

8.1. Introduction

This chapter broadens the argument away from pits by considering deposits in the enclosure ditches of Later Prehistoric settlements and connects discussions of deposition to recent approaches to space and the reproduction of society (see 1.4). In this sense this chapter also builds a bridge between the analysis and interpretation. This will be continued by considering the spatial distributions of material from pit fills in chapter 9. This chapter summarises results of a similar analysis on the Winnall Down enclosure ditch to that carried out on pit contents. The finds assemblages from ditches are often considered to be significantly different and more poorly preserved than those from pits (see 3.7.4.). This chapter shows this is not the case at Winnall and I will suggest that the distinct, irregular, depositional practice identified in pits was found in other features. Previous discussions of the social and cultural importance of enclosure boundaries will be extended (Hingley 1984; Bowden & McOmish 1987; Hingley 1990a), and it will be argued that they provide a way to move from the study of formation processes to wider social questions.

8.2. The Enclosure Ditch at Winnall Down

8.2.1. Previous interpretations of Enclosure Ditches

Since excavations at Little Woodbury, the enclosure ditch and bank have been considered an archetypal component of an Iron Age settlement. Their purpose has been taken for granted (Bowden & McOmish 1987:82) as for keeping out wild men and animals, controlling stock, or simply acting as the "required barrier" (Wainwright 1979:3). The natural processes through which ditches silted up have been exhaustively studied through experimental earthworks (e.g. Jewell 1963; Jewell & Dimbleby 1968; Coles 1973; Reynolds 1984), although how much these have added to previous field observations can be questioned (cf. Pitt-Rivers 1898; Curwen 1930). These experimental and observational studies have emphasised the slow, natural, silting processes at work in ditches to the extent that deliberate infillings are rarely considered in reports and the finds incorporated in ditch fills are generally assumed to have naturally eroded into the feature. Recent work has contrasted finds from ditches and pits, showing how bone (and, by inference, all material) is less well preserved in the open, slow accumulating layers of ditch fills

compared to pits (see 3.7.5). However not all finds were naturally incorporated into ditch fills as has often been assumed and deliberate deposits of bone, pottery and carbonised plant material in ditch fill were common (see 3.5.3; 3.6.2; 3,7.5.)

Such ditches have recently been re-interpreted to have been as much symbolic as practical boundaries (Bowden & McOmish 1987; Hingley 1984, 1990b; Parker-Pearson forthcoming; Hill 1995). Their size would often appear to exceed the basic requirements of keeping animals in their places and simple demarcation; aims achievable with slighter earthworks, fences or hedges. Rather such ditches can be seen as marking significant discontinuities in social/symbolic space, and not simply ecological/economic space. Hingley (1984:79) argued that the significance of the boundary ditch was that in certain circumstances it symbolically defined the social group it enclosed. The enclosure resulted from, defined, and created the isolation and independence of the 'natural' social unit occupying the settlement. Bowden and McOmish (1987) argued that the enclosure ditch at Gussage was back-filled soon after excavation, deliberately incorporating a range of 'trinkets', small finds and human bone fragments. Human remains were selectively deposited in enclosure ditches or on the margins of many sites (C.Wilson 1981:163), as were iron 'currency bars', strip shaped ingots (Hingley 1990c). This suggests an important element in the marking of these boundaries was the deposition of different classes of material, and that ditch fills and functions were not as straightforward as previously thought.

8.2.2. Previous Work on the Winnall Enclosure Ditch

Work at Winnall excavated 29.4% of the total length (267m) of the enclosure ditch (Fasham 1985:11-- Fig.8.1), although little analysis of the finds was attempted. The ditch was discussed in three paragraphs and not directly illustrated. The only published section drawings are as background to illustrate other later features (Fasham 1985:Figs 25,28,29&38). It was concluded "that the ditch... displayed no evidence of cleaning or re-cutting" (Fasham 1985:127) and that "the ditch silted up mainly by natural processes although occasionally there were rubbish deposits" (Fasham 1985:11). No mention is made of the concentrations of animal bone in the upper fills visible in the photographic archive. Although small quantities of bone were found in the ditch, much of the cattle and horse bone was very well preserved, compared to the sheep and pig material. This suggests freshly butchered large animal bone was deposited in ditch (Maltby 1985b:101), contradicting the general conclusion that the ditch finds were 'secondary' rubbish, as opposed to 'primary' rubbish deposited in the pits (Fasham 1985:130).

8.3. A Detailed Analysis of the Winnall Down Enclosure Ditch

To complement the analysis of the Early and Middle Iron Age pits from Winnall, a similar study of the enclosure ditch fills was carried out. In analysing the ditch contents no attempt was made to distinguish the different phases within the fills. The excavators estimated that 85% of the fill dated to the Early Iron Age, and that the ditch would certainly have been a noticeable feature in the Middle Iron Age (up to 50cm deep in places?). However, in attempting to separate the Early Iron Age from later fills, the problems of the re-working of residue material and movement of later material down through the profile, proved insurmountable. Instead, the study lumped all layers together, and totals for each segment inevitably include some Middle Iron Age material in topmost layers. However, the results of this study suggest the presence of later material has not seriously distorted the analyses.

8.3.1. The profile and sequence of ditch fills

The ditch had a V profile with a flat base and was both wider and deeper to the west, where the enclosure was entered (Fig.8.3&5). The 'D' shape of the enclosure may be understood as providing a stretch of the ditch perpendicular to the entrance on either side. Fasham assumed that the excavated profile reflected the original profile, but the ditch was clearly re-cut on several occasions and essentially artificially back-filled. Examination of the pit sections in the archive suggests a complex history with a sequence of re-cuttings and deliberate infillings. Section K (Fig. 8.2) shows three cuts filled with chalk (2049,2019,2018) on the inside of the ditch whose fills can not have naturally eroded from the fills they cut through. In section D the ditch sharply cut the fill of quarry 9558, but shows no signs of subsequent natural erosion which would be expected if left open to slowly naturally infill (Fig. 8.2). Two possible major re-cuts are visible in many archive sections;

1. A steep sided, flat bottomed cut. -- At I and AA it cut through a more U shaped profile and in most segments was immediately infilled with chalk.

2. The shallow excavation of the infilled ditch highlighting the inner edge. -- The inner side of the ditch was acutely cut, the outside shallowly excavated (e.g. section K cutting through the chalk fill of 2018).

These re-cuts were more frequent at the front of the enclosure and the ditch was possibly initially, and certainly later, deeper and wider here, accentuating the boundary on this side. The 'original' profile of the ditch is impossible to establish as the deepest excavations into the chalk were not necessarily the earliest. Where repeated digging and back-filling of the ditch was an important activity, is the importance attached to the 'original profile' valid?

8.3.2. Analyses of Individual Ditch Layers

Analysis of the ditch fills followed the same pattern as used for pit contents, moving from individual layers, through vertical differences, to overall relationships within different segments. Finally, the spatial patterning between ditch segments was investigated.

Individual layer assemblages were similar to those in pits, although with some important differences, e.g. high MSW's corresponded to low number of sherds and bone fragments etc. (see 5.3). But the relationship between the number of bone fragments and the number/weight of pot sherds is not so strongly inverse as found in pits. The behaviour of fine wares (fabrics 14, 15 &16) was considered in detail suggesting they were usually deposited in very small clusters of often large sherds. In general the largest proportions of fine wares occurred in the layers with the smallest assemblages of pottery.

Whether material was deposited from the inside or outside was explored (cf. Barrett & Bond 1988:35), more layers containing finds of any kind came from the inside of the enclosure (63 compared to 38), particularly those with identifiable bone (Table 8.1). However, larger, freshly broken/carefully curated, pot sherds more frequently entered from the outside. This should not be taken as direct evidence for occupation outside the enclosure (cf. 3.5.3). Rather material was deliberately taken outside the enclosure for deposition.

Presence/absence analysis highlighted the presence of human remains, fine ware pottery, and +Std Dev numbers/weight of pottery, bone and MSW. Very large quantities of pottery and/or large sherds were *not* associated with the deposition of bone (prob .0051 & .0222 respectively); another instance of the general antithetical relationship between pot and bone. However, both large weights of pottery and numbers of bone were significantly associated with human remains (prob .0090 & .0074) and fine ware pottery (prob .0084 & .0494).

Relationships with possible ABG's were difficult to assess as the number of ABG's is in doubt. Maltby (1985b:97) records cattle ABG's in four ditch segments (AA, F, MM, N), but does not state which elements were represented. From the context descriptions in the archive, where remarks on bone groups were sometimes made, a case could be made for 10 layers with ABG's in 8 segments

	Layers with +Std Dev Pot Wg	Layers with +Std Dev *MSW*	Layers with +Std Dev %Fw
Cattle (n81)	3	5	10
Horse (n21)	3	1	4
Sheep (n43)	-	-	5
Pig (n19)	-	-	3
Dog (n4)	-	-	-

The distribution of layers with large assemblages of pottery and species of animal bone

(A,F,J,N,AA,FF,JJ & MM). For example, a substantially complete horse skull was noted in the lower fills of the southern entrance terminal (segment A, 552). Animal skulls were also recorded from segments II (6997) and JJ (7063), although neither of these contexts contained any bone according to Maltby's detailed bone archive -- were they bagged separately and subsequently not sent with the rest of the bone? If the possible 10 layers with *ABG's* is reliable, there were significant relationships between +Std Dev overall *MSW* and fine ware *MSW* with *ABG's* (prob .0384 & .0001).

These associations between human remains deposited in the same layers as large quantities of pottery or animal bone *were not* found within pit fills. There human remains were usually deposited discretely, but in close proximity to, discrete deposits of pot or bone (see 5.3.4). In this ditch human remains were mixed with either large quantities of bone or pottery. While freshly broken/carefully curated pot sherds, particularly fine wares, were possibly deposited with *ABG's* -- here skulls or small bone groups -- and other fresh cattle and horse bone placed in the ditch. Although pottery and bone were not strongly associated, the deposition of large sherds and assemblages of pottery, and high proportion of fine wares, would appear connected with this fresh bone.

While the majority of the layers in the ditch were sterile (66% of c530 compared with 54% of c180 in Early Iron Age pits) and many have natural origins, we must envisage occasional events when clearly deliberate quantities of fresh cattle/horse bone, human bone fragments and large quantities &/or large sherds of pottery (often small groups of fine ware) were placed in the ditch. This material was not simply the expedient disposal of rubbish into the ditch from activities close the perimeter inside the settlement. Some of these deposits came from the outside e.g. the majority of the bone, all cattle including an *ABG*, in segment N, in the south corner. Although more mixed than the 'exceptional layer deposits' in pits (see 5.4), they probably derived from similar activities. This mixing possibly implies a longer interval passed before the material was deposited in the ditch compared to the pits. The original discrete groups of material placed together on the surface and then deposited as a whole shortly after. However, such mixing might have been intentional, the distinct categories within the enclosure broken down when deposited in

the liminal zone betwixt and between spaces (cf. McGlade 1990 - see 11.10).

8.3.3 Vertical Differences within Ditch Fills

As with pit fills, each ditch segment was divided into three thirds by depth. There was a notable concentration of all types of material in the upper thirds. However, this may be because the upper third contained c. 50% by volume of each segment's fill, the lowest third only c.15%. If ditches were naturally silted, the lower rapidly forming fills would be expected to contain little material. This was not the case at Winnall where a considerable proportion of lower and middle fills yielded pot and bone (Table 8.3). Densities of bone increase up through the fills. But the wide standard deviations in the lower and middle fills point to large concentrations of bone in these lower and middle fills, which is confirmed by the distribution of those thirds with one standard deviation above mean densities of bone which peak in the middle fills. These large deposits were those of horse and cattle, the highest densities of sheep and pig are found in the upper fills (Table 8.3). Pot densities peak in the middle fills, but again large standard deviations suggest a few segments had very large concentrations of pottery in the lower and middle fills. Sherd size, especially for fine wares, increases with depth, and the middle/lower fills contained high proportions of fine wares (Table 8.3).

Associations between the presence/absence of different factors within thirds suggest the relations between human bone and other factors in layers were swamped by the overall assemblages in thirds. If the *ABG's* discussed above are 'real', then associations with large pot sherds and fine wares are still expressed (prob overall +Std Dev MSW .0013; +Std Dev Fine ware MSW .0084; +Std Dev percentages of fine ware pottery .0106). Above standard deviation densities of pottery were significantly associated with fine ware pottery (prob .0061), but only with horse bone (prob .0055) and not the other species. The presence of small finds was associated with +Std Dev percentage of fine ware (prob .0309), +Std Dev densities of bone (prob .0161) and cattle, horse and pig bone particularly.

Given the complex history of cutting and deliberate fills in this ditch, these patterns do not result from a simple infilling sequence, but a series of depositional episodes - some possibly later dug away. How many such episodes have been truncated or totally destroyed through subsequent re-cutting is impossible to establish. Given the general vertical patterns distinguished in the fills, I would argue that a distinction was made during these repeated backfills between what material should be placed in the bottom of the re-cut and what should be placed after. This is to suggest that the apparent concentration of high densities of pottery and bone in the middle thirds of segments does not relate to any special importance attached to the *middle fill* of the ditch. Rather this was the bottom of the ditch re-cut deliberate back-filled in the last deep re-cuttings of the ditch. Later re-cutting may not have been deep enough to destroy earlier deposits. These lower back-fills contained freshly butchered cattle/horse bone, freshly broken/carefully curated pottery -- often fine ware vessels --, some small finds, human bone and possible *ABG's*. Similar deposits also occurred in the upper fills, although these may relate to the late, shallow re-cutting episode e.g. the pot deposit in L (see 8.4).

8.4. Spatial Variation between Excavated Segments

The overall associations between material within individual segments generally followed those outlined above. More important patterning was found in the spatial distribution of material around the ditch. Although clouded by excavated segments of unequal lengths and distances apart, it is clear that material was not randomly deposited in the ditch (Figs. 8.3-5). It is clear that when the ditch was re-cut, deposits of pottery, animal bone and human bone was placed along its course, as part of a performance I will argue periodically ritually objectified the identity of the community using the enclosure, along with relationships inside that community (see 8.6, 11, 12.3). The deposits and ditch layout were shaped by an interrelationship of four associated variables which it will be suggested structured the organisation of other Wessex enclosures (see 9.7);

1. A concern with the direction of the rising sun, east, and other cardinal points of the compass.

2 A distinction between the inside and outside the enclosure.

3. A distinction between the front and back of the enclosure.

4 . An emphasis on the threshold.

Pottery and animal bone refuse was not a homogeneous category as is seen in the distribution across ditch segments (Figs. 8.3-5). For animal bone density, general trends are discernible, unlike pot

density with its single peaks in individual segments. This might suggest that bone was generally deposited in certain parts of the ditch, but pottery in more spatially discrete dumps. Nevertheless, there were discrete deposits of bone, but not in the same places as those of pot, e.g. pot peaks in F/DG, bone CC, pot MM, bone D, pot C, bone AA etc. (Fig. 8.4). This may read too much into such plots, but densities of bone fragments from different species likewise peak in different segments, although the number of bone fragments is small e.g. cattle density peaks in segment MM between peaks of horse (Fig. 8.3) -- cf. discussion of individual pit layers (see 5.3.4).

These patterns particularly accent the ditch's northern and southern corners, along with the entrance (Figs. 8.5). A concentration of bone in the northern part of the ditch did not result from butchery in that part of the enclosure. Rather, the concentration is the product of two different concentrations of bone deposits -- one either side of the entrance, the other in the north and south corners of the enclosure. These corner deposits (BB to MM, KK to O) were of freshly butchered cattle and horse bone, particularly vertebrae and rib bone (as were the lower densities of cattle/horse bone in segments LL to Q); elsewhere bone assemblages were generally dominated by limb bone fragments. These large bone deposits of particular parts of the carcass, were accompanied by low densities of pottery, but flanked on either side by large pot deposits (C & MM, O & KK). One of these flanking deposit in each corner, both on the left side looking out of the enclosure, contained a high proportion of fine wares (MM, O), although there is a further peak of high proportion of fine ware at F (Fig. 8.4&5).

Either side of the entrance was another preferred location for depositing material. Again, there were pottery deposits (C, FF) flanked those of bone (AA, A) (Fig. 8.4&5). The density of pottery drops off from these peaks towards the entrance, although the proportion of fine wares dramatically increases towards each terminal (Fig. 8.4&5). The terminal deposits were clearly 'structured' (see Table 8.4 for summary). In both almost only fine ware was deposited in the lower and middle fills which also included human bone fragments and cattle bone. Horse bone, including a skull, the remains of a hearth, and small finds -- 3 spindle whorls and 1 loom weight, came from the lower/middle fills in the southern terminal. The only small find in the northern terminal was a loom weight in the upper fills. In the upper fills of both terminals the proportion of fine ware decreases and the proportion of sheep bone increases. More pottery was recovered in the northern terminal (15 sherds, 373g) than the south (11 sherds, 143g). While, more bone was recovered in the south (95 fragments) compared to the north (30 fragments). This could be interpreted as showing that a north-side distinction existed with the following oppositions, particularly in the lower/middle fills:

North	South
Pottery	Bone
	Small
	Finds

These deliberate deposits emphasised the enclosure's entrance, as would the wider/deeper proportions of the ditch (Fasham 1985:127) and the greater re-cutting of the boundary here (Fig. 8.2). The entrance was further marked by a sequence of gate structures not commented on in the report , but which probably went beyond the necessities of stock control (Fasham 1985:11-12, Fig.10). Either side of the gate extended a line of irregular large, shallow, post holes probably from a fence or structural timber work for an earthen bank (Fasham 1985:11). This structure does not extend all around the enclosure (Fig. 8.1). If the absence of postholes in the rear of the site is not due to greater erosion of the natural uphill, this structure was not a effective barrier and, perhaps, more a facade for the site's public face.

The ditch was a slighter feature at the rear, with less evidence of re-cutting. There were also differences in the types and quantities of material deposited in the back and front of the ditch respectively (Fig. 8.6). More animal bone was recovered from the front half of the ditch, with very little bone east of segments CC/KK, in contrast to pottery (Fig. 8.3&6). One very large deposit came from L, 1370g came from a single layer (2034) accompanied by twelve cattle and horse bone fragments. This was deposited in a cut made into the base of the late re-cutting episode (see 8.3.1). All but one sherd was of flint-organic tempered fabric and from at least one vessel, a wide mouthed bowl. Greater numbers of small finds came from the front of the ditch, including a bronze pin and crucible (dated as Late Iron Age/Romano-British in the report although I am not convinced that this dating is sound). Those small finds recovered from the rear of the ditch were all from its north east section. Human remains were even more concentrated to the front (Fig. 8.5&6) and included a complete skull, front up, facing towards the entrance. The only collection of neonatal bones was deposited in the rear of the ditch (M), mirroring the similar fragmented infant skeleton from pit 5777, also in the back of the site. The distinctions between the front and back in can be summarised as:

Front	:	Back
Impressive	:	Slight
Physical Boundary	:	Physical Boundary
Bone	:	Pottery?
Fine ware	:	Coarseware
Small Finds	:	
Adult Human	:	Complete Human
Bone Frgs	:	Infant Burials

The ditch's primary role of dividing inside and outside spaces must not be forgotten. There may be a contrast drawn here in the types of wild animal bone deposited between the interior and exterior. The few bird bones from this phase came from the ditch (Duck) or outside from the quarry (Thrush/Lark). This is despite the poor state of preservation of bone from the quarry which biased the survival of large mammal species and suggests these bird bones were deliberate deposits of fresh material. The only wild animal remains from inside the enclosure were deer antler (three from interior pits, one from ditch & one from the quarry). Dog may also have been preferentially deposited outside; 15 of the 24 dog bones from this phase came from the quarry, 6 from the ditch.

8.5. Comparison with other enclosure ditches

Few other enclosure ditches have been investigated in such detail, and the investigation of substantial proportions of these features must be a priority for future excavations. However, Winnall appears to reflect patterns found on other Late Bronze Age/Iron Age Southern English sites which can be compared to the shrine enclosure at Gournay (Brunaux et al 1985; Brunaux 1988).

At Winnall some of these patterns continued to structure deposition in later centuries. The foundation, not eves drip, gullies of the Middle Iron Age houses contained pottery, carbonised plant remains and bone. This material must have been incorporated *during construction* and in the several instances where the distribution of this material is noted in the report it often showed a concentration on the southern side/ entrance terminal e.g. Houses M & N, Rectangular Structure D (Fasham 1985:18-19). Finds generally from eves-drip gullies need to be re-assessed in this light. Given the deliberate deposits of material in enclosure terminals, the importance of house thresholds suggested in recent studies (Boast & Evans 1985; Wait 1985:177; Parker-Pearson forthcoming; Hill forthcoming a; Oswald 1991) and house foundations deposits in Northern Europe (e.g. Therkorn 1987), are the concentrations of material often found in house gully terminals just fortuitous accumulations of rubbish? For example, was the complete iron bracelet found close to the southern entrance terminal of a house gully on Overton Down really "accidentally lost during the construction of the building" (Fowler 1967:24)?

The Gussage and Winnall enclosure ditches appear to be similar. Bowden and McOmish (1987:81-2) have pointed out that the Gussage ditch was back-filled rapidly (cf. also Little Woodbury - Bersu 1940:39-40). The rear of this, and other Gussage enclosures (Fig. 8.7), was marked by a slight irregular ditch. Bowden & McOmish argue this irregular form was caused by different sections being dug at different times. As deliberately these sections appear to have been quickly back-filled, the complete circuit of the ditch need never have been all open at the same time (1987:82). The distribution of small finds and human bone fragments from this ditch demonstrates a clear front:back distinction (Fig. 8.6) and pottery may have been more common in to the north of the entrance (see 9.6). Evidence for metalworking at Gussage came from either ditch segments or pits close to the entrance in all phases (see Appendix 1). Like Winnall, Gussage I had elaborate post settings at the entrance (Wainwright 1979: Fig7). While it and its neighbours show a particular concern with facading, marking the front and entrance with elaborate antennae ditches (Gussage I & II), or the depth of the entrance passage through three sets of ditches at Gussage IIa (Barrett et al 1991:Fig 6.4). Such antennae may been seen as less for stock control and possibly more comparable to the forecourts and entrance passages of Neolithic tombs (e.g. Sharples 1985; Thomas 1991).

Iron Age enclosure entrances were not only distinguished by elaborate architecture and ditch deposits, but by a quite rigidly prescribed 'correct' facing. The Gussage enclosures, like most in Wessex, followed the easterly orientation of their entrances. Winnall faced due west not east, inverting the standard 'rule'.

Considerable recent attention has been paid to the 'correct' facing of circular buildings and enclosed sites in the First Millennium BC (Evans & Boast 1986; Parker-Pearson forthcoming; Oswald 1991; Hill 1993; 1995; Fitzpatrick 1994a). These studies have shown that the vast bulk of all round houses from the LBA and PRIA faced in an easterly direction (Fig. 8.7). Although this had been noted before, it had always been interpreted in straight forward terms such as avoidance of the prevailing wind etc. (Oswald 1991). Recent studies have argued that this easterly direction can not been explained by these 'functional' causes, but was rather inspired by the importance of entering and leaving a circular buildings whose doorway faced in a particular direction; towards the east, the direction of the rising sun (Parker-Pearson forthcoming). Oswald, in his unpublished dissertation, tested this symbolic interpretation of doorway facing further, conclusively showing that from an environmental architectural point of view, a round house ought to face south in this country if the orientation was to limit some and/or maximise other environment effects. He also plotted the orientation of round building doorways more precisely, showing that most were directly oriented due east, while another significant peak was oriented on midwinter sunrise (Fig. 8.8). This work confirms that it was the rising sun that was an important focus on which round house doorways were oriented.

Other work has shown how this easterly orientation played an important role in deciding the proper orientation for the entrances of enclosures, be they of normal settlements or of hillforts (Parker-Pearson forthcoming; Hill 1993, 1994). Enclosure orientation was not as strict as that for houses, and in both cases examples exist which directly reverse the proper, easterly, orientation (as in the case of the Winnall enclosure). Parker-Pearson (forthcoming) has suggested that this reversed, westerly, direction may have been considered inauspicious.

Front:Back distinctions were evident at Late Bronze Age enclosures in the Lower Thames Valley. At both Mucking and Springfield Lyons a distinction between a 'clean' front and 'dirty' back can be seen, caused by artefact deposition concentrated in subsoil features at the rear, connected with revealed front and hidden back spaces at Mucking (Parker-Pearson forthcoming). Both sites were enclosed by circular ditches, with fine ware pottery selectively deposited in/near the terminals at Lofts Farm and Mucking North Ring - "possible deliberate deposition during a ritual activity" (N. Brown 1988:270) (see 3.5.3). The association between 'north' and pottery is clear at Mucking, where seven times more sherds were recovered from the northern than southern ditch terminal (Barrett & Bond 1988:35). Pottery was equally distributed in both terminals at Lofts Farm, but struck flints were particularly associated with the north, burnt flints and carbonised cereals with the south; bone was not preserved on this site (N. Brown 1988: figs 20, 24, 25). At Springfield Lyons, the northern terminals of the east and west entrances contained large dumps of bronze working debris -- cf. Gussage & Winnall (Parker-Pearson forthcoming). Metalworking debris was also found in the ditch at Mucking. Bronze objects were deposited in enclosure ditches on a range of Late Bronze Age sites (Parker-Pearson forthcoming) and this boundary location may also be reflected in the position of the Danebury Late Bronze Age bronze hoard close to the line of the later rampart (Cunliffe 1984a:335).

At the Late Bronze Age/Early Iron Age Sussex hilltop enclosure of Harting Beacon, excavation of the west entrance revealed that the terminals were re-cut and soon back-filled. The southern terminal contained bone, pot and a human skull. This material was interpreted as originating from the clearing the site as a final act of its use/occupation the site which was deposited in the re-cuts of the terminals which were "simply rubbish pits" (Bedwin 1979:25). However, earlier excavations challenge this functional interpretation. These found in the northern terminal two gold penannular ornaments which must have been placed in the re-cut as "... a sort of foundation deposit... heirlooms sacrificed on the occasion of renewing the fortifications" (Keef 1953:205). Other examples of similar deposits in Late Bronze Age enclosures with deposits placed at their entrances are given in Needham (1992).

8.6. The Winnall Enclosure Ditch - Some Conclusions

The boundary ditch was an important feature of Later Prehistoric sites from the 'appearance' of settlements in the Middle Bronze Age onwards, and emerging out of an earlier tradition of using earthworks as boundaries to demarcate space at communal and funerary monuments. Set within this tradition, interpretations of the symbolic nature of settlement enclosures ought to be more readily understood, and are strengthened by this study which show that the importance of the ditch was reinforced by intentional, structured, deposits.

Ditch fills should be seen as neither simple nor essentially natural in origin. Their finds should not be taken as an indication of the location of past activity areas. Deliberate deposits of material, intentional back-filling, and re-cutting were common. Much of the material excavated from the Winnall ditch came from distinct, irregular, depositional practices involving similar material and associations as suggested for pits. The simple distinction between pits, as receptacles of primary refuse, and ditches, as receptacles of secondary refuse, is insupportable in this case. The specific depositional practices isolated in previous chapters were not restricted to just pits, similar deposits governed by a common set of ideas may be found in enclosure ditches, and also in gullies, 'working hollows' (see 11.8), well/shaft fills (see 11.8), linear earthwork ditches (see 11.8) and house wall trenches (see 8.5).

Interpreting boundaries as symbolic is becoming common place, the enclosure boundary defining the occupants as the basic natural unit in Iron Age society (Hingley 1984; Hill 1995). Boundaries classify the world into meaningful units, enabling it to be understood and acted upon (e.g. Durkheim 1915:23; De Certeau 1984:120-127; A.Cohen 1985:117). However, in the majority of ethnographic case studies on such boundaries, the boundary has no permanent physical manifestation (e.g. A.Cohen 1985; 1986 *esp.* Mewett 1986; Thornton 1980), and the physical nature of Iron Age settlement boundaries must not be over looked. Boundaries were projects (cf. Evans 1988), not just predispositions. Their creation required people to act together and through their construction specific ideas about the relationships between the participating individuals were objectified. For Neolithic communal monuments this is usually considered in terms of creating/manifesting corporate identity as different groups worked together. While bringing into the world the Winnall enclosure (re-)defined the social distinctness of its inhabitants, I would not envisage it was (re-)dug by just the occupants alone. Through participation of people from neighbouring settlements (and possibly further afield) relationships between groups, particularly who were on the inside and outside, were (re-)affirmed.

Simultaneously participation created/paid social obligations and relations necessary for the wider reproduction of society -- particularly in the atomised relations of production I envisaged for Early and Middle Iron Age Wessex (Hill 1995). At Winnall this was an on-going, intermittent, practice through which the traditional significance and associations of the enclosure, and its contents, were re-affirmed and re-inscribed -- a 'rhetoric of re-enactment' (Connerton 1989).

Although ditches were often back-filled, their course was probably still visible and acted to define sites in later phases, e.g. Gussage, Winnall and Old Down Farm. However, it is likely that the Gussage antennae ditches and the front of Winnall were also real barriers and more than just ideas. They physically constrained how people entered enclosures and what they could have seen. Such materiality would harden the mental predispositions of the symbolic boundaries discussed in ethnographies, which would be open to greater re- and mis-interpretation were they not physically manifested to constantly shape and determine the daily movement and observations of the enclosure's inhabitants. These boundaries created a sharp divide between inside and outside; spaces which would have been ascribed different values and expected behaviours. However, these highly structured spaces had to meet and where the boundary was heavily invested, the crossing was likely to be marked and controlled. Crossing the threshold provided a point in time and space during which distinctions between people, spaces, and things could be clearly drawn. The architecture forced people to approach from a proper direction in a proper way. Yet the ditch deposits which played an important role in (re-)affirming the associated ideas and values of the boundary would have only been directly known by those who witnessed, or were told of, their creation, particularly the inhabitants (cf. discussion of Neolithic chamber tomb contents -- Shanks & Tilley 1982; Thomas & Whittle 1986; Barrett 1991a). The fresh nature of the bone and pottery at Winnall suggests that these deposits were not exposed and visible for any length of time.

Van Gennep's (1960) ritual model of rites of passage was drawn from a discussion of the symbolism and ritual surrounding thresholds in many cultures. The liminal nature of the boundary, a space between, a non-space, has been suggested by McGlade (1990) as why it was an appropriate place to bury infants on some Iron Age sites. This betwixt and between nature of the boundary and threshold, the transition and transformation of space and social categories, may also explain why it was an appropriate position to deposit some of the debris from transforming metal. Similar reasons may apply to the deposition of currency bars and coins, mediums by which value may be transferred between things through exchange and relationships between groups established. As such it may not be surprisingly that coins were 'lost' at site entrances in Wessex, as an important element in marking the front and threshold of enclosures was to structure the context through which the site and its inhabitants met the outside world.

In the context of a time/space geography (cf. Johnson 1986:485-7; Pred 1986 - see 1.4.) of Iron Age Wessex with clearly defined, highly competitive, settlement units isolated from each other and dispersed across the landscape, accidental meetings between inhabitants of different settlements would have been comparatively rare (Hill 1995; cf. Pred 1986). I would argue as a consequence, great importance for the wider constitution of society would have rested on the rarer intentional meetings between inhabitants of different settlements. In such situations the facade of Winnall was more than just to impress. Hospitality and meeting the wider world took place through the forecourts of these enclosures, and such ideas may explain why fine ware pottery in particular was deposited around the threshold. The deposition of such pottery, not routinely used (by all the inhabitants?), served to presence such ideas and activities where these vessels were used during the sharing of food and drink with others through which relations of alliance, dependency, and domination were (re-)established.

This chapter has taken the discussion of deposition practices further by connecting them to understandings of space. It has been suggested that the architecture and deposits in the Winnall enclosure ditch were integral to each other, and structured through three important dimensions.

Inside:Outside
Front:Back
North:South

The enclosure has been interpreted in terms of a "structuring structure" (c.f. Donley-Reid 1992; Robbens 1989), it both physically and symbolically contained, defined and reproduced the settlement and its inhabitants. In these terms, the Winnall enclosure acted as a cultural template which served to inculcate the generative structures required for the routine reproduction of human life and society into its inhabitants. An axis onto which were mapped a grid of categories, reference points, which enabled individuals to situate themselves in a complex, but limited, range of historically specific values and associations.

This mapping is witnessed in the ditch deposits and enclosure layout. The boundary itself provided a basic means of dividing up the world and shaping the social group within: "The consciousness of community is... encapsulated in perception of its boundaries" (A.Cohen 1985:3). Facading provided a further dimension of classification, front:back. These distinctions were tied into wider cosmological categories, through the correct easterly orientation of the entrance which threw up the other cardinal points to build into the classification schemes. As Barrett has suggested (1991d), this proper orientation of house and enclosure tied the daily movements of people in and around the settlement into the movement of the heavens and the seasons. Here settlement space was clearly linked to time and also allowed possible links to be conceptually/morally made with classifications of the body, left and right, and between categories of objects through the different types of deposit in the entrance terminals. For example, the distinction between pot:bone was linked to those of north:south, and right:left, and shows that this distinction between pottery and bone, seen in detailed studies of layer assemblages (see 5.3.4), was itself consciously recognised and articulated by Iron Age peoples themselves.

This brief discussion of the spatial organisation of Iron Age settlement enclosures accentuates the inadequacies of functional explanations of this evidence, and highlights one way in which to recognise the difference of the European past (Hill 1989, 1993). Later Prehistoric enclosures were not simply convenient or neutral spatial containers. They were produced in the context of, and helped reproduce, a rationality, a common sense, that was not our own. The chapter has demonstrated the close links between the deposition of material, space and the structuration of Iron Age societies (see 1.4.). Both Hingley and I have argued that Iron Age social relations only had an existence in so far as they existed spatially and that they inscribed themselves in space while producing it. As such settlement enclosures re-produced the communities that occupied them, although greater future attention needs to be paid to the role such definition played in re-producing power structures within those communities. While such practices may have been intended by the group staging them as a display of solidarity, particularly defining themselves in relation to outsiders, it is also a display -- possibly implicit, possibly overt, of the current state of the contested power relations within the group itself (Harrison 1992:225 - see 12). The enclosure not only defined, but it created an analytical space in which activities could be perceived and controlled. At the same time as the physical boundary included and excluded, it also contained and constrained -- possibly even to the point it penned in animals and (certain groups of) people (cf. Spencer 1988:15).

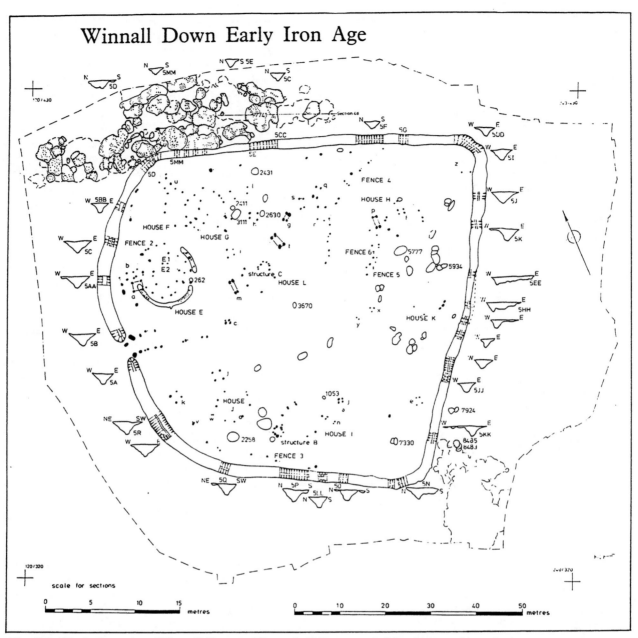

Fig. 8.1. Early Iron Age Winnall Down: Plan of all Features belonging to phase 3

(Fasham 1985:Fig 9)

Note - North is not at the top of the page

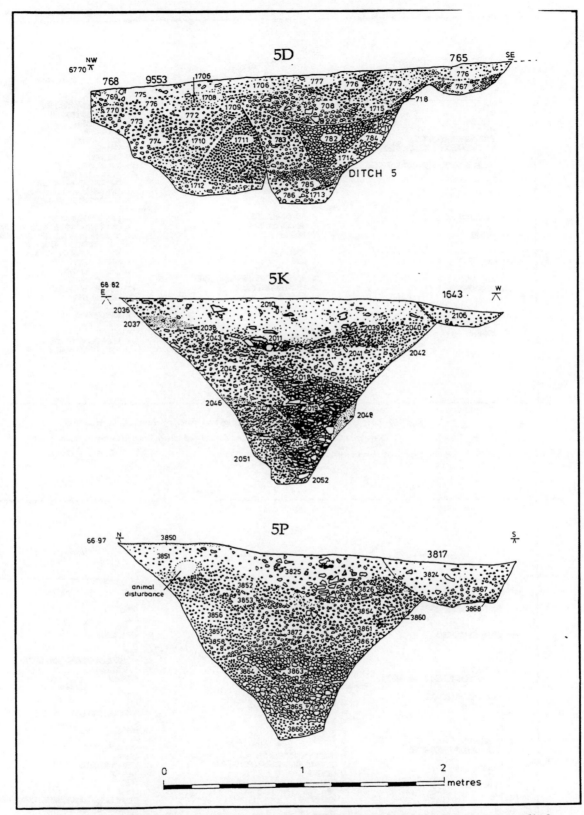

Fig. 8.2. Early Iron Age Winnall Down: Sections through the fills of the enclosure ditch
(Fasham 1985: Figs 25,28, 29, & 38).

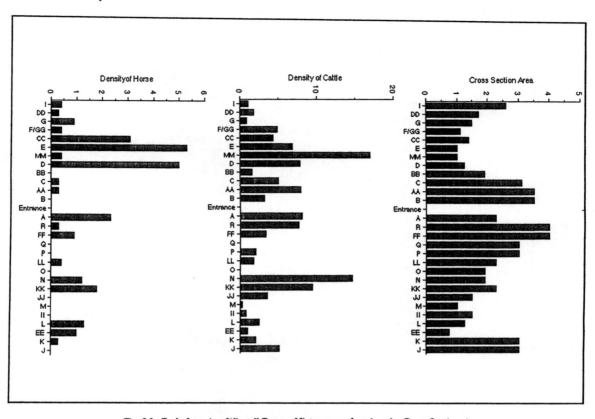

Fig. 8.3. Early Iron Age Winnall Down: Histograms showing the Cross Section Area,
Density of Cattle Bone Fragments and Density of Horse Bone Fragments from
different sections of the enclosure ditch.

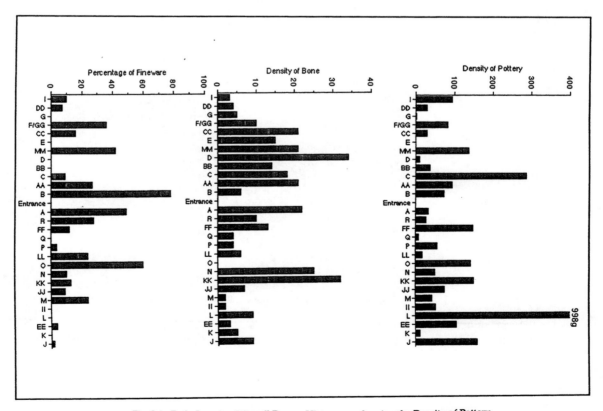

Fig. 8.4. Early Iron Age Winnall Down: Histograms showing the Density of Pottery,
Density of all Bone Fragments and Percentage of Fineware pottery from different
sections of the enclosure ditch.

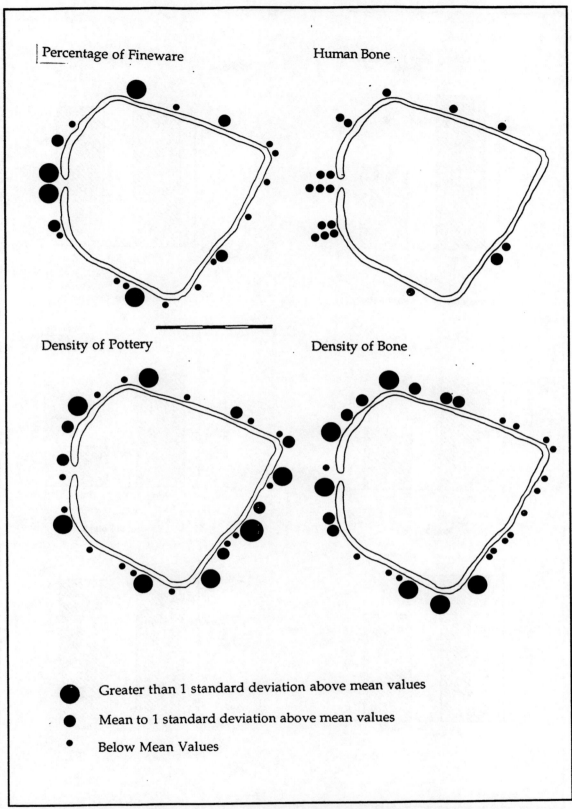

Fig. 8.5. Early Iron Age Winnall Down: Schematic plans showing the distribution of pottery, animal bone fragments and human remains, along with the proportions of fineware pottery around the fill of the enclosure ditch.

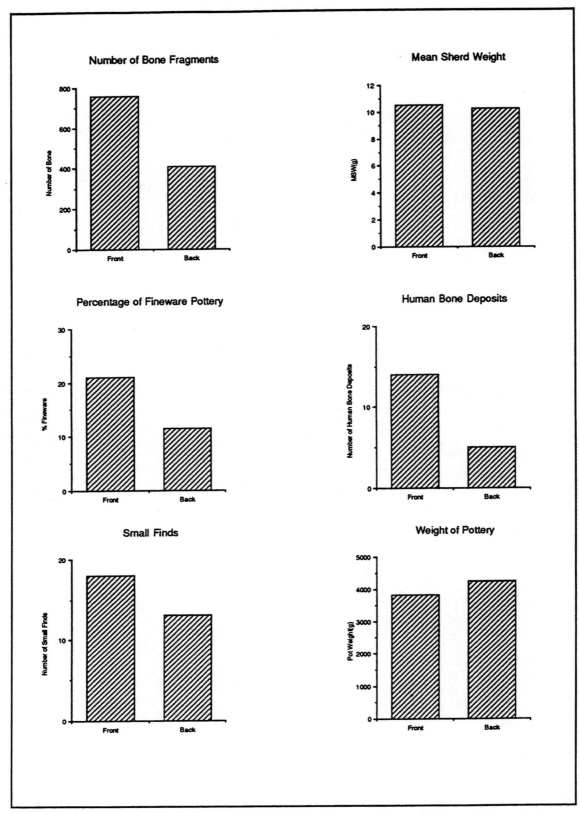

Fig. 8.6. Early Iron Age Winnall Down: Histograms showing the characteristics of finds assemblages from the front and back of the enclosure ditch. The ditch fills were divided between MM&E, KK&JJ.

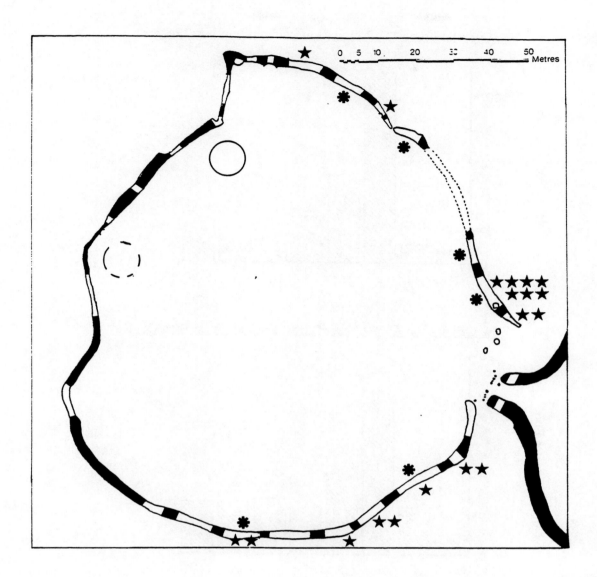

Key: Human Remains ✱   Small Finds ★

Fig. 8.7. Middle Iron Age Gussage: Plan of the enclosure ditch showing the distribution of
human remains and small finds.

The Orientation of 233 Round Houses from Southern England

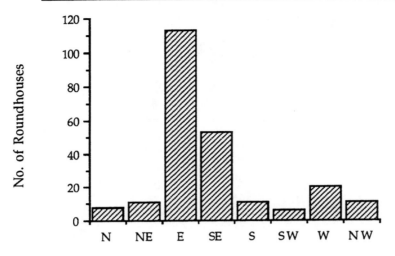

The Orientation of 139 Non-Hillfort Enclosures in Wessex

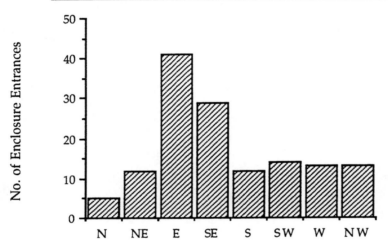

The Orientation of 75 Hillfort Entrances in Southern England

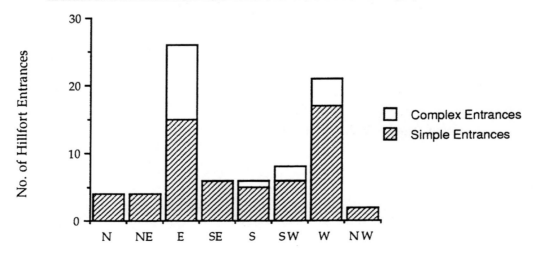

Fig. 8.7. The orientation of circular structures, non-hillfort enclosures and hillforts

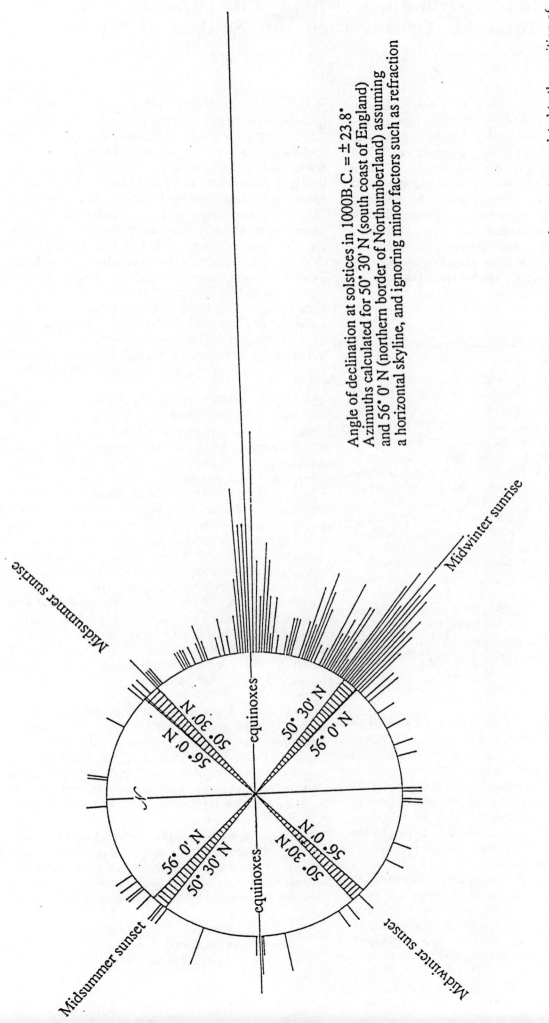

Angle of declination at solstices in 1000 B.C. = ± 23.8°
Azimuths calculated for 50° 30' N (south coast of England)
and 56° 0' N (northern border of Northumberland) assuming
a horizontal skyline, and ignoring minor factors such as refraction

Midsummer sunrise

Midwinter sunrise

equinoxes

50° 30' N

56° 0' N

56° 0' N

50° 30' N

S

50° 30' N

56° 0' N

equinoxes

Midsummer sunset

Midwinter sunset

Fig. 8.8. Oswald's (1991) plot of the exact orientation of Iron Age circular structures related to the position of sunrise.

Chapter 9
Spatial Distributions within Pit Deposits and the Internal Organisation of Settlement Space

9.1. Introduction

Deposits in enclosure ditches were spatially structured and played an important role in the habitus(es) of Iron Age peoples. This chapter will show that similar patterns existed with pit deposits. A detailed discussion of Winnall Down/Easton Lane complex of sites will show the development of a specific sequence of the changing structuring principles and their manifestations at work in organising settlement layout and deposition at these sites. These patterns were not restricted to this one site sequence, and the chapter concludes by summarising comparable patterns from Gussage All Saints and Winklebury.

9.2. Winnall Down/Easton Lane: Introduction

Excavations in advance of the M3 north-east of Winchester provided important evidence for the development and sequence of Later Prehistoric settlement over 15 hectares (Fasham 1985; Fasham et al 1989). Iron Age settlements were found at the Winnall Down site and the Easton Lane site, approximately 150m further west along a spur covered with traces of 'Celtic Fields' on the east side of the Itchen valley. Other Iron Age settlement traces were found on neighbouring spurs (Fasham et al 1989:2-3 esp. Fig.1), while a further D-shaped enclosure was located only c200m to the North-East of the excavated enclosure, close to a possible Romano-British shrine. Close by are known many contemporary sites including St Catherine's Hill (4km S - Hawkes et al 1929), Winchester 'enclosed oppidum' (2 km SW - Biddle 1970), Owslebury (6km S - Collis 1968, 1970), Bramdean (13km E - Perry 1972. 1982) and Micheldever Wood (7km N - Fasham 1987).

9.3 The Early Iron Age Enclosure

During the Middle Bronze Age two north-south linear earthworks were constructed, framing a 'Celtic Field System', which structured the landscape into Romano-British times. In the Late Bronze Age these linears were re-cut, and settlement activity focused at the Winnall Down site (Fig. 9.1). Activities presumably previously divided between houses were brought into a single compound with the construction of the Early Iron Age D-shaped enclosure -- and its neighbour(?) (Barrett 1989a:312). The shape of the ditched enclosure was probably determined by a pre-existing field system perpendicular to the north-south linear ditch, suggesting that the Late Bronze Age settlement backed onto a square plot of land. Quarrying

predated the enclosure and it seems likely that quarries were dug north of an existing boundary (Fig. 8.1, 9.2). The 'D' shape of the enclosure meant that the enclosure was not entered through the acute angle of a corner (see 8.4). The curve of the 'D' enabling the entrance to be sided by short sections of ditch perpendicular to it for at least a short distance. The entrance of the this enclosure reverses the common easterly orientation for such sites (see Fig 8.7), and continued to follow the orientation of the Late Bronze Age houses over which it was built. That the enclosure entrance was directly superimposed on the location of the former Late Bronze Age buildings may not have been co-incidental. Some Early Iron Age activities are evident immediately through material and features immediately outside the enclosure and at the site of the subsequent Easton Lane settlement 200m away.

The important distinctions drawn between inside and outside this enclosure have been elaborated (see 8.4&6.) and are evident in the distribution of dog and bird bones which concentrate in the ditch and exterior quarry hollow fills. Fasham (1985:127-130) interpreted the site to be a "self-contained unit" comprised of four activity areas. Only four circular structures probably stood at any one time, a main porched house -- the major domestic focus -- and three ancillary structures (cf. 3.8.2). A sequence of three porched round houses (only one standing at anyone time) stood at the North-West corner of the site, associated with various post settings and a pit cluster (Fig. 9.3). To the south were remains of two houses and another pit cluster between, while the back of the site contained slighter circular structures and shallow scoops/pits. Parker-Pearson (forthcoming) suggests the site was divided into two household units, north and south.

The enclosure ditch was argued in the last chapter to have been more than just the settlement's container, stressing the importance of the entrance, a front and back distinction, and a marking the cardinal 'compass' points (see 8.4&6). Some of these distinctions also appear to be evident in the organisation of the interior.

The pits inside the enclosure can be divided into four groups (different to Fasham's areas), which can ultimately combined to suggest that the enclosure was divided into two unequal halves along a line from the entrance to the eastern corner (Fig. 9.4);

Group 1 in the North
Group 3 in the Centre   Group 4 in the East
Group 2 in the South

84

Group 1

This area consisted of the porched houses and associated pit group to the north of the entrance. These pits contained the highest densities of and best preserved animal bone (Fig. 9.5). Two pits (2341 & 3111) contained large deposits of freshly butchered bone (Maltby 1985b:98), two others contained 'hoards' of loom weights (2630 & 2676). These deposits can not be taken as direct evidence for the location of activities within the enclosure and this close proximity of animal bones and weaving kit is reminiscent of the southern ditch terminal (see 8.4).

Group 2

This group is in the area of the buildings in the south of the site and had the greatest below ground storage capacity (Fig. 9.5). Although numbers of pot and bone were high, densities were low (Fig. 9.5). Pit 2258 contained the only other *ABG* from this phase, mirroring those in the north, and also a human bone fragment and early saucepan pot dating the deposit to late in the Early Iron Age phase, if not later (Fig. 9.7). An unexpected result of this study was the clear differential deposition of different fabric groups across the enclosure. Flint-grog, sand and organic tempered fabrics, all predominantly associated with jar forms (Hawkes 1985: Table 6) show a southern distribution (Fig. 9.6).

Group 3

The four pits in the middle of the enclosure. At the centre of the enclosure was pit 3670 with poorly preserved pot and bone, but the large part of a saddle quern rubber. The other pits lay in a row, possibly aligned with post structures k, j, j & x , dividing the enclosure north-south (Fig. 8.1). Bone densities were low, but well preserved (Figs. 9.5). Pot density was higher than both areas 1 and 2, with the largest proportion of fine wares on the site (Fig. 9.6) in pits 4156 and 3936 (very large sherds of a substantially complete scratched cordon ware bowl).

Group 4

The back of the enclosure contained two circular structures and shallow pits/scoops between them, like area 2. The characteristic deposits in the shallow pits in this group are similar to deposits in the back ditch (see 8.4) and in Area 2 with low densities of poorly preserved bone, highest densities of pottery and high proportions of minority pot fabrics -- here shell, coarse flint and flint/organic fabrics (Figs. 9.6). The major deposit in segment L in the rear of the ditch was of at least one flint/organic tempered vessel. The only vessel form found in shell fabric was a jar, in flint/organic wide-mouthed bowls. The back of the enclosure was the location for the only two complete human corpses, both infant 'burials', in pit 5777 and in ditch segment M (Fig 9.7).

Outside the enclosure was a small cluster of pits with some very poorly preserved bone, but a few large pot sherds (Figs. 9.4). Bone and pot from the quarry and the features on the Easton Lane site were poorly preserved, occurred in low densities and were generally not well preserved.

The organisation of the enclosure's built space and locations of the pit deposits, like the ditch, were spatially structured. These spatial organisations could be understood as operating on two interlinked time scales. The architectural and semi-permanent fixtures provided the setting for the choreography of daily, routine activities. However, the depositional patterns are not a direct indication of the locations of some of these routine activities, as previously assumed (see 3.9), but were created through brief events spaced over years/decades/centuries. There is a general, but not a direct, correlation between patterning in the ditch and pit deposits, although the general structures, i.e. front:back and north:south distinctions are evident in both. The interior depositional patterns represent a coherent entity, and are not divided into two clear elements as might be expected if the enclosure contained two spatially distinct household units.

In summary, we may imagine approaching up hill, eastwards, from the river Itchen to the enclosure, aware of its neighbour to the left/north. As an inhabitant or frequent visitor we would know of the occasions when the ditch was re-cut, accompanied by the placing of deposits which served to emphasise the entrance and the north/south corners of the ditch. Crossing the threshold, drawing on visual cues, memories and deeper predispositions we would be alerted that we were entering a different quality of space, not least that one's actions were observable and could scrutinised by others inside the compound. We would be aware on entering that the interior was divided into two halves, right and left, south and north, heightened in one phase by a stretch of fence running some 20m into the centre of the site on the south side from the entrance. On our left, to the north, lay the porched house(s), with the unporched house L directly in front -- circular structures directly in front of others were common in later phases -- and associated structures and pits, partially bounded by fence 4 (Fig. 8.1). This would present an image of dense structures/activities compared to the open space of the centre and south. Through most of a summer day, the fronts of the southern structures would have been in shadow, light falling on the fronts of the northern structures.

Fresh bone and loom weights were deposited in the north of the enclosure, reversing the pattern found in the ditch terminals. However, this bone was deposited to the left side on leaving the porched houses as it would have been on the left leaving the enclosure. Deposits of human remains were rare inside the enclosure, compared to Middle Iron Age sites, with just one infant body in a pit and another

Group 1 in the North
Fine/Medium Flint Gritted Wares

Entrance Terminals
Fine Wares

Group 3 in the Centre
Fine Wares

Group 4 in the East
Shell & Flint/Organic Wares

Group 2 in the South
Sandy & Organic Wares

The Unusual Characteristics of the Pot Fabrics in Different Parts of the Enclosure

in the ditch at the rear of the site (cf. the one infant burial at Gussage in the Early Iron Age). The rest of the enclosure contained both other pairs of unporched circular structures and the largest pits. Bone here was not deposited in a fresh state, and pottery was particularly deposited in the rear features, as it was in the back of the enclosure ditch (see 8.4). It was in this area that the minor/odd pot fabrics were selectively deposited. Many of these, but not all, were mainly associated with jar forms. Fine wares were _not_ predominantly associated with the porched structures (cf. 3.5.2&3), but their deposition in features was concentrated in the centre of the enclosure, and, particularly, at the entrance ditch terminals. Again, all these deposits of pottery can not be taken as a direct indication of the routine locations in which these fabrics were used or deposited. Many, such as the fine wares, were deliberate deposits of a few large sherds, separated by years, if not decades. All but one pit in the north contained small finds, only five of 21 in the south. Querns were not found in the far south of the enclosure (in 2411 & 3111 in area 1; 3670 in area 3; 5797 in area 4). Human bone fragments And infant corpses were only deposited in the southern half of the site (Fig. 9.7).

This is to confirm Fasham's original interpretation of this phase, with the primary houses in the north, ancillary structures in the rest of the enclosure. Whether two porched houses existed at any one time is impossible to assess. It is possible to conceive both a single porched house, or a pair. If the latter each might have been associated with one pair of ancillary structures. Although this would imply each household unit using different minor fabrics. Alternatively (and more plausibly?) there could have been a chronological distinction between the use of the minority fabrics; with the filling of pits in area 2 later than those in area 4? Either would see the continuity of the basic Bronze Age household unit of primary porched and ancillary houses (Ellison 1980) into the Early Iron Age. However, this need not suggest the same activities/values/gender division were always expressed through this opposition.

9.4. Early/Middle Iron Age Easton Lane

The settlement moved down the slope c.100-150m, close to the linear earthwork, for a time when Early Iron Age pottery styles ceased to be used here (Fig. 9.8). Discussions of settlement shifts and abandonment in Later Prehistory usually assume sharp breaks, especially where associated with a change of ceramic style. However, Fasham (et al 1989:151) recognised the possibility of "continuous movement rather than episodic phases". Discussions are further clouded by the assumption that all Later Prehistoric settlements were self contained units. Perhaps _locale_ -- "a physically bounded area which provides a setting for institutionally embedded social encounters and practices" (Giddens 1984:118-9; Johnson et al 1986:263-4; Barrett et al 1991:7-8 -- see critique in Soja 1989:138-155) -- is a more useful concept, seeing sites/enclosures as points in the landscape where people repeatedly came together to perform a range of activities. As such, they need not all be perceived as 'settlements', or have been 'settlements' throughout their use. If so, we need not envisage both D-shaped enclosures as self contained units, they may have formed parts of a larger unit, or even occupation and other activities oscillated between the two. Equally if we stop seeing 'sites' as self contained settlement units, we need not think in terms of a total break in use between the old enclosure and new settlement down the slope. Even after the abandonment, the front of the enclosure would have been visible a short distance up the slope to the east every time people left their easterly oriented houses and it is possible that the enclosure was still the focus of activities which might have included depositing the human bone fragments and _ABG's_ in pit 2258.

However, the association between shifting settlement and new ceramic styles requires further attention. If the shift in settlement was simply the result of increasing population why was the existing settlement neither enlarged or replicated? Why did the shift coincide with the adoption of new ceramic styles? This is to focus on the Early-Middle Iron Age transition, not usually regarded as a major change. Ceramic styles were not incidental, but can be seen as created and used in particular social practices which sustained/challenged particular social structures and systems (Barrett 1991b). The distinct forms of Early Iron Age or Middle Iron Age pottery did not result from just (random) change in a tradition of craft production but can be understood as related to significant changes in the structures and practices of everyday life.

Such differences are also indicated by the change in settlement layout. The demarcation and the layout/use of the interior of the Early Iron Age enclosure have been interpreted as a paramount cultural resource. Boundaries only exist as long as that which they bound and define as a natural social unit continues to serve a purpose (Mewett 1986:83). Given the social importance of the boundary, the failure to replicate it when the settlement moved westward implies a major change in the natural unit it defined. Not least, spatially and symbolically not living in a confined, contained, demarcated space would have been an important (ontologically unsettling?) change. The new settlement was comprised of two, probably contemporary, clusters of structures. Whether both social units these represent came from the original enclosure, or if the other enclosure was abandoned at the same time, continuing the pairing of settlements, is not known. Both clusters now faced east, up hill, and were bounded on three sides by slight ditches (Fig. 9.9). The spatial logic of the settlement was now shaped by the strict rules that determined how round houses should be oriented (Parker-Pearson forthcoming; Hill forthcoming a&b; Oswald 1991). The southern cluster was only partially excavated, but is assumed to have been similar to its counterpart 50m way. They were separated by open ground and a curving ditch which was originally dug in the preceding phase. It is suggested that this and two linear arrangements of post holes "formed part of a rather grand entrance" to the northern cluster (Fasham et al 1989:67-8).

The northern cluster was divided into two halves and as on other Iron Age sites no attempt was made to spatially integrate the settlement's components. The north comprised of two buildings facing east, one directly in front of the other. Fasham suggests that the smaller, rear building was a dwelling unit for a "dependent relative group" of the main house in front. The southern structures in each cluster were probably ancillary buildings. This organisation was retained when the settlement subsequently moved, where a grading of front (public?) to back (private?) space is more apparent (see below). From such a valuation of space, Fasham's interpretation of the smaller, rear, northern circular structure is sustainable, but so are others suggesting that the rear 'houses' were more private areas shared by a single household unit, and the front structures were for more 'public' activities.

Only basic spatial analysis was carried out at this site, and there is a problem fully phasing the pits Only eight pits were definitely assigned to the

Early/Middle Iron Age, a further eight contained a mix of Early/Middle Iron Age (EL phase 7) and Middle Iron Age (EL phase 8) pottery. Fasham (et al 1989:68) suggests that the earlier pottery was residual, but interestingly, these latter pits contained more small finds than those definitely assigned to phase 7, and also those definitely in phase 8. When combined with those 'pure' Early/Middle Iron Age pits they form a consistent pattern.

Human remains were distributed to the rear of the structure clusters, the three corpses (1 infant, 2 adult) all coming from the rear ditch. Human bone fragments came from pit 409 in the south and in the north from the southern door post hole in CS2404. A goat and a sheep *ABG* were recovered from post holes in the south (Fig.9.10a). Other *ABG's* were recovered from three pits, notable four complete cattle skulls which appeared to have been exposed (displayed?) for some time before deposition (Maltby 1989:125) buried in pit 329 after a massive initial dump of pottery (Fig.9.11) Various deposits in both settlement units appear to have mirrored each other and the *Mustellae ABG's* can not be easily interpreted as natural pit fall victims (see 7.5) (Fig. 9.10a). Similar patterns are found for the two stone measuring weights, both from pits with *ABG's*, and the illustrated (hence largest?) quern fragments -- interestingly only saddle querns in the south, but rotary querns in the north -- and other small finds (Fig. 9.10b). Most of these deposits were particularly associated with the 'ancillary structures' in both the north and south parts of the settlement.

9.5. Middle Iron Age Winnall Down

The shift back to the site of the former Early Iron Age enclosure was probably a less dramatic spatial/social re-organisation, and may have taken place only after a short period of time. There is no evidence of rebuilding in any of the Easton Lane structures and the low ratio of pits to structures compared to the Middle Iron Age settlement might imply a short occupation of the Easton Lane site. (Fasham et al 1989:150). Certainly, early saucepan forms were deposited at Winnall, and the early Middle Iron Age sandy fabrics was predominant in some pits suggesting that the settlement shifted uphill before the switch to flint tempered fabrics. Alternatively, these pits could have been filled before the Middle Iron Age settlement, activities but not 'occupation' continuing inside the old enclosure when settlement focused at the Easton Lane site.

The new layout and orientation were determined by the old enclosure ditch which was still a visible feature that had to be levelled up around where the houses were built. The houses/circular structures faced the morning sun across a zone of pits 10-20m wide delimited in front by the back of the former

		North	South
Human Bone Fragments		post hole 907	pit 409
Articulated Animal Bone Groups		pit 329	pit 4567
		(4 Cattle Skulls)	(Cattle lower hind limb)
			pit 4560
			(Horse lower hind limb)
			post hole 4632, MS5633
			(Sheep partial skeleton)
			post hole 4573, CS5602
			(Goat bones)
		pit 317	pit 4567
		(Pine Martin)	(Weasel)
Small Finds	Measuring Wgt	pit 329	pit 4567
	Spindle Whorls	pit 316 (bone)	pit 4560 (clay)
	Bone Point/Gouge	pit 238	pit 4560
	Querns	pits 316,317	pits 409, 4567
		(Rotary)	(Saddle)
	Loom Weights	pits 317 (clay)	pit 496 (clay)
		pits 329 (1 chalk)	pits 4560, 4567 (14 chalk)

The distribution of different types of deposits between the north and south hut clusters at Easton Lane

enclosure (Fig. 9.12). Fasham (1985:130-134) discussed the social/spatial organisation of the phase, suggesting six circular structures were in existence at any time. These were arranged north-south in three pairings, one in front of the other (V&E, M&D/R, U&T/P&S/W). A solitary structure, N, lay to the north, separated by fences and four posters (Fig. 9.12). Set apart, care was taken to secure firm foundations for this structure and it lay over the north corner of the former enclosure ditch. Human remains were deposited to its rear and this was one of the only two structures to definitely contain interior pits, the other occurs in house T - also at the north end of the settlement. In both, the pit was very large, centrally placed, and contained 'special deposits';

Circular Structure N   Dog A ABG's and a dense concentration of flints
Circular Structure T   A complete quern, human infants burials, and slow natural fills
                rare at Winnall (see 7.9).

There is no reason to suggest that V was not a complete circular structure (Fasham 1985:130) as it had a complete inner post ring. Structure E was a compound with, its southern stretch following the inside of the former enclosure ditch (Fig. 9.12). Structure D, replaced by circular structure R, was rectangular and interpreted as a sheep fold or shrine (Fasham 1985:130). It had a central position and it is possible to see its entrance aligned to a gap, 'path', through the zone of pits (Fig. 9.12). If animal stock were socially/symbolically an important resource, there is no reason why stock compounds should not be given a prominent position, as has been suggested to explain the large front

spaces in North English Iron Age enclosures (Ferrell 1995).

The main cluster of structures could be seen as an enlarged version of the one clusters of structures in the previous settlement, again with no integration of house thresholds. As at Easton Lane, structures were paired, one in front of the other. At least two of the front structures were probably animal compounds (E and D), although there are problems in interpreting the northern structures in this light. This phase could be seen in terms of a series of bands of space from east to west, front to back. After entering the site from the east, across the rear of the old enclosure, was a large open area containing the bulk of the pits and some four posters. This was the settlement's open, front, public space and the location of the main storage facilities, like the animal compounds, in front of the settlement was probably not coincidental. Next were the first band of buildings, compounds/workshops/ancillary structures. Behind these structures were the main 'dwelling' structures, private space, with largely unobserved, back, space to their rear.

Analysis of pit contents revealed several spatial patterns, including a distinction between the house and pit zones shown by compressing the variability into a single slice across the settlement's orientation (Fig. 9.13). Densities of animal bone drop markedly away from the houses and become less well preserved as indicated by increasing percentages of loose teeth, eroded and gnawed bone (Fig. 9.13). These patterns could be taken to indicate that bone was dumped on middens/yard floors close to the houses and subsequently swept further away. However, the infilling of a pit was a very irregular event and its contents often not a fortuitous selection of the material being produced in or laying around the vicinity. The high densities and good preservation of bone near the houses was due to the preferential deposition of both *ABG's*, and fresh unarticulated/associated bone (dominated by cattle/horse) close to the houses (Fig. 9.13, 14b/c). Maltby (1985b:104-5) suggested that such deposits of fresh butchery waste meant "such butchery may have been more common at the outskirts of the settlement". However, I would not regard pits such as 6595 or 4006 (see 7.9), only a few meters from houses/structures (or 3111 in the Early Iron Age) as particularly marginal. Four of the five dog class A *ABG's* came from around the houses, the other associated with a human deposit in 8585. However, all but one sheep ABG's were deposited away from the houses (Fig. 9.14b/c) as were wild animal remains (Fig. 9.14d).

Pot density did not follow the same pattern as bone, peaking both around the houses and in the main pit zone. The southern group of pits is particularly marked by high densities of pottery, small finds, and sheep and pig bone. Burnished and decorated pottery both occurred in higher percentages around the houses, but the decorated pottery came from just two pits at the north and south of the back houses/structures (Fig. 9.14e). Burnt clay and daub were deposited away from the structures (Fasham 1985:134), while Monk's (1985:115) study of the carbonised plant remains showed wheat dominant in the west, barley in the east.

Within the zone of pits there was a contrast between the north and the south sides of the gap/path in front of Structure D/House R. The southern cluster contained the highest densities of material of all classes. This can not be simply due to its proximity to the houses. Would taking material an extra 20-40m from the northern, compared to the southern structures make that much of an inconvenience, especially if it happened only once or twice a decade? In both groups a similar proportion of pits contained above mean *MSW's* and densities of pottery, although decorated pottery concentrates in the far south. Bone was more frequently deposited in the south. In terms of both simple presence and distribution of highest densities, cattle, sheep, but especially pig, horse, dog and bird were more commonly deposited in the southern group.

If divided by a path -- although movement would not be hindered by a few sealed pits -- the pits on either side could be compared to ditch terminals. Although no clear patterns emerge, the northern edge of the southern pit cluster is marked by several notable deposits. Bone was absent from four pits, but 7372 contained high bone densities, a dog class D *ABG*, two unusual small finds -- a decorated stone weight and a bronze 'torque'/collar fragment -- and two human infants (see 7.9). Neighbouring pits contained above mean pot densities and *MSW's* and in 7399 another concentration of small finds.

The north-south axis was particularly expressed through the deposition of a tiny proportion of the settlements' population (estimated at 75-109 -- Fasham 1985:141). There were two clusters of deposits of complete bodies (Fig. 9.14a). Behind house N, an adult female and three children were deposited in the former northern quarry area. In the southern part of the southern pit group were deposited two adult males, one female and five plus infants. Only those in southern pits were deposited with other classes of finds. Those from the quarry were buried with virtually sterile fills. This might suggest that a north:south axis was important to the site's users. This raises the importance of the former enclosure boundary in this phase. Did it simply shape the organisation of the settlement by demarcating the available building plot, or were its associated meanings still felt?

When the course of the former ditch is plotted over the distribution of Middle Iron Age deposits it is clear that a further dimension of variability, inside/outside the old enclosure, operated. Both clusters of humans lay outside the former ditch, as did the two other adult female burials (Fig. 9.14a). The human deposits inside were only infant burials and bone fragments, except the one *partial* adult corpse in pit 5548 (Fasham 1985:26). Depositing mature human remains outside settlements was a feature of later Durotrigean and Aylesford burial rites. Although the corpses of mature individuals were deposited in the interior of other Middle Iron Age Wessex sites, these were often on the periphery of settlements in contrast to most *ABG's* (see 2.2&3). Although acknowledging the small sample and problems of ageing skeletons, is it purely co-incidence that five of the six complete 'mature' corpses found inside the enclosures at Micheldever, Old Down Farm, Gussage and Little Somborne were aged between 12-22, as was the complete mature male burial in the ditch at Micheldever Wood. That is they do not reflect the expected age profile of an total Iron Age population, in which I would expect more mature individuals over the age of 22. The age profile of complete/partial human carcasses at Danebury is also mark by a higher than expected proportion of 'adolescent' and young adult bodies (Cunliffe & Poole 1991) (see next page).

A similar contrast was made with the deposition of *ABG's* (Fig 9.14b/c). For example, just outside the former enclosure ditch came the only complete horse skull and partial corpse. Class A horse deposits were unusual and could even be seen as a substitute for a human deposition (see 7.3). Those horse deposits inside the former enclosure were all limb or vertebrae groups. In contrast, the only near complete sheep carcass and sheep skull came from inside the enclosure, a limb and vertebrae from outside (see next page).

	Interior	Enclosure Ditch	Exterior
Gussage Little Somborne	F 13-15yrs M 18-20yrs		
Micheldever	M 25-25yrs F 12-15yrs	M 18-20 yrs	
Old Down Farm	M.18-22 yrs		
Winnall	F 15-16 ? 17-25 yrs (partial corpse)	M <15 yrs F "mature, but not elderly"	F 20-25 yrs F 25+ yrs F 18-20 yrs M 35-40 yrs

The Ages and Sexes of Mature Human Corpses deposited at Gussage, Little Somborne, Micheldever, Old Down Farm and Winnall Down

Type of ABG	INSIDE	OUTSIDE
Type A (Almost) Complete Carcass	Dog, Dog, Sheep	Horse, Dog, Dog, Dog, Pig
Type B Heads/Skulls	Dog, Sheep	Horse, Cattle
Type C Limbs	Horse, Horse, Horse, Horse,	Sheep Horse, Cattle, Cattle, Cattle
Type D Trunk (vertebrae)	Horse, Horse, Dog,	Dog, Sheep
Wild Species	Pig Thrush(?)A, HeronC	Hare A

The Type and Species of Articulated/Associated Animal Bone Groups deposited Inside and Outside the limits of the former enclosure at Middle Iron Age Winnall Down

Decorated pottery was significantly associated with human bone (see 7.8.3), particularly in those pits with human burials south of the enclosure ditch. Of the other eight pits with above mean percentages of decorated pottery, half came from outside the former enclosure (Fig. 9.14e). It would appear that both pig and bird bone were contained within the enclosure, although their *ABG's* were on the south of their distributions (Figs. 9.14d). Of the three contexts with hare remains, the two associated with other species *ABG's* came from outside the former enclosure.

Pit 4475 (see 7.9) had a potentially significant position. On the northern limit of the southern human burial cluster, this pit cut the enclosure ditch. This pit is unique through the association between complete adolescent male, small finds, large quantities of fresh pottery, bone etc. Does this pit's liminal position in the boundary help explain the very complex sequence of deposits, the only presence of 'grave goods' -- shale bracelet and bronze thumb ring -- with any Winnall skeleton, the young age of this male -- all other complete corpses were aged as adults, and the only complete bird skeleton etc. ? The former ditch still acted as a pertinent boundary and some memory of the older associations can be argued for, set within broader cultural context which continued to stress boundaries and north-south oppositions. Throughout the Iron Age complete adult remains were not deposited inside the enclosure, although other patterns were deliberately reversed. In the Early Iron Age bird remains came from the ditch and outside, in the Middle Iron Age from the ditch area and inside.

To summarise, in the Middle Iron Age the deposition of material in pits was spatially structured. The site continued to face up-hill, towards the rising sun, its back to the river valley. The settlement was contained within the old enclosure and memories of its associated structuring principles appear to have continued in some form, although space and deposition were not structured in identical ways. It has been argued that the settlement continued to use the former enclosure ditch to express a contrast between the inside and outside of the settlement without a major project of earthwork construction. In the light of the discussion of the Early/Middle Iron Age transition, might the occupation of Easton Lane be seen as a short lived episode to escape the ingrained structures reproduced by the Early Iron Age enclosure? Could the contradictions that built up by changing realities in the Early Iron Age not bring about a gradual spatial re-organisation of the settlement, necessitating a fresh start and location to escape the spatial tyranny of the enclosure and its past?. Inside the settlement a front:back distinction was welded to a continuing concern with the cardinal points of the compass. Certain classes of material were selectively deposited away from the houses, others not. Within these deposits a distinction

between, and importance of, north and south were marked over the centuries of the site's use.

9.6. Other Examples: Gussage and Winklebury

Other sites were studied as part of this research, revealing similar spatial structures to those at found at Winnall. As extra examples, I will briefly discuss some of the patterns found at Gussage All Saints and Winklebury.

9.6.1 Gussage All Saints

At Gussage All Saints (the Gussage I enclosure) a series of north:south contrasts through the site's history can be distinguished using the published material. These evident patterns point to the potential the archive for the site offers for further work. The Early Iron Age site was apparently concentrically organised with a central area with four-posters surrounded by a band of pits broken in line with the enclosure's entrance. No traces of circular structures were recovered from this phase. Greater densities of small finds were found in those pits in the north and front of the site (Fig. 9.15). It has already been shown that bone gouges/'knifes' were usually deposited in pairs in this phase (see 7.6), 8 of 10 of these pairs were in the north.

In the Middle Iron Age, this north-south division was strengthened through the actual layout of the enclosure. Now the majority of the pits and both identified houses were in the northern half of the enclosure (Fig. 9.16). If the selection of ceramic groups illustrated in the report reflects the deposition of large quantities and/or large pot sherds, it is noticeable that all came from the south of the enclosure. However, all three ceramic groups illustrated from the ditch came from the front of the site, close to the entrance (Fig. 9.17). These possible patterns need to be confirmed by more detailed work from the archive.

The distribution of small finds and human bone fragments in the front of the enclosure ditch have been discussed (see 8.5 esp. Fig. 8.7). Similarly, small finds of all kinds were apparently deposited in pits close to the enclosure's boundary and at the front of the site (Fig. 9.16). This included 209, well known for its concentration of metalworking moulds, hearth material, crucibles and bone tools and its possible twin, pit 437 to the north of the entrance, with its large accumulation of scrap iron (see 7.3).

The deposition of human remains in this phase again stresses the front of the enclosure and the perimeter. A human bone fragment came from the south of the entrance in pit 209 along with the metalworking debris, but to the north were an infant burial (along with a bronze balance, bone gouge and worked antler) in 439, close to the only complete adult deposit of this phase of an adolescent female in 435. As shown in Fig. A.9.18, the majority of the other remains were deposited close to, or in the enclosure ditch. At the rear, two pits (428 & 426), each containing human bone fragments, along with quern fragments, two iron objects and either an worked bone or antler object, may have been as intentionally deposited aligned with the entrance.

In the Late Iron Age Gussage I underwent a major re-organisation (Fig. 9.19). Although still contained within the former enclosure, the front part of the site was divided into at least three ditched compounds surrounded by a scatter of pits. The earlier enclosure was still a prominent feature (possibly hedged on the outside - Wainwright 1979:25) and was remained gated. Pottery deposition may have concentrated outside the smaller enclosures at their rear, using those illustrated ceramic groups as a guide (Fig. 9.19). However, this was not the case for the deposition of imported ceramics (Fig. 9.21). Overall, small find deposition was concentrated at the front of the site, around the enclosures, with a contrast between the main northern and southern compounds (Fig. 9.20).

The more massively defined northern enclosure 310, defined by a ditch and possible external bank was probably dug late in the period. The sub-circular enclosure is of a similar size to those of contemporary Banjo enclosures such as Micheldever Wood and Bramdean, and also shares, a possible, external bank, internal ditch arrangement. The area around Gussage is noted for is unusual concentration of Banjo enclosures (Barrett et al 1991). The ditch rapidly silted up and was not re-cut. Wainwright (1979:27) suggests it was "clearly dug in response to a particular need which was of a temporary nature", possibly related to the violent death of a "robust young male" in 285 (this pit also contained two infants) and the Roman conquest (Wainwright 1979:194). The spatial patterning of small finds and human remains discussed below suggest important contrasts between this and the other main enclosure, and its interior and exterior, which can not be adequately explained as a shift through time. While this enclosure may have been constructed late in the site's history, this need not be a defensive ditch and it is possible that the area was previously demarcated in some way.

The northern enclosure (310) contained far more pits than the southern enclosure, although as the ditch cut several inside and out, not all may be contemporary with the ditch's existence. The entrance contained two massive post holes and faced towards the older enclosure's threshold. The published ditch sections do suggest rapid silting, which included dumps of burnt flint, flint noodles and large pot sherds (Wainwright 1979:Fig 21). The southern terminal was deliberately back filled and contained an iron nail. The northern terminal contained no small finds. Sherds of Gallo-Belgic imported flagons were found in forward segments of the ditch (Fig. 9.21). The interior was divided into a central open area, a cluster of post holes in the

centre (a house?), flanked by pits. Two of the three contexts with human bone fragments in this phase came from this enclosure (Fig. 9.22). Including those pits in close proximity outside the enclosure (within 10m), this part of the site contained half of the brooches from this phase, brooches deposited in pits to the south of 310's entrance (293, 290, 289, 220) (Fig. 9.23).

At the centre, one pit (517) contained a tiny sherd of Arretine, two broken bronze brooches, an arrowhead and other finds. Of the imported pot from this phase, only Arretine and Samian were deposited inside the main compounds, a Gallo-Belgic jar in the centre of the small enclosure 25 (Fig. 9.21). It could be argued that imported pot sherds, except amphorae, was selectively deposited in the front of the site. This particularly applies to samian. One pit (302) just south of 310 contained an unusual concentration sherds from at least four Gallo-Belgic beakers and a platter throughout its fills. The only Gallo-Belgic jar sherds, as opposed to flagons and bowls, came from the back of the site. The bulk of amphorae sherds were deposited away from the main enclosures (Fig. 9.21). Other finds from the interior of enclosure 310 included loom weights, spindle whorls (one of shale), and one worked bone object, none of these objects was found inside the main southern compound.

The southern compound was less massively enclosed, with slight entrance post holes and the ditch re-cut. The southern terminal held an infant burial. Although containing fewer pits, a greater proportion contained small finds than inside 310 (Fig. 9.20). At the rear, (139) a single pit contained an adult female and two infant humans. The two central pits (155, 156) both contained sherds of samian (cf. 517 above). In contrast to the north compound, the ditch of 130 yielded relatively few small finds (2 cf. 14), but more infant burials (8 cf. 2) than 310.

Over these patterns a clear north:south gender divide can be seen (Wait 1985). The division between the main enclosures/compounds matching one in the biological sex of the adult inhumations in this phase: the three adult male inhumations all from the north, the adult female burials in the south (Fig. 9.22).

9.6.2. Winklebury

As final example, the distribution of finds within the excavated area of the hillfort at Winklebury will be considered. Fisher's (1985) previous study of the finds from this site concentrated on the spatial patterning within the Early Iron Age material, unlike the Middle Iron Age material considered here. The pit fills at Winklebury had frequent episodes of natural silting (see 7.9), which I suggested was a feature of both Hampshire hillforts (see 3.2). The idealised sequence of fills proposed for Danebury (see 3.2) would suggest similarly abbreviated pit filling sequences as found at Winklebury. Hampshire hillforts have been interpreted as communal monuments which intervened at key points in the agricultural year (Stopford 1987; Barrett 1989a; Hill 1995). In this context, the pit sequences at Winklebury might be seen as deposits placed originally during activities in late summer/autumn, but completed in subsequent springs if not late summer/autumns. This suggests these pits were left open after the initial deposits not just because there was no need to infill them because of low density/seasonal occupation, but because the infilling was intentionally to take months, even years.

In terms of the distribution of pit deposits a north:south contrast is evident, in part explained by differences in the deposits within and outside a rectangular enclosure. This enclosure, 1800m by possibly 3000m was marked by insubstantial, but re-cut, gullies and contained a large working hollow as well as a few pits. The excavation report was uncertain of its function, and little importance was attached to the enclosure (Smith 1977:50-2). Only eight pits were found inside the enclosure, but only two were beehive shaped, in contrast to the large proportion of beehive pits outside (Fig. 9.28). Decorated pottery was deposited in pits in, or close to the enclosure (Figs. 9.24). A higher proportion of pits inside the enclosure contained small finds and *ABG's*. The finds include a fragment of an iron currency bar, a class of object usually deposited on the margins of sites (Hingley 1990c), found in a small, artificially filled beehive pit along with a human skull and two horse skulls (pit 2893). Both the horse *ABG's* from pits on the site, all skulls, came from the enclosure, as did the deposits of a complete red deer, with 12 foxes and a hare, (3825) and the deposit of complete badgers and a calf (240) (Fig. 9.25-26) - the only deposits of wild mammal carcasses on the site.

This enclosure was marked at as distinct, although there is no evidence for a square, possible shrine, structure as at South Cadbury or Danebury, and the extensive 'working hollow' inside the compound was interpreted flint extraction for burning (Smith 1977:54). I personally would not simply see this as a 'ritual compound'; a space set aside for ritual and worship. Rather, we should avoid working from within a rigid sacred:profane divide that leads to either or arguments. This space could both be used for ritual deposits and 'practical' purposes, as an animal kraal etc. An appropriate situation for deposits in a society where livestock were symbolically and ideological important? If so, were the wild animal deposits an inversion, a deliberate bringing in of the wild to an arena of heavily endowed with the domesticated to highlight the distinctions between both?

This concentration in and around the compound helped to produce a general north:south division in the distribution of finds in the excavated area. The concentration of decorated pottery in the north is mirrored is a similar distribution of type XII storage jars. Other pot forms were generally distributed across the site, except bipartite jars which were only found in the south. A greater proportion of pits in the north of the site contained small finds. Horse bone was concentrated in the north of the site, and it could be argued dog was deposited in the south. Only three pits contained dog bone, the only *ABG* (a complete skeleton) came from the far south of the excavated area (Fig. 9.27). Human skeletons were only deposited outside the compound as were sheep and pig *ABG's* (Fig. 9.25-26).

9.7   Conclusions

These other examples confirm the basic patterns seen at Winnall. They all show that the material deposited in Iron Age pits was as spatially structured as deposits in enclosure ditches (see 8.6). At Winnall the changing settlement form shows the continuing importance of several basic structuring principles;

A distinction between the inside and outside of the enclosure.

A concern with the cardinal points of the compass.

An emphasis on the threshold.

A distinction between the front and back of the enclosure.

These 'rules' would appear to have actively structured the layout of many Later Prehistoric settlements in southern England. The four basic divisions can be understood in terms of the coming together of two basic ways of organising space; the distinction between inside and the outside of a settlement created by the act of enclosure and the importance attached the direction of the rising sun, the east. This basic principles can be seen to come together to create the primary grid, so to speak, of spatial distinctions/divisions made in settlements

Similar spatial patterns are evident on other Later Prehistoric sites (e.g. Parker-Pearson forthcoming; Ferrell 1995). These principles were interlinked to form a rich spatial grid, chronically structuring and structured by the choreography of activities that took place on these sites. But this was as much a temporal as a spatial social map; "space contains compressed time. That is what space is for" (Bachelard in Harvey 1989:217 cf. Hall 1966:163). Time, the cycles of the day and seasons, the lifetime of peoples, is inseparable from space in the constitution of society (e.g. Johnson et al 1986:451-3, 485-487; Giddens 1984; Pred 1986; Soja 1989), even if it is rarely given a voice in archaeological accounts were seem obsessed with plans and distribution maps. This is an area for future discussion, especially as the central principle of the proper   .

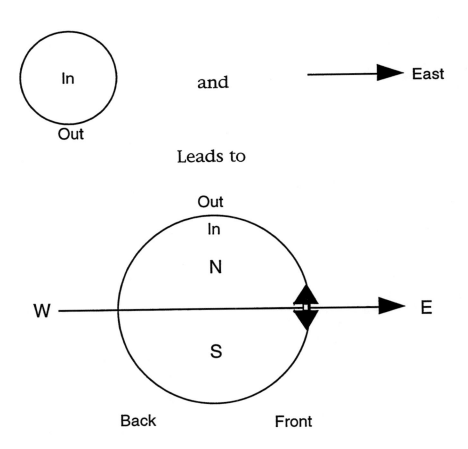

Basic principles behind the ordering of space on a Later Prehistoric settlement in Wessex

easterly orientation of buildings and enclosures, and the north-south distinctions this spatial axis allowed, clearly linked the spatialities and temporalities, and through the selective deposition of different classes of material, the materialities of Iron Age life (cf. Barrett 1991d; Oswald 1991; Fitzpatrick 1991b).

I have already shown that the majority of material recovered from pits came from a distinct, irregular practice and only a tiny minority of the total finds from these subsoil features can be directly related to activities/material laying around the surface close to a feature. As such, the contents of sub-soil features are a very poor indication of the locations of past activity areas. This is simply to confirm the conclusions of *Behavioural Archaeology* (Schiffer 1976); the archaeological record records the location of deposition, not of activities (see 1.2).

This distinct, infrequent, social practice of depositing a range of material in pits and ditches etc. did not take place randomly across a site. In the unusual practice of deliberately depositing material found in pits and other sub-soil features, where certain types of material were put was an integral element the structuring already shown in these deposits (confirming observations by Wait 1985 and esp. Parker-Pearson forthcoming). For example, within the overall significant association shown between bird bone and human remains at Middle Iron Age Winnall, the spatial distributions make clear that this association was particularly between bird bone and human infants and bone fragments in the interior, but not with complete adult burials outside the former enclosure ditch. The spatial patterning found in these pits can be understood in the same ways as those found in enclosure ditches (see 8.6) and I will argue that the location of these deposits provides evidence for the structuring principles and pre-dispositions drawn on in daily social re-production, and suggest that these deposits were a key practice for maintaining those structures (see 11&12.).

94

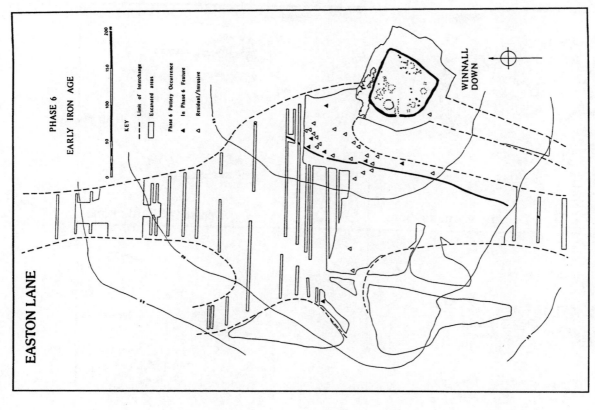

Fig. 9.2. Winnall Down/Easton Lane: Distribution plan of Early Iron Age features
(Fasham et al 1989: Figs 66).

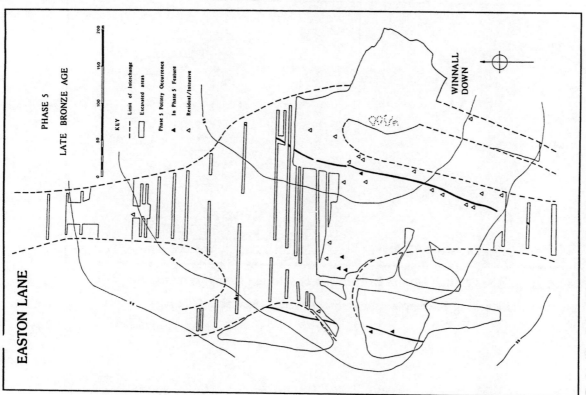

Fig. 9.1. Winnall Down/Easton Lane: Distribution plan of Late Bronze Age features
(Fasham et al 1989: Figs 64).

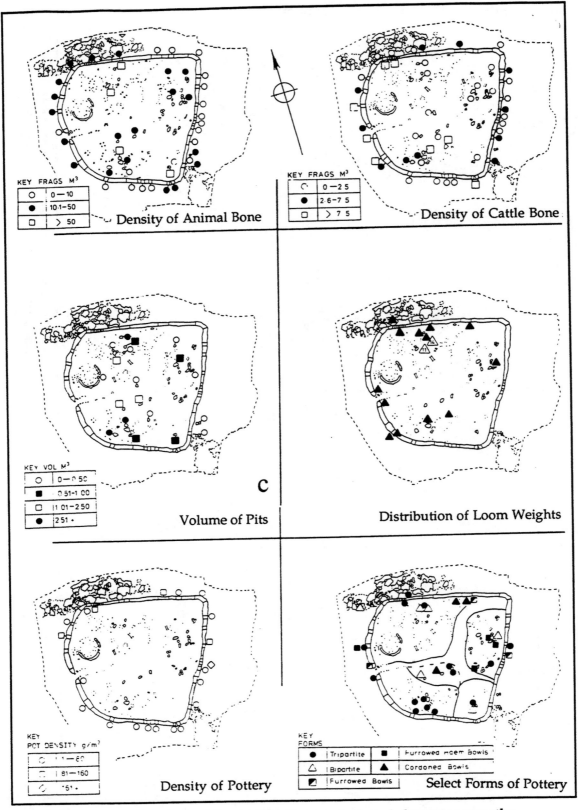

KEY FRAGS M³

○	0 — 10
●	10.1 – 50
□	> 50

Density of Animal Bone

KEY FRAGS M³

○	0 — 2.5
●	2.6 – 7.5
□	> 7.5

Density of Cattle Bone

KEY VOL M³

○	0 — 0.50
■	0.51 – 1.00
□	1.01 – 2.50
●	2.51 +

Volume of Pits

Distribution of Loom Weights

KEY
POT DENSITY g/m³

○	1 — 80
○	81 – 160
○	161 +

Density of Pottery

KEY
FORMS

●	Tripartite	■	Furrowed Haem Bowls
△	Bipartite	▲	Cordoned Bowls
◨	Furrowed Bowls		

Select Forms of Pottery

Fig. 9.3. Early Iron Age Winnall Down: Distributon of selected elements across the enclosure, including Fasham's four *Activity Areas* (Fasham 1985: Figs 84).

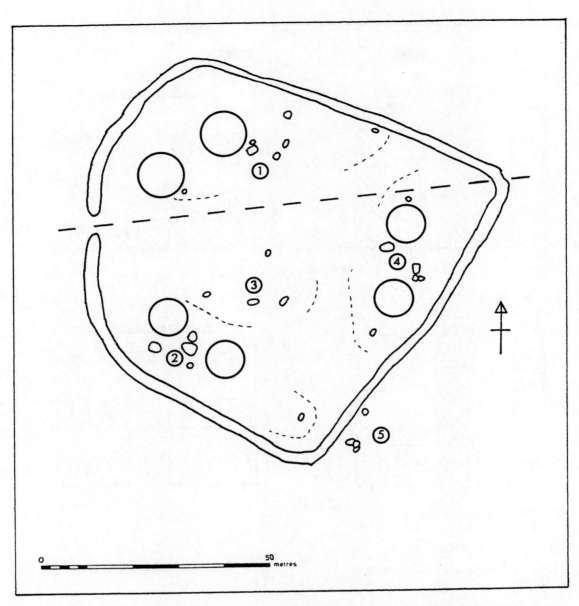

Fig. 9.4. Early Iron Age Winnall Down: Distribution plan of Early Iron Age pits showing the location of the five *Pit Groups* used in this study

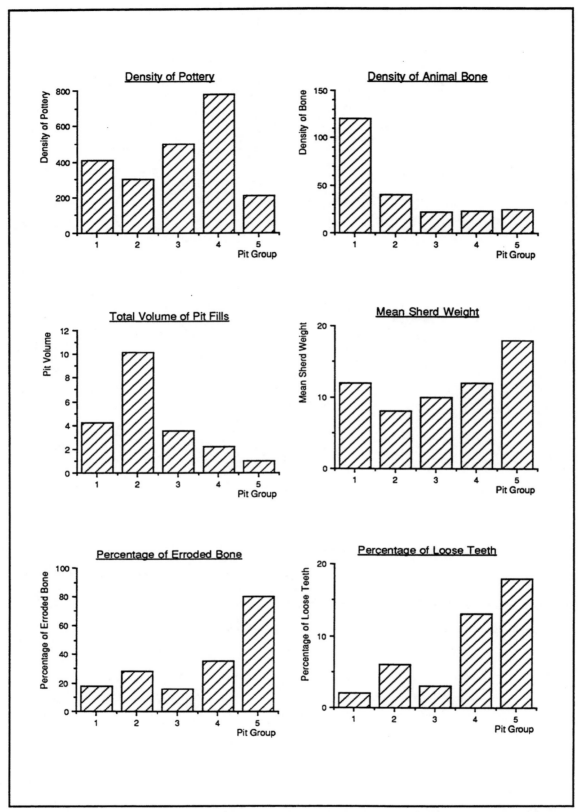

Fig. 9.5. Early Iron Age Winnall Down: Histograms showing the different characteristics of the finds assemblages and storage volumes of the five Pit Groups

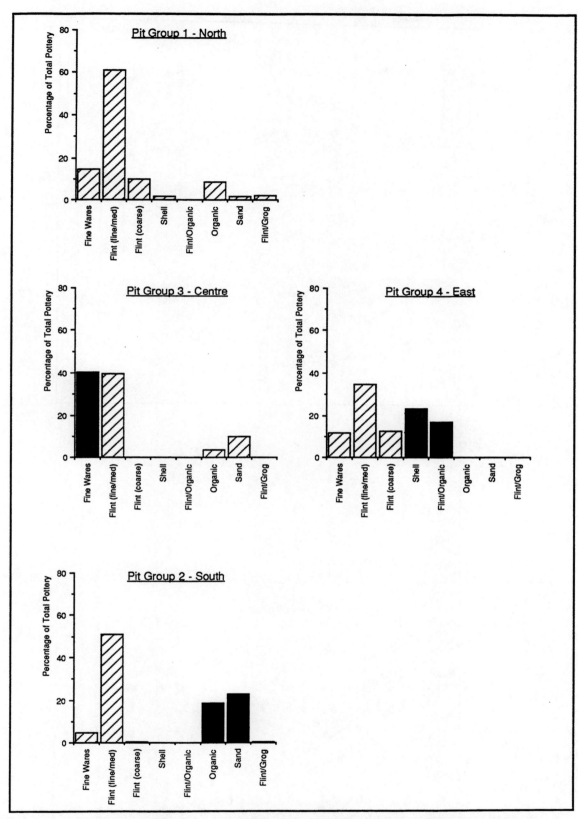

Fig. 9.6. Early Iron Age Winnall Down: Pie Charts showing the proportions of the main groups of pottery fabrics in the five Pit Groups

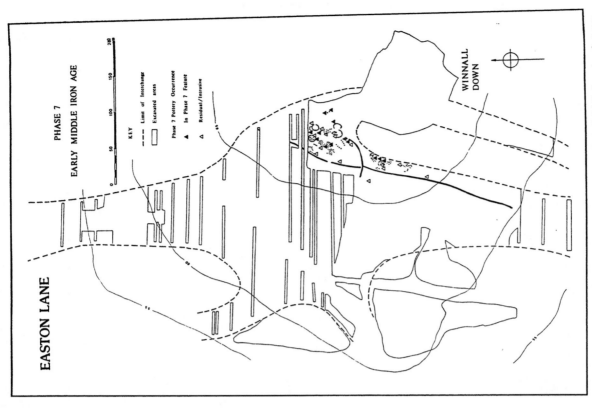

Fig. 9.8. Winnall Down/Easton Lane: Distribution plan of Early/Middle Iron Age features
(Fasham et al 1989: Figs 67).

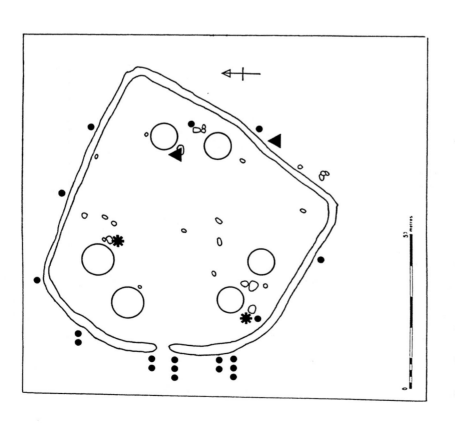

Key   Group of Human Infant Bones
        Fragment of Adult Human Bone

        Articulated/Associated Animal Bone Groups in pits

Fig. 9.7. Early Iron Age Winnall Down: The distribution of human remains and articulated
groups of animal bones.

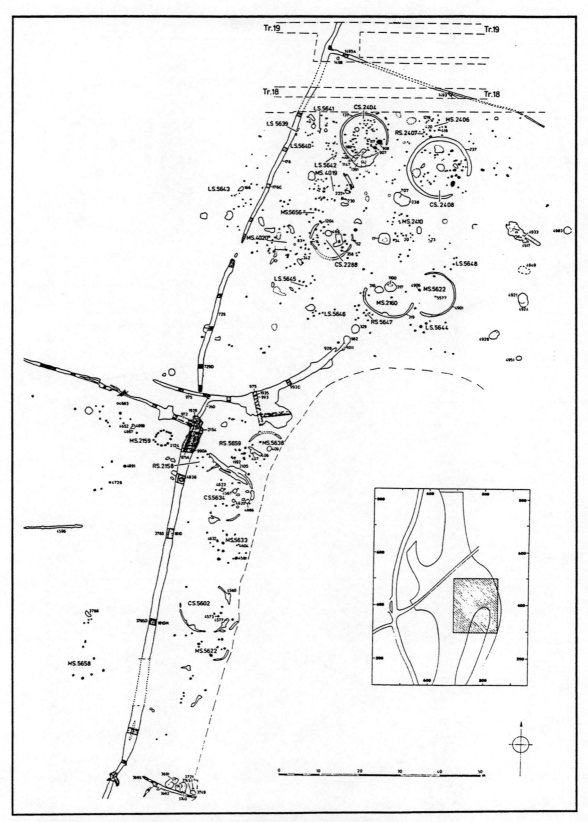

Fig. 9.9. Easton Lane: Plan of the Early/Middle Iron Age settlement
(Fasham et al 1989: Figs 67).

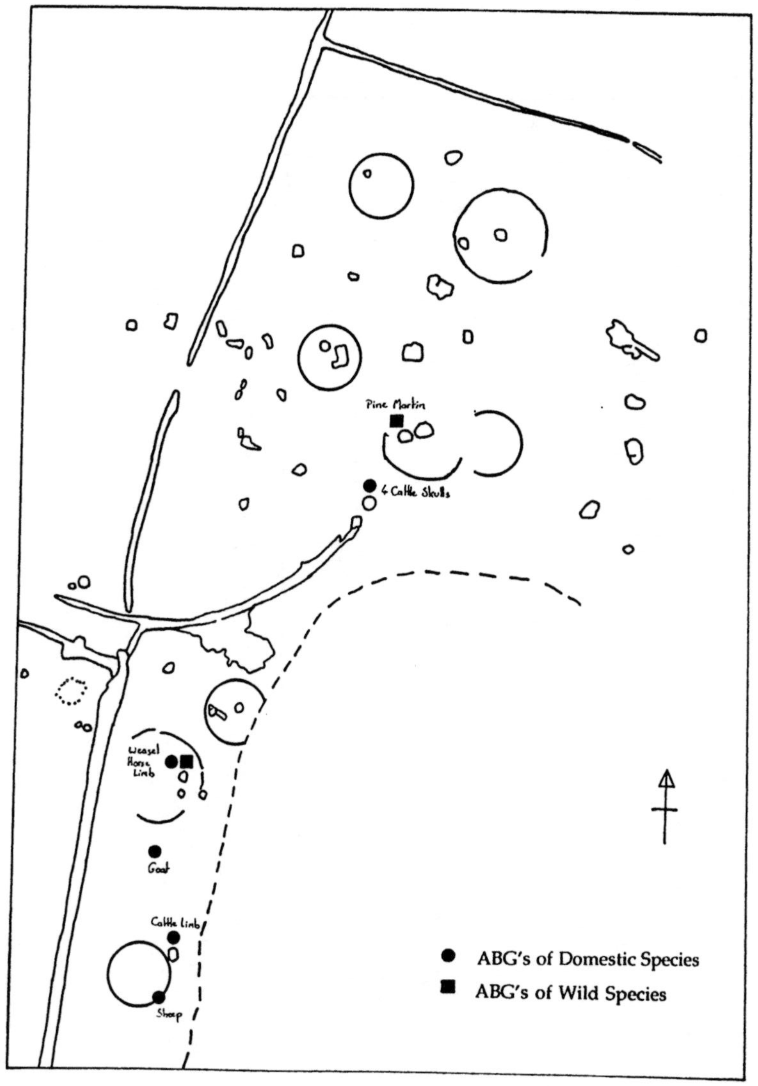

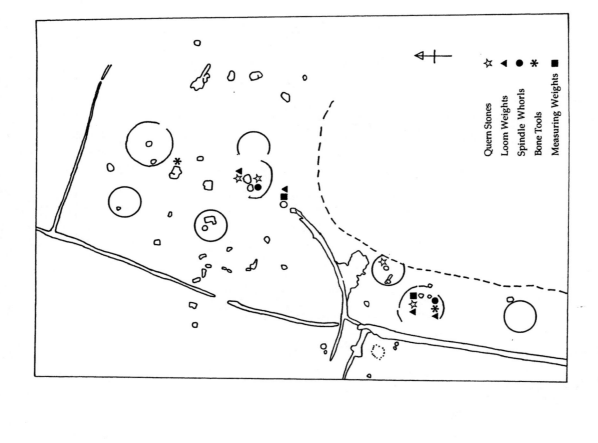

Fig. 9.10b. Early/Middle Iron Age Easton Lane: The distribution of different types of small finds.

Quern Stones ☆
Loom Weights ▲
Spindle Whorls ●
Bone Tools ✳
Measuring Weights ■

Fig. 9.10a. Early/Middle Iron Age Easton Lane: The distribution of articulated animal bone groups.

ABG's of Domestic Species ●
ABG's of Wild Species ■

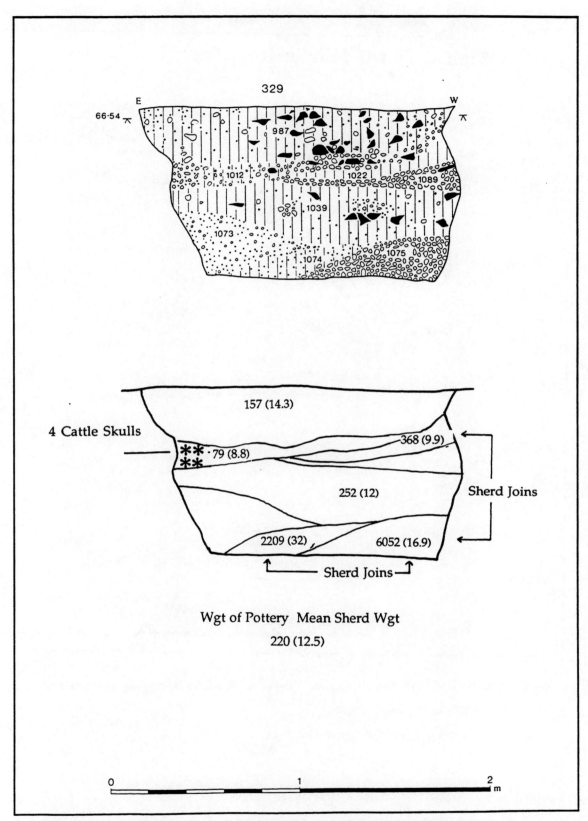

Fig. 9.11. Early/Middle Iron Age Easton Lane: Pit 329. This pit contained four well preserved cattle skulls, whose lack of teeth suggested they were only buried some time after their slaughter. This pit also contained a stone measuring weight, loom weight and quern fragment (specific contexts unknown).

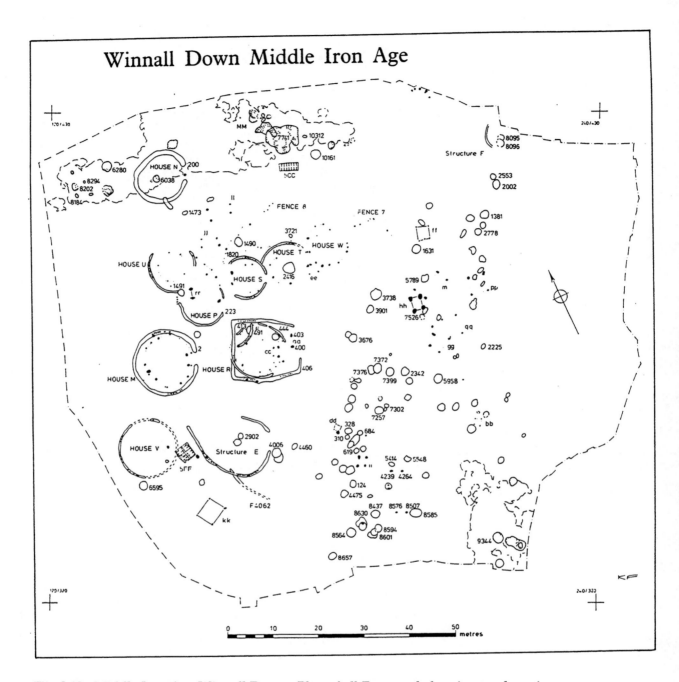

Fig. 9.12. Middle Iron Age Winnall Down: Plan of all Features belonging to phase 4
(Fasham 1985:Fig 15)

Note - North is not at the top of the page

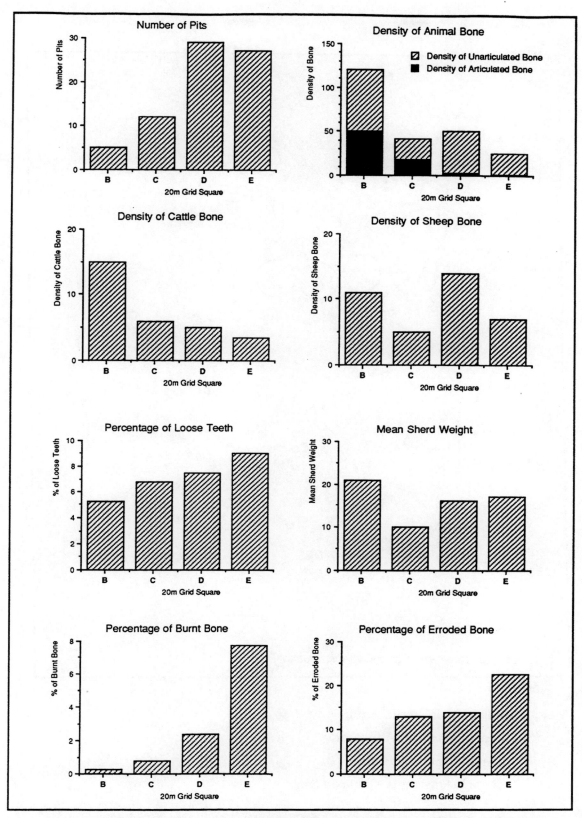

Fig. 9.13. Middle Iron Age Winnall Down: Histograms compressing the variability in the characteristics of assemblages in pits into a 'slice' through the settlement north-west/south east - the alignment of the circular structure's entrances.

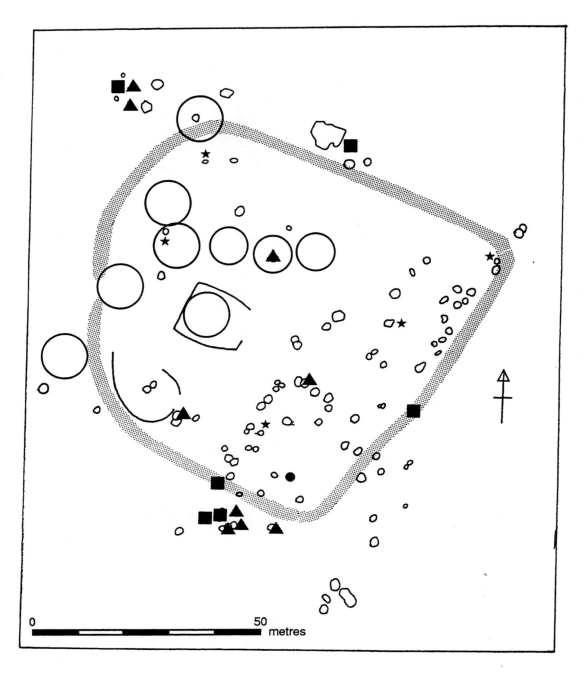

Key: Complete Adolescent/Adult Body ■

Partial Adolescent/Adult Body ●

Neo-natal/Infant Remains ▲

Individual Fragments of Human Bone ★

Fig. 9.14.a. Middle Iron Age Winnall Down: The distribution of Human Remains

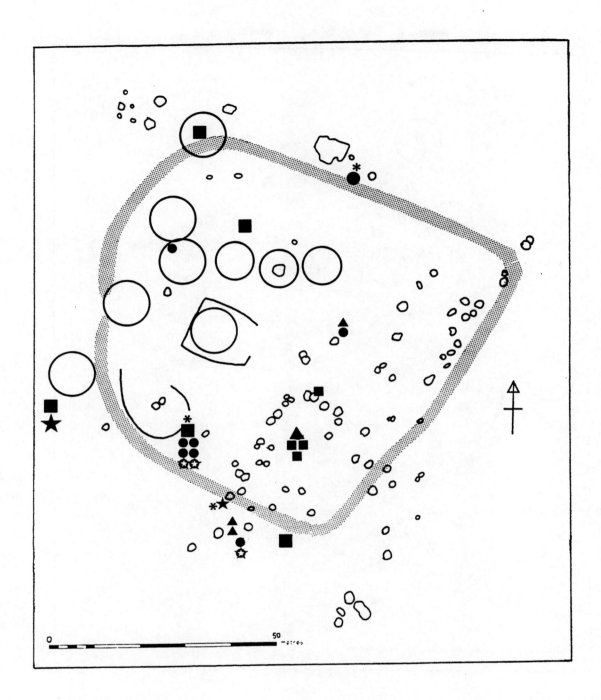

Key:

Horse	●	
Cattle	☆	
Sheep	▲	
Pig	★	
Dog	■	
Bird/Hare	*	

Fig. 9.14.b. Middle Iron Age Winnall Down: The distribution of Articulated/Associated Animal Bone Groups of different species

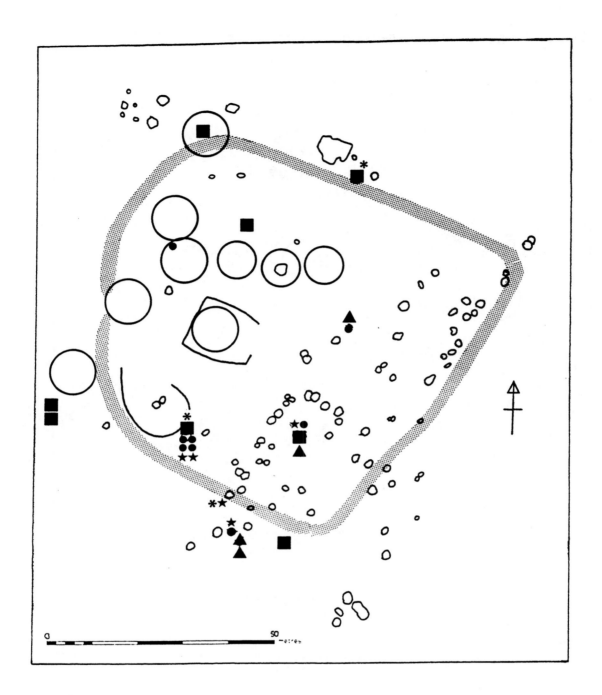

Key: Complete/Partial Carcass   A ■
        Complete Skull   B ▲
        Articulated/Associated Limbs   C ●
        Articulated/Associated Vertebrae D ★
        Birds/Hare

Fig. 9.14.c. Middle Iron Age Winnall Down: The distribution of Articulated/Associated Animal Bone Groups of different types.

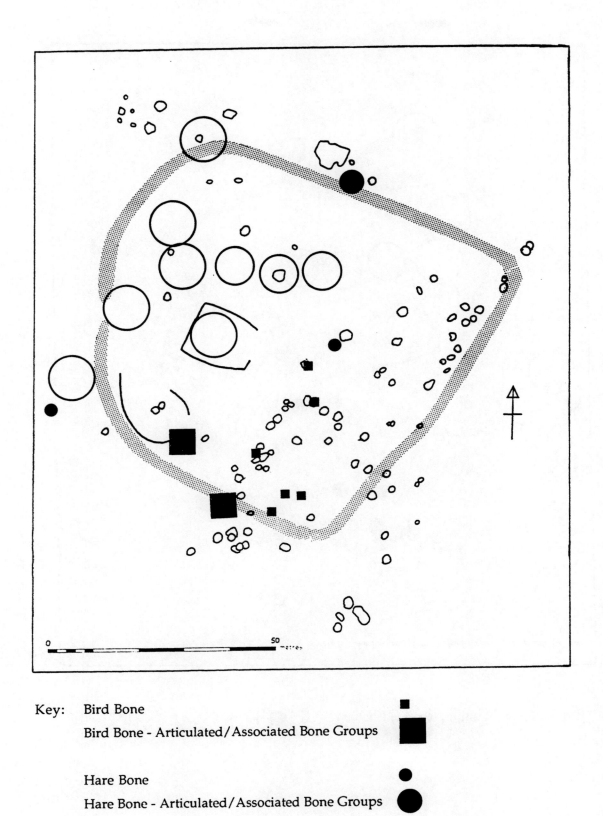

Key:　Bird Bone

　　　　Bird Bone - Articulated/Associated Bone Groups

　　　　Hare Bone

　　　　Hare Bone - Articulated/Associated Bone Groups

Fig. 9.14.d. Middle Iron Age Winnall Down: The distribution of pits with Bird and Hare bone.

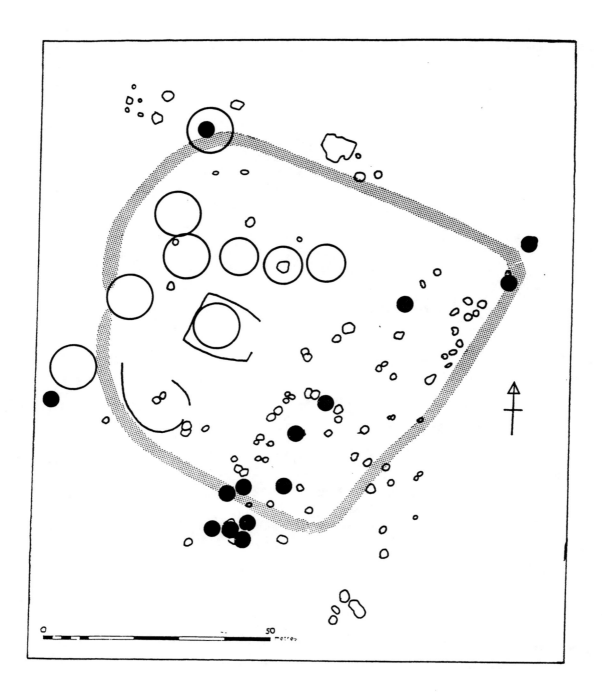

Key: Pits containing decorated pottery.   ●

Fig. 9.14.e. Middle Iron Age Winnall Down: The distribution of pits with decorated pottery.

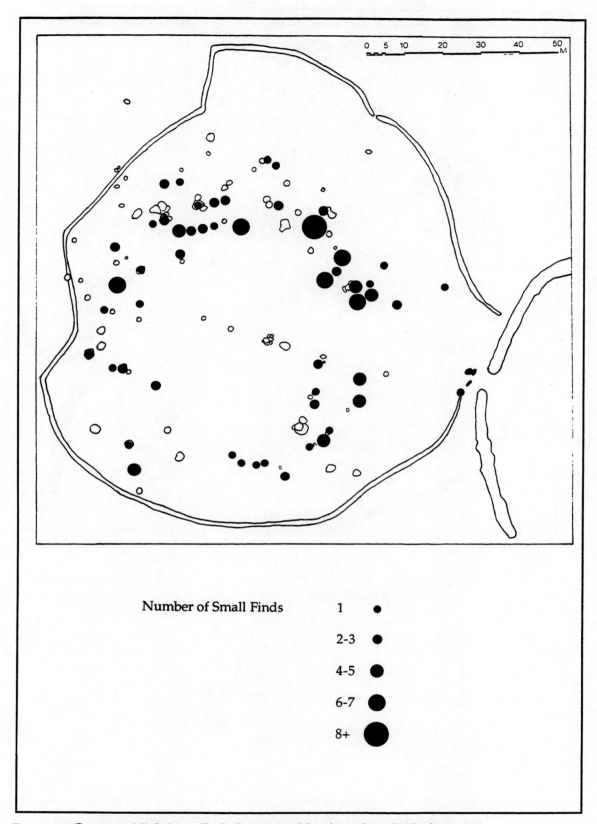

Fig. 9.15 **Gussage All Saints:** Early Iron Age. Number of smalls finds per pit

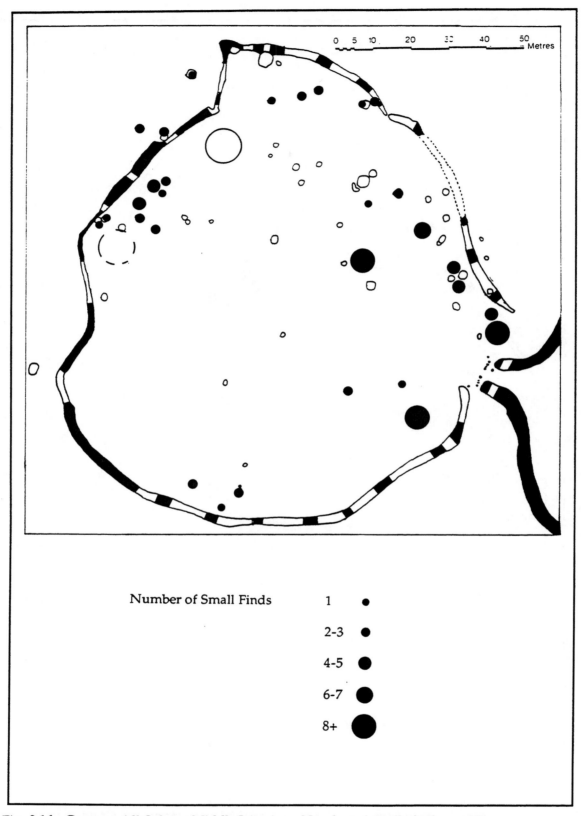

Number of Small Finds

1	•
2-3	●
4-5	●
6-7	●
8+	●

Fig. 9.16 **Gussage All Saints:** Middle Iron Age. Number of smalls finds per pit

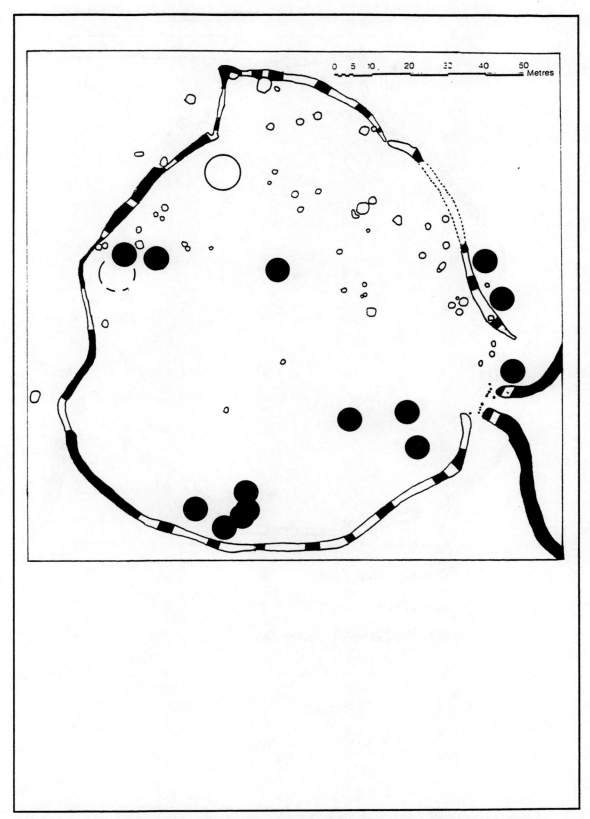

Fig. 9.17. **Gussage All Saints:** Middle Iron Age. Distribution of illustrated pot groups
(a guide to the location of the large densities of pottery?).

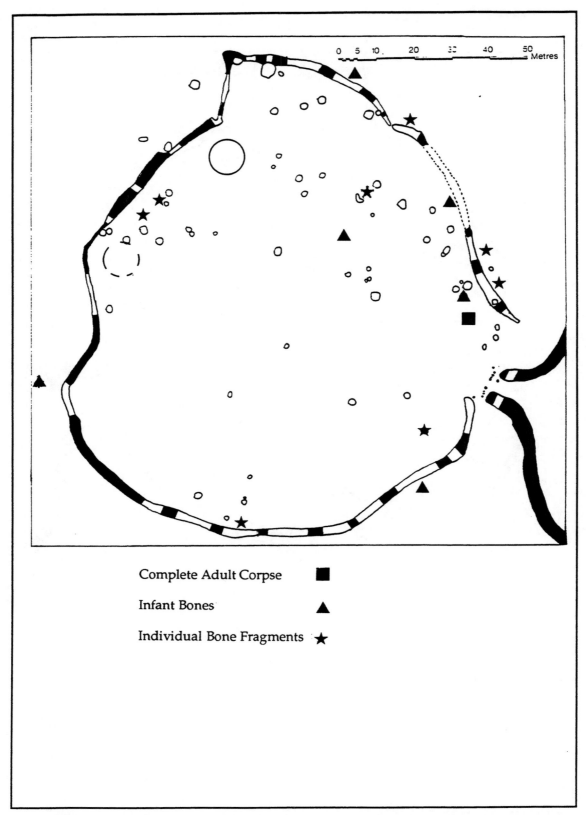

Complete Adult Corpse ■

Infant Bones ▲

Individual Bone Fragments ★

Fig 9.18. **Gussage All Saints:** Middle Iron Age. Distribution of Human Remains

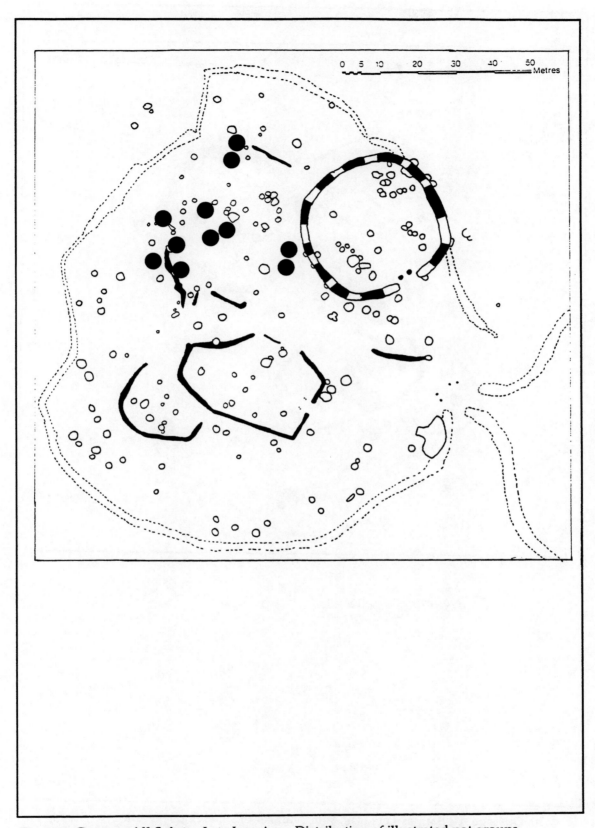

Fig 9.19. **Gussage All Saints:** Late Iron Age. Distribution of illustrated pot groups
(a guide to the location of the large densities of pottery?).

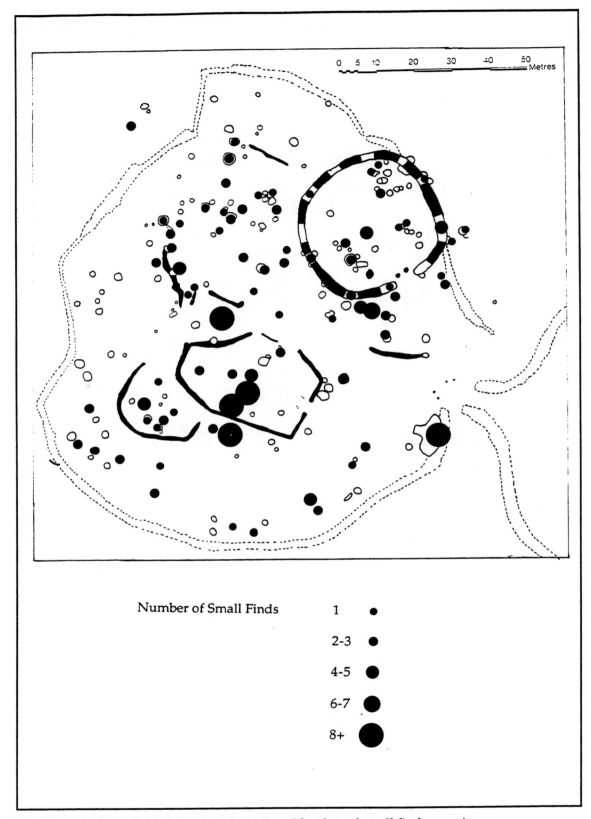

Number of Small Finds

1	•
2-3	•
4-5	●
6-7	●
8+	●

Fig. 9.20. **Gussage All Saints:** Late Iron Age. Number of small finds per pit.

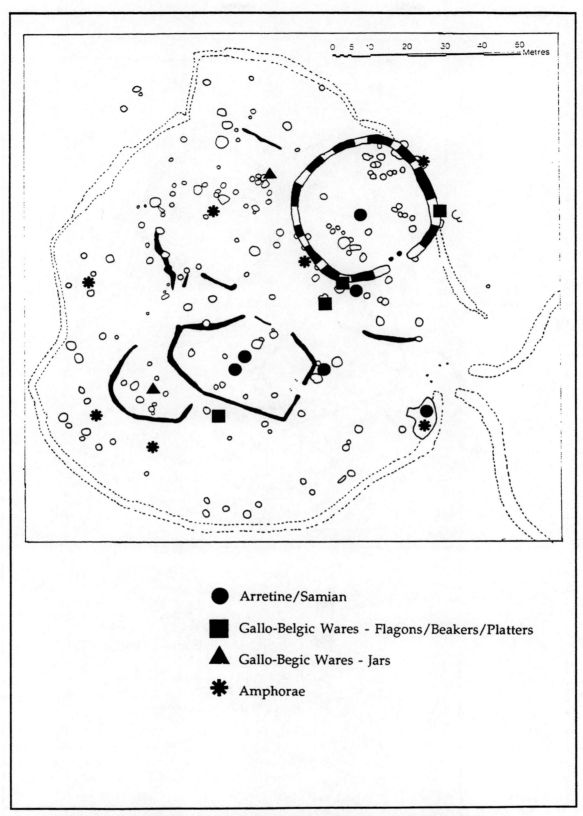

Legend

● Arretine/Samian

■ Gallo-Belgic Wares - Flagons/Beakers/Platters

▲ Gallo-Begic Wares - Jars

✳ Amphorae

Fig 9.21. **Gussage All Saints:** Late Iron Age. Distribution of imported ceramics.

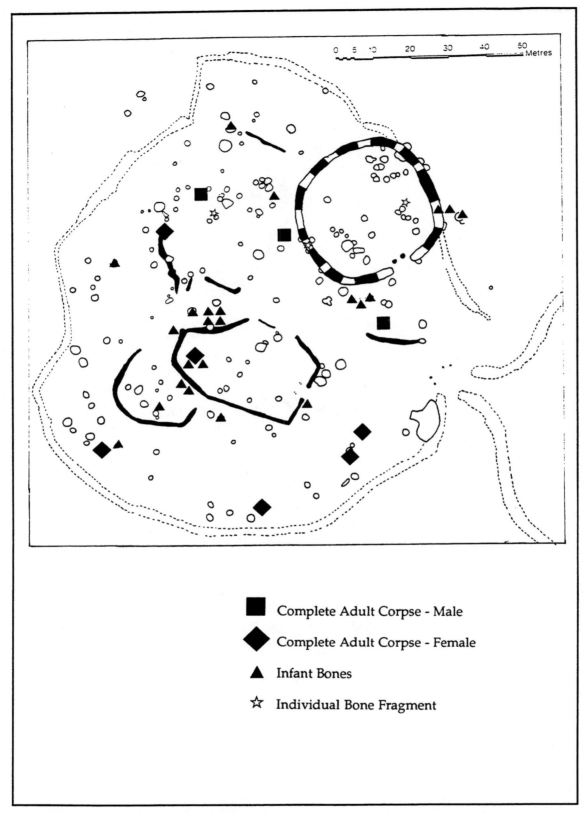

Complete Adult Corpse - Male

Complete Adult Corpse - Female

▲ Infant Bones

☆ Individual Bone Fragment

Fig. 9.22. **Gussage All Saints:** Late Iron Age. Distribution of Human Remains.

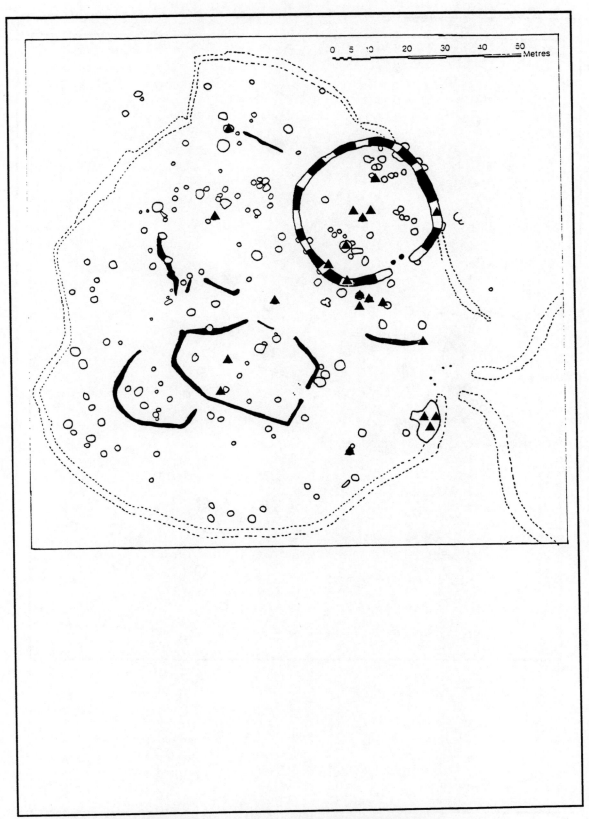

Fig, 9.23. **Gussage All Saints:** Late Iron Age. Distribution of brooches.

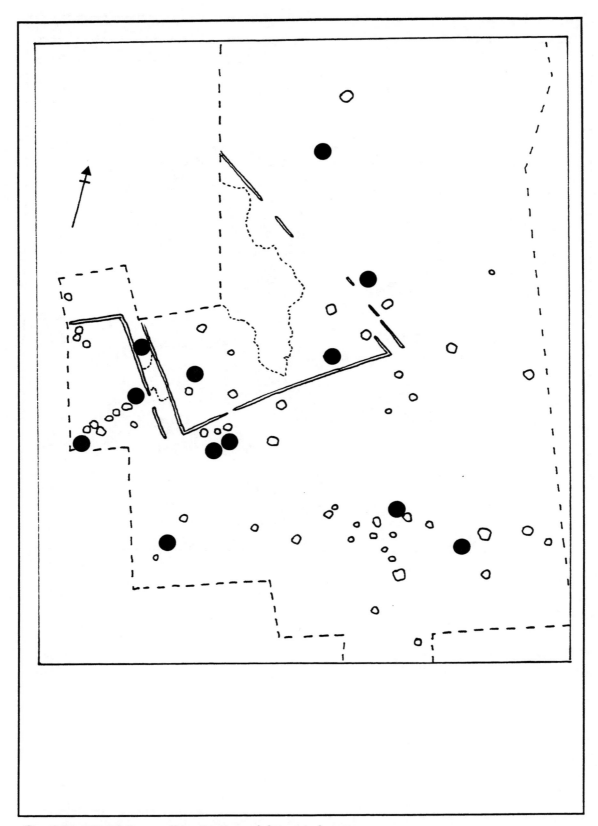

Fig. 9.24. **Winklebury:** Distribution of decorated pottery.

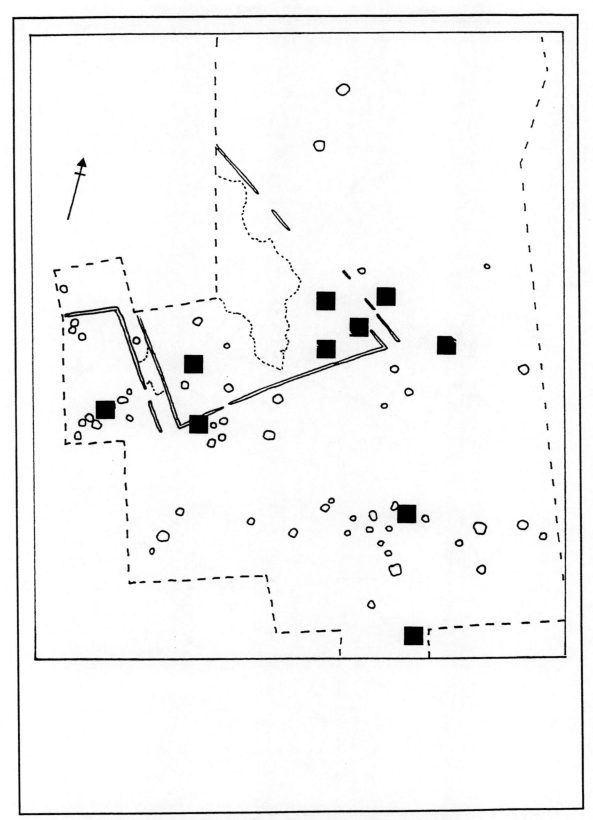

Fig. 9.25. **Winklebury:** Distribution of Articulated Animal Bone Groups.

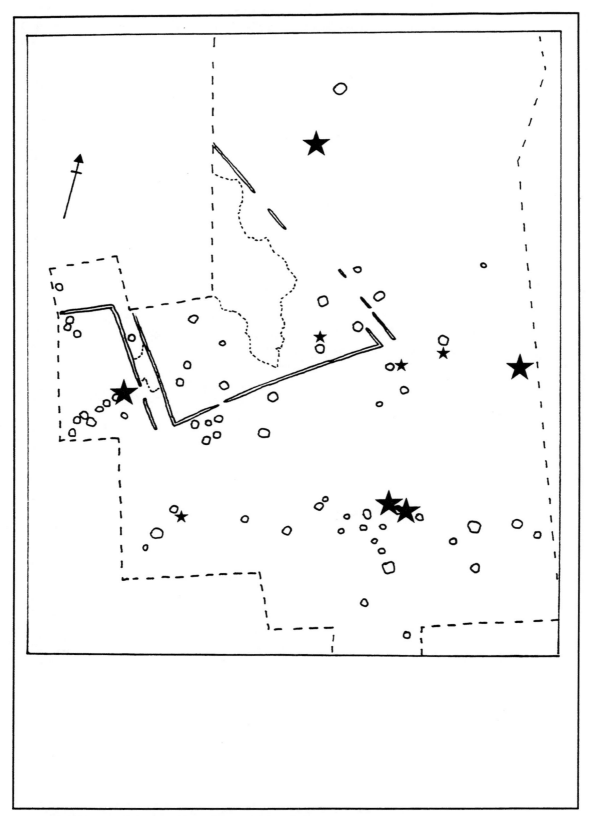

Fig. 9.26. **Winklebury:** Distribution of Human Remians.

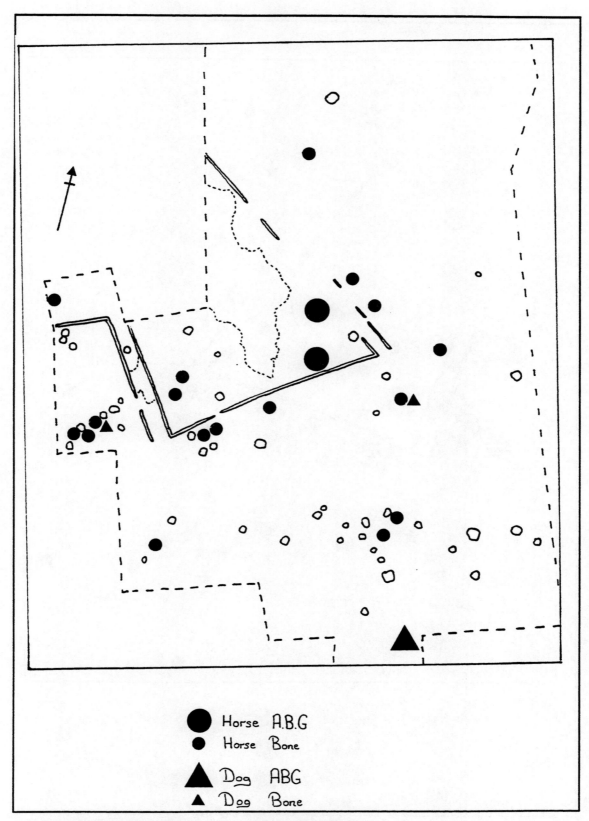

Fig. 9.27. **Winklebury:** Distribution of horse and dog bone.

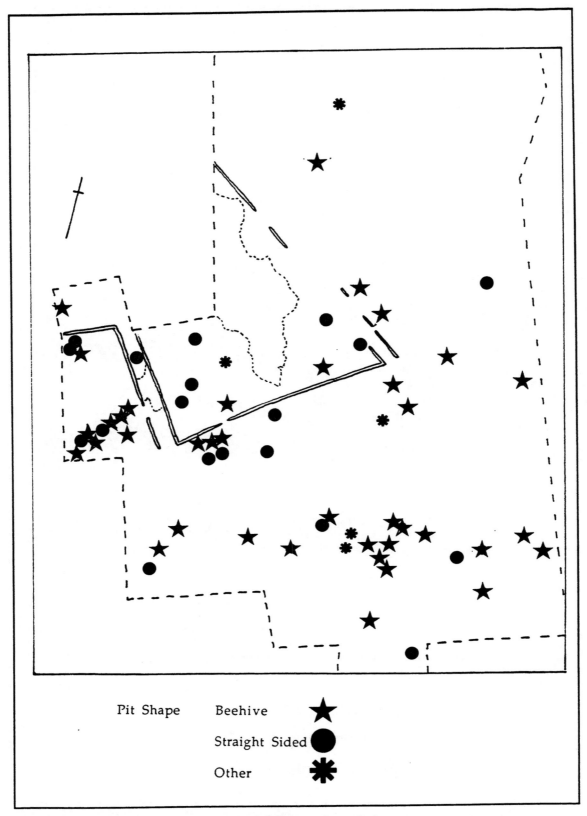

Fig. 9.28. **Winklebury:** Distribution of different shaped pits.

Chapter 10
'Special', 'Structured' or 'Ritual' Deposition?

10.1. Resume

Time has come to grasp the nettle and decide whether these were ritual deposits. The previous chapters provide a 'thick description' of deposits from sub-soil features on Later Prehistoric sites in Wessex to understand how this particular archaeological record was produced. I have shown that only a tiny fraction of all the material discarded on Iron Age sites entered archaeologically recoverable contexts and this was not a random sample -- certain types of finds were regularly deposited together, in a certain order and in certain places, while others were generally excluded. Importantly, it can be shown that this patterning is not a product of natural processes, but essentially produced through the way people deposited material in pits, ditches, post holes etc. Individual acts of deposition were usually separated by months and years on most sites, not hours or days.

Using the assumption that there was an average pit fill, my analyses show that most atypical pits are those which contained what others have considered 'special deposits' of humans or animals. Investigations began considering the characteristics of individual layers, arguing the need to understand these basic building blocks of our assemblages. How individual layers were combined to produce the overall associations found in pit fills shows deliberate sequences of fills, and that vertical differences within fills were not largely a product of *in situ* differential preservation. An essential dimension of variability in these deposits was their location, with certain types of material deposited in particular parts of settlements, but not others. From these, and studies of the overall contents of pits, a series of associations has emerged between different factors which typify these atypical pits. Some of these include the deliberate deposition of human remains, *ABG's*, small finds, certain species of animal, certain types of pottery etc. and represent *a distinct, infrequent, social practice.* This is to emphasise the active role of people in these practices; we recover individual depositional events, not a generalised system of behaviour. These results may have been demonstrable from a detailed study of a single site. However, I have shown that this was a widespread practice across a large area, although with significant local differences in the way it was manifested on different sites.

10.2. Is This 'Structured Deposition'?

In this chapter I will argue that the exceptional deposits I have described from pits and other sub-soil features are an example of 'structured deposition' and should be further interpreted as ritual deposits. However, as I will argue, 'structured deposition' and 'ritual' are not the same thing. Demonstrating the existence of the former in archaeological deposits does not necessarily act as a litmus test for recognising ritual in the past. It, in fact, may be a more secure way of showing that deposits contain well preserved material, whatever their origin.

The term ritual is confused in archaeology and social anthropology. There is general agreement that rituals are of focal importance for understanding small-scale societies, but there has been considerable doubt within archaeology about how the material correlates of ritual can be identified or recognised (e.g. Barrett 1991a; Garwood et al 1991; Hodder 1982c; Levy 1982; Renfrew 1985; Richards & Thomas 1984).

Rather than directly considering whether these deposits were the result of ritual, it is easier to ask if this is 'structured deposition'. 'Structured deposition' was a term introduced by Richards and Thomas (1984) to help understand a range of deposits found on Neolithic sites variously described as "non-domestic", "unusual" (Whittle 1985:220,233), "symbolic or placed" (Pryor 1988:114), "purposeful" (Richards and Thomas 1984:214), "intentional... symbolic" (Evans 1988:89) etc. such as material which Bradley (1990:4) notes, probably falls into Schiffer's category of *Ritual Caches and Discards*: "a residual category that labels a diverse set of deposits apparently produced in a ritual or ceremonial context" (Schiffer 1987:79-80). If it turns out that much of the material excavated on Late Bronze Age and Iron Age settlements are shown to fall into this category, then it would appear that the vast majority of all the evidence available to understand the British Neolithic, Bronze Age and Iron Age comes from ritual deposits, be they burials or ritual caches and discards.

Richards and Thomas (1984:215) argued that these deposits could be shown to have been ritual because...

> "the performance of ritual involves formalised, repetitive actions which may be detected archaeologically through a highly structured mode of deposition".

Although introduced as a criterion for archaeologically identifying ritual, it is recognised that this is not an unambiguous ritual litmus test (see 1.2). Demonstrating structured deposition relies on showing archaeological deposits are recurrently patterned both in terms of associations and disassociations between different types of finds and their spatial distribution. Furthermore, these patterns, in Schiffer's terms (see 1.2), must be shown to be the product of *C-transforms* and not subsequent *N-transforms*. In these terms the bulk of the deposits from Iron Age pits and ditches from Wessex are clearly structured. I have shown a series of relationships and spatial patterns across and between different classes of archaeological finds that cannot be the result of natural formation processes. Associations and distributions showing that;

> "what is significant is that when the material was deposited, it was done in a particular manner, obeying certain rules which were important to the actors involved" (Richards and Thomas 1984:214-5).

However, the basic recognition of structured deposition goes no further than saying this is symbolic behaviour. As has been pointed out, all human activities are symbolically structured, drawing on and reproducing cultural norms and structures. As such any human activity, such as the arrangement and use of settlement space, or the preparation, cooking and consuming of food, is open to symbolic analysis and interpretation. As has already been noted (see 1.2), various ethnographic and archaeological studies have shown that this situation also applies to garbage, its classification and disposal. All daily refuse maintenance strategies will be structured through deep-rooted cultural norms. It will be structured deposition, even if such patterning will be quickly broken down as material is subjected to a range of natural processes (see 1.2).

As such, demonstrating the existence of structured deposition does not demonstrate the existence of ritual deposits, particularly where possible ritual deposits are of apparently (broken) domestic/agricultural material. If my pit deposits were only of complete human burials with grave goods, or just fine objects or figurines, I doubt if there would be need for this study. Fortunately, this is not the case and these deposits, ritual or otherwise, contain material that can legitimately be described as *rubbish*.

In this sense, finding 'structure' in archaeological deposits is primarily telling us something about how well that material has been preserved; how soon it entered a feature that protected it from further attrition and displacement. This is similar to Bob Wilson's (1989) criticisms of Annie Grant's (1984a) initial criteria for identifying animal 'special deposits'; that these deposits are simply of primarily butchery waste that has by some accident escaped the destruction and dispersal caused by normal taphonomic processes. In trying to understand how this specific archaeological record was created, how these 'accidents' took place must be the next crucial question.

However, does it matter whether or not these deposits, 'accidents', were the result of ritual practices? On one level, the answer is *no*. To misappropriate a phrase Gilbert Lewis (1980:20) applied to ritual, any structured deposition is important for its *Alerting Quality*. The patterning and associations of structured deposition says to us, "This is odd". It immediately confronts us with the otherness, the difference, of the past if we are prepared to listen (Hill 1989; 1993), and shows us where to concentrate our efforts at interpretation. This is because any structured deposition is the result of human practice. The structures witnessed in these archaeological deposits are direct evidence for the culturally specific predisposition's that produced and were reproduced by these human practices in the past. Ritual, as practice, draws on the same structures as any other, daily, practice (see 11.9). As such, even if these deposits are shown to be the result of purely domestic, non-ritual, regular activities, the complex patterning shown in the deposits remains. If all refuse maintenance strategies produce what we can term structured deposition, then it must be recognised that the deposits are the *direct* evidence for the structuring principles at work on the deposits after natural transformation processes have been taken into account. It may mean that it is easier to study the concerns of symbolic and structural analyses, than the reconstruction of economy, exchange and agricultural systems from assemblages of animal bone and pottery. Or, to put it another way, perhaps Hawkes' (1956) 'Ladder of Inference' is upside down?

As such, the study of structured deposition should allow interpretations to go further than saying "this is odd". It shows us where to look for the dominant structural principles through which people thought about and acted on their worlds, central to any archaeology of practice. As all human actions draw on and reproduce such structures, simultaneously with the reproduction of society with its relations of signification, legitimation and domination, elucidating the nature of these historically specific structures is essential to any understanding of the past. At a basic level, for studies concerned with the changing cultural rules and norms which articulated daily life, it does not matter if the material came from formal deposits, or was the result of daily routine refuse maintenance strategies. Or to put it another way;

I may not convincingly show you, the reader, that the contents of these Iron Age ditches and pits etc. were the result of rituals. But the clear examples of structured deposition that I have shown, all the results in the previous chapters, are not going to go away regardless of whether they are ritual deposits or not.

10.3. Are these Ritual deposits?

From a basic understanding of the structuration of past societies (see 1.4), we can possibly defuse much of the controversy surrounding the "misused term" *ritual* (Garwood et al 1991: v). This is not to argue that recognition of ritual is a non-question. As the archaeologist's task is to say what the past was like, clearly whether a pit deposit resulted from an Iron Age wife's daily household chores (sic) or a communal ceremony marking a key event of a person's life, is of vital importance for our understanding of Iron Age society.

By recognising that ritual is a form of social practice, an action, might we avoid the hobbling sacred:profane dichotomy that pervades many interpretations? This is a divide that appears to eliminate any archaeological evidence's ability to illuminate the 'real', everyday, world as soon as it is labelled 'ritual' (see 2). These sentiments would appear to play a strong part in many archaeozoologists' reluctance to interpret animal bone assemblages. Is perhaps because they feel any bone labelled 'ritual' cannot be used to reconstruct diet, herd management and the practical matters of the economic? Equally, this sacred:profane distinction is linked to others, such as that between thought and action, the symbolic and practical. But as I argued above, all human actions, including the cultural classification of and the actual practicalities of disposing of rubbish, embody a symbolic dimension. As Bell (1992) has emphasised, this sacred:profane distinction is a feature of recent Western thought, arguing for a deconstruction of these historically specific categories, one of *our* basic structuring principles, and so examining why such questions as the definition of ritual have become a *problem for us*.

By emphasising ritual as a social practice, an action, it is also easier to distinguish between ritual and religion. Ritauls are actions, practices, and are not the sum total of religious life. As such, examples of the manifestation of religious ideas and prescriptions in daily life, be it the orientation of household space, or Medieval Christians not eating fish on Fridays, are not rituals in the sense I use here.

It is often argued that archaeologists apply the term ritual to phenomena they fail to interpret, which do not appear to be practical, technological or rational (e.g. Garwood et al 1991; Hodder 1982c: Orme 1981). Such non-technological or non-rational views of ritual in archaeology and anthropology usually (mis-)interpret rituals as not doing anything 'real' (e.g. Turner 1968:15; Leach 1964; see Lewis 1980:15 for critique). In archaeology it is often felt that ritual is more difficult to pin down, let alone interpret, than other aspects of life. This legacy of functionalism is evident in Hawkes' (1954) 'ladder of inference', and has lead to attempts to provide a universal criterion to identify ritual archaeologically (e.g. Renfrew 1985; Levy 1982; Richards and Thomas 1984). These all stress the formal, stereotyped and repetitive nature of ritual, and their general definitions are hard to disagree with, e.g.

A definition of a ritual offering or deposit, then, is a deposit made in a stereotyped way, of symbolically valuable objects..., with the conscious purpose of communicating with the supernatural (Levy 1982:20).

However, the detailed "check lists" (Renfrew 1985:20) that usually follow to identify objectively ritual are not as universally applicable as claimed. Indeed, they may be usually less a universal assay for ritual, and more a series of justifications for something specific already known/felt to be ritual (cf. Barrett 1991a:1; Lewis 1980:6). Thus, Levy's (1982) criteria for defining ritual deposits of Danish Bronze Age metalwork are not applicable to my material, or even to all Bronze Age hoards (Bradley 1990:10).

Yet, despite the supposed difficulty and insecurity over identifying ritual, (the same) archaeologists show little hesitation in finding and interpreting ritual in the past. Here the schizophrenic quality of the term ritual is most keenly felt. The ability to provide a neat identification of ritual would surprise most anthropologists amongst whom there is "the widest possible disagreement as to how the word ritual should be used and how the performance of ritual should be understood" (Leach 1968:526 cf. Goody 1961, 1977; S.Moore & Meyerhoff 1977; see Bell 1993; Lewis 1980:6-38 & Bloch 1986:1-11 for summaries of these arguments). Yet, like archaeologists, most social anthropologists have little problem studying specific rituals in the context of the specific societies they study, even if there is disagreement over their interpretations of these rituals. No one, to my knowledge, has ever suggested a Neur sacrifice, or a Christian wedding were not rituals.

This is to suggest that ritual is not difficult to *recognise* or *study*, even if it might be impossible to *identify* or *define* ritual's essential form or qualities. This suggests to me two, overlapping, approaches.

1). Recognising that it has proven impossible to define a universally applicable rigorous definition, or 'litmus test', for ritual we should concentrate on interpreting the specific material at hand, rather than wasting further time in pursuit of the unobtainable.

2). Rather than searching for a universal definition of 'ritual', we could outline more clearly what each of us has in mind when we use the word 'ritual' by giving examples of the sorts of social practices in different societies we recognise as rituals -- and then studying different accounts and interpretations of such 'rituals' to prompt and inspire us how to approach the social practices we study. This is to suggest that we could all probably agree on a common list of social practices in different cultures we would call rituals (Parkin 1992:15); "There is a central area of general agreement, it is the periphery and the boundaries that are dispute" (Lewis 1980:7). When using ritual here I am thinking about social practices such the Merina ceremony of the royal bath (Bloch 1987), a Nembu Isoma ceremony (Turner 1967), a Nuer cattle sacrifice (Evans-Pritchard 1956), a Berawan funeral (Huntingdon & Metcalf 1979), or a Anglican wedding service.

This is not to argue for an universal definition, but rather to see ritual as a <u>polythetic concept</u> encompassing a multiplicity of phenomena between which there are overlapping family resemblances but no fixed criterion (Parkin 1991:218).

I take *some* of these family resemblance's *could* include (after Gerholm 1988:198ff);

Formal, rigidly prescribed action

A finite province of meaning - exclusive from mundane /everyday

Practices which focus and intensify attention

Doing things - instrumental action guided by people's interests in controlling and regulating the world, man-made and natural.

These are not the platonic essence of ritual which a cross-cultural, universalising archaeology can bottle as a middle range theory. Rather they are a starting point in the interpretation of specific practices. They are generalities which should be increasingly critically examined and pushed to the back if the study is successful in understanding the nature, context and history of these particular southern English Iron Age practices (cf. Barrett 1991a:1). This is again to focus on the specific practices in question, trying to understanding their nature and context, rather than seeing the central issue as whether these practices were, or were not, rituals. The latter is a "taxonomic enterprise" (Bell 1993:69) which can only be answered yes or no.

The problem in this particular case is the apparently 'domestic' character of both the location and nature of the deposits (cf. Renfrew 1985:21). Or rather, the problem is the straight-jacket of the sacred:profane dichotomy evident in previous discussions of this material (see above & 2.5). Although first articulated by Durkheim (1915), the opposition between sacred and profane is an important feature of western thought. It is historically specific and in other cultures "most people in most societies have the haziest ideas about the distinction... between sacred and profane" (Leach 1968:523). The sacred is a relational concept with no fixed boundaries (Van Gennep 196:12-13) and in other cultures the sacred and profane need not be mutually exclusive. For example, Parkin (1991:7) has argued that the Giriama of Kenya think in terms of more or less sacredness.

The distinction of ritual from non-ritual practice is usually wrongly equated with the sacred:profane opposition. Neither the content nor location of ritual need be clearly distinct from profane activities. It is perfectly possible to have ritual practices which used and deposited daily domestic garbage (just as it is perfectly possible for human remains to be treated just as rubbish). In such situations, it is not what was being deposited or where it was deposited that can be used as criterion for identifying this deposit as ritual, and that as not. I would suggest it is how the deposit was created.

This is to see *ritual as a particular form of practice* distinct from everyday practices which typify the ordinary, the commonplace, the routine, but which are still practices. Such a position stresses that ritual does not belong in a box separate from other activities. It drew on and reproduced structures, habituses, like other practices, but in a somewhat different manner (J. Turner 1992). This argument also supports recent discussions that suggest that theories of social practice need to consider the differing ways different social practices reproduced structure and the constitution of society. Or as Kelly and Kaplan (1990:141) ask: What is the place of ritual, and structure, in practice?

The distinction between rituals (as I have defined them above) and mundane, daily, activities is often stressed by discussion of the formality, repetition and stereotyped nature of rituals. However, emphasising these aspects of ritual presents problems. It may tend to cast ritual as constrained action, and consequently see non-ritual action as more free (a possible danger with Barrett 1991a, 1994?). As the problems structured deposition encounter in demonstrating ritual show, stereotyped behaviour is found in mundane activities. Indeed, repetition and routinisation (whatever is done habitually) are *the character* of everyday activity (Giddens 1984:xxii&84).

In most mundane social practices people are usually only tacitly aware of the skills and procedures involved. Such actions are performed without direct motivation, their change usually unintended (Giddens 1979:59, 218). Daily routine activities are largely a realm of *practical consciousness*, i.e. "what actors know (believe) about social conditions, including especially the conditions of their own actions, but cannot express" (Giddens 1984), which can be distinguished from *discursive consciousness*, i.e. "a level of awareness determined by the ability to put things into words" (I. Cohen 1987:286; cf. Giddens 1984:41-5). Discursive consciousness is also the ability to be aware of, explicit about, reflect upon, and consciously attempt to change the nature of practices and the structures which are their

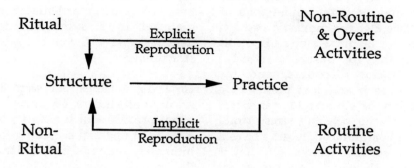

Ritual		Non-Routine & Overt Activities
	Explicit Reproduction	
Structure	→ Practice	
Non- Ritual	Implicit Reproduction	Routine Activities

<u>The relationship between 'ritual' and 'non-ritual' practices in terms of how they reproduce social structures in differing ways</u>

medium and outcome. Here may lie a potential difference between ritual and non-ritual practice, one again not concentrating on the content of ritual. This can be compared with Barrett's (1991a, 1994) distinction between ritual and non-ritual discourse as being text-like and speech-like still does.

The sorts of practices I see as ritual (listed above) share much with mundane activities. Indeed it would be surprising if animal sacrifice and feasting did not share similar technologies, procedures and metaphorical links with more mundane cuisine (see 11.2, 11.9). As such ritual draws from and reproduces the same generative principles as other social practices (J.Turner 1992). Rather, what may distinguish rituals from everyday activities is the way in which these generative principles, metaphors, symbolic structures, are drawn on and reproduced. In daily situations, such structures, habitual actions, are drawn on and reproduced with little or no reflection. They are habits. But in ritual, the underlying metaphors and linkages, the religious basis so to speak, of these actions or the use of space etc. are exposed far more overtly. The same categories of animate and inanimate things encountered in everyday life are used, but according to more stringent, stronger, combinatorial rules (Traube 1984:21-3, C.Hugh-Jones 1978) (see 11.9). This is to distinguish some practices, including those that I would see as rituals, on the basis of the *degree* of explicit reproduction of structure. It implies a gradation between ritual and non-ritual, practices explicitly and implicitly reproducing structures.

Here the irregularity of these deposits is essential. It is this separation from daily/other activities which Bell (1993:74) calls *Ritualisation* and is often strongly marked by the formal behaviour,

forms of speech, movement etc. It is such features that distinguish rituals from riots, another class of irregular, non-mundane, activity, and are part of the alerting quality of ritual -- to use Lewis's term properly. In such situations the rules and sequence of the event are clear and explicit to the participants creating a peculiar arena where gestures and actions may have a significance they would not have otherwise have (Lewis 1980:7&20). Formalised behaviour may also be necessary because participants are less secure of their tacit knowledges of how to go on in these situations. While the discussion of structured deposition shows the problems of using the existence of repetitive, symbolic patterning to demonstrate ritual, one approach is to go into more detail about the nature of the events that created the deposits. This is not to treat the material just as patterns on site plans, however pretty and revealing they are. Rather, it is to consider in detail, using all the available evidence, how the specific material in a specific feature actually ended up there. It is here that both the 'formality', consideration, care and overt/strong statement of symbolic structuring principles can be discerned, as, in cases, can something of the scale and planning of the event (e.g. Winnall 6595; see 7.9). This is not an exercise in empathy, but simply reconstruction fully as possible terms of the history of individual features and their fills.

As such I am arguing that rituals are one situation which are far more discursive than routine daily activities, although the degree and nature of this discursive element will vary between different participants (and non-participants). The infrequency of the events has been particularly stressed here, because I am trying to understand practices separated by probably years in most circumstances. Clearly, the less frequent the activity, the more distinctive, alerting and discursive it will be.

Ritual is just a form of practice and, as such, certain things called rituals may be better understood as habitual daily practices e.g. the monastic routine, hand shakes on meeting, or prayers at daily meals etc. This is similar to Barrett's (1991a) characterisation of ritual discourse, and his distinction between speech and text points to a similar characterisation of ritual and non-ritual practice, although this may possibly stress ritual too much as a form of communication and not as a technology which does real things (cf. Lewis 1980:16). Although both ritual and non-ritual practices draw on and reproduce the same structures, the overt, alerting quality of ritual results in a more precise, heavy manner, than in routine activities, where the duality of structure is more variable and fuzzy; "ritual is a piece of frozen objectified social action, with all contingency and indeterminacy reduced to a minimum" (Harrison 1992:235).

With these guidelines let us return to the deposits in pits, ditches and other features. When recognising ritual archaeologically I have argued we must consider form not content, suggesting it is what is done with the content and how that matters. I particularly stressed the irregular nature of ritual and the separation from the mundane and everyday. The infilling of a pit or ditch was not a daily event. As perhaps only a third of all pits contain the range of deposits distinguished in previous chapters, such deposits were possibly made only once or twice a year at Danebury, once or twice a decade on other sites - if pit fills are seen as regular events. Depositing material in pits was not a part of the daily refuse maintenance strategies. Background assemblages (mostly stages III and IV in Fig.5.10) can be regarded as a fortuitous incorporation of rubbish in convenient holes, but not 'normal' rubbish. But this would not explain those 'exceptional' deposits which have been shown often to have involved considerable effort and care in placing material in pits and ditches, following sequences and 'rules' such as those which meant different categories of material had to treated separately in different layers, or that certain objects/material could be deposited in the lower or upper parts of pits, or not in pits at all.

Nor would the fortuitous accident argument support the evidence provided by cases such as Winnall pit 6595 for the scale of meat slaughter in a relatively short time span by inference suggests a large gathering of people, larger than the resident population, to eat the large quantities of the meat. Nor do such arguments account for the planning involved to have the large numbers of adult animals available to slaughter in these cases. Deposits such as Winnall pits 4475 and 6595 (see 7.9), or the re-cutting of the Winnall enclosure ditch with the subsequent placing of different material in set positions along its course, were clearly intentional, motivated, discursive practices. As such, they would have been exceptional activities, the separation of which from the mundane and explicit content could act to focus and intensify attention. Events explicitly articulated a specific range of material in a symbolic manner, as already demonstrated in the clear evidence for pattern and structure.

However, whether they were the result of a ritual, or another kind of irregular, distinct and explicit social practice which clearly and overtly deposited a range of material according to cultural 'rules' etc., ultimately may not matter. In terms of the model illustrated above, I could still argue that these deposits were not ritual, although through their discursive, non-contingent, nature, they still performed a similar role in the (more) explicit re-production of structuring principles. Is this another reason why the need to ascribe the R-label is ultimately a non-problem?

10.4. Conclusions

I have interpreted these practices as ritual by trying to avoid arguing from the contents, more from the nature and shape of activities. The involvement of human remains in this tradition could be used to demonstrate its ritual nature. Throughout this thesis I have stressed the importance of a contextual approach, showing that all the elements of this depositional practice were treated in similar ways and formed part of a web of associations. Concentrating on a single category of finds, say animal bones, cannot adequately explain the nature of these deposits, and arguments against *ABG's* as ritual deposits must take into account the strong similarities with the treatment of human remains. Not only were human remains and *ABG's* deposited in the same contexts and in similar ways, but the apparent classification of human and animal deposits was identical (see 2.2&3, 11.3.4). Note I am not arguing here that human remains in archaeological deposits have to be ritual (I would be happy to see them as 'rubbish'), but those archaeologists who accept that the treatment of human remains is ritual must extend this interpretation to animal remains, pottery or small finds treated in similar ways. Equally, those who argue that *ABG's* were not the result of ritual, must then explain these human deposits.

In this chapter I have argued that these deposits were acts made during rituals conducted by groups of peoples living in Iron Age Wessex. I have argued in the previous chapters that these deposits are clearly an example of 'structured deposition' but have argued in this chapter that this on its own is not a secure guide to identifying ritual activities in the archaeological record. Rather, I have suggested that we need to consider the actual nature of the activities which created these deposits, not to consider gross general patterns but real people doing things in the world. This is to suggest that neither the content nor the location of a deposit is a secure guide to its ritual origins, but evidence for the irregularity, form, procedure and ways in which the deposit was made is. In this sense, this chapter's discussion might be considered by some to be unnecessary after the detailed descriptions of how a sample of individual pits was infilled, given in earlier chapter (see 7.10).

The factors I am using here to argue that these were ritual deposits include;

That this material was not simply shot into pits on a regular basis, but represents episodes on many settlements separated by years.

That these episodic deposits often involved material deposited in features according to a proper sequence, and with people often actually carefully placing material in, stamping down fills etc. in the pits themselves.

That there is evidence that these deposits often took place in the context of gatherings involving large numbers of people.

This is to place emphasis on the definition which *I use*. As I have suggested above, one way to defuse the dead-lock over the definition/recognition of ritual deposits in archaeology is to recognise that no universal definition of ritual is possible. Rather than be hobbled by this fact, we can go forward by being explicit about those human practices that we individually would recognise as ritual or non-ritual. This is to acknowledge that ritual is not a fixed category in any society. As such, we should expect that the boundaries between ritual and non-ritual in a situation where ritual takes place on settlements, and uses the elements of daily life, would be blurred and open to negotiation by Iron Age peoples themselves.

However, as the discussion of structured deposition above suggested, this does not mean that we can neatly separate off material in ritual deposits from those in non-ritual deposits and interpret each separately. All well-preserved deposits on these Iron Age sites are structured, and the need to understand these structuring principles does not go away if the deposit can be clearly shown to be non-ritual. Equally, the importance of sacrifice and ritual in prehistoric societies is not diminished in the majority of situations where people did not deposit the sacrificed items in the ground or other archaeologically recoverable contexts in their rituals.

Much of this chapter and the thesis have been concerned with establishing whether certain features of the archaeological record were the product of ritual or non-ritual activities. I have tried here to outline a way of showing that these can be consider as ritual deposits. However, it is has not been my intention to produce a new universally applicable archaeological litmus test for ritual. I have argued that whether or not these deposits were the result of 'ritual' activity, their nature suggests that they may have played an important, if infrequent, role in explicit reproducing the structuring principles drawn on in other, more regular and less 'heavy' situations. Indeed, I would suggest that we need to find ways to dissolve the self evident problem the definitions and identification of 'ritual' appears to have for British archaeologists (see 2). One way I have suggested is by being explicit about what we each mean by a ritual when we used the word. Another is to recognise that the answer to the question this study posed at the outset, 'are these deposits ritual', is not the end in itself of our analyses.

After all, the question *Is this ritual?* can only be answered Yes or No. How much does it tell us about the actual nature and context of these deposits, or the societies who made them? Perhaps the question ought to be;
What was the nature and context of this practice of putting a range of items in the ground during the Southern English Iron Age?

101

Chapter 11
A Life-Giving Technique:
The Elements of this Ritual Tradition

11.1. Introduction

I have argued that the deposition of a range of material on Iron Age sites in Hampshire and Dorset was a ritual practice. This practice was widespread across Wessex and other parts of Southern England (Whimster 1981; C.Wilson 1981; Wait 1985; Cunliffe 1991), and this has been variously labelled *the Pit Burial Tradition* (Whimster 1981), *the Pit Ritual Tradition* (Hill forthcoming a), and *the Pit Belief System* (Cunliffe 1991:536). None of these labels is satisfactory, since they run the risk of over-emphasising the pit as the primary location for these ritual deposits (see 11.7). Equally, I would suggest that to call a tradition of social practices/actions, a 'belief system', is misleading and wrongly assumes the neat identification of a particular set of 'beliefs' with a set of rituals (see 12.2.1).

Ritual, as a social practice, draws on and reproduces historically specific structural principles in a particular way. A consequence of this is that the archaeological study of ritual must always try to understand the nature of this tradition in its historically specific context. This is not to look for the ritual's meaning, which is always dangerous in the anthropological study of ritual and perhaps more so within archaeology. Due to the very nature of interpretation, a ritual has no single meaning, even when static in form and context through time and space (see 12.2). Archaeological, like ethnographic, interpretations of rituals should not be the pursuit of any imagined 'real meaning', but the eliciting of possible readings that could have been given to those rituals within the specific cultural context studied (Charsley 1987). More importantly,

> "ritual is not done solely to be interpreted...
> it is done (and from the point of view of the performers this might be more important) to resolve, alter, or demonstrate a situation" (Lewis 1980:35).

This is to stress ritual's ultimate practical quality. It some sense ritual can be seen as a technology; it does things in the real world, and is not 'just' to do with symbols or theology. In this chapter I will discuss the content and elements of this specific tradition, starting an understanding of its nature and the dominant ideas it drew upon and reproduced. I will argue that the essence of this ritual tradition lay in the deliberate deposition and sacrifice of things, living and inanimate, through which the division and demarcation of the boundaries between elements of the social world, the (re)definition of people and things, were sanctioned.

11.2. Animals; Good to sacrifice, Good to think

11.2.1 Sacrifice

The role of animals in the ritual tradition outlined here exemplified the themes of sacrifice and classification. Patterns in animal bone assemblages from pits, ditches, and other features outlined in this thesis were not the product of 'functional' or natural taphonomic processes. Grant has been one of the few archaeozoologists to consider possible symbolic interpretations of bone assemblages, and she has interpreted *ABG's* from Danebury as sacrifices (see 2.3). This study supports and deepens her interpretation. Critics have stressed that such animal remains should be considered in the context of 'normal' butchery and disposal practices, while others think *ABG's* and large bone deposits resulted from celebrations and feasting (see 3.7.7.). A sharp sacred:profane distinction is assumed here, leading to the expectation that ritual uses of animals should be archaeologically distinct from secular (a problem with Grant's own interpretation which rigidly separates *ABG's* from other bone assemblages). I have argued that a rigid sacred:profane dichotomy is inappropriate, and that it is impossible to distinguish sacrifice from feasting. A more appropriate term may then be *ritual consumption* .

Sacrifice is much discussed in the anthropology of religion. Sacrifice may be defined as "a rite in the course of which something is forfeited or destroyed" (James 1920:1). With its chief object "being to establish relations between a source of spiritual strength and one in need of such strength, for the benefit of the latter" (*ibid*). No single explanation, such as the expiation of sin (Evans-Pritchard 1940, 1956), can be offered to explain all sacrifice and sacrifice is often employed for a range of purposes/occasions. Hubert and Mauss' (1964) study on its nature and function has been particularly influential, defining sacrifice as a "means of communication between the sacred and profane worlds through the mediation of a victim" (1964:97). More recent studies have criticised the Indo-European and Judeao-Christian basis of Hubert and Mauss' approach for its grounding in Durkheim's division of sacred and profane, and argue that in other cultures there exist different models of sacrifice (De Heusch 1985; Valeri 1985). These critiques reject that sacrifice "always implies consecration" (Hubert & Mauss 1964:8), and argue that sacrifices may be seen as the "conjunction and disjunction of spaces, human and non-human" (De Heusch 1985:213, cf. opening definition).

I have shown that no one species was preferred in these sacrifices in Iron Age Wessex, , although it would appear that different species were normally ritually consumed together (see 7.3.4), with body size being important in determining how much of the carcass was reserved for the gods/spirits/ancestors (see 7.3.3). Using raw *ABG* counts it would appear that some species were preferable to sacrifice than others. A grading is evident: the smaller the overall proportion of animal bones assemblages to which a species contributes to, the greater the proportion of the number of *ABG's* and total bone from *ABG's* to which that species contributes (see 7.3.1). Minority species are also marked out by their associations with other factors and by their spatial distributions (see 5.4.2, 6.3.3, 9.5 etc.). Dog, horse, and wild species were treated in special ways, though I cannot definitely say that these species were particularly favoured for sacrifice. The evidence indicates that they were particularly favoured for reservation, for deposition as whole/parts of the carcass, rather than for complete consumption. Dog, horse, and some wild resources were occasionally eaten, but were these meats considered a delicacy or its use regulated? The choice of species and type of *ABG* may be considered as an Iron Age "hierarchy of taste" (Spencer 1988:255), possibly with the head in particular being an important cut.

One variable for manipulation within a rite was the proportion of animal reserved by the host/organiser (a greater or lesser proportion of an animal could be eaten by the living participants or offered to the spiritual participants - deposited in the ground). In this way, ritual consumption can be considered in terms of gift giving, even as the archetypal gift in these communities (cf. Leach 1976:82). Meat shared with the human and other participants was one method to build and repay social obligations/acquire prestige. Ritual consumption can also be seen as ritualised cooking, in which close actual and conceptual links may have existed between ritual and similar daily activities, with the methods and rules of ritual food preparation being similar to those of mundane cuisine. Even if normal roles in preparation were reversed during ritual consumption (e.g. men doing women's work), these activities would act as a strong model for daily preparation and consumption (e.g. C, Hugh-Jones 1978), even making them legitimate or pious (e.g. Vernant on Classical Greece discussed in De Heusch 1985:18-19).

11.2.2 Classification

A common theme in the interpretation of sacrifice is the mediating role of the victim between this world and another. During sacrifice, animals were not only manipulated to mediate spiritually, but also spatially and socially (Gibson 1986:182). Therefore, where and how animal remains were deposited on Iron Age sites, both from ritual or mundane consumption, may provide a unique opportunity in understanding some of the ways in which animals

were perceived/treated in these communities, and how their classification related to other social categories; "Sacrifice burrows into the deepest part of the animal to extract some meaning" (De Heusch 1985:215).

Within archaeology human-animal interactions are almost exclusively studied in ecological, economic and functional terms. However, animals are as good to think with as they are good to eat (Shanklin 1985; Tambiah 1969). Such issues have been recognised in archaeozoology (Hesse & Whipnash 1985:5-12; Moore 1981), but as yet little realised (e.g. Richards & Thomas 1984; Hodder 1990; Thomas 1991; Grant 1984a, 1991 etc.).

The choice of animal in sacrifice (species, sex, age, colour) often related to the basic classifications through which a culture structured its world. Classification is an essential process for understanding one's environment, and is the basis of all social actions (including agriculture: Willis 1990). Similarities and differences drawn between animals, things, and humans "allow the natural and social universe to be grasped as an organised whole" (Levi-Strauss 1963:135). Ethnotaxonomists have established universal principles in an attempt to understand how cultures classify the natural world, but with only limited success (e.g. Berlin et al 1973, Berlin 1992). Usually such systems recognise the same domestic species as the Linnaean system, but larger groupings and the classification of wild animals are often different, while the meanings and metaphorical associations people make with biological categories are extremely diverse. Care must be taken to avoid imposing our strong notion of a culture-nature opposition on the past. It is possible that past societies need not have had similar important distinctions. Although a wide number of examples have shown that some forms of wild:tame, nature:culture/humanity distinctions are common in many societies, the exact nature of these distinctions and the valuations and meaning ascribed to them vary considerably. Classifications of animals are often expressed in spatial terms (literally and metaphorically), and a common element is a concentric discrimination according to the conceptual distance of a species from a human centre (Leach 1964, Buxton 1968, Tambiah 1969).

The above principles cannot predict how a particular species will be valued in a specific culture. The dog is often accorded a special status through its social proximity to humans, but this value may be contradictory in different cultures. The dog can at times be considered a positive species, regarded as clean, as a human friend, even almost human (Leach 1964; Buxton 1968; Sahlins 1976). This may mean it was not eaten, or was a delicacy, or in both situations was possibly disguised by calling its meat another name (Olowo Ojoade 1990; Sahlins 1976). In other cultures it is a negative animal, considered dirty and polluting because it scavenges food waste and even human

{Large Body}	Cattle		Horse
			Wild Species
{Small Body}	Sheep	Pig	Dog

<u>A possible Iron Age cultural classification of animal species</u>

faeces. Alternatively, this may be because of its uninhibited sexual behaviour where constrained sexual behaviour is morally advocated, or because of the dog's ambiguous relationship to humans that is itself so close and almost human (e.g. Bulmer 1967; Tambiah 1969; Wijeyewardene 1968). How the dog is considered and treated is always related to other aspects of a culture, attitudes to sex, notions of dirt and pollution, what it is to be human. As such, social distance may well be a useful concept in understanding how Iron Age animals were perceived and disposed of, but this has always to be set in its wider context.

The special treatment of wild animal remains from Iron Age sites (see 7.5), and patterns in the disposal of worked bone and antler objects, raises the possibility of a distinction between tame:wild/culture:nature (see 7.6). Although such an opposition may be present within all agriculturally-based societies, its relative importance and manifestation varies considerably. Most of the scant finds of wild mammal and bird bones in this study came from occasional, ritual, deposits, and this suggests that in Iron Age Wessex a culture:nature division was of central importance to the dominant cultural symbols that were articulated in these practices.

This treatment of wild remains can be fitted into a broader scheme which encompasses all animal remains. Different species can be graded according to their treatment in deposits. Calculations of both the number of *ABG* deposits, and the overall proportion of the total bone of a species from *ABG's*, shows a gradation where the smaller a species' contribution to the overall total number of bone fragments, the more marked its treatment (see 7.2.2). This not only relates to pig, dog, and horse *ABG's*, but also demonstrates that unarticulated bone from these species (not all from ritual/exceptional deposits) had marked associations with other factors and distinct spatial distributions.

This gradation could be interpreted in terms of cattle and sheep (the main domesticates in Iron Age Wessex) at one end of the scale, wild animals at the other. Is this a 'typical' discrimination radiating set, ordered in relation to a central, domestic and probably human reference point (but see 11.3.4)? Iron Age bone assemblages represented only those wild species that were eaten (especially birds, hares), or deposited (foxes, mustids) on sites. The status of other wild animals could be guessed/approximated, with deer, boar, bustard, wolf and bear-set on the extreme right of this proposed classification. Dog and horse appear to be intermediary species, the previous discussion of the special status of these species having stressed their close relationship with humans and their associations with 'Celtic' deities (Wait 1985:155; Cunliffe 1983:159). An argument for the proximity of dog and horse to humanity may appear paradoxical if these two species lay on the boundary between culture and nature (away from the putative human centre). However, horses were probably not bred on Wessex sites, but rather came from (managed) wild herds outside the area (Harcourt 1979:158; Grant 1984a:521-22; Maltby & Coy 1991:103).

It is important to emphasise that these ritual deposits explicitly reveal something of Iron Age animal classifications, and the ways in which these were given meaning through association with other categories of objects, people and space. From these relationships, we can begin to understand the procedures by which

> "animals are brought into human social categories by a simple extension to them of the principles that serve for ordering human relationships" (Douglas 1990:36).

The patterns suggest that a domestic:wild opposition of some form was a central metaphor articulated in Iron Age rituals (a similar approach has been argued in understanding the European Neolithic, see Hodder 1990 and Thomas 1991).

I have argued that the status of wild animals was ambiguous within Iron Age animal classification procedures, and the cultural treatment of animals. Hunting and fishing played a minor role in Iron Age diets in Southern England (in terms of overall bone assemblages, and the inferences drawn from them). However, the special deposition of wild remains suggests that the absence of wild resources from Iron Age diets was not due to a lack of time to hunt, or the availability of prey. Wild animals were probably surrounded by prohibitions, so that their occasional hunting, the use of their feathers and skins, and consumption were probably heavily regulated or proscribed. Perhaps wild animals were only brought onto sites and eaten as part of feasting and sacrifice (c.f. Bulmer 1967; Tambiah 1969)?

The choice of species hunted was not directly related to a species' abundance or economic value, but was in terms of cultural factors. Therefore, the absence of certain species from the archaeological evidence is as important as the presence of others. Evidence for hedgehog is extremely rare on Iron Age sites, although they would have been common around, if not on, sites, and they are edible. Although weasels and martins are sometimes present (e.g. as *ABG's* at Easton Lane - see 9.4), otter is not represented in bone assemblages and I wonder if this related to the absence of fish (c.f. Douglas 1966 on Leviticus). Fish bone was rarely recovered, even on sites with excellent conditions for preservation and locations for exploitation such as Runnymede and Haddenham V (Sergeantson *pers com*), and even though water fowl made up a considerable proportion of all non-Corvid bird bone. Were creatures that lived in water proscribed in Iron Age classifications?

Birds would appear to have been given an important symbolic association during the Iron Age. It is tempting to link the symbolism of bird remains, particularly the concentration on wings/feathers (see 3.7.8, 7.5), to flight and a meeting of opposites, the deposition of creatures of air below the ground. Feathers may have been an important Iron Age resource, and specialist exploitation of wild fowl and beaver for feathers and pelts has been demonstrated at Haddenham V in the Fens (Evans & Serjeantson 1988). A concentration on ducks and geese, along with other species in these deposits, may be related to the iconographic importance of water birds seen in Urnfield/Hallstatt symbolism (Coles & Harding 1979:368-370, Kossack 1954). However Southern England was beyond the main Central European concentration of this bird imagery, although a few examples are known from Britain and Ireland (Dunaverney flesh hook - Megaw & Simpson 1979:338). These include a small bronze bird fitting excavated at the Iron Age hillfort of St Catherine's Hill, Winchester (Hawkes et al 1929).

The animal categories articulated within Iron Age ritual tradition must not be regarded as incidental to daily agricultural cooking, dining and refuse maintenance practices. Instead they were the cognitive basis for these practices. Food was a ubiquitous metaphor through which people demarcated their social and cultural identity (Fiddes 1991), and as such "it could be argued that changes of diet are more important than changes of dynasty or even of religion" (Orwell 1984:82). It is within this context that innovations and changes in farming practice or cuisine must be set. For example, the proportion of pig bone increased on some Late Iron Age sites (especially those interpreted as elite centres and/or oppida), and this has been connected to feasting (see Grant 1989b). However, the 'appropriateness' of pork has not been investigated by archaeologists, and pig was already treated differently from cattle and sheep in its deposition on Early/Middle Iron Age Wessex sites (e.g. 7.4., 9.5.). Equally, the importance attached to birds and hares in Early/Middle Iron Age Wessex provided the cultural setting into which domestic fowl were introduced in the later Iron Age, and in which to

place Caesar's odd comments about British fowl and hares:

> "Hares, fowl, and geese they think it unlawful to eat, but rear them for pleasure and amusement". (Caesar V.12 - 1982:111)

11.3. Human Remains

11.3.1. Introduction

The deposition of human remains has been the most obvious component of an Iron Age ritual tradition (see 2.2). Human remains (from individual bone fragments to complete carcasses), were regularly deposited in association, and in a particular sequence, with different classes of material (see 2.2). The context of deposition (pits and ditches filled with apparently domestic rubbish), and the small numbers of people represented, have raised the question as to who these people were. Thus, complete 'burials' have been discussed in terms of social outcasts (or possibly sacrifice), partial skeletons as proof that the majority of the population was excarnated, and individual bones as part of the excarnated body retained and utilised in various ways (see Fig. 2.3.a). Complete skulls were considered 'easy' to interpret in terms of 'Celtic' head hunting (Cunliffe 1983:164).

11.3.2. Mortuary Practice or Human Sacrifice?

A fundamental failure of previous interpretations was not to recognise basic parallels between the treatment of human remains and animal remains in similar deposits (Fitzpatrick 1991:125). Although recognised by Bradley and Cunliffe, any consequences from this have not been followed up (Bradley 1990:161-164, Cunliffe 1992). The range of human deposits (from complete body through to single bone fragment) are remarkably similar to the range of different types of animal *ABG's*. Both human and animal remains occur as complete carcasses, partial carcasses often with missing/displaced limbs or skulls, complete skulls, although proportions of the different types of deposit differ. Also, both complete/partial carcasses of humans and animals occur as associated, but not articulated, groups of bones (see Fig 11.1).

A dominant distinction between humans and animals will appear 'natural' within present Western ideals, and human remains in archaeology are regarded as a distinct category which has its own separate body of theory, namely Mortuary Theory. Recent critiques of mortuary theory (Barrett 1988; Thomas 1991a&b) argue that the dead take on a different significance in different societies, stressing a need to set human remains in their specific historical context. Similarly, the deposition of a range of human remains in Iron Age features does not necessarily fit into our conventional understanding of mortuary rituals (either ancestor or funerary rites), and it is perhaps misleading to treat these remains as reflecting a minority mortuary rite. The vast majority of Iron Age populations were disposed of in archaeologically untraceable ways, as is the case for all British prehistory. I would argue that we should stop approaching prehistoric human remains from a perspective which expects the majority of these populations to be archaeologically visible. Instead we should recognise that from the Neolithic onwards archaeological deposits of human remains are never *simply* to do with the treatment of the dead.

Human remain deposits may have been connected with the construction/celebration of passages between human life and death, but this was just one part of a wider ritual tradition in which social/cultural categories were (re)defined and transformed. It is therefore wrong to limit discussion of human remains to mortuary practice, and human sacrifice must be seriously reconsidered in terms of the origin of some of these remains. Sacrifice and cannibalism have in the past been considered as suitable propositions, for example Cunliffe (1983) considered sacrifice as the origin of all burials but ultimately found the explanation of social outcasts more attractive. Similarly, Bradley (1990:164) considered the possibility of human sacrifice, but did not interpret these remains as offerings (see 2.4.). Is a hesitancy to accept human sacrifice more to do with our own expectations? Humans were treated in similar ways, and deposited in the same features, as the animals which archaeologists have interpreted as having been deliberately killed in sacrifice. This association at least suggests a strong metaphorical link between animal sacrifices and human remains, if not actual human sacrifice.

It would be wrong to argue for either sacrifice or natural death as a total explanation for human remains (especially given the variability in an Iron Age ritual tradition). Whether deliberate or natural death, complete carcass or hip fragments, these human remains carried the heavy burden of standing for something; they were metaphors and metonyms for humanity and particular types of humans. In this sense the individuals' personal identities were of little importance. Nevertheless, obfuscating the identity of the individual should not be seen as the purpose of these rituals, as Sharples implies (1991c:87). It was probably an unintended consequence of their more important role of mediation between this world and the next/other.

11.3.3. Strategies of Representation: What it was to be an Iron Age person

The procedures by which the body was treated in death and particularly in sacrifice were "strategies of representation", "practices which formed a given community's expectation of what it is to be a person" (Thomas 1991:140). Notions of the subject, the person, and image of the body, are not identical but are closely linked, and were different things in different times. Human subjectivities are primarily formed through the social spaces, relationships and material environments they grew up in and

inhabited (Bourdieu 1977; Giddens 1984; I.Cohen 1990; Pred 1986 etc. see Hill 1993). We should, therefore, expect what it was to be an Iron Age person to be different from our own notions in the present, especially because of the demonstrably different organisation of Iron Age space (Hill 1993). The ways in which the human body was classified, manipulated, broken down, and deposited, provide evidence for these forms of representation. The human body was used, amongst other items, as part of a complex strategy of representation, as metonyms for different types of humanity particularly related to age and completeness of the body/subject/agent. These strategies were possibly more 'heavy'/explicit than in many mortuary practices, since this type of ritual tradition was primarily concerned with establishing the relationships that made sense of the world as a whole, rather than 'merely' coping with the death of an individual.

The classification of the body constitutes the most basic human predisposition (Bourdieu 1977, 1990; Blacking 1979, Shanks & Tilley 1982). It is in this light that an emphasis on the right side of the body, in individual bone deposits, can be set for Danebury (Walker 1984: 454-455). This was linked to left:right spatial distinctions further connected with valuations of north and south, and other cultural connotations seen in the spatial organisation of settlement space and the location of deposits (see 8, 9). Similar arguments apply to the singling out of the head, in humans and animals, for special treatment. Between Early and Middle Iron Age Hampshire hillfort and non-hillfort sites there were differences between the proportion of deposits of women and children (more within non-hillfort sites, see Hill 1995 - see 2.2), and there also appeared to be few obvious gender differences in the associations with different types of find on any site (see 7.2.4). Age would appear to be a more important distinction, with infants often particularly deposited inside or at the rear of settlements, and often associated with particular types of finds, such as querns (see 7.2.3).

At Winnall, the vast majority of the population that lived/used these locales were disposed of in an untraceable manner (including high levels of expected infant mortality). We must assume that people were disposed or excarnated away from the site (on the edges?), although a small number of human deposits were made in different parts of the site. It would appear in both Early and Middle phases that infant, and also individual bone fragments were restricted to the inside settlement and enclosure ditch. In contrast, adult burials were either absent (Early Iron Age), or deposited outside but very close to the boundary of the former enclosure (Middle Iron Age) (see 9.5). Similar patterns were found on other sites (although not all show the same peripheral preference for complete, adult deposits e.g. Little Somborne, Old Down Farm). The human deposits recovered at Winnall mediated and stood

```
      Cattle              Horse
                          Humans      Wild Species
         Sheep      Pig   Dog
```

A possible Iron Age cultural classification of humans and animal species

for social values and ideas which were explicitly articulated during the course of ritual. It may, therefore, have been 'appropriate' to deposit infant deaths in the settlement. Though not all infant mortalities were deposited inside sites, a selected few (both 'natural deaths' and sacrifices) represented children and the associations/values ascribed to youth generally.

A direct association may have been made between deposits of children, and where children spent most of their lives (this would not explain the similarities in the treatment of individual bone fragments, which shared similar preferred locations and associations). Another explanation may lie in the way infants are often differentially treated in death because they are not considered to be full persons. A possible distinction was being made between young and incomplete persons/ whole adult persons, which gave value to different spaces, and shaped the expectations of what it was to be a person. This could be linked with individual bone fragments, and also the only partial corpse from Middle Iron Age Winnall which was deposited inside the former boundary (see 9.5.).

11.3.4. Humanity's Place in the Natural Order

What it was to be human appeared as a central element within the practices discussed above, and this was also closely associated with animal classification. Spatial distributions and associations clearly related human and animal categories. It is at this point that we must be careful of imposing an arbitrary distinction between humanity and nature. In these deposits humanity does not stand apart from nature in a sharp manner. Humans could be understood as having been treated in the same ways as any other animal species in these deposits. Humans/animals were deposited in the same contexts, in the same manner, and their bodies divided up and classified similarly. There are, at the same time, differences between humans and animals, for example at Winnall (and to a lesser extent Winklebury) human remains were placed in the middle /upper pit-fills, often above ABG's and other deposits. There are also differences in location, and in the proportions of the different types of deposit between human and animal ABG's. However, are these differences no greater than differences between types of animal species, or are humans remains more marked out in their deposition and associations than other species.

Certainly humans were not radically distinguished from animals; humans and animals carcasses were broken down in similar typologies, and treated in similar ways when deposited in the ground. Humans can also be fitted into the proposed scheme of animal classification (see 11.2.2.). Although figures on the number of human bones are not usually calculated, a very high proportion of all human bone came from what could be called *articulated/associated human bone groups*. In the gradation of species, in terms of the proportion of bone from *ABG's*, human bone could probably be placed between horse/dog and wild animals. Humanity (or one form of humanity) was not the centre of these classifications but appeared on the boundary between the domestic and the wild, just as spatially they were often deposited on the margins of the settlement (see 9.5.):

The above scheme runs against
> "the hypothesis, not very extensively tested, that domesticated animals occupy an intermediate position between human (culture) and the wild (nature)" (Shanklin 1985:397).

From my proposed classification, we can understand the position of horse and dog in terms of their proximity (metaphorical and real) to humanity (or at least one form of it), and also in terms of their relationship between domestic and wild. However, it may be wrong to assume that because horse and dog held similar classificatory positions that it was due to identical reasons and qualities. Nor was their position simply due to a close involvement with people, since horse and dog could also be considered as quite different from one another (or opposed, as the evidence from Winklebury would suggest, see 8).

Horses were probably brought to Wessex settlements from the outside, since they do not appear to have been bred on Wessex sites but probably in semi-wild herds outside the Chalk Downlands akin to New Forest or moorland ponies today (see 11.2.2). In contrast, dogs were raised on Iron Age settlements (neo-natal/young dog ABG's are common). Both horses and dogs may have been considered to have personalities, even to be subjects in some senses, but like humans both horses and dogs require training, disciplining, to fulfil their roles or act as companions. Horses, particularly if raised in semi-wild herds, had to be broken and trained in order to be ridden or used to draw vehicles. It is this process of bringing in from the wild, taming, controlling, that made them a potent metaphor to express ideas about culture and nature within society (e.g. Lawrence 1990). Likewise, dogs had to be trained, brought to heel, if they were to play an active role in human life, be it as a watch dog, hunting dog, or sheep dog.

Animal classifications and valuations are created by people, therefore animals naturally share the same patterns of relations as those of humans, because humans understand animals to act according to the same principles as themselves (Douglas 1990:33). The treatment and perception of animals is homologous to that of people. The position of humans on the boundary between culture and nature was a spatial metaphor physically embodied when representative humans were deposited during ritual. This is to relate the contrast between infants/bone fragments and complete adult deposits directly with the classifications of the natural world and to notions of human demeanour and discipline. From Winnall's interior, the evidence would suggest that infants were treated in the same ways, and were possibly conceived, as incomplete adults remains (cf. the different species of *ABG'* associated with complete and incomplete human deposits at Danebury, see Table 7.4). I would argue that an important metaphor that was sustained during these practices was the division, and controlled transformation of humanity into children and adults - initiation. In this transformation the coming of age was thought of conceptually and spatially in terms of becoming a complete person.

Breaking, controlling, disciplining, training, may have been important metaphors about the perception and treatment of humans, and as I have argued were reflected upon the animal world. As with dogs and horses, to become a complete person required training, education, socialisation, processes that took place largely within the settlement. The idea that complete humanity was a boundary to be crossed, spatially expressed as such, perhaps gave emphasis and an appreciation to the values bound up in the settlement boundary. Thus, settlement boundaries created analytical spaces in which activities (such as the upbringing and socialisation of children?) could be observed, constrained and disciplined (see 8.6).

11.4. Small Finds

There are other elements within an Iron Age ritual tradition that can be interpreted as evidence for offerings/sacrifice. Items, *produced* and *used* in specific fields of social practice especially those associated with field and home, became objectified, identified with particular sets of ideas and associations, during rituals. In general, only certain types of small finds were offered. The majority of these could be labelled 'domestic', although this word fails to capture the sense of a world in which work and home were neither spatially, nor conceptually, divided. These were the items used in

routine, mundane, agricultural, craft production, and food preparation activities. Examples ranged from textile production and repair (loom-weights, spindle whorls, combs, needles), leather-working (knifes and gouges), woodworking (saws, chisels, adzes), crop production and processing (ard points, 'pruning hooks', querns), to small-scale metalworking.

Certain classes of objects appeared to have been more specifically marked out (querns, iron objects and objects made of worked bone and antler, see 7.2.3, 7.6 etc.). What all these objects have in common was that they were (by procedures similar to the treatment of human and animal remains) involved in the transformation of a cultured nature. These objects were the tools involved in the daily processes of transforming the products of field and managed woodland into food, clothing, buildings etc. and were in turn the products of such processes (e.g. bone and antler tools). The involvement and manipulation of such objects in these rituals served to presence the activities in which they were involved, and the objects themselves within the ritual field. It imbued these activities with considerable symbolical and metaphorical importance and connected them with concerns of cosmology, mortality and social reproduction. Some objects, such as bone and antler tools, also carried with them the important distinctions seen in the treatment of other animal bone between 'culture' and 'nature', the special treatment of antler fitting in with the special treatment accorded to other body parts of wild animals.

The theme of transformation (of nature into culture, of young into old) was also drawn on in those deposits involving material from metal-working (e.g. Gussage All Saints pit 209). Querns often seem to have been given a special place in this ritual tradition, and I have suggested that fragments from a substantial proportion of all the querns used on a site are represented in deposits (Appendix 2). These clear and important associations between the manufacture, use and deposition of a range of tools, may suggest that the acquisition of raw materials, their transformation and use should be understood in ways far more akin to those employed to understand Neolithic lithics than hitherto thought. Was the quarrying of quern stones in Iron Age southern England far more like the quarrying, knapping and distribution of Neolithic flint axes (Bradley and Edmonds 1993), than the familiar, 'commercial', picture often implied for this and other areas of Iron Age exchange?

The majority of these small finds had been used; in one sense they were 'dead' things since the majority were broken and could be considered rubbish. There were very few complete, or deliberately broken items, and many appeared to have been broken through use and curated before deposition. This was clear with most bone combs and points, but was also true for other objects such as the stone measuring weights from Winnall/Easton Lane, and with substantially complete querns (though only one of the pair of rotary stones was usually deposited). These items only served to strengthen the links between actual activities and the concerns of ritual because these were not objects (in the main) made specifically to be used in these rituals, but actual objects used in a range of actual mundane activities and contexts; they were the actual products and instruments of praxis. Bringing such items into a sacred sphere made the qualities, powers, and values they represented malleable and re-definable in the grid of daily predispositions. These artefacts would have acted as metaphors and mnemonics presencing in routine activities the symbols and concepts 'played with' in the ritual sphere - and vice versa. Objects within ritual stood for other objects of the same type, but also for the circumstances and particular human agents that had been involved in their use and production.

In this ritual process, a primary distinction made was between those activities, ideas, and associated objects which could be brought into a sacred space (were valued), and those which were excluded. Here the relative rarity, especially compared to later centuries, of fine objects such as weaponry, vehicle/horse fittings, and especially personal ornaments was particularly striking in the EIA and MIA. Such items and their qualities were not part of the "models of experience" (Valeri 1985:345) articulated in these sacrifices, and this points to ways in which the ritual practices studied here stood in contrast to the practices of metalwork deposition in both the Late Bronze Age and Late Iron Age.

11.5. Pottery

Pottery can be seen as akin to both small finds and animal bones. Like animal bone, pottery deposits belong to a continuum which runs from the rare deposition of a complete vessel (complete or already broken), large sherds, to mixed assemblages of degraded sherds. Also, like animal bone there need be no sharp divide drawn between complete or substantial portions of single vessels, and groups of mixed sherds. Broken vessels and large fresh sherds may be derived from a variety of activities. Yet, basic interpretations see such assemblages, especially in pits with ABG's or fresh bone, as the direct result of sacrifices/feasting. This would point to the deliberate smashing, 'killing', of pottery (a new perspective in which to set the demand for Iron Age ceramic production and exchange). However, it was also likely that some of the pottery was, like some small finds, broken in daily use but curated for later use (cf. human bone fragments).

In these deposits, conscious differentiations were made between pottery and bone, and between different types of vessel/fabric, providing evidence to compare our typologies to theirs (see 7.8.). The deposition of certain types of pottery in certain types of contexts and associations suggests their use was ritually, ideally restricted to certain types of people, activities or spheres of practice (Thomas 1991a). Iron Age pots were more than 'just pots' (containers for storing, preparing and serving food), they were also objects to be thought with and fitted into the conceptual and social order (cf. Barrett 1991b). At Early Iron Age Winnall, the less common fabrics were deposited in specific parts of the site. While a few large sherds of fine ware vessels were deliberately deposited at the enclosure's entrance, associating this pottery with a range of axiomatic values constructed around the crossing of the settlement's boundary and its public face, mediating between different social arenas.

Early Iron Age fine wares were often decorated, while course wares were usually plain. Decoration continued in importance in the Middle Iron Age, where it appeared to have been selectively placed in certain deposits. Decoration was not simply a stylistic convention; the surface treatment and form of pottery played an active part in the reproduction and transformation of society. This implies far more than mapping style zones to distinguish ethnic/social groupings (see 3.5). Braithwaite's (1982:87-8) suggestions may be particularly useful for further work on these issues;

> "decoration functions as a...marker of particular areas of ambiguity and concern brought about by actions of people in the course of everyday life", in, "encounters of opposed categories".

Decorated pottery appeared to have been deposited at spatial and conceptual boundaries, for example at enclosure entrances or with adult humans. Moreover different types of pottery were also integral to more general spatial divisions, especially north-south, mapped on to pot vs. animal bone (e.g. Early Iron Age and Middle Iron Age Winnall, see 9). It is also in this context that the use and deposition of non-local pottery most be set. The work from Gussage (see 8) shows that the few LIA vessels of continental manufacture were clearly recognised as different, if not as anomalous, in their deposition - and by extension, their use.

11.6. Rubbish and Grain

Deposits of plant material (especially cleaned grain at Danebury) may have been important within these rituals (see 7.10). At present it is impossible to say whether there has been equal concern given to the classification of plant species as to that of animals, or if deposits of plant remains were deliberately marked off from those of pottery and bone. The representation of plant remains during sacrifice was, at the same time, in association with other dominant symbols linked to agricultural and domestic food preparation activities. This form of representation should not be explained simply in terms of food storage (as is often emphasised in discussions of pits, see 11.7.), but in terms of a theme of transformation that pervaded all elements of these types of deposit (see 11.10). The carbonised material (some deliberately dumped and not accidentally incorporated into features - see 3.6., 7.10), came from the processing, the transformation, of crops. Equally, it seems particularly important that those layers of grain found in pits were deliberately carbonised/burnt.

Further work should consider, more thoroughly, the specific matrices of layers in features. Parker-Pearson (forthcoming) has suggested that midden deposits might have had considerable significance as stores of fertility. Layers of midden soil (mixed compound rubbish or pure dung), in feature-fills may have been an important component in these ritual deposits. In particular contemporary cultures, hearth ash is an important symbol, often disposed of distinctively from other 'rubbish' and used in a variety of practices (Moore 1986; Hodder 1987b). Layers of ash and hearth material were sometimes dumped into features on Iron Age sites and, like other layers, were usually distinct and not mixed with other categories of material. That the remains of a complete hearth were deposited in the southern ditch terminal at Winnall Down, as part of the opposed north:south deposits, suggests such material may have been another component of ritual offering.

11.7. Pits and Ditches

> Explanation must necessarily lie in the realms of guesswork, but the context of these deposits -- in storage pits -- is suggestive of a rite to ensure the maintenance of crop fertility. If we are correct in supposing that these pits were used for storing seed-corn then to ensure a good harvest or in retrospect to give thanks for one (Cunliffe 1991:518).

Dominant interpretations have emphasised where plant remain deposits were made, *the pit* (Wait 1985:251; Bradley 1984:159, Bradley 1990:163-4; Cunliffe 1992). This has become so common, that the very act of digging, and the use of pits for storage has been interpreted as ritual activity and opposed to functionally determined above-ground storage of grain (Cunliffe 1991; 1992; Cunliffe & Poole 1991:162). But I would argue that we should be wary of an over-emphasis on the pit (see 2.4.).

From Bersu (1940) onwards, calculations have assumed that pits had an average life-span of ten years, that pits were all used for crop storage until they became unsuitable, then they were infilled and replaced (Bowen & Wood 1968; Wainwright 1979; Cunliffe 1984a; Fasham 1985). Any possibility of pit re-use after storage has not been considered. However, if pits were the prime locations for ritual deposits, the decision to take them out of storage

service may have been more to do with ritual and social requirements, than an ability to store crops effectively. Deposits were not restricted to eroded pits, and were found in well-preserved bee-hive pits that have shown no obvious sign of becoming unusable. Indeed, some pits were specifically dug only to receive deposits (see 3.2). It is also possible that the original location in which a storage pit was dug was governed by concerns of ritual. As such Danebury's 'apparent' and massive below-ground storage capacity may be illusory if the very high numbers of ritual deposits at the site meant pits were being filled in frequently for ritual purposes.

Studies at Winnall and Winklebury have shown that bee-hive shaped pits were specifically chosen to receive certain types of ritual deposits, especially of human remains. However, it must be stressed that *ABG's* were not significantly associated with bee-hive shaped pits (see 7.7). This is *only* understandable if the key element of these rituals had a connection with crop storage. It has been argued that this form of pit was the most optimally shaped for cereal storage (see 3.2), although it has not been proven whether these rather than other pit-forms were used for storage. The question of why there were different shaped pits is a problem, since all pits could have been used for crop storage (for cereals or other crops - or the storage of non-crops), and it may be wrong to assume that a particular shape had a single function.

Links between pits, grain storage and a ritual tradition are not necessarily as simply indicated, or as central, as Cunliffe and Bradley have argued. The disputed function of pits must be considered first: were pits used only for storing grain, or might other possible functions be just as important? Deposits were only placed in approximately one third of all pits, so if storage was central and all pit-storage was ritual as Cunliffe (1992) has argued, why were deposits not made in every pit? In addition to this, evidence would suggest that the infilling of a pit was not a regular event, which would refute the argument that every opportunity was taken to "ensure a good harvest or in retrospect to give thanks for one" (Cunliffe 1992:77).

We may have placed too much importance on the specific function of these features (from crop storage to the ritual deposition of human remains), for such deposits were not only restricted to pits. Chapter 8 showed similar deposits of materials were made in the fills of enclosure ditches. It can be shown that a range of similar deliberate deposits involving the same range of materials, and whose deposition was ordered by similar general principles, to those shown to occur in pits were made in the enclosure ditches around Later Prehistoric sites. Similar deposits have been found in a range of other sub-soil features on Iron Age sites in Wessex. Examples from house wall foundation trenches and the eaves drip gullies surrounding circular structures have already been mentioned, and such deposits are also known from post-holes and 'working hollows'/quarries (see 8.5, 9.4, 8). However, it is also important to realise that such deposits were not just restricted to settlements.

At the Wilsford shaft (Ashbee et al 1989), Early Iron Age material was recovered from the erosion cone around the top of a shaft in the centre of a Bronze Age pond barrow. This was considered as 'casual' or 'accidental', from either a surface scatter or exposed pit fill. However, I would argue that human bone fragments, a complete jar, articulated portions of sheep carcasses and the limbs of dog, cattle skull(s), deer bone, and worked bone and antler, in with 'scattered sherds and animals bones' suggest that this was a deliberate ritual deposit similar to others discussed in this thesis. This 'off-settlement' deposit was not unique. Recent work on other parts of Salisbury Plain have shown how the Late Bronze Age linear ditches were re-dug in the Iron Age, where the reinstatement of these boundaries was accompanied by deposits of cattle and horse *ABG's* (Bradley *pers com.*).

It is not then the case that these deposits were exclusively associated with pits. There was equally significant emphasis placed on the boundary ditch surrounding many settlements and on other humanly created holes in the ground. Given that such deposits occurred in a range of subsoil features, and had earlier been found on hut floors (see 12.2.2.), it is unlikely that deposits in pits were either the primary focus of this ritual tradition or primarily because of the pits' storage function. It seems more important that the associations between people, things, activities and spaces ritually objectified in these sacrifices were physically etched onto settlement space and the landscape. That is, it was their placement in features - cut by people - and penetrating the ground, that linked these deposits. Barrett has begun to elaborate on the important vertical distinctions within mounds in Bronze Age mortuary practices, where the ground surface acted as an important datum for structuring the position of deposits (Barrett et al 1991:128, cf. Mizoguchi forthcoming). One of the important changes that occurred during the Middle Bronze Age, when the components of this ritual tradition took form (see 12.2.2.), was that mortuary deposits were cut into the ground surface - rather than lain on the ground surface (Barrett et al 1991:224). Iron Age offerings continued this pattern, pointing to an important contrast between *above* and *below* ground (see 11.10). Therefore, these deposits could not simply be to do with thanking the gods of the underworld for the safe storage of grain, and the assumption that this was a fertility cult needs re-appraisal (see 11.10).

11.8. Everything in its Place

A cluster of elements, concrete symbols, have been identified in this ritual tradition which were rarely all found together in the same deposits. Oppositions or correspondences between elements were primarily expressed through space as deposits were made over long periods of time on the same sites. Previous chapters have demonstrated several key spatial axes (the site's boundary, orientation, and facing), which formed a grid onto which were mapped the associations and disassociations found in various deposits (see 8.5-6, 9). This work demonstrates that Iron Age spaces were not organised according to a Western functional rationale (Hill 1993), but rather confirm the existence of the Later Prehistoric 'symbolic settlement' (Parker-Pearson forthcoming). This is not to argue for any universal structuralism, which identification of front:back, inside:out oppositions often seems to imply. An opposition between the inside and outside of a settlement may be an almost universal potential, but rarely is the boundary symbolically accentuated through architecture and deposits in the specific ways it was in the Southern British Iron Age.

Space is both the medium and outcome, presupposition and embodiment, of society (Bourdieu 1977, 1990; Giddens 1984; H.Moore 1986; Pred 1986; Soja 1989). Iron Age settlement sites and landscapes were not simply a backdrop to, nor merely a product, of Iron Age societies, but they played a key role in their constitution. The farmsteads and hamlets of these landscapes, where the spaces of work/home/growing up were the same, acted as 'structuring structures'. Through their homologous structures of physical and symbolic oppositions, these were the pre-eminent locations for the creation and experience of cultural order during this period.

In growing up, in living through the daily routines in and around such settlements, people inculcated their culture's tangible classifying system and gained the ontological security provided by this world of certainties. These spaces were read through the movement of the human body, by human actions (Bourdieu 1990; De Certeau 1984; H.Moore 1986). These actions created, sustained or manipulated the meanings of different spaces:

> "Space comes to have meaning through practice. Such practice is informed by a set of schemes which are represented in the order of space" (H. Moore 1986:77).

Such a process might be schematised as follows;

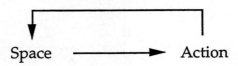

A model for the general relationship between structure and practice could be presented as (see 1.4);

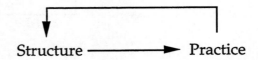

Given the different possible readings of the same spaces, little attention has been paid to how dominant readings are sustained. Physical architecture limits the movement of the body and the emotional responses of encountering certain spaces, so closing down the range of possible readings (e.g. Foster 1989; Thomas 1991). However, the common explicit connection between settlement organisation and cosmology, pictures of the universe in spatial terms (Parker-Pearson forthcoming), provided a powerful medium for further limiting the possible meanings of spaces. The relationship between space and cosmology is reproduced through a diverse network of practices and *need not* include any categorical statement of their connection through ritual (Kus & Raharijaona 1990). In Later Prehistoric Wessex, however, I would argue that ritual was the principal mechanism by which meaning was invested/controlled in the built environment (cf. C. Hugh-Jones 1979). Ritual deposits physically engraved, writ large in an explicit way, a dominant reading of space that would have been heavily felt in the routine activities that took place in and through those spaces. The re-cutting and backfilling of the Winnall enclosure ditch did not simply redefine the natural social unit it contained, but renewed that people's connectedness to their cosmology (cf. Lawrence and Low 1990:415). The 'symbolic settlement', with its orientation to the east and concern with marking north and south etc. (see 8 & 9), intruded mythic and cosmic images into all daily actions (and vice versa), to bond theologies and moralities with space and time through the medium of the body and its daily activities.

The movement of peoples within these charged spaces of houses, settlements and landscapes must be central to our understanding of Later Prehistory (cf. Barrett 1991d - see 1.4.). Space is primary for the constitution of any society, but this particular attention to physical boundaries and the marked spatial patterning in sacrificial deposits was unique to these Iron Age societies. It may suggest that thinking spatially about the world was particularly strong in Later Prehistoric Wessex cultures. In this ritual tradition, a series of key spatial axes provided the way of organising the cognitive connections between its different elements and meanings. Offerings explicitly linked different types of people, objects, animals, and the ideas they symbolised, to different parts of the settlement. Memories of such offerings and corresponding ideas would have been ever present in the use of such spaces, and in encounters with the objects, animals and peoples inscribed on them: "Sacrifice introduces guidelines into the universe; it already sketches out a topology even a cosmology" (De Heusch 1985:213).

11.9. Ritual Deposition and the Everyday

I have argued in this thesis against a disjuncture between ritual and daily activities, the sacred and the profane in the Iron Age. Ritual draws from and reproduces the same generative principles as other social practices (J.Turner 1992). As such all rituals are related to daily practices, but the intimacy and potency of that inter relation varies considerably with the particular nature of ritual traditions. Compared to the ritual consumption of Bronze Age or Late Iron Age fine metalwork, these deposits of materials represented a range of routine activities, and the people involved and therefore had a far greater direct semantic continuity with the everyday. The same categories of animate and inanimate things encountered in everyday life were used in these rituals but according to more stringent combinatorial rules (Traube 1984:21-3, C.Hugh-Jones 1978). Such associations have been discussed for cooking and eating, where the ritual consumption evidenced in these deposits was not totally divorced from daily activities. Rather they were the same, but stronger, extended, versions of the latter (see 12.2.1); "Sacrifice is efficacious insofar as ideas order or even constitute praxis" (Valeri 1985:ix-x). Ritual and everyday practices are structured in terms of the same categories, rules and resources. They necessarily flow into each other, and as I have argued in the thesis,

> "they are informed by the same meaning (and) ...as a consequence ritual resonates with the 'truths' that are affirmed in daily life and everyday practice is linked to the sacred" (J.Turner 1991:294).

This relationship I have already schematised as follows. However, it is important to stress that the distinction between ritual and routine activities was probably not sharply drawn, but blurred.

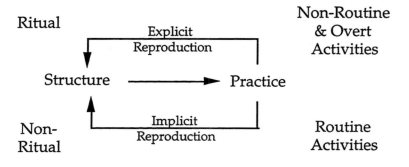

11.10.   A Life-Giving Technique

> In religious belief and practice a people's style of life...is rendered intellectually reasonable; it is shown to represent a way of life ideally adapted to the world 'as it really...is'. At the same time, the supposed basic structure of reality is rendered emotionally convincing because it is presented as an actual state of affairs uniquely accommodated to such a way of life... (Geertz 1968:406).

This chapter began with a detailed interpretation of the practices that produced the majority of the material excavated from Later Prehistoric Wessex sites. I have suggested that these deposits were offerings, sacrifices, in which certain classes of material were 'presenced' (Turner 1967). Particular items were represented with their associated values, activities and kinds of persons, but others were excluded. A range of dominant symbols from the daily world of home and field were handled in these sacrifices. Pottery, animals, tools, crops, and people were manipulated as metaphors and metonyms in similar ways. It is therefore meaningless to discuss the deposition of animal bone as a coherent entity separated from the deposits of pot-sherds, or the treatment of human remains as a distinct mortuary practice.

Not all structured deposition can be interpreted as ritual during the Iron Age, and not all the material evidence excavated on Wessex Iron Age sites derived from offerings. However, many of the layers/features which are not obviously 'exceptional' deposits demonstrate structured relationships between different classes of material which are still, albeit fuzzily, evident. This *explicit* articulation of key classifying principles through the deposition of material in particular parts of sites was not a universal, cross-cultural phenomena. Instead deliberate ritual deposits of a range of material began in the Neolithic and the effect of this long accumulation of practice was to create what was a particular *long-term* characteristic of north-west European prehistory.

The essence of this Iron Age ritual process was the building of definitions in a clarified form to create understandings of the premises of a cultural system (Turner 1969; Kelly & Kaplan 1990;Valeri 1985). Three connecting themes could be discerned through all the elements of these Iron Age sacrifices:

Classification
Mediation
Transformation

Classification is visible in the clear differentiation of categories of the same classes of phenomena such as pit shape, pottery type, animal species, spaces, or type of person. Similar explicit differences were also made between different classes of material, such as pottery and animal bone. The details and sequences of feature-fills showed how classification and mediation were linked in individual layers, dominated by single classes of things, and were combined in an orderly way. Relationships expressed in the "model experiences" of sacrifice (Valeri 1985:345) must be recognised as pervading all routine activities. Thus the mediation between species expressed in the ritual consumption of different species together (see 7.3.3), and even as parts of individuals brought together to make a composite whole *ABG* (see 7.3.2), probably extended to any eating of meat (see 5.4.2.). Marking, and by implication controlling, transformations cross-cut the spaces, objects, and persons brought together in these deposits, be it a transformation involved in the changing of agricultural products (working bone, processing crops, cooking), or the changing of the human body (both marking its coming of age and physical dissolution on death). While such transformations may appear connected to natural processes, they, like the classifications of nature evident in these deposits, were all brought about by human actions.

Through sanctioning demarcations and their mediations of the social world, ritual deposits publicly made concrete ties between diverse parts of that world. The bringing together of spaces, pots, animals, people, even rubbish, into the sacred arena made the qualities they represented malleable. Associations made would have been felt most whenever actions involved specific spaces, objects or people, and provided a pattern of homology for the definition of human groups. The importance of space in this ritual process has been stressed. The explicit ordering of space was with grand outlines of cosmology, material culture, and repetitive daily routines (cf. Kus & Raharijaona 1990). Cosmology should remind archaeologists to consider those dimensions often forgotten through a blinkered concentration on two-dimensional site plans. To distinctions such as in:out, left:right, east:west, must be added up:down, hinted at in this chapter through the importance of birds, the placing of deposits in holes penetrating the ground surface, and the sequence of those fills (see 7.9, 11.2, 11.7).

The deliberately interrupted sequences of pit-fills at Winklebury (see 7.9) emphasised the importance of time. Different time periods were inscribed in Iron Age deposits, which included daily and seasonal cycles of activities around settlements, and structures locked into the passage of the sun and seasons through their easterly orientations (see 9). Other time periods represented included those of the passage through human life (that included the time period of the final dissolution of the corpse through excarnation). The importance of space/time in these deposits cannot be over-emphasised, especially as a minimal definition of ritual may be formulaic spatiality;

Formulaic Spatiality : "...the capacity to create and act through idioms of passage, movement, including exchange, journey, axis, concentricism, and up-and-down directions" (Parkin 1992:18).

Previous discussions of these deposits have argued that "it is probably natural fertility which is the goal of the ritual" (Wait 1985:251, see 2.4.). However, I have argued that a detailed understanding of this tradition cannot be neatly put in a box marked 'fertility', denoting a concern with the origins and regeneration of the natural world. During these Iron Age sacrifices certain materials/symbols could generally not be 'presenced', for example particularly impressive metalwork, weaponry, and personal adornments. Those materials/symbols which were 'presenced' were heavily redolent of the domestic and agricultural; the indistinguishable world in which 'home', craft and farming activities were inseparable and for which we have no adequate word to translate. Animals and plants, and their transformations, were involved in depositional practices through human actions (and control). Concern was for the reproduction and ordering of a social world in which it was wrong to distinguish agricultural products from other components. This can be understood as a world of *culture* (summoning up a play around *cult, cultivation* of plants and animals, and *cultivation* of manners, habits, people), set against the wild worlds of 'nature' (e.g. undomesticated animals) and people (social discourses of individuals, weapons, objects associated with individuals).

Although this ritual tradition has been described by me as 'a life-giving technique', even a 'technology' (Traube 1984:12), this is not due to any previous notions of fertility. Bradley's comment that "the link with storage pits is so pervasive that it seems possible the dead were believed to exert influence over the agricultural cycle" (1991:61), wrongly distinguished human remains as a special part of these deposits and over-emphasised the role of the storage pit. Pits were not the sole location of these deposits, and as such it is hard to argue that their role of crop storage was as central an element in these rituals as previously thought. Therefore, this Iron Age ritual tradition was neither a 'pit ritual tradition' nor a 'pit belief system'.

This chapter has outlined something of the specific substance of the material symbols used and articulated in the tradition of ritual deposits I have discussed in this study. I have previously argued against studies of prehistoric ritual which simply use the 'R' word as a label or a box in which to put phenomena in. The danger with this approach is that the labelling becomes far more important than actually understanding the nature of the specific rituals we are studying. Neolithic mortuary enclosures, deposits in grooved ware pits, bronzes from wet deposits and hoards, LIA shrines can all be labelled 'ritual', but are quite clearly very different sorts of activities in very different contexts from one other. We need to attempt to understand something of the specific nature of different rituals. This means a study of the crucial symbols different rituals employed which recognise that these were not arbitrarily selected. Rather the central symbols and metaphors articulated in a ritual tradition reflect fundamental concepts and social practices in the societies that practise those rituals. To understand a ritual tradition is then to know something of substance of the societies which practise that tradition. Or as Geertz eloquently put it; "in ritual, the world as lived and the world as imagined... turn out to be the same world" (1973:112).

Chapter 12
Deposits in History,
Deposits making History

12.1. Introduction

Fitzpatrick (1991:127) has argued that a serious flaw in previous studies of Iron Age/Celtic religion is that time and place seem incidental. This is a danger with the last chapter's discussion of the main themes articulated in this tradition of deposits. However, traditions of social practices are not timeless, rather they are changing to meet, and to initiate, changes in their wider social context. This chapter briefly elaborates this view of ritual practices by showing both the changes that can be seen in this tradition of deposits through the first millenium BC, and the different ways the tradition was manifested in different parts of southern England. This is to situate these practices in history. The chapter then moves further to begin to consider the relationship between these practices and the organisation of Wessex Iron Age societies, outlining the central role such rituals played in sustaining the dominant social discourses through which Iron Age societies were constituted. This is to understand how these deposits helped make history.

12.2. Deposits in History
12.2.1 Variation in Ritual Traditions

Important differences in depositional practices on contemporary sites are evident across Later Prehistoric Wessex. Some differences have been claimed between the types of deposits on hillforts and non-hillforts (Wait 1985:133-121; Hill 1995), while other variations are evident on a 'sub-regional' scale. For example in different parts of Wessex human deposits were more common than in others, e.g. Early and Middle Iron Age sites in Dorset and South Wiltshire had relatively few human deposits compared to North Wiltshire and Hampshire (Hill nd1, 1990). Also the orientation of complete human carcasses in pits and graves varied considerably across the region, although in North Wiltshire human burials unusually shared a strict northerly orientation (Whimster 1981:14).

However, although clouded by the problems of directly comparing sites excavated to different standards, differences existed within this Later Prehistoric ritual tradition between sites within the same 'sub-region' and these local peculiarities remained constant on some sites for several centuries. Thus at Middle Iron Age Danebury there were differences in how plain:decorated combs were deposited (see 7.2.3). Only at Danebury were combs particularly marked out in this way; at Early Iron Age Gussage it was bone gouges (see 7.6.3), while at Middle Iron Age Winnall it was any worked bone/antler (see 7.2.3, 7.3.5). Clearly bone and antler objects were a general category of objects marked out in these deposits, but the specific way this theme was expressed could be extremely varied, if not contradictory.

Similar variability was found in a wide range of parts of this tradition. Wild animal and bird remains have been given considerable emphasis in my study. But again how their importance was manifest could vary considerably. There is no simple black and white rule book in operation here, nor a fixed liturgy. The species 'played' with and their associations could vary over time, even on the same site. At Middle Iron Age Winnall bird bone was significantly associated with human remains, while at Danebury with ABG's (see 7.5). At some sites the body position of human remains was strictly controlled through time, but not at other sites (Whimster 1981:13-14; C.Wilson 1981). In addition to this, the choice of favoured species and type of ABG could vary. For example complete/partial carcasses were not recorded during the excavations at Micheldever, and at Poundbury almost all the deposits were of sheep (Green 1987), while at Middle Iron Age Balksbury pig was unusually common. This diversity is set within the same shared culture and ritual traditions, in which general trends and common structuring principles are discernible, but the way in which these specific principles were materialised, and their elements combined, was not according to a liturgical rigidity. The transformation of bone and antler was an important concrete symbol within this tradition, but how it was specifically manifest (and interpreted) could vary considerably. Do differences between deposits on various sites, or different phases, really matter or was this variability superficial?

Archaeological and ethnographic analyses usually assume a high degree of homogeneity in cultural/social phenomena in time and space. Ethnographies rarely consider the evident differences between a ritual in neighbouring communities or how rituals change through time, although there are notable exceptions which suggest a generative approach to such cultural variation (Barth 1987; Keesing 1981a:210-217; Parkin 1992). For example, Barth modelled cosmological communication and innovation to explain the "raucous variation" between the conscious reconstruction of male initiation rites separated by up to ten years in Highland Papua New Guinea. This work demonstrates how local differences in ritual practices can be approached and how deeply felt they can be for the people concerned. Local groups linked through language, culture, kinship, exchange, even participation in the same communal rituals, know of and can be deeply shocked by the differences in their ritual practices. On the other hand there need be no constant relationship between ritual, mythology or exegesis, and symbols need not have universal discrete meanings within the same 'culture'. Concrete symbols are multi-vocal; their different potentials can be elaborated and used differently by different 'sub-traditions', if used at all. For example the human skull, water, and the wild boar are all important symbols in Ok ritual and thought, but their use by, and meaning to, different groups can be varied and contradictory (Barth 1987:3-4,34-36). More importantly, these are not alternative vocabularies in which the same message of a ritual is expressed. The metaphors of ritual are read literally; the 'vocabulary' is integral to the message and so involves real differences in bodies of knowledge about the world.

From such ethnographic studies I suggest that diversity should be expected in non-literate cultural and ritual traditions, and that its effect is not superficial. This warns against constructing neat interpretations of the common core of symbols, and dimensions of differentiation, identified in Iron Age deposits; their particular manifestations may have had different dominant meanings. As such, the human skulls encountered in deposits need not have had the same types of origins, or if they had, almost certainly did not always have the same meaning. Equally, the broad cultural content objectified in this tradition could imply that in one part of Wessex complete human skeletons were sacrifices, while in another place or at another time they were natural deaths. This is to emphasise how cultures are transmitted and transformed, that is, through a multitude of individual practices and sub-traditions.

Traditions are transmissions, not slavish replications. The re-enactment of an intermittent social practice involves its reconstruction from memory, and the knowledge of other practices, mythology, cultural products and the dominant symbols that permeate daily routine. Through this creative process each re-enactment, in different circumstances, will vary and unintentionally or intentionally build cumulative changes. There are limits to the possible variation in any particular enactment, since any change or borrowing must be plausible within its specific context and replication may depend on their effectiveness. People would have known of, and witnessed, the differences in ritual practice amongst their neighbours. Differences in practice, between sites only a few kilometres apart, in a context where the identity of individual settlements appeared important (Hingley 1984; Stopford 1987; Hill 1995), could be seen as conscious difference-making to re-emphasise a group's individuality. The existence of such differences would have turned them into a resource

to be ignored or borrowed. Keesing stresses that such innovations or borrowings in ritual must be set within the "politics of innovation" (1981a:215). Which innovations and changes were adopted may relate both to the exchange of rituals and sacred knowledge as an object of exchange between groups (Harrison 1992). Alternatively, they may relate to the conscious adoption of ritual forms from what are perceived as more successful groups (an explanation of the spread of cremation in the LIA?). Such emulation may be related to the perception that a group's political or subsistence success is directly related to their ritual forms (Kessing 1981a).

The diversity in depositional practices between Wessex Iron Age sites is important. It points to real differences in the knowledge and readings of culture between inter-communicating groups. Therefore, specific histories represent an interplay of divergent creativity and modification, and convergent cross-influence which has important consequences. We should not assume that a 'Culture' or 'Social System' or 'Ritual Tradition' constitutes a single unity. Rather we should work from the assumption that there exists an aggregation of various sub-traditions. This would lead us away from "The very concept of culture as a tidy bundle of meaningful traditions handed down by a particular social group" (Goody in Barth 1987:viii).

We should not expect prehistoric rituals, especially those as irregularly spaced as these, to demonstrate exactly the same, constant, and repeatable form and content, as our expectations drawn from literate liturgical traditions lead us to expect. This has important implications. It is unlikely that a single, fixed meaning existed for any element in this ritual tradition. As such, trying to interpret one category of human remains as having the same constant origin, or having come from the same sort of person, across the region and throughout the many centuries of the Iron Age, is probably futile. Equally, it is unlikely that these ritual deposits represented the same type of ritual event throughout space and time. They were probably not *all* harvest thanksgivings, or marking initiation rites. Rather, we should think of them in terms of the same basic ritual form articulating the same basic repertoire of key cultural symbols, but to meet a possible wide range of different circumstances and events. An analogy would be with the basic nature of the Christian communion service/mass which forms the basic format for a Christian act of worship for a wide range of different celebrations and rituals, and can be creatively drawn on to produce an act of worship to meet new, unexpected circumstances etc. In one way this is to suggest that through a study such as this we can get at the grammar and the vocabulary of a prehistoric ritual 'language', even if the specific meaning of each ritual statement is far, far harder to comprehend.

12.2.2. Change Through Time

Diversity in ritual practice provides the basis for a fuller understanding of the nature of cultural traditions and how, through their transmission, they are open to change. From the diversity of practices across communities there are discernible general trends through time, particularly in the treatment of human remains (C.Wilson 1981, Whimster 1981, Wait 1985). However, previous discussions of Iron Age ritual (Wait 1985; Cunliffe 1992), and society (Bradley 1984; Cunliffe 1984b, 1991), are hobbled by the assumption that the Iron Age was a coherent entity, distinct from previous periods (Bradley 1990). If preceding centuries are mentioned in these discussions, it is merely as a 'background' or contrast, and is not recognised as essential for understanding the continuous flow of human conduct.

I would accept that in terms of house and ceramic forms, and hence the social discourses they structured/were structured by, there was no radical break during the Eighth Century BC, and that Late Bronze Age/Early Iron Age traditions have direct histories reaching back to the Middle Bronze Age, when an apparently secular world of settlement sites and field systems increasingly replaced the former ritual landscapes of communal monuments and barrows (Childe 1940:187ff, Bradley 1991, Barrett et al 1991). Changes in the nature and symbolic/political importance of agricultural and other daily routine practices meant that settlement sites and fields became the main monumental, hence archaeologically visible, form (Barrett 1989, 1993). It is in these transformations that the practices studied here must ultimately be set. The Middle Bronze Age was a period of radical transformation of pre-existing practices, social discourse focused on the daily and longer cycles of human and agricultural reproduction. A dominant symbolism emerged through which relationships of gender, age, and kin groups were structured. A discourse which turned the products of agricultural labour, the locations of its transformation and consumption, and the humans themselves into the resources of an explicit ideology/hegemony (Barrett 1989, Barrett et al 1991:223-6).

This is seen in the types of material deposited on the settlements that now become an increasingly important part of the archaeological record. Middle Bronze Age settlements seem to have been surprisingly frequently abandoned, with material left on the floors of their huts (e.g. Itford Hill, Black Patch, Trethellan Farm). These deposits may not be *De Facto* refuse, as Drewett (1982) interpreted them, but deposits made during the ritual closing of the site (Nowakowski 1990). Thus at Itford Hill, one small hut contained a large quantity of carbonized grain, while another had a partial cattle carcass placed on its floor (Burstow & Holleyman 1957:188 - cf. Dean Bottom - Gingell 1992). Such animal or plant deposits were not a common component of either Early or Middle Bronze

Age mortuary rites, and their appearance on settlements and in other contents during the Middle and Late Bronze marks a significant departure. Not only are the basic elements of the ritual traditions witnessed in Iron Age Wessex evident in the Middle Iron Age, but so are many of the basic structuring principles which ordered them. For example, at South Lodge (Barrett et al 1991), a north:south distinction was drawn between animal bone and pottery. Hut 1 to the north contained a partial cattle carcass buried in a shallow pit on its western side. Hut 2, to its south, contained a shallow pit on its south-east side which was covered by a mound of pot-sherds with a quern fragment. Here the primary distinction between pot and bone, mapped onto that between north and south, and the importance of deposits on the south-east side of a house or enclosure are all evident. Again, at South Lodge, deposits making the crossing of the site's threshold are evident, with another mound of pottery to the south of the enclosure's entrance. Again, the enclosure ditches of both South Lodge and Down Farm were deliberately backfilled, the fillings containing the now very similar deposits of fresh cattle bone, dog skulls and pot groups.

12.2.2.1. The Late Bronze Age and Early Iron Age

The Late Bronze Age, ceramically 'post-Deverel Rimbury' (Barrett 1980), marked a significant transformation in daily and ritual practices in Wessex (Barrett & Bradley 1980; Bradley 1984; Cunliffe 1984b). New ceramic forms demonstrated an increased cultural and political importance in eating and drinking (Barrett 1980). Settlement use became longer lived, with more and larger storage facilities at individual sites. The landscape was physically re-shaped with linear earthworks and the new foci of large, 'lightly' defended, enclosures such as Balksbury and Winklebury. It was from this period onwards that the distinct tradition of Iron Age social practices outlined in this study began its transformation.

During the Middle Bronze Age in Wessex three distinct areas of ritual practice can be discerned. The first was the mortuary rite involving cremations deposited with urns in small clusters, sometimes associated with an older barrow. The Deveril-Rimbury rite is a clear development of pre-existing mortuary practices. Alongside these practices directly centred on the body were those involving the deposition of bronze objects, singly or in hoards. Middle and Late Bronze Age hoards in Wessex did not involve the quantities or wide range of object types, or take place as frequently, as those in the Thames valley. However, this form of ritual consumption nevertheless remained an important part of social life. Finally, there was a range of ritual deposits of animal remains, pottery and other objects on settlements and other enclosures.

The transformation from Deveril-Rimbury to post-Deveril-Rimbury ceramic assemblages c.1000 b.c. was also accompanied by important changes in ritual which most also be related to those in the structures and practices of daily life evidenced by the change in settlement organisation and ceramic assemblages (c.f. Barrett & Bradley 1980; Barrett et al 1991). From this time onwards distinct formal mortuary practices - graves, burials, barrows etc. - become extremely uncommon. Instead, human remains now are increasingly represented on settlements, although this should not be seen simply as a shift of location. If cremation continues to be the dominant technology to transform the body on death, then the remains are now almost never deposited in archaeologically recoverable ways. However, from this time pieces of human bones become a common find on sites, implying that excarnation was being practised for some, if not most people. While similar to cremation in that the individual and the corpse were destroyed, excarnation significantly prolonged this important liminal period of transition (cf. Barrett 1988b). Excarnation also represented a significant change in the medium of the corpse's transformation, from fire to natural decay. Late Bronze Age/Early Iron Age human remains were generally complete or fragmentary bones, some of which were worked (further physically transformed, see C.Wilson 1981; Hill nd1; Brück forthcoming). While Middle Bronze Age mortuary practices see a shift in focus from barrows shaping their landscape, to the dead fitting within a landscape of fields (Barrett et al 1991), the Late Bronze Age saw the bringing in of (some) dead into the settlement itself. However, this still places too much emphasis on these human remains being seen solely in terms of mortuary practice. I argued in the last chapter that these deposits of human remains were something more and different from the simple treatment of the dead. These human remains joined with the pre-existing tradition of deposits involving animal remains, pottery and small finds etc.

These deposits are clearly the same phenomena as those found on Early and Middle Iron Age sites. The same elements, but also the same spatial concerns can be seen in these Late Bronze Age deposits as in those I have outlined in this study (see Needham 1992). With the earliest traces of occupation at Old Down Farm, Andover (Davies 1980), which date to c. 800-700 BC, the same basic pattern seen in the interior at South Lodge is repeated. This early phase contains only three excavated pits. Fortuitously (?), the one pit (937) in the north of the later enclosed site contained over 1000 bone fragments from at least 8 sheep ABG's along with 1163g of pottery (2 recognisable vessels, both jars). Two pits were clearly spatially separated from, and to the south of 937. Pit 2492 contained only 100g of pottery (one recognisable vessel - a bowl), and 236 bone fragments from a complete dog skeleton complete apart from its head. Pit 2493 contained only 114 animal bone fragments, but 5297g of pottery from a minimum of 12 recognisable vessels including 4 bowls, and a quern stone. Again, there appears to be a distinction being made in deposits between a

dominance of bone and pot & quern, equated with north and south. It is also in this period that substantial, multi-post ringed circular buildings were constructed, with their easterly facing porched entrances. Three of these buildings have now been excavated on separate sites which appear to have been destroyed by fire, preserving something of the nature and location of their contexts (Longbridge Deveril Cow Down - Chadwick-Hawkes 1994; Brighton Hill South, Basingstoke - Coe et al. 1992; Dunston Park -Fitzpatrick 1994a). Whether these burnings should be seen as accidents, or, as appears more likely to me, as equivalents to the ritual abandonments/closings of some Middle Bronze Age settlements has not been established. However, as Fitzpatrick (1994a) has shown, these buildings all appear to have pottery concentrating in the south-east quadrant, south of the entrance.

From the Middle Bronze Age onwards it is possible to see the emergence and the development of a series of themes which were to be a dominant force in creating the archaeological record over the next thousand years. Through this dominant social discourse, articulated through a ritual tradition of depositing a limited range of materials in the ground, people encountered their world, motivating and giving shape to all their activities. This was not a single unchanging system, in the systemic sense. Through these structures, which threw up, unintentionally, human and agricultural reproduction as a dominant symbolism, relations of age, gender, status etc. were articulated. They also gave the historically specific forms that the nature of surplus production and its consumption took, the vehicle for establishing prestige and building social relations. It is in this light that it is important to recognise that quite different social discourses were probably available throughout the Later Bronze Age and Iron Age. It is in this context that the relationship between Iron Age practices, and those which define the Bronze Age must be considered.

It is important to ask what the relationship might have been between these settlement-centred deposits and the other dominant ritual form, the use and deposition of bronze artefacts. Need they have been complementary to each, or represent alternative ritual discourses (c.f. Braithwaite 1984)? The deposition of bronze objects singly or in hoards did not take place in Wessex on the same scale as in the Thames Valley. Such practices have been interpreted in terms of a 'prestige goods system' (Rowlands 1980) and as central to the reproduction of Bronze Age societies. If such is the case, then it must be recognised that such practices and the discourse they maintained became (if they were not originally) an alternative to discourse structured around the cycles, and symbolism, of undifferentiated human and agricultural reproduction.

	Mortuary Practice	Settlements	Hoards
Early Bronze Age	Inhumations & Cremations in Prominent Barrows with Grave Goods		Bronze Hoards
Middle Bronze Age	Cremation Mortuary practices in cemeteries close to settlements	Animal, Grain & Pot deposits on settlements	Bronze Hoards
Late Bronze Age		Animal, Grain, Pot & Human deposits on settlements	Bronze Hoards
Early Iron Age		Animal, Grain, Pot & Human deposits on settlements	

A simplified chronology of changing foci of ritual deposition in Southern Britain c.2000-400 BC

In the Late Bronze Age it would seem that these two discourses became dominant in different parts of southern England: the former in the Thames valley, the latter in Wessex. In Wessex, Barrett et al (1991:240) have argued that the lesser frequency of bronze objects deposited here, compared to the Thames Valley, only *displayed* "social and cultural distinctions, which were structured through the divisions of labour associated with agricultural production". Some bronze objects were clearly in circulation, even as 'prestige goods' but this was "not *central* to strategies of social reproduction" (my emphasis). However, I would want to explore the possibility that the use, circulation and deposition of bronze objects could have been more active, even offering an alternative strategy of social reproduction. This is to see these as alternative, rival, ritual traditions articulating different social discourses, legitimating contradictory forms for the nature of surplus production and its consumption. While clearly one or the other was dominant at any one time and place in the Late Bronze, it should not be assumed that individuals could not participate in both. In Wessex, at different times and places, groups and individuals could have attempted to use the circulation of bronze objects as an alternative competitive strategy for establishing rank and prestige. This might have been an attractive strategy to those marginalised by, or those seeking to escape the existing obligations and constraints of the dominant discourse. Such an alternative would rarely, perhaps, have been a sharp either/or situation, and we must envisage individuals participating in both, contradictory, discourses to varying degrees. This situation was probably not unique to the Late Bronze Age (cf. Braithwaite 1984), but the normal course of events. Such similar explanations are applicable to the changes visible in the Late Iron Age, but probably were a constant feature of the Early and Middle Iron Ages as well. The problem with the archaeological manifestation of a dominant social discourse is that, because it was dominant, it is difficult to see failed alternatives in the archaeological record. In such a perspective, it should not be seen as inevitable that, due to any inherent property, the ritual discourse outlined in this study should have become dominant. The Iron Age was possibly not the inevitable outcome of the Bronze Age.

It is from such a perspective that we could approach the brief fluorescence of ritual bronze consumption in Wessex during Hallstatt C, or the Llyn Fawr phase as it is called in Britain. This period marked the Bronze Age/Iron Age transition in Britain and western Europe. In the Thames Valley, a major region for the deposition of bronzes in preceding centuries, deposits of bronzes almost totally stopped.

However, at the same time, those parts of southern Britain that had witnessed few hoards and single deposits previously are marked by a flourish of hoarding at this stage (Thomas 1989). Some of these hoards contain iron objects for the first time, usually copies of bronze forms, while the character of the bronze objects has lead to suggestions they were increasingly tokens for exchange and competition (Thomas 1989). Thomas has argued that this flourish in Wessex, at a time when bronze consumption had apparently dropped steeply in the previous 'core' area, was because areas like Wessex now had access to metal no longer socially required elsewhere. Such consumption in Wessex can be seen as an attempt to participate in the competitive network of exchange and consumption of bronze objects, even if the metal was by now largely non-functional except as a medium/symbol of exchange and status. The flourish of Llyn Fawr deposits perhaps attests to the long-lasting attractiveness of the social discourses articulated through 'playing the bronze game' even for those communities largely excluded from them for several centuries. Was the 'failure' of this Llyn Fawr phase to continue longer in Wessex 'simply' due to the collapse of the international bronze exchange networks, or because direct control of land and agricultural production were of greater 'real' and 'ideological' importance than the manipulation of the exchange and alliance networks evidenced in bronze deposits? Was the ritual tradition of using bronze objects not strong enough to succeed? Or, was the success of those individuals and groups engaged in this different strategy translated into the traditional resources drawn on in the existing dominant strategies centred on the reproduction of the local community?

EIA Iron objects were generally not common in deposits, especially compared to the proportions of worked bone or antler. This need not directly indicate the abundance of iron during this period; the new dominant metal (as with bronze) may generally have been excluded from these deposits.

12.2.2.2. Subsequent Early and Middle Iron Age Transformations

There is no discernible break in settlement or ritual deposits with the beginning of the Iron Age, rather an end to bronze hoarding. The next five centuries show the continuity of the ritual tradition outlined in this study, with its changes through drift, changed circumstances and conscious modification. There appears to be no radical break between the EIA and MIA, but general trends are hard to discern in the considerable variability in the tradition. Because of this variability between sites, I would suggest that some of the differences that Wait's (1985) initial investigations showed of change in this tradition through time, are more a product of this considerable variation, than real chronological trends. The Hampshire sites studied in detail here do not show a decrease in the deposition of complete/partial animal carcasses from the EIA to the MIA, nor a decrease in the frequency of cattle

and pig deposits. At Balksbury in the MIA pig increase to form a significant proportion of all *ABGs*. Although based on so few sites, one possible change with time was the increased frequency of dog *ABG's* on settlement sites such as Winnall, Balksbury and Old Down Farm. Spatial evidence at Winnall Down suggests that here (and elsewhere?) dog bones were deposited beyond the site's margins in the EIA, and possibly treated in analogous ways to human remains. If this is an important trend, then the general absence of dog *ABG's* at both the hillforts of Danebury and Winklebury in the MIA may be significant.

Hingley (1990c) has shown that towards the end of the MIA large deposits of iron objects and scrap become common on Wessex sites. These include hoards of 'currency bars' and appear to have been deposited on preferably a site's margins. Major deposits of metal working debris may also be considered in this context (e.g. Gussage All Saints MIA pit 209). These deposits cannot be directly read as an increase in the volume of metal production or exchange during the Third to First Centuries BC. Rather its increasing importance in the discourse is articulated in these ritual deposits, perhaps because increased scale of production and exchange were highly ambiguous notions in the context of the apparent emphasis on the immediate, agrarian and local in this discourse.

The clearest general trend was in the treatment of human remains. There was an increased deposition of complete human carcasses on sites through time. Evidence for complete adult corpses became steadily more frequent during the Middle and Late Iron Ages, sometimes accompanied by something possibly describeable as 'grave goods', with increased numbers in graves. These deposits were usually made just beyond the settlement's limits or close to a settlement's margin (e.g. Winnall see 9.5, C.Wilson 1981, Durotrigian burials - Whimster 1981:37-59). That this might have been the normal location for excarnation/disposal of excarnated remains is hinted at by C.Wilson, who suggested that, through the period, human burials "gradually infiltrated" onto sites (1981:141). Some complete human carcasses were deposited in all types of features in the EIA. However, a particular group include those under hillfort ramparts, which from Whimster's (1981) distribution map would appear to be confined to the limited area similar to Hingley's (1990c) later MIA distribution of iron 'currency bar' hoards in settlement boundary contexts. Partial corpses, skulls, and articulated limbs appeared to peak in the Middle Iron Age (especially on hillforts, see Hill forthcoming a; Wait 1985:116-120). Therefore, an increased number of individuals (not allowed a natural dissolution through excarnation), were increasingly deposited in features distinctively created for this sole purpose. This trend represented a significant transformation in the strategies of representation of the human body - and we should think in terms of these bodies being viewed in the grave, pit or ditch - and what these human metonyms consequently signified. Coarsely described, such changes represented a gradual separating out of those categories formerly mixed and mediated, increasingly to emphasise (certain) people as distinct individuals. Such changes engendered the emergence of a more distinct mortuary tradition.

12.2.2.3. The Late Iron Age: Ritual fracture and alternative discourses

Socially and ritually the Middle and Late Iron Ages was a period of fragmentation in Wessex, complicated by the lack of extensively excavated Late Iron Age sites. I suggest that there was a decrease in the number of *ABG* depositions. Complete/partial animal skeletons appear to be rarer, possibly since complete human skeletons were more common (a direct relationship if substitutes for each other). This does not imply that animal sacrifice was less common, nor that animal bone assemblages had more 'rational' origins. Ritual consumption was a feature of all prehistoric societies, but it is only archaeologically visible if the end results were deposited in a recoverable manner. Rather than a decline in sacrifice during the Late Iron Age, more meat was possibly employed in strategies for building social obligations amongst the living (instead of being reserved for offerings).

Other evidence points to the continued, if distinctly changed, importance of consumption. Eating, both routine and ritualised, played a key part in competing social discourses in Later Iron Age Southern England. New specialised ceramic (and metal/wood) forms emerged to augment the basic Middle Iron Age bowls and jars. A compartmentalisation of function and form accompanied the appearance of 'sets' of eating equipment and, for the first time, specific drinking vessels. This suggests an increased concern with the structure (and presentation) of the meal, the meal being a key symbolic code in the articulation of relationships of gender and status. This representation of food formed a new area of 'ritual consumption', especially with the incorporation of food vessels in ritual deposits such as Aylesford style cremations, 'Durotrigian' burials. These incorporations of specific ceramic forms in burials explicitly constructed specific metaphorical links between categories of material culture, types of humans and areas of social practice. Similar links were also made through the ways new, imported, ceramics were incorporated or excluded in formal deposits made in pits and ditches (e.g. Gussage see 9.6).

Attention is usually paid to the fine metalwork and coinage deposited in considerable numbers during this period, but personal ornaments also became more common in archaeological deposits and may offer different insights into general changes during the period. Brooches, bracelets, beads occurred in graves as part of the strategies which represented a

whole individual. Ornaments were also found in larger numbers on settlements, and this *cannot* be taken as a reflection of their increasing abundance. Rather, the 'rules' that had previously excluded such objects from deposition were transformed as ornaments became incorporated into the existing tradition of formal deposits (see 7.6.3). For example, the number of brooches recovered from Gussage All Saints dramatically increases in the last phase of occupation, and this flourish of fibulae - so typical of the Early Roman period - represents a distinct change in how we see the past which might even be called *The Fibulae Event Horizon* (with apologies to Adams 1989). As such the dramatic increase in the numbers of brooches found on sites in the First Centuries BC/AD, along with other small 'trinkets' associated with the adornment of the body (these include objects such as toilet objects) must be set in the context of changes in the strategies of representation of the body and the increased archaeological importance of the individual noted by Sharples (1991c). This is to emphasise that new categories of material culture and 'imports' (and the ideas they embodied) did not enter a cultural vacuum, but were incorporated into existing social categorisations and transformed existing practices.

The Fibulae Event Horizon as seen at Gussage All Saints

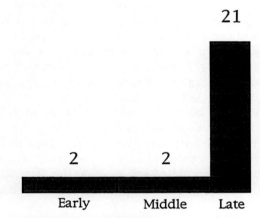

Number of Fibulae deposited per phase

Distinctly different forms of mortuary practice emerged or were incorporated during the Later Iron Age. In Southern Dorset 'Durotrigian' burial practices appeared where previously there had been relatively few deposits of human remains (Whimster 1981:37-59; Sharples 1991c:87). These deposits were clustered in small cemeteries of oval-shaped graves on the edge of settlements, with older children and adults (never younger children) deposited with a specific range of grave goods. Here gender distinctions were clearly represented for the first time through the particular species of meat joints placed in graves; pig with females, cattle with men, sheep/goat with either (Parker-Pearson forthcoming; Sharples 1990a:92-3). Significantly, neither dog nor horse was represented. This rite was restricted geographically to the area between Portland and the Isle of Purbeck. In north Dorset, but still within the area supposedly held by the 'Durotriges', a different transformation took place which involved unprovisioned inhumations of all ages (though this did not represent all the population) in pits and ditches without grave goods, e.g. Rotherley, Woodcutts and Gussage. A north:south spatial gender distinction was also apparent at Gussage (see 8).

There is evidence for regional traditions of practice on the Isle of Wight, with a localised group of crouched inhumations in cists around Ventnor (Whimster 1981), and in East Hampshire and West Sussex. In these latter areas a distinct sub-type of the Late Iron Age cremation rite (well-known in South Eastern England) was practised into the Early Roman period (Millett 1987). Generally these were small cemeteries of cremations buried on the edges of settlements (for example at Owslebury, Collis 1977), although a larger cemetery was recently excavated near Chichester (Fitzpatrick 1994b). The adoption of cremation, which had been a non-local rite, might be understood in terms of a deliberate rejection of the dominant authoritative symbols of the excarnated body and the use of its parts, although there is a danger of equating cremation or inhumation with a single universal meaning. Late Iron Age cremation was practised within a different historical context from Middle Bronze Age cremation. However, if this was an opposition to the previous norm of excarnation and secondary burial, might this mean that cremation was viewed in terms of purification, in contrast to the prolonged physical decay of the corpse, direct human intervention by speeding up the liminal phase between 'primary' and 'secondary burial'? This contrast also led to increased concern with controlling the body's transformation through the physical, technological, intervention of the pyre. Equally, both inhumation and, especially, cremation prevented parts of an individual's skeleton being circulated and used -as the deposits of individual bone fragments reflect- after excarnation

It is important not to see Wessex divided into distinct regions of ritual practice in the LIA. Some areas lacked distinctive mortuary practices, for example West Hampshire and Wiltshire, or followed the general trend towards pit and grave inhumations. However, even in apparently homogeneous areas different practices are evident. Pit deposits continued on many sites, often becoming increasingly 'pit burials', but several complex mixed human, animal and small finds deposits are known from this period (e.g. Flagstones, Dorset and Viables Farm, Basingstoke) Alongside 'pit burials' on Cranborne Chase, certain individuals were cremated and buried (unfurnished) in square barrows (White 1970; Barrett et al 1991:227-242). This alternate strategy appeared widespread, and a scattering of square barrows and/or rich cremations (often associated with the dyke systems/'territorial oppida'), are known across the region (Corney 1989). Within the 'Durotrigian burial' area there were

notable differences. A Late Iron Age pit with a human infant skull, adult skeleton, and articulated cattle and horse limbs was excavated amongst a typical cemetery at Flagstones, Dorchester (Bullock nd), while individual stone cists, with few grave goods, were used on the Isle of Purbeck (Whimster 1981; Sunter & Woodward 1987). Three 'Durotrigian' burials contained mirrors, and two swords (Whimster 1981), drawing on a similar repertoire of specific objects found in a scatter of burials across Southern Britain (Whimster 1981:129-146; Collis 1972). Comparable sword inhumations were found on the Isle of Wight (Whimster 1981:134) and Owslebury (Collis 1970, 1972). The Owslebury 'warrior' was surrounded by a cluster of cremations. Nevertheless, furnished cremation was not the sole mortuary practice around Winchester. At Winnall Down, 6 kilometres to the north, a few unaccompanied pit burials were deposited in the south of the site into the Roman period, while the majority of the population was still archaeologically undetectable in death. This continuance of an existing tradition, could have been increasingly recognised as *traditional* (Giddens 1979:200) in the face of alternative ritual discourses. This is to argue that there existed broad social, ritual and physical landscapes of fracture during the Late Iron Age which are unpredicted, let alone explained, through existing archaeological interpretations of the period.

Later Iron Age transformations have generally been interpreted as the result of a spreading Roman world. However, the gradual shift in emphasis, toward the complete corpse, highlighted the existence of longer-term cultural trends. A shift towards the complete individual was only one component of a gradual change expressed in all aspects of life across North-West Europe. For example, from a previously narrow ceramic corpus a wide range of specialist forms appeared with different vessels for particular functions. The perception and organisation of space similarly changed with an increased emphasis on division. Later Iron Age settlement sites, such as Gussage or Winnall, were no longer large, single enclosures, but clusters of smaller units with possibly distinct functions (compare plans in Cunliffe 1984b:Figs 2.12 & 2.18). In Dorset a previously largely open landscape was increasingly enclosed with small square fields, compounds, and settlements (Sharples 1991c). We may perceive similar ontological changes, with an increased emphasis on the individual (Sharples 1992c:86-7; Pearce 1992), in terms of the strategies of representation of the body, the emergence of distinct arenas of mortuary practice, and also the greater quantities of personal ornaments and objects that were deposited on sites. While beyond the scope of this study, I would suggest that the supposed impact of the Roman world was writ upon deeper long-term changes of compartmentalisation, specialisation, and individualisation (of all aspects of culture, society and people). Long-term changes were also evident in the form and location of ritual practices, and a general model may be proposed with a shift from undifferentiated practices on settlements, to an increase in different types of practice in different locations, often away from the settlement. This possible changes can be visualised in the model outlined in Fig. 12.1. Parkin (1991:2) has argued that to think about the sacred is to think about space, and to some extent vice versa. In this case, the spatial distinctions drawn between different activities and ritual practices during the Late Iron Age may have implied that some form of sacred:profane distinction began to be drawn on in the specific context of local cultures at this time.

12.2.3 Transmission, Variability and Change in Ritual Tradition

This section has sketched one history of ritual deposition in Wessex from c1500 BC to the Roman conquest. It offers a diachronic perspective that has illustrated several trends within these 'ritual' deposits throughout the First Millenium BC in Wessex. Although at any one time there existed considerable real differences in the form of these sacrifices and the specific knowledges about the world they articulated across the region, certain elements within this culture were more variable than others. House and enclosure orientation were heavily fixed throughout the period, as was the basic distinction between pottery and animal bone. Long-term changes in the form of human deposits, and the specific associations drawn between wild animal or types of object were more variable. The recognition of such diversity should make us wary of any neat interpretation of these practices, and Iron Age ritual must be recognised as central to the nature and reproduction of Iron Age societies. More specifically, this tradition should not be regarded as being of one particular type of ritual, uniquely related just to initiation ceremonies or harvest. Rather, as a tradition these practices and the dominant symbols they employed were creatively drawn upon in a variety of situations.

The particular form of depositional practice constantly changed through time and space, changes that were intimately related to the inconstant interpretations of these practices, and the social worlds they maintained and altered. A central minimal core is recognisable, but this should not be envisaged as an *Ur*-ritual. To some extent this theme was a distillation of many particular performances, outside of which this tradition had no existence. This illustration of the diversity of ritual practices questions the tendency to interpret ritual as "an area of human activity very low indeed in creativity" (Bloch 1986:13). Bloch (1986) has specifically argued that rituals were static in form through time, despite considerable change in their social content and interpretation. My study contradicts Bloch's view, Instead, from this study I understand ritual to be a highly discursive and creative realm of social practice. To argue that rituals have "consistency of form and variability of

interpretation" (Harrison 1992:231), is falsely to separate ideas and practice, since the interpretation of a tradition of ritual practice in non-literate societies directly affect the nature and form of the ritual's performance. Given the important role ascribed to ritual in this study, that it explicitly reproduced the generative principles behind all daily activities and thought, it could be argued that ritual was an area of social practice more open to (and the vehicle for) change/manipulation than more habitual practices. Ritual forms, or at least these Iron Age ritual forms, did *not* "tend to be slower to change than many other aspects of culture, as any student of Western religions knows" (Bloch 1986:12). Therefore, these deposits must *not* be seen as simply happening in history, taking place in or justifying social relationships structured outside ritual, but as playing a significant role in creating those relationships; making that history.

12.3 Deposits Making History

Recent interpretations of prehistoric ritual have stressed its importance for sustaining and challenging social organisation and power relations. However, there is a danger that these approaches reduce ritual to a basic concern of domination and legitimation, or as secondary to the 'real' workings of society (e.g. Bloch 1986). Ritual cannot be bracketed off from other social phenomena, nor can power, dominance, or legitimation be separated out from economic or domestic activities. The reproduction of Iron Age societies through practice (ritual or otherwise) was an on going process in which relations of dominance, human subjectivity and structuring principles were reproduced simultaneously and undivisibly (see 1.4). Moreover, structures were not drawn on and reproduced in practice as slavish imitations. Differences will have occurred by default, but more importantly they also occurred because of differing circumstances, and due to people being able to reflect (particularly through the discursive nature of ritual), creatively draw on, and so alter structures. Ritual was "essentially an act of the possible", allowing the transposition of cosmological structures onto systems which people were able to change (C.Hugh-Jones 1979:280).

The dominant symbols articulated in the Iron Age depositional practices that I have discussed were the principal content of the discourses through which Iron Age worlds were perceived and structured. Symbols facilitated the acceptance of particular actions and sayings, but effectively excluded others. The problem with symbols is that their meanings are various and slippery. In ritual, where such symbols and the associations between them are explicitly exposed, particular interpretations of such can be made and reified (made 'natural', 'timeless', the will of the ancestors/gods). These readings directly relate to how such symbols and categorisations will be drawn on in routine activities, so that a dominant reading will permeate daily life (e.g. Traube 1984; J.Turner 1991). This is to understand:

"ritual as a distinctive form of practice" through whose "highly formalised drama...that dominant readings of cultural symbols are constructed" (Barrett et al 1991:7).

Iron Age sacrifices were probably evoked to legitimate changing sectional interests, but relations of dominance and authority were not just flagged or sanctioned through these rituals, they were actually created through such performances. This is again to stress ritual as practice. The current stress on ritual's role in producing dominant social discourses is possibly too passive and intellectual. While accepting that the authority to reinterpret dominant generative principles and the ideas drawn on in routine activities was important, ritual practice usually had more immediate consequences. The effect of ritual practice was to do real things in the world, and the people in control were of prime importance. The classification of the world expressed through these deposits included also the ability to control the world and may have had direct, immediate effects. For example, the (re)enclosure of sites and their associated rituals was also a political act (Thornton 1980). Ritual practice did not simply mark various transformations, but controlled, or at least was the cause of such transformations. I have suggested that coming of age may have been an important element of these rituals (see 11.3.4), and we may envisage the rite of passage of initiation as either actually *making* the change, or trying to intervene and influence the natural processes of ageing. Whatever the form of representation, those in power, acting on behalf of the community, exercised control over others in the most potent of ways. I would envisage control over the natural processes of decay through excarnation, or intervention through burial or cremation of the dead in similar ways (cf. Parkin 1992:23).

Relations of authority and power were integral to the conduct of ritual, but they did not simply reflect a static current state of political and social affairs; interpretations often implies that relationships of dominance between individuals and groups were fixed before ritual. Alternatively, "for rituals in particular, and for rituals in general, there must be contestation" (Parkin 1992:18). Who has the authority to conduct a ritual and who will take which role is often the object of intense rivalry and struggle (e.g. Turner 1967:98, Harrison 1992:225). The very act of holding a ritual, especially involving ritual consumption, may have been a vehicle for individuals and groups to build and challenge positions of rank and prestige. Even during rituals it is not necessarily the case that those organising the event will remain in control; particularly in large gatherings things may get out of control (Parkin 1991:10). Equally, it is wrong to assume that the ability to hold rituals was the 'property' of any

'ruling' group, or that ritual only worked for those in power. In hierarchical social situations the subordinate groups (the Late Iron Age?), and in relatively 'egalitarian' situations the juniors and women (Early and Middle Iron Age?), may have drawn on the same traditions for their own ritual practices which overtly or subversively challenged and altered prevailing social circumstances. Iron Age ritual practices did not simply legitimate, or passively reflect a status quo. They were central to the working out of social relations: "A history of rituals is a history of reproduction, contestation, transformation and, ... deconstruction of authority" (Kelly & Kaplan 1990:141).

Ritual practice in Iron Age societies was not separable nor secondary to political and economic realities. Rituals did not simply give meaning to, maintain, or reflect as a cosmic image, social relations. If ritual processes are seen as logically independent of economic and political relations between people it is impossible to comprehend prehistoric societies. This is to suggest that, in Marxist terminology, ritual practice 'determined' the nature and the form of the consumption of surplus production in these societies, constituting the mechanisms through which individuals/groups competed and acquired prestige. Since ritual provided the model experiences for these societies, so the nature and valued medium of exchange between people was strongly drawn on through sacrifice; the 'model' and morally sanctioned exchanges between men and gods (Mauss 1967:13-15). It is here that the important contrasts between a ritual discourse centred on the sacrifice of metal objects and those centred on the sacrifice of agricultural and craft produce must be centred. It is the ritual discourse that shaped the way a surplus is exchanged/consumed and the form that surplus takes. In this ritual discourse sacrificing and feasting was one important element, probably providing the key underlying motivation Indeed, as most of these Iron Age offerings, unlike bronze hoarding?, were probably directly associated with feasting and sacrifice, social and cosmological obligations were thoroughly intermingled in these practices. In this sense ritual practice did not just regulate or unify Iron Age societies, nor simply reflect them, but was the medium for their social organisation. It is important to remember that rituals in prehistoric societies were continually acting in this way, even when we have no direct archaeological evidence for ritual. Therefore, the recognition that the majority of material excavated on Wessex Iron Age sites came from ritual deposits is not the end of a social archaeology- as logically it must be for those who work within a functionalist framework, or at least one that still clings to a Hawkesean ladder of inference. Rather this could be see as the beginning of a fresh approach to hillforts and an understanding of the people who used (and did not use) them. Such recognition would see such rituals as a principal focus through which Iron Age history was made.

MIA NO CLEAR DIVIDE BETWEEN
SACRIFICE & BURIAL or
SACRED & PROFANE
Everyday and ritual activities in the same location: the settlement

Humans, animals &
inaminate objects placed
in pits and ditches

LIA Moves towards divide between Sacred & Profane
and also sacrifice/offerings & burial.
Activities (daily and religious divided up and take place in different
locations)

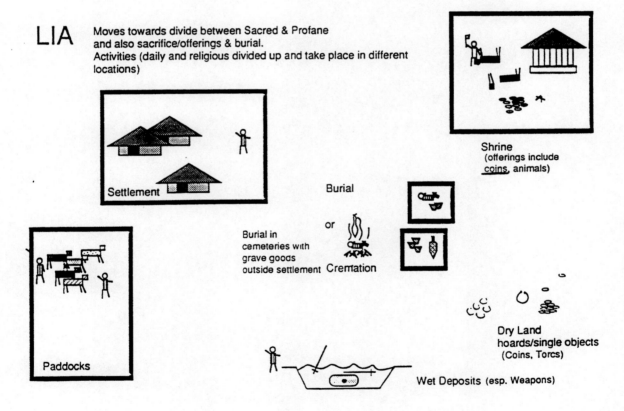

Settlement

Shrine
(offerings include
coins, animals)

Burial

Burial in
cemeteries with
grave goods
outside settlement

or

Cremation

Paddocks

Dry Land
hoards/single objects
(Coins, Torcs)

Wet Deposits (esp. Weapons)

Fig. 12.1. A Schematic Model of Change in Ritual Practices during the Later Iron Age.

Chapter 13
Ritual and Rubbish in the Iron Age of Wessex:
A Conclusion

'Why is there an archaeological record' may appear at first a somewhat silly question, but asking it forces us to examine critically perhaps the most basic assumption in archaeology; namely that there is an archaeological *record* (Patrik 1985). We take for granted that the material evidences we recover speak in a direct way about the past, and take it for granted that such evidences exist. In concentrating our efforts on interpreting this record, our interpretations take place in front of the 'text', which as a *record* is often assumed to be a passive *reflection*, inscription, of the past. Such assumptions do not encourage a great concern with how that record was formed, except to assess how good a *reflection* it might be.

However, asking 'why is there an archaeological record' should force us to reconsider these basic assumptions. That we find apparently abundant evidence for Iron Age societies should not lull us into a false sense of statistical security. If this study has achieved anything, it should be the conclusion that you cannot take for granted how any past society is represented through its archaeological traces in the present. How the Wessex Iron Age, or Bronze Age or Mesolithic 'look' today is not determined by their 'subsistence economy'. I can envisage possible Iron Ages and Mesolithics with the same 'subsistence strategies' that would leave radically different archaeological evidences. This is not to argue that there is no relationship between past society and their traces in the present; far from it. But I have tried to show that to make valid interpretations of archaeological data we must understand more of the processes through which that evidence was made. This must consider the natural processes, Schiffer's *N-transforms* (see 1.2), at work transforming the archaeological record, but also, more importantly, those original activities that created the materials we recover. These *C-transforms* (see 1.2) are central as the way any period looks today is a direct product of historically specific social practices drawing on and reproducing specific structuring principles, that were an essential part of the ways specific societies in the past were maintained and changed.

As such these are not *cultural transforms* that stand between a living Behavioural System and its archaeological *record*. Rather, following Barrett (e.g. 1989, 1993), I have argued that the activities that lead to the creation of the Iron Age we excavate and survey in the present were an integral part of how those societies were 'constituted'. The archaeological record is not a passive record, a fall out, but *evidences* for the specific practices, activities, that reproduced past social life (Barrett 1988a). As such, no amount of attempting to account for the distortion caused by the cultural and natural transformations of the archaeological record will get us closer to the

unbiased Behavioral System, be it herd composition, exchange networks or social organisation. In 'accounting for the biases' caused by those C-transforms you actually lose the very object of your study - society itself.

Hopefully, I have succeeded in achieving my objectives in this thesis (see 4.1). I have attempted to understand how past societies in Wessex c. 800BC-AD50 produced the specific archaeological evidences we recover today. I have emphasised that only tiny amounts of the material used and created on Later Prehistoric sites entered archaeologically recoverable contexts (see 1.1), and illuminated some of the processes through which those small quantities of material got there and their subsequent transformation due to natural factors. This leads me to make two important general statements;

What material is recovered is not a direct reflection of their original abundance.
This applies to all class as of material, be they the proportions of locally and non-locally produced pottery, animal species and ages, or, the abundance of brooches.

The finds from Later Prehistoric settlements are just as structured as those from graves or hoards.
As such we should consider the relationships between material from contemporary settlements, graves and other contexts - and how these change through time - , but also avoid falling into the trap that evidence from settlement evidence is somehow a better reflection of social realities than that from obvious 'ritual' contexts such as hoards or burials.

These factors have led me to suggest that in one way *all material* recovered in excavations of these sites is *special*, in that it has actually survived (see 1.2). We should *expect to find nothing* excavating Later Prehistoric settlements anywhere in Europe. However, we should not just be pleasantly surprised when we do find material, but always ask how this material has escaped the normal processes of dispersion and destruction at work on rural, sedentary sites.

Bearing this in mind, I then questioned whether the pottery, bone and small finds from pits and ditches were 'rubbish', investigating the consequences of the presence of human remains on the other finds found in the same archaeological features. I have shown that the rubbish deposited in the same features as human remains was significantly different from that in those features without human remains. Similar associations are also present in those features with articulated/associated groups of animal bones, confirming Grant's suggestions that 'Animal Special Deposits' were ritual deposits.

To answer such questions, it has been necessary to develop a detailed understanding of the nature and formation of archaeological deposits on Iron Age sites in Wessex, their transformation by natural processes, and, especially, the culturally/historically specific social practices which produced them. This is to concentrate on the pathways by which material has passed from the activities in the past, on how it entered the record, and on how that material may have been subsequently transformed after deposition. A thoroughly contextual approach was essential for this study, bringing together all the finds recovered from the same features and stressing the limitations in current practices of treating pottery, bones, seeds and small finds etc. in isolation. The work has shown the considerable potential that very detailed studies on the assemblages recovered from individual layers within feature fills offer and also shows that the fills of a feature should not be considered as homogeneous.

The results of these analyses revealed a series of specific associations between different classes of finds. Individual categories of material were often deposited in large quantities on their own in individual layers. However, following general rules, these exceptional layers were built up into complex sequences of fills to produce clear associations between different types of finds within the overall contents of a pit or ditch segment. It was also shown that where certain categories of material were deposited on sites was not random, nor a direct reflection of the location of different activities. Rather, these patterns demonstrate that excavated settlement evidence, and the associated artefacts and ecofacts, were structured according to symbolic schemes, rationalities and common senses very different from our own.

I have argued that such deposits, often separated by many years, were not a result of the daily disposal of refuse, but were made during irregular rituals which engraved a cosmology into the physical setting and daily lives of Iron Age people. The main themes of the mediation, transformation and classification of people, animals, spaces and things were outlined, including the suggestion that people were not radically bracketed off from animals in Iron Age thought as in our own. This is to emphasize that the content, the imagery of the symbols, of these rituals was not unimportant, nor arbitrary. They were central metaphors in these Iron Age societies which reflected their fundamental concepts and social practices. To understand these ritual symbols in their fullness and complexity is to know something essential about the societies that practised those rituals.

Throughout, I have emphasised that ritual has to be understood as a specific form of social practice, and have outlined how ritual relates to everyday life. This perspective stresses the fluid nature of these practices, providing a basis for understanding both how these practices change through time, but also how they could differ between neighbouring areas. Finally, situating ritual in an archaeology of practice provides the framework to construct a very different social archaeology of Wessex c.800BC-AD50.

This ritual tradition was not restricted to 'Wessex'. Similar sorts of deposits have been found on other Late Bronze Age and Iron Age sites across southern England. The specific nature and possible considerable differences between the practices discussed here and those in other parts of the country, and beyond, fall outside the scope of this study.

By nature this has been a contextual study, building towards its final conclusions through drawing the connections between different sites, levels of analysis and classes of finds. Any one part of the argument could probably be criticised, particularly because of the poor quality of the data often employed, but it is the way they are all interlinked that provides the strength of the argument. More rigorous statistical methods could have been employed, and more attention paid to any one part of the study. However, such a positivist and reductionist tendency would fail to see the broader picture considered here. Ultimately, I am not totally satisfied with how this study has been structured. While the study has been written to follow a simple narrative plan, I recognise that the detailed analysis chapters are often too dense, and ultimately too separated in both location and style from the later discussion. Ideally, I should have integrated discussion and analysis far more. I did consider an alternative structure. Here the argument would be centred on discussions of individual pits, showing how the overall relationships found within a pit's fills were built up through sequences of layers, how these relate to the pit's location, and thoroughly integrating interpretations. However, ultimately this was not suited to either the needs or expectations of a thesis, and are more suited to a shorter paper, or presentation.

There is not space here to consider the full implications this study has for the Iron Age or other periods. Hopefully, I have shown the potential which detailed contextual studies combining different classes of material have for all settlement excavations and have pointed towards both more detailed studies of Iron Age material, but also an extension of these approaches to Roman, Migration period and other archaeologies. This is not to suggest that deposits on Roman and Migration period sites are going to be ritual deposits like those for which I have argued here. Rather, detailed contextual studies can unwrap the historically specific conditions which produced historically specific types of archaeological evidence, and help to gain a better understanding of those different societies. The results of these study should directly bear on the current excavation strategies used on Later Prehistoric sites, providing new research questions and influencing what/how much is sampled.

This is not to advocate any radically different way of excavating and recording Iron Age sites - as some have suggested I do. This work could have only been undertaken because of the detailed recording of current approaches, a level of detail which is largely redundant for most contemporary studies of archaeological material. However, this does not mean I am arguing for any complacency. Greater attention to detail is suggested by this study. There is a need for methodological experiments exploring different excavation strategies for pits, ditches and other features to assess the quantity and quality of the information they provide. I would suggest we need to compare half sectioning to excavation by horizontal spits in terms of the data they record. Equally, I would see the need for the detailed studies of a few pits, throwing all possible techniques, especially from soil science, on-to the data, and wet-sieving the total fill.

One important consequence of this work regards the limited excavation and sampling of sites. Winnall Down implies the need to excavate very large portions of enclosure ditches, at least 25%, to understand fully the complex nature of these features. At present the limited number of samples for plant remains taken on most excavations limits our understanding of the formation processes at work on this important class of data. Do plant remains show the same structured deposition shown here for other classes of material? Equally, as the location for depositing certain classes of material was clearly important, limited sampling of a site will not necessarily reflect to total proportions of species bone, pot fabrics and types etc. obtained from a total excavation. Constantly stressing the need to understand how archaeological deposits were created should seriously question any interpretations of material which assume that what we excavate is a straightforward reflection of past subsistence, exchange and economic systems.

Winnall Down Pit 6595 revisited

Above all I hope the contextual approach used here shows how thoroughly interconnected both the different classes of material we excavate are, and different aspects of Iron Age life were. The pottery, bone and small finds from Winnall pit 6595 (see 7.9) do not speak about different, distinct, spheres of Iron Age life. Pottery cannot be separated to talk just about exchange, distinct from animal bones which speak of subsistence (distinct from articulated bone groups which speak of ritual). Iron Age society cannot be conceived of as an abstract network of sub-systems. These different sub-systems, self-contained boxes, must be dissolved, in order to see the different aspects of social life as operating simultaneously in the constant flow of human activities through which they, gender relations, the socialisation of the individual and the symbolic classifications of Iron Age societies, were constantly produced, reproduced and changed. Pit 6595 is evidence for a specific practice through which key definitions and knowledges about the world were socially defined through ritual. It is evidence for a single event in which relationships between individuals, groups, age sets and genders would have been reproduced.

This was a communal feast and sacrifice which involved the consumption of over twelve cattle and horses, a sheep, a pig, and a hare. This number of large animals slaughtered and consumed at once would have been a rare event. Ensuring this quantity of meat was available would probably have been the result of many years planning and preparation, and/or have involved animals raised on a number of settlements. In short, it should be seen as one of the principal objectives of the 'subsistence economies' of this and connected settlements for, probably, some time (several years?). The need for this feast, and others, was determining the form in which these economies produced and consumed their surplus. The event involved the hunting and probably consumption of a hare, which as I have suggested, would not have been a common event, but rather one surrounded by ritual and taboo, even one in which only certain sorts of people would have been involved. The preparation of the meal itself would have possibly involved considerable time and the involvement of people from outside the immediate household group. If the large sherds of pottery in this deposit were deliberately smashed, then motivation for the making or acquiring of certain pots through exchange may have been for this one event. Indeed if a large number of vessels were used for the cooking and eating at such a meal, this may have been more than the normal complement in the settlement. Were vessels borrowed from neighbours before, or brought by the participants? May some of those in attendance for such an major event have travelled over long distances (10km or more) to attend, bringing pottery and livestock with them?

The scale of the animals consumed in this event does suggest a considerable number of people were present. As such this single event has also to be seen in the political context of the relationships between the local households in the community. Hosting such a event was part of these competitive relationships through which households and their heads sought to establish prestige, rank, and repay/create social debts and obligations. This is to emphasise again that the raising of the meat and other food-stuffs eaten at this and other similar events were not for subsistence, but intimately part of the Iron Age political process. Who was responsible for the cooking, and which parts of the cooking, and who sat with whom, eating which portions of the meat (if meat at all), were all parts of the means through which relationships and status between guests, and between genders and age groups, were signalled, established and challenged. Finally, the ritualised context in which parts, or all, of this event were set helped to extrude cosmological concerns into this unusual specific event, and into the objects and spaces through which the household lived its daily life. Where this deposit was placed on the settlement, the order and care with which it was made, and the material symbols it utilised served to articulate explicitly the structuring principles, and a dominant reading of them, through which society was reproduced. Whether, or not, you agree with me in calling such an event a ritual does not alter the fact that this pit deposit is evidence for all of the interconnected processes outlined above.

Recognising that the archaeological record is evidence of particular practices in the past through which society was reproduced implies an end to the division between ecofact and artifact. In an archaeology of practice there can be only social facts. It should also inform our studies of all classes of archaeological data with new questions. However, these are not just supplements to the existing agendas of archaeobotany, archaeozoology, ceramic studies, or social reconstruction etc. If we are to understand the genesis of the archaeological record, it is not that we *can*, which will be a shock to many, but that we *cannot avoid* moving from Iron Age cosmology to ceramics, from pits to power.

Appendix 1
'Guessimating' the quantities of originally material discarded on Iron Age settlements

This appendix offers a series of simple calculations which give a sense of the quantities of material that could have been originally discarded on a 'typical' Iron Age settlement. These 'games' do suggest that a vast quantity of the material used and thrown away on settlements such as Danebury or Gussage All Saints has not entered those traps, the sub-soil features, that enable material to escape the normal processes of degradation and destruction on a site. The calculations sketched below do support the suggestion provided by both a working from taphonomic first principles and ethnoarchaeological studies; that the vast majority of material originally discarded on a settlement has not entered the archaeological record. If only a tiny proportion of the material used and discarded on a site is preserved, it must be asked how representative this tiny proportion is of the range and scale of activities that took place on a site in the past?

Detailed studies of contemporary pottery use in different parts of the world provide some guidelines to the possible breakage rates of domestic Later Prehistoric pottery (e.g. David 1971; DeBoer 1974; DeBoer & Lathrap 1979 see also Schiffer 1976). As such, greater attention is paid here to ceramics than to other classes of finds. While not arguing for any direct application between these studies and the British Iron Age, such figures provide a guide to show just how much material was potentially broken and discarded -- and failed to enter the archaeological record -- on a typical Iron Age settlement. Mills (1989 esp. Tables 4 & 5) usefully summarises the data produced in a range of ethnoarchaeological studies in Africa and Latin American. Using such data it is possible to calculate mean values for breakage, vessels per household, and proportions of different types of vessel in these studies. These figures are summarised on the next page and have been used to calculate possible breakage rates for the lowest, mean and highest values for breakage rate and vessels per household.

A calculation of the overall mean breakage rate makes no allowance for the often considerable differences in the breakage rates between different functional categories of pottery. Storage vessels, because they are rarely moved are rarely broken, unlike vessels that are used daily for cooking and serving food. Cooking vessels also have to suffer repeated heating and cooling which may lead to thermal shock breakage. Using the mean proportions of different classes of vessel summarised by Mills, more 'refined' figures can be estimated. Using an mean value of 10.85 pots per household, 4.1 vessels would be discarded annually (2.4 cooking vessels, 1.1 serving vessels, 0.35 storage vessels, 0.3

other vessels. These can be compared to actual figures produced by DeBoar and Lathrap (1979) for Shipibo-Conibo communities. This study produced the highest breakage rates summarised by Mills. An average household using 13.4 pots at a time, broke and discarded 21 vessels a year (3.36 cooking vessels, 13.06 serving vessels, 1.87 storage vessels, 2.67 other vessels).

It is not possible to calculate exact figures for the proportions of different classes of vessels, their use life or numbers per Southern English households in different places and times during the First Millennium BC. However, I would consider it likely that these fell within the ranges summarised above. Certainly, in those rare occasions in which houses were destroyed and then well preserved *in situ.* with something of their contents, it is possible to make a better 'guestimate' of the number of pots per household, such as the three well preserved Late Bronze Age/Early Iron Age double ringed round houses from Northern Wessex e.g. Longbridge Deveril Cow Down (Chadwick-Hawkes 1994), Dunston Park (Fitzpatrick 1994a), Brighton Hill South (Coe, Newman & Morris 1992). These large houses appear to have contained c.10-15 vessels each. This should be taken as a minimum number of vessels in such households, as it is likely that such large porched structures did not contain all the pottery in use on the settlement. Large storage/cooking jars would appear not to have been represented in the assemblages at all three houses. These were presumably kept elsewhere. Nor would I assume that the average number of vessels per household remained constant throughout the First Millennium BC in Southern England.

What ever the actual size of the pottery assemblages used by Iron Age households, these 'guessitimations' do demonstrate the considerable quantities of pottery we are lacking on the Later Prehistoric settlements we study. They clearly question how representative of the overall pottery assemblage used on a site, the excavated remnant is. Assuming the mean figures outlined above (2.7 broken per annum), and assuming an average vessel weight of 1kg, a single Early Iron Age household continuously resident in a single location for 200 years could have broken c.550 kg of pottery. This can be compared to the 34kg of Early Iron Age pottery recovered at Winnall Down, and puts the total of 1400kgs of pottery recovered at Danebury (Brown 1990) in a similar perspective (using the highest discard rates outlined by Mills, the total pottery from Danebury represents the total breakage/discard of only *one* household in less than a century!). Such calculations also give some

	Cooking Vessels	Serving Vessels	Storage Vessels	Other* Vessels
Mean % of vessels in this class per household	51%	17%	18.7%	20.8%
Range	28-65%	8-36%	3-46%	5-46%
Mean use life in years	2.14 n11	1.5 n5	5.4 n8	6.4 n7
Range	0.4-2.6	0.25-2.7	1.2-12.5	0.75-13.8

Overall Mean Use life   = 3.9 years

Overall Mean No. of vessels per household   = 26.5 n11

Overall Mean No. of vessels per household excluding Mayan households**   = 10.85 n8

*   Includes special occasion and fiesta pots

**   Mayan households consistently had much larger numbers of pots per household (57-85) and it was, by myself and others, felt that such high numbers were not to be expected in an Iron Age Southern English household. This could be a wrong assumption. If it is then even higher quantities of pottery are missing from Iron Age sites.

<u>Calculations of mean vessel use life, number of vessels per household and proportion of vessel types using figure summarised by Mills (1989: Table 4&5)</u>

	Lowest Overall Use life 0.95 yrs	Mean Overall Use life 3.9 yrs	Highest Overall Use life 8.8 yrs
Lowest Vessel Number per Household 5.6	5.9 per yr	1.4 per yr	0.6 per yr
	590 per 100yrs	140 per 100yrs	60 per 100 yrs
Mean Vessel Number per Household 10.8	11.4 per yr	2.7 per yr	1.2 per yr
	114 per 100 yrs	270 per 100yrs	120 per 100yrs
Highest Vessel Number per Household 20.9	22 per yr	5.4 per yr	2.4 per yr
	2200 per 100 yrs	540 per 100 yrs	240 per 100 yrs

<u>Calculations of the minimum, mean and maximum pottery vessels broken and discarded per year and per century using Mills' (1989) figures.</u>

impression of the scale of pottery production and exchange within the Iron Age.

Similar games can be played with all classes of finds recovered on Later Prehistoric settlements, with similar results. For example, during the first ten years excavations at Danebury Grant (1984a:500) calculated the Minimum Number of Individuals represented for the main domestic animal species. Divided by an approximate 500 year occupation of the site, this produces a result of a 2.3 MNI of domestic animals a year. This makes no allowance for the limited sample of the site excavated, making such allowances provides the following figures -- 6.5 Sheep an annum, 1.1 Cattle, 1.2 Pig, 0.2 Dog, 0.3 Horse per year. Such figures may be a close approximation to the actual numbers slaughtered at the site if it was only an infrequently visited ritual centre. However, they are extremely low if one expects a large resident population. There are well known problems in the calculation of MNI. However, alternative games using overall recovered bone fragments produce similar results. There were only 6572 bone fragments recovered from Middle Iron Age features at Winnall Down (Maltby 1985b). When it is remembered that the domestic mammal skeleton contains several hundred complete bones, even making allowance for poor recovery of the smaller bones and making the totally unrealistic assumption that all larger bones remained complete, or just broke into just two fragments, it is clear how potentially few of the bones produced by butchery and consumption on a site have been preserved. It is

the recognition of these problems, and the potential little correlation between the recovered archaeological bone assemblage and original herd structures etc. that have driven the important developments in taphonomy (see 3.7).

The general rule that a potentially unrepresentative tiny fraction of the original discarded material has entered the archaeological record, may have one notably exception; quern stones. Comparatively large number of quern stone fragments are recovered from typical Iron Age excavations. I have been unable to find any published studies of the use life of either saddle querns or hand rotatory querns, but David Peacock (*pers com.*) would not feel it unlikely if a hand rotatory quern had a typical use life of a ten years. If such figures are representative for Iron Age Wessex, and only one quern was owned by a household at any one time, it would suggest that at least a small fragment from the majority/large proportion of querns used on a site did enter the archaeological record. This may not be too surprisingly, given the bulk and inconvenience of disposing of a large, broken quern stone. But it should be noted most querns are represented as small fragments, and this study shows this class of finds is particularly marked out in terms of its associations when deposited. Given the possible connections between gender, food preparation and life cycle of the household unit, querns may have been ascribed important symbolic attributes in the Iron Age.

Numbers of Querns: Estimated Minimum Numbers of Different Stones

EIA Winnall Down	20
Easton Lane	13
MIA Winnall Down	61

after - Fasham 1985, Fasham & Hawkes 1989

Bibliography

Adams, D. 1978. *The Hitch-hiker's Guide to the Galaxy* BBC Radio 4.

Aitken, G & Aitken G. 1990. Excavations at Whitcombe 1965-1967. Proceedings of the Dorset Natural History and Archaeological Society 112, pp57-94.

Alcock, L. 1969. Excavations at South Cadbury Castle, 1968. A summary report. Antiquaries Journal 49, pp30-40.

Alcock, L. 1970. Excavations at South Cadbury Castle, 1969. A summary report. Antiquaries Journal 50, pp14-25.

Alcock, L. 1971. Excavations at South Cadbury Castle, 1970. A summary report. Antiquaries Journal 51, pp1-8.

Alcock, L. 1972. By Cadbury is that Camelot? London, Thames & Hudson.

Allen, T., Miles, D. & Palmer, S. 1984. Iron Age buildings in the Upper Thames Region. In BW. Cunliffe & D. Miles (eds.), Aspects of the Iron Age in Central Southern Britain. Oxford, Oxford University Committee for Archaeology Monograph 2, pp89-101.

Allen, T. and Robinson, M. 1993. The prehistoric landscape and Iron Age enclosed settlement at Mingies Ditch, Hardwick-with-Yelford, Oxon, Oxford, Oxford University Committee for Archaeology/Oxford Archaeological Unit.

Armour Chelu, M. 1991. The animal bones. In N. Sharples, Maiden Castle: Excavations and Field Survey 1985-6. London, English Heritage Archaeological Reports 19, pp131-151.

Arnold, P. 1990. The organisation of refuse disposal and ceramic production within contemporary Mexican houselots. American Anthropology 92, pp915-932.

Ashbee, P. 1978. The Ancient British. Norwich, Geo Abstracts, University of East Anglia.

Ashbee, P., Bell, M. & Proudfoot, E. 1989. The Wilsford Shaft: Excavations 1960-1962. London, English Heritage Archaeological Reports 11.

Audouze, F. & Buchenschutz, O. 1989. Villes, Villages et Campagnes de l'Europe Celtique. Paris, Hachette.

Austin, D. & Thomas, J. 1990. The 'proper study' of medieval archaeology. In D. Austin & L. Alcock (eds.), From the Baltic to the Black Sea: Studies in Medieval Archaeology. London, Unwin Hyman, One World Archaeology 18, pp43-78.

Baily, C. 1967. An Early Iron Age and Romano-British site at Pins Knoll, Litton Cheny. Proceedings of the Dorset Natural History and Archaeological Society 89, pp147-159.

Baily C. & Flatters, E. 1972. Trial excavations of an Iron Age and Romano-British site at Quarry Lodden, Bincombe, Dorset. Proceedings of the Dorset Natural History and Archaeological Society 93, pp135-143.

Barbar, J. 1988. Ibister, Quanterness and the Point of Cott: The formulation and testing of some middle range theory. In J.C. Barrett & I.A. Kinnes (eds.), The Archaeology of Context in the Neolithic and Bronze Age: Recent Trends. Sheffield, The Department of Archaeology and Prehistory, University of Sheffield, pp57-62.

Barbar, J., Halstead, P., James, H. & Lee, F. 1989. An unusual Iron Age burial at Hornish Point, South Uist. Antiquity 241, pp773-778.

Barker, G. 1975. To sieve or not to sieve? Antiquity 49, pp61-63.

Barrett, J. 1980. The pottery of the Later Bronze Age in Lowland England. Proceedings of the Prehistoric Society 46, pp297-319.

Barrett, J. 1981. Aspects of the Iron Age in Atlantic Scotland. A case study in the problem of interpretation. Proceedings of the Society of Antiquarians, Scotland 111, pp205-219.

Barrett, J. 1985. Hoards and related metalwork. In: D.V. Clarke, T. Cowie and A. Foxon, Symbols of Power at the Time of Stonehenge, Edinburgh: National Museum of Antiquities, pp93-106

Barrett, J. 1988a. Fields of discourse: reconstituting a social archaeology. Critique of Anthropology 7:3, pp5-16.

Barrett, J. 1988b. The living, the dead, and the ancestors: Neolithic and early Bronze Age mortuary practices. In J.C. Barrett & I.A. Kinnes (eds.), The Archaeology of Context in the Neolithic and Bronze Age: Recent Trends. Sheffield, The Department of Archaeology and Prehistory, University of Sheffield, pp30-41.

Barrett, J. 1989. Food, gender and metal: Questions of social reproduction. In MLS. Sørensen & R. Thomas (eds.), The Bronze Age-Iron Age Transition in Europe. Oxford, British Archaeological Reports (International Series 483), pp304-320.

Barrett, J. 1991a. Towards an archaeology of ritual. In P. Garwood, D. Jennings, R. Skeates & J. Toms (eds.), Sacred and Profane. Oxford, Oxford University Committee for Archaeology Monograph No. 32, pp1-9.

Barrett, J. 1991b. Bronze Age pottery and the problems of classification. In J. Barrett, R. Bradley & M. Hall (eds.), Papers on the Prehistoric Archaeology of Cranborne Chase. Oxford, Oxbow Books, Oxbow Monographs 11, pp201-230.

Barrett, J. 1991c. Review of R. Bradley, *The Passage of Arms*. Antiquity 65, pp743-744.

Barrett, J. 1991d. Later Prehistoric Landscapes: Creating biographies of space. Paper presented at TAG, Leicester, December 1991.

Barrett, J. 1994. Fragments of Antiquity. Blackwells, Oxford.

Barrett, J. & Bond, D. 1988. The pottery In D. Bond Excavation at the North Ring, Mucking, Essex. East Anglian Archaeology 43, Chelmsford, Essex County Council, pp25-36.

Barrett, J., Bradley, R. & Green, M. 1991. Landscape, Monuments and Society; The Prehistory of Cranborne Chase. Cambridge, The University Press.

Barth, F. 1987. Cosmologies in the Making: A generative approach to cultural variation in inner New Guinea. Cambridge, The University Press.

Bedwin, O. 1978a. Iron Age Sussex - the Downs and the Coastal Plain. In P. Drewett (ed.), Archaeology in Sussex to AD 1500. London, The Council for British Archaeology (Research Report 29), pp41-58.

Bedwin, O. 1978b. Excavtions inside Harting Beacon 1976. Sussex Archaeological Collections 116, pp225-240.

Bedwin, O. 1979. Excavations at Harting Beacon, West Sussex; Second Season 1977. Sussex Archaeological Collections 117, 23-35.

Bedwin, O. 1980. Excavations at Chanctonbury Ring, Wiston, West Sussex, 1977. Britannia 11, pp173-222.

Bedwin, O. 1994. Copse Farm, Oving, West Sussex. In A.P. Fitzpatrick & E. Morris (eds.) The Iron Age in Wessex: Recent Work, Salisbury, Association Francaise D'Etude de L'Age du Fer/Trust for Wessex Archaeology, pp112-114.

Bedwin, O & Holgate, R. 1985. Excavations at Copse Farm, Oving, West Sussex. Proceedings of the Prehistoric Society 51, pp215-245.

Bedwin, O & Pitts, M. 1978. The excavation of an Iron Age settlement at North Bersted, Bognor Regis 1975-1976. Sussex Archaeological Collections 116, pp293-346.

Bell, C. 1992. Ritual Theory, Ritual Practice. Oxford, The University Press.

Ben-Ari, E. 1987. On acknowledgements in ethnography. Journal Anthropological Research 43, pp63-84.

Benfield, E. 1946. The Town of Maiden Castle. London, Robert Hale.

Bersu, G. 1940. Excavations at Little Woodbury, Wiltshire. Part 1. Proceedings of the Prehistoric Society 6, pp30-111.

Bertin, B. 1992. Ethnobiological Classification. Princeton, The University Press.

Bertin, B., Breedlove, D., Raven, P. 1973. General principles in classification And nomenclature in folk biology. American Anthropologist 75, pp214-242.

Biddle, M. 1983. The study of Winchester: Archaeology and history in a British town, 1961-1983. Proceedings of the BritishAcademy 69, pp93-135.

Binford, L. 1964. A consideration of archaeological research design. American Antiquity 29, pp425-441.

Binford, L. 1981. Bones: Ancient Men and Modern Myths. New York, The Academic Press.

Binford, L. 1987. Researching ambiguity: Frames of reference and site structure. In S. Kent (ed.), Method and Theory for Activity Area Research: An Ethnoarchaeological Approach. New York. Columbia University Press, pp449-512.

Binford, L. & Bertram, J. 1977. Bone frequencies and attritional processes. In L. Binford (ed.), For Theory Building in Archaeology. New York, The Academic Press, pp77-153.

Blacking, J. 1979. Towards an anthropology of the body. In J. Blacking (ed.), The Anthropology of the Body. London, Academic Press, pp1-28.

Blackmore, C., Braithwaite, M. & Hodder, I. 1979. Social and cultural patterning in the Late Iron Age in Southern England. In B. Burnham & J. Kingsbury (eds.), Space, Hierarchy and Society. Oxford, British Archaeological Reports (International Series 59), pp93-117.

Bloch, M. 1985. From cognition to ideology. In R. Fardon (ed.), Power and Knowledge: Anthropological and Sociological Approaches. Edinburgh, Scottish Academic Press, pp21-48.

Bloch, M. 1986. From Blessing to Violence. Cambridge, The University Press.

Bloch, M. 1987. The ritual of the royal bath in Madagascar: the dissolution of death, birth and fertility into authority. In D. Cannadine & S. Price (eds.), Rituals of Royalty. Cambridge, The University Press, pp271-297.

Bloch, M. 1992. Prey into Hunter: The Politics of Religious Exprience. Cambridge, The University Press.

Boast, R. & Evans, C. 1986. The transformation of space: two examples from British prehistory. Archaeological Review from Cambridge 5:2, pp193-205.

Bond, D. 1988. Excavation at the North Ring, Mucking, Essex. East Anglian Archaeology 43, Chelmsford, Essex County Council.

Bonte, P. 1977. Non-stratified social formations among pastoral nomads. In J. Friedman & M. Rowlands (eds.), The Evolution of Social Systems. London, Duckworth, pp173-200,

Bonte, P. 1979. Marxist analyses and social anthropology. A review article. Critique of Anthropology 13/14, pp145-163.

Bonte, P. 1981. Marxist theory and anthropological analysis: The study of nomad pastoralist societies. In JS. Kahn & JR. Llobera (eds.), 1981. The Anthropology of Pre-Capitalist Societies. London, Macmillan, pp22-56.

Bourdieu, P. 1977. Outline of a Theory of Practice. Cambridge, The University Press.

Bourdieu, P. 1979. Symbolic power. <u>Critique of Anthropology</u> 13-14, pp77-85.

Bourdieu, P. 1990. <u>The Logic of Practice</u>. Cambridge, Polity Press.

Bowden, M. & McOrmish, D. 1987. The required barrier. <u>Scottish Archaeological Review</u> 4. pp97-84.

Bowden, M. & McOrmish, D. 1989. Little boxes: More about hillforts. <u>Scottish Archaeological Review</u> 6, pp12-16.

Bowen, H. & Wood, P. 1968. Experimental storage of corn underground and its implications for Iron Age settlements. <u>Bulletin of the Institute of Archaeology, London</u> 7, pp1-14.

Bowen, H. 1969. The Celtic background. In A. Rivet (ed.), <u>The Roman Villa in Britain</u>, London, Routledge Kegan & Paul, pp1-48.

Bowen, H. 1990 <u>The Archaeology of Bokerley Dyke</u>. London, HMSO for RCHME.

Boyd Dawkins, W. 1862. Traces of the early Britons in the neighbourhood of Oxford. <u>Proccedings of Oxford Architectural and Historical Society</u> 1, pp108-116.

Boyd Dawkins, W. 1917. The inhabitants of the Lake Village. In A. Bullied & H. St.G. Gray, <u>The Glastonbury Lake Village</u> vol2, Glastonbury, Glastonbury Antiquarian Society, pp673-680.

Bradley, R. 1981a. 'Various styles of urns': Cemeteries and settlement in Southern England c1400-1100bc. In R. Chapman, I. Kinnes, & K.Randsborg (eds.), <u>The Archaeology of Death</u>. Cambridge, The University Press, pp93-105.

Bradley, R. 1981b. Economic growth and social change: Two examples from prehistoric Europe. In A. Sheridan & G. Bailey (eds.), <u>Economic Archaeology</u> , Oxford, British Archaeological Reports (International Series 96), pp231-238.

Bradley, R. 1984. <u>The Social Foundations of British Prehistory</u>. London, Longman.

Bradley, R. 1990. <u>The Passage of Arms: An archaeological analysis of prehistoric hoards and votive deposits</u>. Cambridge, The University Press.

Bradley, R. 1991. The patterns of change in British Prehistory. In T. Earle (ed.), <u>Chiefdoms: Power, Economy, and Ideology</u>. Cambridge, The University Press, pp44-70.

Bradley, R. & Fulford, M. 1980. Sherd size in the analysis of occupation debris. <u>Bulletin of the Institute of Archaeology</u> 17, pp85-94.

Bradley, R., Lobb, S., Richards, J. & Robinson, M. 1980. Two Late Bronze Age settlements on the Kennett gravels: Excavations at Aldermaston Wharf and Knights Farm, Burghfield, Berkshire. <u>Proceedings of the Prehistoric Society</u> 46, 217-295.

Brailsford, J. 1948. Excavations at Little Woodbury, Wiltshire (1938-39), Part II: The pottery. <u>Proceedings of the Prehistoric Society</u> 14, pp1-18.

Braithwaite, M. 1982. Decoration as ritual symbol: a theoretical proposal and an ethnographic study in Southern Sudan. In I. Hodder (ed.). <u>Symbolic and Structural Archaeology</u>. Cambridge, The University Press, pp80-88.

Braithwaite, M. 1984. Ritual and prestige in the prehistory of Wessex c.2200-1400 BC: a new dimension to the archaeological evidence. In D. Miller & C. Tilley (eds.) <u>Ideology, Power and Prehistory</u>. Cambridge, The University Press, pp 93-110.

Britnall, W. 1989. The Collfryn hillslope enclosure, Llansantffraid Deuddwr, Powys: Excavations 1980-1982. <u>Proceedings of the Prehistoric Society</u> 55, pp89-134.

Brown, A. 1991. Structured deposition and technological change among the flaked stone artefacts from Cranborne Chase. In J. Barrett, R. Bradley & M. Hall (eds.), <u>Papers on the Prehistoric Archaeology of Cranborne Chase</u>. Oxford, Oxbow Books, Oxbow Monographs 11, pp101-133.

Brown, G., Field, D. & McOmish, D. 1994. East Chisenbury midden complex, Wiltshire. In A.P. Fitzpatrick & E. Morris (eds.) <u>The Iron Age in Wessex: Recent Work</u>, Salisbury, Association Francaise D'Etude de L'Age du Fer/Trust for Wessex Archaeology, pp46-49.

Brown, L. 1984. The Iron Age pottery. In B.Cunliffe, 1984. <u>Danebury: An Iron Age Hillfort in Hampshire.</u> vol 2. London, Council for British Archaeology, pp231-331

Brown, L. 1987. The late prehistoric pottery. In B. Cunliffe, <u>Hengistbury Head, Dorset: Vol 1 The Prehistoric and Roman Settlement, 3500BC-AD500.</u> Oxford, Oxford University Committee for Archaeology, pp207-321.

Brown, L. 1991a. The Iron Age pottery. In B. Cunliffe & C. Poole (eds.), <u>Danebury: An Iron Age Hillfort in Hampshire</u> vol 5. London, Council for British Archaeology, pp277-318.

Brown, L. 1991b. The Later Prehistoric pottery. In N. Sharples, <u>Maiden Castle: Excavations and Field Survey 1985-86</u>. London, English Heritage Archaeological Reports, pp185-202.

Brown, N. 1988. A Late Bronze Age enclosure at Lofts Farm, Essex. <u>Proceedings of the Prehistoric Society</u> 54, pp249-304.

Brunaux, JL. 1988. <u>The Celtic Guals: Gods, Rites and Sanctuaries</u>. London, Seaby.

Brunaux, JL., Meniel, P., & Poplin, F. 1985. <u>Gourney I. Fouilles sur le sanctuaire et l'oppidum</u>. Revue Archéologique de Picardies, numéro spécial.

Bullied, A. & Gray, H. 1911. <u>The Glastonbury Lake Village</u> Vol 1, Glastonbury, Glastonbury Antiquarian Society.

Bullied, A. & Gray, H. 1917. <u>The Glastonbury Lake Village</u> Vol 2, Glastonbury, Glastonbury Antiquarian Society.

Bulmer, R. 1967. Why is the Cassowary not a bird? <u>Man</u> 2, pp5-25.

Bulmer, R. 1976. Selectivity in hunting and in disposal of animal bone by the Kalam of the New Guinea Highlands. In G. Sieveking, I. Longworth & K. Wilson (eds.), <u>Papers in Economic and Social Archaeology</u>. London, Duckworth, pp169-186.

Burstow, G. & Holleyman, G. 1957. Late Bronze Age settlement on Itford Hill, Sussex. <u>Proceedings of the Prehistoric Society</u> 27, pp167-212.

Buxton, J. 1968. Animal Identity and human peril: some Mandari images. <u>Man</u> 3,pp35-49.

Bølviken, E., Helskog, E., Helskog, K. , Holm-Olsen, I., Solheim, L. & Bertelsen, R. 1982. Correspondence analysis: an alternative to principle components. <u>World Archaeology</u> 14, pp41-60.

Caesar, J. 1982. <u>The Conquest of Gaul</u>. (trans. S. Handford), Harmondsworth, Penguin.

Chadwick, S. 1958. Early Iron Age enclosures on Longbridge Deverill Cow Down, Wiltshire. In S. Frere (ed.), <u>Problems of the Iron Age in Southern Britain</u>, London, Institute of Archaeology, University of London, pp18-20.

Chadwick-Hawkes, S. 1994. Longbridge Deveril Cow Down, Wiltshire, house 3: A major round house of the early Iron Age. <u>Oxford Journal of Archaeology</u> 13, pp49-69.

Champion, S. & Champion, T. 1981. The Iron Age in Hampshire. In S. Shennan & T. Schadla-Hall (eds.), <u>The Archaeology of Hampshire</u>. Winchester, Hampshire Field Club Monograph No. 1.

Champion, T. 1975. Britain in the European Iron Age. <u>Archaeologia Atlantica</u> 1, pp127-145.

Champion, T. 1987. The European Iron Age: Assessing the state of the art. <u>Scottish Archaeological Review</u> 4, pp98-107.

Champion, T. 1990. . Medieval archaeology and the tryany of the historical record. In D. Austin & L. Alcock (eds.), <u>From the Baltic to the Black Sea: Studies in Medieval Archaeology</u>. London, Unwin Hyman, One World Archaeology 18, pp79-95.

Champion, T. 1991. Theoretical archaeology in Britain. In I. Hodder (ed.), <u>Archaeological Theory in Europe: The last three decades</u>. London, Routledge, pp129-160.

Chapman, M. 1992. <u>The Celts: The construction of a myth</u>. London, Macmillan Press.

Charsley, S. 1987. Interpretation and Custom: The case of the wedding cake. <u>MAN</u> 22, pp93-110.

Childe, G. 1936. <u>Scotland Before The Scots</u>. London, Methuen

Childe, G. 1940. <u>Prehistoric Cummunities of the British Isles</u>. London, Chambers. (1st edition, 3rd edition 1949)

Clark, G. 1940. <u>Prehistoric England</u>. London, Batsford.

Clark, G. 1966. The invasion hypothesis in British archaeology. <u>Antiquity</u> 40, pp172-189.

Clark, J. 1990. Anthony Giddens, sociology and modern social theory. In J. Clark, C. Modgil & S. Modgil (eds.), <u>Anthony Giddens: Consensus and Controversy</u>. London, The Falmer Press, pp21-27.

Clarke. DL. 1972. A provisional model of an Iron Age society and its settlement system. In DL Clarke (ed.), <u>Models in Archaeology</u>. London, pp801-869.

Clarke, DL. 1977. Spatial information in archaeology. In DL. Clarke (ed.), <u>Spatial Archaeology</u>. London, Academic Press, pp1-28.

Clay, R. 1924. An Early Iron Age site on Fifield Bavant Down. <u>Wiltshire Archaeological Magazine</u> 43, pp457-496.

Clay, R. 1925. An inhabited site of La Tene 1 data on Swallowcliffe Down. <u>Wiltshire Archaeological Magazine</u> 43, pp59-93.

Cleal, R. 1991. Cranborne Chase - The earliest prehistoric pottery. In J. Barrett, R. Bradley & M. Hall (eds.), <u>Papers on the Prehistoric Archaeology of Cranborne Chase</u>. Oxford, Oxbow Books, Oxbow Monographs 11, pp134-200.

Coe, D. , Newman, R. & Morris, E. 1992. Excavations of an Early Iron Age building and Romano-British enclosure at Brighton Hill South, Basingstoke, Hampshire. <u>Proceedings of the Hampshire Field Club</u> 48, pp5-21.

Cohen, A. 1985. <u>The Symbolic Construction of Community</u>. Chichester, Ellis Horwood.

Cohen, A. (ed.), 1986. <u>Symbolizing Boundaries: Identity and diversity in British culture</u>. Manchester, The University Press.

Cohen, I. 1989. <u>Structuration Theory: Anthony Giddens and the constitution of social life</u>. London, Macmillan.

Cohen, I. 1990. Structuration theory and social order: Five issues in brief. In J. Clark, C. Modgil & S. Modgil (eds.), <u>Anthony Giddens: Consensus and Controversy</u>. London, The Falmer Press, pp33-45.

Coles, B. & Coles, J. 1986. <u>Sweet Track to Glastonbury: The Somerset Levels in Prehistory</u>. London, Thames & Hudson.

Coles, J. 1973. <u>Archaeology by Experiment</u>. London, Hutchinson University Library.

Coles, J. 1987. <u>Maere Village East: The excavations of A. Bullied and H. St George Gray 1932-1956</u>. Exeter, Somerset Levels Project, Somerset Levels Papers 13.

Coles, J. & Harding, A. 1979. <u>The Bronze Age in Europe</u>. London, Methuen.

Collis, J. 1968. Excavations at Owslebury, Hants: an interim report. <u>Antiquaries Journal</u> 48, pp18-31.

Collis, J. 1970. Excavations at Owslebury, Hants: a second interim report. <u>Antiquaries Journal</u> 50, pp246-261.

Collis, J. 1972. Burials with weapons in Iron Age Britain. Germania 50, pp121-133.

Collis, J. 1977a. The Iron Age in Britain: A Review. Sheffield, The Department of Prehistory and Archaeology.

Collis, J. 1977b. An approach to the Iron Age. In J. Collis (ed.), The Iron Age in Britain: A Review. Sheffield, The Department of Archaeology and Prehistory, pp1-7.

Collis, J. 1977c. Owslebury (Hants) and the problem of burials on rural settlements. In R.Reece (ed.), Burial in the Roman World. London, Council for British Archaeology, pp26-34.

Collis, J. 1978. Winchester Excavations Vol II. 1949-1960. Winchester, City Council.

Collis, J. 1985. Review of Danebury, An Iron Age Hillfort in Hampshire. Proceedings of the Prehistoric Society 51, pp348-349.

Collis, J. 1990. L'impact des processus d'urbanisation sur les sites ruroux: Le cas d'Owslebury, Hants, Angleterre. Revue Archéologie Ouest Supplement 3, pp209-222.

Combs-Schling, E. 1989. Sacred Performances: Islam, Sexuality and Sacrifice. New York, Columbia University Press.

Connerton, P. 1989. How Societies Remember, Cambridge, The University Press.

Corney, M. 1989. Multiple ditch systems and Late Iron Age settlement in central Wessex. In M. Bowden, D. Mackay & P. Topping (ed.), From Cornwall to Caithness: Some aspects of British Field Archaeology. Oxford, British Archaeological Reports (British Series 209), pp 111-128.

Cosgrove, D. 1984. Social Formation and Symbolic Landscape. London, Croom Helm.

Coy, J. 1984a. The small mammals and amphiba. In B.Cunliffe, 1984. Danebury: An Iron Age Hillfort in Hampshire. vol 2. London, Council for British Archaeology, pp526-527.

Coy, J. 1984b. The bird bones. In B.Cunliffe (ed.), 1984. Danebury: An Iron Age Hillfort in Hampshire. 2vols. London, Council for British Archaeology, pp527-531.

Coy, J. 1987. The animal bone. In P. Fasham A Banjo Enclosure in Micheldever Wood, Hampshire. Winchester, Hampshire Field Club Monograph No. 5, pp45-53.

Coy, J. 1992. The animal bones (from Lains Farm). In P. Bellamy, The investigation of the prehistoric landscape along the route of the A303 improvement between Andover and Amesbury, Wiltshires, 1984-7. Proceedings of the Hampshire Field Club 47, pp32-36.

Crummy, N. 1983. The Roman Small Finds form Excavations in Colchester 1971-1979. Colchester Archaeological Reports 2.

Cunliffe, B. 1968. Excavations at Eldon's Seat, Encombe, Dorset. Proceedings of the Prehistoric Society 34, pp191-237.

Cunliffe, B. 1974. Iron Age Communities in Britain, London, Routledge Kegan & Paul (1st edition).

Cunliffe, B. 1983. Danebury: The anatomy of an Iron Age hillfort. London, Batsford.

Cunliffe, B. 1984a. Danebury: An Iron Age Hillfort in Hampshire. 2 vols. London, Council for British Archaeology.

Cunliffe, B. 1984b. Iron Age Wessex: Continuity and change. In BW. Cunliffe & D. Miles (eds.), Aspects of the Iron Age in Central Southern Britain. Oxford, Oxford University Committee for Archaeology Monograph 2, pp12-45.

Cunliffe, B. 1987. Hengistbury Head, Dorset: Vol 1 The Prehistoric and Roman Settlement, 3500BC-AD500. Oxford, Oxford University Committee for Archaeology.

Cunliffe, B. 1991. Iron Age Communities in Britain. London, Routledge (3rd edition).

Cunliffe, B. 1992. Pits, preconceptions and propitiation in the British Iron Age. Oxford Journal of Archaeology 11, pp69-84.

Cunliffe, B. 1993. Wessex to AD 1000. London, Longman.

Cunliffe, B. & Poole, C. 1991. Danebury: An Iron Age Hillfort in Hampshire. vols 4&5. London, Council for British Archaeology.

Cunliffe, B. & Orton, C. 1984. Radiocarbon age assessment. In B. Cunliffe, 1984. Danebury: An Iron Age Hillfort in Hampshire. London, Council for British Archaeology, pp190-198.

Cunnington, M. 1923. The Early Iron Age Inhabited Site at All Cannings Cross. Devizes, Privately Published.

Cunnington, M. 1925. Figsbury Rings: An account of excavations in 1924. Wiltshire Archaeological Magazine 43, pp48-58.

Cunnington, M. 1932. Was there a second Belgic invasion represented by bead-rim pottery? Antiuaries Journal 12, pp48-58.

Cunnington, M. 1933. Excavations in Yarnbury Castle Camp. Wiltshire Archaeological Magazine 46, pp198-213.

Cunnington, M. &.Cunnington, L. 1913. Casterley Camp excavations. Wiltshire Archaeological Magazine 38, pp53-105.

Cunnington, M. & Cunnington, L. 1913. Lidbury Camp. Wiltshire Archaeological Magazine 40, pp12-36.

Curwen, EC. 1930. The silting of ditches in chalk. Antiquity 4, pp97-100.

David, N. 1971. The Fulani compound and the archaeologist. World Archaeology 3, pp111-131.

David, N. 1972. On the life span of pottery, type requencies, and archaeological inference. <u>American Antiquity</u> 37, pp141-2.

Davies, S. 1981, The excavations at Old Down Farm, Andover. Part 2 Prehistoric and Roman. <u>Proceedings of the Hampshire Field Club</u> 37, pp81-163.

Davies, S. 1994. Old Down Farm, Andover, Hampshire. In A.P. Fitzpatrick & E. Morris (eds.) <u>The Iron Age in Wessex: Recent Work,</u> Salisbury, Association Francaise D'Etude de L'Age du Fer/Trust for Wessex Archaeology, pp57-62.

Davies, S., Stacey, L. & Woodward, P. 1985. Excavations at Alington Avenue, Fordington, Dorchester 1984-5: Interim report. <u>Proceedings of the Dorset Natural History and Archaeological Society</u> 107, pp101-110.

Deal, M. 1985. Household patterns of disposal in the Maya highlands: An ethnoarchaeological interpretation. <u>Journal of Anthropological Archaeology</u> 4, pp243-291.

DeBoer, W. & Lathrap, D. 1979. The making and breaking of Shipibo-Conibo ceramics. In C. Kramer (ed.), <u>Ethnoarchaeology: Implications of ethnography for archaeology</u>. New York, Columbia University Press, pp102-138.

De Certeau, M. 1984. <u>The Practice of Everyday Life</u>. Berkeley, The University of California Press.

De Heusch, J. 1985. <u>Sacrifice in Africa: A Structuralist Approach</u>. Manchester, The University Press.

Demoule, J-P. & Illett, M. 1985. First Millennium settlement and society in northern France: A case study from the Aisne Valley. In T. Champion & V. Megaw (eds.), <u>Settlement and Society: Aspects of West European prehistory in the first millennium BC</u>. Leicester, The University Press, pp193-221.

Dennel, R. 1974. Botanical evidence for prehistoric crop processing activities. <u>Journal of Archaeological Science</u> 1, pp275-284.

Dewar, H. 1969. Hippophagy or Horse sacrifice among the Durotriges. <u>Proceedings of the Dorset Natural History and Archaeological Society</u> 91, pp194-195.

Dietler, M. 1990. Driven by drink: The role of drinking in the political economy and the case of Early Iron Age France. <u>Journal of Anthropological Archaeology</u> 9, pp352-408.

Donaldson, P. n.d. <u>Further Excavations at Balksbury Camp, Andover, Hampshire, 1973 & 1981</u>. Unpublished preliminary site report, Trust for Wessex Archaeology.

Donley-Reid, L. 1990. A structuring structure: The Swahili house. In S. Kent (ed.), <u>Domestic Architecture and the Use of Space</u>, Cambridge, The University Press, pp114-126.

Douglas, M. 1957. Animals and Lele religious symbolism. <u>Africa</u> 27, 46-58.

Douglas, M. 1966. <u>Purity and Danger.</u> London: Routledge and Kegan Paul.

Douglas, M. 1990. The pangolin revisited: a new approach to animal symbolism. In R. Willis (ed.), <u>Signifying Animals: Human meaning in the natural world</u>. London, Unwin Hyman, One World Archaeology 16, pp25-36.

Drewett, P. 1982. Later Bronze Age downland economy and excavation at Black Patch, East Sussex. <u>Proceedings of the Prehistoric Society</u> 48, pp321-400.

Dunning, G. 1976. Salmonsbury, Burton-on-the-Water, Gloucestershire. In D. Harding (ed.), <u>Later Prehistoric Earthworks in Britain and Ireland.</u>, London, Routledge, pp75-118.

Durkheim, E. 1915. <u>The Elementary Forms of Religious Life</u>. London, Allen & Unwin.

Dwyer, P. 1977. An analysis of Rofaifo mammal taxonomy. <u>American Ethnologist</u> 3, pp425-445.

Ehrenreich, R. 1994. Ironworking in Iron Age Wessex. In A.P. Fitzpatrick & E. Morris (eds.) <u>The Iron Age in Wessex: Recent Work,</u> Salisbury, Association Francaise D'Etude de L'Age du Fer/Trust for Wessex Archaeology, pp16-19.

Ellison, A. & Drewett, P. 1971. Pits and postholes in the British Early Iron Age. <u>Proceedings of the Prehistoric Society</u> 31, pp183-194.

Ellison, A. 1981. Towards a socioeconomic model for the Middle Bronze Age in Southern England. In I. Hodder, G. Issaca & N. Hammond (eds.), <u>Pattern of the Past</u>. Cambridge, The University Press, pp413-438.

Ellison, A. 1987. The Finds. In S. Green, <u>Excavations at Poundbury. Volume 1: The Settlements.</u> Dorchester, Dorset Natural History and Archaeological Society Monograph No.7.

Ellison, A. & Rhatz, P. 1987. Excavations at Whitsbury Castle Ditch, Hampshire 1960. <u>Proceedings of Prehistoric Society</u> 43, pp63-81.

Evans, C. 1988. Acts of enclosure: a consideration of concentrically-organised causewayed enclosures. In J.C. Barrett & I.A. Kinnes (eds.), <u>The Archaeology of Context in the Neolithic and Bronze Age: Recent Trends.</u> Sheffield, The University Press, pp85-96.

Evans, C. 1989. Archaeology and modern times: Bersu's Woodbury 1938 & 1939. <u>Antiquity</u> 63, pp436-50.

Evans, C. & Boast, R. 1986. The transformation of space: two examples from British prehistory. <u>Archaeological Review from Cambridge</u> 5(2), pp193-205.

Evans, C. & Serjeantson, D. 1988. The blackwater economy and excavation of a Fen-edge community in the Iron Age: the Upper Delps, Haddenham. <u>Antiquity</u> 62, 381-400.

Evans, J. & Millett, M. 1992. Residuality revisited. <u>Oxford Journal of Archaeology</u> 11, pp225-240.

Evans-Pritchard, E. 1940. <u>The Nuer</u>. Oxford, The University Press.

Evans-Pritchard, E. 1956. <u>Nuer Religion</u>. Oxford, The University Press.

Fasham, P. 1983. Fieldwork in and around Micheldever wood, Hampshire 1973-1980. <u>Proceedings of the Hampshire Field Club</u> 39, pp5-45.

Fasham, P. 1985. <u>The Prehistoric Settlement at Winnall Down, Winchester.</u> Winchester, Hampshire Field Club Monograph No.2.

Fasham, P. 1988. <u>A Banjo Enclosure in Micheldever Wood, Hampshire.</u> Winchester, Hampshire Field Club Monograph No. 5.

Fasham, P., Farwell, D. & Whinney, R. 1989. <u>The Archaeological Site at Easton Lane, Winchester.</u> Winchester, Hampshire Field Club Monograph No. 6.

Fasham, P. & Whinney, R. 1992. <u>Archaeology and the M3</u>. Winchester, Hampshire Field Club Monograph 7.

Fasham, P. & Keevil, T. Forthcoming. <u>Brighton Hill South Heritage Project</u>. Winchester, Hampshire Field Club Monograph.

Fell, V. 1988. Iron Age metalworking tools from Gussage All Saints, Dorset. <u>Proceedings of the Dorset Natural History and Archaeological Society</u> 110, pp73-76.

Fenton, A. 1983. Grain storage in pits: Experiment and fact. In A. O'Connor & DV. Clarke (eds.), <u>From the Stone Age to the 'Forty Five</u>. Edinburgh, J.Donald, pp567-588.

Ferrell, G. (I1995). Space and society: new perspectives on the Iron Age of North-East England. In Hill, J. and Cumberpatch, C. (eds.), <u>Different Iron Ages: Studies on the Iron Age in temperate Europe</u>, British Archaeological Reports (International Series), Oxford.

Fiddes, N. 1991. <u>Meat: A natural symbol</u>. London, Routledge.

Field, N. 1982. The Iron Age and Romano-British settlement on Bradford Down, Pamphill, Dorset. <u>Proceedings of the Dorset Natural History and Archaeological Society</u> 104, pp71-91.

Firth, R. 1963. Offering and sacrifice: Problems of organisation. <u>Journal of the Royal Anthropological Institute</u> 93, pp12-24.

Fisher, A.R. 1985. Winklebury Hillfort: a study of artefact distribution from subsoil features. <u>Proceedings of the Prehistoric Society</u> 51, pp167-180.

Fitzpatrick, AF. 1984. The deposition of La Tene Iron Age metalwork in watery contexts in Southern England. In BW. Cunliffe & D. Miles (eds.), <u>Aspects of the Iron Age in Central Southern Britain</u>. Oxford, Oxford University Committee for Archaeology Monograph 2, pp178-190.

Fitzpatrick, A. 1989. The uses of Roman imperialism by the Celtic barbarians in the later Republic. In JC. Barrett, AF. Fitzpatrick, & I. Macinnes (eds.), <u>Barbarians and Romans in North-West Europe</u>. Oxford, British Archaeological Reports (International Series 471), pp27-54.

Fitzpatrick, A. 1991. 'Celtic (Iron Age) Religion' - Traditional and Timeless? <u>Scottish Archaeological Review</u> 8, pp123-128.

Fitzpatrick, A. 1991b. Everyday life in the Later Iron Age of European Britain. Paper presented to the 5th conference of the Institute of Field Archaeologists, Birmingham.

Fitzpatrick, A. 1994a. Outside in: the structure of an Early Iron Age house at Dunston Park, Thatcham, Berkshire. In A.P. Fitzpatrick & E. Morris (eds.) <u>The Iron Age in Wessex: Recent Work</u>, Salisbury, Association Francaise D'Etude de L'Age du Fer/Trust for Wessex Archaeology, pp68-72.

Fitzpatrick, A. 1994b. The Late Iron Age cremation cemetery at Westhampnett, West Sussex. In A.P. Fitzpatrick & E. Morris (eds.) <u>The Iron Age in Wessex: Recent Work</u>, Salisbury, Association Francaise D'Etude de L'Age du Fer/Trust for Wessex Archaeology, pp108-111.

Fitzpatrick, A. & Morris, E. (eds.) 1994. <u>The Iron Age in Wessex: Recent Work</u>, Salisbury, Association Francaise D'Etude de L'Age du Fer/Trust for Wessex Archaeology.

Flannery, K. (ed.), 1976. <u>The Early Mesoamerican Village</u>. New York, Academic Press.

Foster, J. 1980. <u>The Iron Age Moulds from Gussage All Saints</u>. London, British Museum Press, British Museum Occasional Papers 12.

Foster, S. 1989. Transformations in social space: The Iron Age of Orkney and Caithness. <u>Scottish Archaeological Review</u> 6, pp34-54.

Fowler, P. 1967. The archaeology of Fyfield and Overton Downs, Wiltshire; Third interim report. <u>Wiltshire Archaeological Magazine</u> 62, pp16-33.

Fowler, P., Musty, J., Taylor, C. 1965. Some earthwork enclosures in Witlshire. <u>Wiltshire Archaeological Magazine</u>. 60, pp52-74.

Fox, C. & Wolseley, G.R. 1928. The Early Iron Age Site at Findon Park, Sussex. <u>Antiquaries Journal</u> 8, pp449-460.

Franks, A.W. 1858. Acount of a recent exploration of an ancient pit at Dunbury Hill... <u>Proceedings of the Society of Antiquaries</u> 1st Series 4, pp241-242.

Garwood, P., Jennings, D., Skeates, R. & Toms, J. (eds.), 1991. <u>Sacred and Profane; Proceedings of a conference on archaeology, ritual and religion, Oxford, 1989</u>. Oxford, Oxford University Committee for Archaeology Monograph No. 32.

Geertz, C. 1968. Religion: The anthropolgcial study of. In <u>International Encyclopedia of the Social Sciences</u>. London, Macmillan & The Free Press, pp398-406.

Geertz, C. 1973. <u>The Interpretation of Cultures</u>. New York, Basic Books.

Geertz, C. 1984. Anti Anti-relativism *American Anthropologist* 86, pp263-278.

Geertz, C. 1986. The uses of diversity. In S. McMurrin (ed.). *The Tanner Lectures on Human Values.* VII, Salt Lake City & Cambridge, The University Presses of Utah & Cambridge. pp251-276.

Gerholm, G. 1988. On ritual: A postmodernist view. *Ethnos* 53, pp190-203.

Gero, J. & Conkey, M. 1991. *Engendering Archaeology.* Oxford, Blackwells.

Gibson, D. & Geselowitz, M. (eds.), 1986. *Tribe and Polity in Late Prehistoric Europe.* New York, Plenum Press.

Gibson, T. 1986. *Sacrifice and sharing in the Philippine highlands: Religion and society among the Buid of Mindora.* London, Athlone Press (LSE Monographs in Social Anthropology 53).

Giddens, A. 1979. *Central Problems in Social Theory.* London, Macmillan.

Giddens, A. 1984. *The Constitution of Society: Outline of the Theory of Structuration.* Cambridge, Polity Press.

Gifford, D. 1981. Taphonomy and palaeoecology: A critical review of archaeology's sister disciplines. In M. Schiffer (ed.), *Advances in Archaeoliogical Method and Theory* 4, pp345-438.

Gingell, C. 1982. The excavation of an Iron Age enclosure at Groundwell Farm. *Wiltshire Archaeological Magazine* 76, pp33-76.

Gingell, C. 1992. *The Marlborough Downs: A Later Bronze Age landscape and its origins.* Devizes, Wiltshire Archaeological and Natural History Monograph 1.

Gingell, C. & Lawson, A.J. 1983. The Potterne project: excavation and research at a major settlement of the Late Bronze Age. *Wiltshire Archaeological Magazine* 78, pp31-34.

Gingell, C. & Lawson, A.J. 1985. Excavations at Potterne 1984. *Wiltshire Archaeological Magazine* 79, pp101-108.

Gleghorn, G. 1992. *The Representation of Gender at King Harry Lane, St Albans.* Part II Dissertation, Department of Archaeology, University of Cambridge.

Gosden, C. 1989. Debt, production and prehistory. *Journal of Anthropological Archaeology* 8, pp355-387.

Goody, J. 1961. Religion and ritual: the definitional problem. *British Journal of Sociology* 12, pp142-164.

Goody, J. 1977. Against 'ritual': Loosely structured thoughts on a loosely defined topic. In SF. Moore & BG. Meyerhoff (eds.), *Secular Ritual.* Assen, Van Gorcum.

Goody, J. 1982. *Cooking, Cuisine and Class.* Cambridge, The University Press.

Grant, A. 1981. The significance of deer remains at occupation sites of the Iron Age to the Anglo-Saxon period. In G. Dimbleby and M. Jones (eds.), *The Environment of Man: The Iron Age to the Anglo-Saxon Period,* Oxford, British Archaeological Reports (British Series 87), pp205-213.

Grant, A. 1984a. Animal husbandry. In B.Cunliffe (ed.), *Danebury: An Iron Age Hillfort in Hampshire.* vol 2. London, Council for British Archaeology, pp496-547.

Grant, A. 1984b. Animal husbandry in Wessex and in the Thames Valley. In BW. Cunliffe & D. Miles (eds.), *Aspects of the Iron Age in Central Southern Britain.* Oxford, Oxford University Committee for Archaeology Monograph 2, pp102-119.

Grant, A. 1984c. Survivial or sacrifice? A critical appraisal of animal burials in Britain in the Iron Age. In C. Grigson & J. Clutton-Brock (eds.), *Animals and Archaeology.* Oxford, British Archaeological Reports (International Series 227), pp221-227.

Grant, A. 1989a. Animals and ritual in Early Britain: the visible and the invisible. *Anthropozoologica* 3, pp341-355.

Grant, A. 1989b. Animals in Roman Britain. In M. Todd (ed.), *Research on Roman Britain: 1960-89.* London, Society for the Promotion of Roman Studies (Britannia Monograph 11), pp135-146.

Grant, A. 1991. Economic or symbolic? Animals and ritual behaviour. In P. Garwood, D. Jennings, R. Skeates & J. Toms (eds.), *Sacred and Profane.* Oxford, Oxford University Committee for Archaeology Monograph No. 32, pp109-114.

Green, F. 1994. Early Iron Age stream deposits at La Sagesse, Romsey, Hampshire. In A.P. Fitzpatrick & E. Morris (eds.) *The Iron Age in Wessex: Recent Work,* Salisbury, Association Francaise D'Etude de L'Age du Fer/Trust for Wessex Archaeology, pp49-52.

Green, S. 1987. *Excavations at Poundbury. Volume 1: The Settlements.* Dorchester, Dorset Natural History and Archaeological Society Monograph No.7.

Gregory, D. & Urry, J. (eds.), 1985. *Social Relations and Spatial Structures.* London, Macmillan.

Guilbert, G. 1981. Double-ring round houses, probable and possible. *Proceedings of the Prehistoric Society* 47, pp299-317.

Guilbert, G. 1982. Post-ring symmetry in roundhouses at Moel y Gaer and some other sites in prehistoric Britain. In P.Drury (ed.), *Structural Reconstructions,* Oxford, British Archaeological Reports (British Series 110), pp67-86.

Halstead, P., Hodder, I. & Jones, G. 1978. Behavioural archaeology and refuse patterns: A case study. *Norwegian Archaeological Review* 11, pp118-131.

Hamilton, S. 1985. Iron Age pottery. In O. Bedwin & R. Holgate, Excavations at Copse Farm, Oving, West Sussex. *Proceedings of the Prehistoric Society* 51, pp220-227.

Harcourt, R. 1979. The animal bones. In G.Wainwright. *Gussage All Saints: An Iron Age Settlement in Dorset.* DOE Archaeological Reports 10, London, HMSO, pp150-161.

Harding, D. 1974. The Iron Age in Lowland Britain. London, Routledge, Kegan & Paul.

Harris, M. 1974. Cows, Pigs, Wars and Witches: The riddle of culture. New York, Random House.

Harrison, S. 1992. Ritual as intellectual property. MAN 27, pp225-244.

Harvey, D. 1989. The Condition of Post-Modernity. Oxford, Blackwells.

Hasdorf, C. 1991. Gender, space and food in prehistory. In J. Gero & M. Conkey (eds.), Engendering Archaeology. Oxford, Blackwell, pp132-162.

Haselgrove, C. 1982. Wealth, prestige and power: The dynamics of Late Iron Age Centralization in South Eastern England. In C.Renfrew & S.Shennan (eds.), Ranking, Resource and Exchange. Cambridge, The University Press, pp79-88.

Haselgrove, C. 1984. Romanisation before the conquest: Gaulish precedents and British consequences. In T. Blagg & A King (eds.), Military and Civilian in Roman Britain. Oxford, British Archaeological Reports (British Series 136), pp 5-63.

Haselgrove, C. 1986a. Central places in British Iron Age studies: A review and some problems. In E. Grant (ed.), 1986. Central Places, Archaeology and History. Sheffield, Department of Archaeology and Prehistory, pp3-12.

Haselgrove, C. 1986b. An Iron Age community and its hillfort: The excavations at Danebury, Hampshire, 1969-79. A review. Archaeological Journal 143, pp363-369.

Haselgrove, C. 1987. Iron Age Coinage in South-East England: The Archaeological Context. Oxford, British Archaeological Reports (British Series 174).

Haselgrove, C. 1989. The later Iron Age in Southern Britain and beyond. In M. Todd (ed.), Research on Roman Britain: 1960-89. London, Society for the Promotion of Roman Studies (Britannia Monograph 11), pp1-18.

Haselgrove, C. 1994a. Social organisation in Iron Age Wessex. In A.P. Fitzpatrick & E. Morris (eds.) The Iron Age in Wessex: Recent Work, Salisbury, Association Francaise D'Etude de L'Age du Fer/Trust for Wessex Archaeology, pp1-4.

Haselgrove, C. 1994b. Coinage and currency in Iron Age Wessex. In A.P. Fitzpatrick & E. Morris (eds.) The Iron Age in Wessex: Recent Work, Salisbury, Association Francaise D'Etude de L'Age du Fer/Trust for Wessex Archaeology, pp22-26.

Haselgrove, C. & Allon, V. 1982. An Iron Age settlement at West House, Coxhoe, County Durham. Archaeologica Aeliana (5th series) 10, pp25-51.

Hawkes, C. 1931. Hill Forts. Antiquity 5, 60-97.

Hawkes, C. 1939. The excavations at Quarley Hill 1938. Proceedings of the Hampshire Field Club. 13, pp136-194.

Hawkes, C. 1940. The excavations at Bury Hill 1939. Proceedings of the Hampshire Field Club. 14, pp291-237.

Hawkes, C. 1947. Britons, Romans and Saxons round Salisbury and in Cranborne Chase: reviewing the excavations of General Pitt-Rivers, 1881-1898. Archaeological Journal 104, pp27-81.

Hawkes, C. 1954. Archaeological method and theory: some suggestions from the Old World. American Anthropologist 56, pp158-168.

Hawkes, C., Myres, J., & Stevens, C. 1929. Excavations at St Catherine's Hill. Proceedings of the Hampshire Field Club 11, pp1-188.

Hawkes, J. 1985. The pottery. In P. Fasham. The Prehistoric Settlement at Winnall Down, Winchester. Winchester, Hampshire Field Club Monograph No.2, pp48-76.

Hawkes, J. 1989. Later prehistoric pottery. In P. Fasham et al. The Archaeological Site at Easton Lane, Winchester. Winchester, Hampshire Field Club Monograph No. 6, pp91-97.

Hayden, B. & Cannon, A. 1983. Where all the garbage goes: Refuse disposal in the Maya highlands. Journal of Anthropological Archaeology 2, pp117-163.

Helbaek, H. 1952. Early crops in Southern England. Proceedings of the Prehistoric Society 18, pp194-233.

Hearne, C. & Cox, P. 1994. The development of settlement, industry and trade on the Purbeck heath and southern shore of Poole Harbour, Poole. In A.P. Fitzpatrick & E. Morris (eds.) The Iron Age in Wessex: Recent Work, Salisbury, Association Francaise D'Etude de L'Age du Fer/Trust for Wessex Archaeology, pp102-106.

Henderson, J. 1991. Industrial specialization in late Iron Age Britain and Europe. Archaological Journal 148, pp104-148.

Hesse, B. & Whipnash, P. 1985. Animal bone Archaeology Washington DC, Taraxacum (Manuels in Archaeology 5).

Hill, JD. 1987. The confessions of an archaeologist who dug in school. Archaeological Review from Cambridge 6:2, pp143-155.

Hill, J.D. 1988. Celtic Castles in the Air. Unpublished M.Phil Dissertation, Department of Archaeology, University of Cambridge.

Hill, J.D. 1989. Rethinking the Iron Age. Scottish Archaeological Review 6, pp16-24.

Hill, JD. 1992. Feasting, Sacrifice and the interpretation of Iron Age animal bone. Paper presented at TAG, Southampton, 1992.

Hill, J.D. 1993. Can we concieve of a different Europe in the past: A Contrastive archaeology of Later Prehistoric settlement in Southern England. Journal of European Archaeology 1. pp57-76.

Hill, J.D. 1994. Why we should not take the data from Iron Age settlements for granted: Recent studies of intra-settlement patterning. In A.P. Fitzpatrick & E. Morris (eds.) The Iron Age in Wessex: Recent Work, Salisbury, Association Francaise D'Etude de L'Age du Fer/Trust for Wessex Archaeology, pp4-8.

Hill, J. D. 1995. How should we understand Iron Age societies and hillforts? A contextual study from Southern Britain. In JD. Hill & C. Cumberpatch (eds.) Different Iron Ages: Studies on the Iron Age in Temperate Europe, Oxford, British Archaeological Reports.

Hill, J.D. Forthcoming a. Hillforts and the Iron Age of Wessex. In T. Champion & J. Collis (eds.), Recent Trends in the Archaeology of Iron Age Britain, Sheffield, JR Collis publications, The University.

Hill, J.D. Forthcoming b. The Iron Age in Britain and Ireland; An overview. Journal of World Prehistory

Hill, JD. nd1 (1989). Investigating mortuary and other ritual deposits on Wessex Iron Age settlements. Unpublished paper.

Hill, JD., Mays, S. & C. Overy. 1989. The Iron Age: A project for schools. Archaeology and Education Publication No.9, University of Southampton

Hillman, G. 1981. Reconstructing crop husbandry practices from charred remains of crops. In R. Mercer (ed.), Farming Practice in British Prehistory, Edinburgh, The University Press, pp123-163.

Hingley, R. 1984. Towards Social Analysis in Archaeology: Celtic Society in the Iron Age of the Upper Thames Valley. In BW. Cunliffe,. & D. Miles (eds.), Aspects of the Iron Age in Central Southern Britain. Oxford, Oxford University Committee for Archaeology Monograph 2, pp72-88.

Hingley, R. 1988. The influence of Rome on idigenous social groups in the upper Thames valley. In R. Jones, J Bloemers, S. Dyson & M. Biddle (eds.), First Millennium Papers. Oxford, British Archaeological Reports (International Series 401, pp73-98.

Hingley, R. 1989a.Rural Settlement in Roman Britain. London, Seaby.

Hingley, R. 1989b. Iron Age settlement and society in central and southern Warwickshire. In A. Gibson (ed.), Midlands Prehistory. Oxford, British Archaeological Reports (British Series 204), pp122-157.

Hingley, R. 1990a. Boundaries surrounding Iron Age and Romano-British Settlements. Scottish Archaeological Review 7, pp96-103.

Hingley, R. 1990b. Domestic organisation and gender relations in Iron Age and Romano-British households. In R. Samson (ed.), The Social Archaeology of Houses. Edinburgh, The University Press, pp125-149.

Hingley, R. 1990c. Iron Age 'currency bars': The archaeological and social context. Archaeological Journal 147, pp91-117.

Hingley. R. 1992. Society in Scotland from 700BC to AD 200. Proceedings of the Society of Antiquaries of Scotland 122, pp7-53.

Hingley, R. & Miles, D. 1984. Aspects of Iron Age settlement in the Upper Thames Valley. In BW. Cunliffe & D. Miles (eds.), Aspects of the Iron Age in Central Southern Britain. Oxford, Oxrord University Committee for Archaeology Monograph 2, pp52-71.

Hodder, I. 1977. How are we to study the distribution of Iron Age material? In J. Collis (ed.), The Iron Age in Britain: A Review. Sheffield, The Department of Archaeology and Prehistory, pp8-16.

Hodder, I. 1982a. Symbols in Action. Cambridge, The University Press.

Hodder, I. (ed.), 1982b. Symbolic and Structural Archaeology. Cambridge, The University Press.

Hodder, I. 1982c. The Present Past. London, Batsford.

Hodder, I. 1982d. The Archaeology of the M11: Excavations at Wendens Ambo. London, Passmore Edwards Museum.

Hodder, I. 1986. Reading the Past. Cambridge, The University Press.

Hodder, I. 1987a. The contextual analysis of symbolic meaning. In I. Hodder (ed.), The Archaeology of Contextual Meanings. Cambridge, The University Press, pp1-8.

Hodder, I. 1987b. The meaning of discard: Ash and domestic space in Baringo. In S. Kent (ed.), Method and Theory for Activity Area Research: An Ethnoarchaeological Approach. New York. Columbia University Press, pp424-448.

Hodder, I. 1989a. This is not an article about material culture as text. Journal of Anthropological Archaeology 8, pp250-269.

Hodder, I. 1989b. Writing archaeology: site reports in context. Antiquity 63, pp268-274.

Hodder, I. 1990. The Domestication of Europe. Oxford, Blackwells.

Hodder, I. 1991a. Interpretive archaeology and its role. American Antiquity 56, pp7-18.

Hodder, I. 1991b. To interpret is to act: The need for an interpretative archaeology. Scottish Archaeological Review 8, pp8-15.

Hodder, I. & Hedges, J. 1977. 'Weaving combs': Their typology and distribution with some introductory remarks on date and function. In J. Collis (ed.), The Iron Age in Britain: A Review. Sheffield, The Department of Archaeology and Prehistory, The University, p17-28.

Hodson, F. 1960 . Reflections on the 'ABC of the British Iron Age'. <u>Antiquity</u> 33, pp170-181.

Hodson, F. 1964. Cultural grouping within the British pre-Roman Iron Age. <u>Proceedings of the Prehistoric Society</u> 30, pp99-110.

Holleyman, G. 1937. Harrow Hill excavations 1936. <u>Sussex Archaeological Collections</u> 78, pp230-252.

Hooley, R.. 1929. Excavation of an Early Iron Age village on Worthy Down, Winchester. <u>Proceedings of the Hampshire Field Club</u> 10, pp178-192.

Hubert, H. & Mauss, M. 1964. <u>Sacrifice: Its nature and functions</u>. Chicago, The University Press.

Hugh-Jones, C. 1978. Food for thought: patterns of production and consumption in Pira-Pirana society. In: J.S. LaFontaine (ed.) <u>Age and Sex as Principles of Social Differentiation</u>, London:, Academic Press, pp41-66.

Hugh-Jones, C. 1979. <u>From the Milk River: Spatial and Temporal Processes in Northwest Amazonia</u>. Cambridge, The University Press.

Hugh-Jones, S. 1979. <u>The Palm and The Pleiades: Initiation and Cosmology in Northwest Amazonia</u>. Cambridge, The University Press.

Huntingdon, R. and Metcalf, P. 1979 <u>Celebrations of Death</u>. Cambridge, The University Press.

Hynes, S. 1987. Hardy's historians. <u>Thomas Hardy Annual</u> 5, pp102-118.

Jackson, W. 1925. Report on the animal remains. In R. Clay, An inhabited site of La Tene 1 data on Swallowcliffe Down. <u>Wiltshire Archaeological Magazine</u> 43, pp90-93.

Jackson, W. 1943. The animal bones. In REM. Wheeler, <u>Maiden Castle, Dorset</u>. London, Society of Antiquaries, pp360-371.

Jackson, W. 1948. Excavations at Little Woodbury, Wiltshire (1938-39), Part III: The animal remians. <u>Proceedings of the Prehistoric Society</u> 14, pp19-23.

James, E. 1920. Sacrifice. <u>Encyclopedia of Religion and Ethics</u>, 11, Edinburgh, T&T Clark, pp1-7.

Jamous, R. 1992. The brother-married sister relationship and marriage ceremonies as sacrificial rites: a case study from northern India. In D. de Coppe (ed.), <u>Understanding Rituals</u>. Routledge, London, pp52-73.

Jefferies, J. 1979. The pits. In G. Wainwright, <u>Gussage All Saints: An Iron Age Settlement in Dorset</u>, pp9-15.

Jessen, K. & Helbaek, H. 1944. Cereals in Great Britain and Ireland in Prehistoric and early Historic times. <u>Wet Kongelige Danske Videnskaernes Selsab Biologiske Skrifter</u> 3, pp1-68.

Jewell, P. 1963. <u>The Experimental Earthwork on Overton Down, Wiltshire, 1960</u>. British Association for the Advancement of Science.

Jewell, P. & Dimbleby, G. 1968. The Experimental Earthwork on Overton Down, Wiltshire, England: the first four years. <u>Proceedings of the Prehistoric Society</u> 32, pp313-342.

Johnson, R., Gregory, D., & Smith, D. (eds.), 1986. <u>The Dictionary of Human Geography</u>. Oxford, Blackwells (2nd Edition).

Jones, M. 1984a. The Plant Remains. In Cunliffe, B., <u>Danebury: An Iron Age Hillfort in Hampshire.</u> vol 2. London, Council for British Archaeology, pp 483-495.

Jones, M. 1984b. Regional patterns in crop production. In BW. Cunliffe & D. Miles (eds.), <u>Aspects of the Iron Age in Central Southern Britain</u>. Oxford, Oxford University Committee for Archaeology Monograph 2, pp120-125.

Jones, M. 1985. Archaeobotany beyond subsistence reconstruction. In G. Barker & C. Gamble (eds.), <u>Beyond Domestication in Prehistoric Europe</u>. pp107-128.

Jones, M. 1989. Agriculture in Roman Britain: The dynamics of change. In M. Todd (ed.), <u>Research on Roman Britain: 1960-89.</u> London, Society for the Promotion of Roman Studies (Britannia Monograph 11), pp127-134.

Jones, M. forthcoming. Plant exploitation. In T. Champion & J. Collis (eds.), <u>Recent Trends in the Archaeology of Iron Age Britain</u>, Sheffield, JR Collis publications, The University.

Jones, M. & Nye, S. 1991. The plant remains: a quantitative analysis of crop debris. In B. Cunliffe & C. Poole (eds.), <u>Danebury: An Iron Age Hillfort in Hampshire</u> vol 5. London, Council for British Archaeology, pp439-446.

Jones, R. 1977a. The animal bones. In K. Smith, The excavation of Winklebury Camp, Basingstoke, Hampshire. <u>Proceedings of the Prehistoric Society</u> 43, pp58-66.

Jones, R. 1977b. Small mammal bone. In K. Smith, 1977. The excavation of Winklebury Camp, Basingstoke, Hampshire. <u>Proceedings of the Prehistoric Society</u> 43, pp66-69.

Karp, I., & Maynard, K. 1983. Reading *The Nuer*. <u>Current Anthropology</u> 24(4), pp481-503.

Keef, P. 1953. Two gold penannular ornaments from Harting Beacon, Sussex. <u>Antiquaries Journal</u> 33, pp204-206.

Keesing, R. 1982a. <u>Kwaio Religion</u>. New York, University of Columbia Press.

Keesing, R. 1982b. Introduction. In G. Herdt (ed.), <u>Rituals of Manhood: Male Initiation in Papua New Guinea</u>. Berkeley, University of California Press.

Kent, S. 1981. The dog: An archaeologist's best friend or worst enemy. <u>Journal of Field Archaeology</u> 8, pp367-372.

Kent, S. 1984. <u>Analyzing Activity Areas: An ethnoarchaeological study of the use of space</u>. Albuquerque, University of New Mexico Press.

Kent, S. 1987. Understanding the use of space: An ethnoarchaeological approach. In S. Kent (ed.), Method and Theory for Activity Area Research: An Ethnoarchaeological Approach. New York. Columbia University Press, pp1-62.

Kelly, J. & Kaplan, M. 1990. History, structure and ritual. Annual Reveiw of Anthropology 19, pp119-150.

King, A. 1978. A comparative survey of bone assemblages from Roman sites in Britain. Bulletin of the Institute of Archaeology of the University of London 15, pp207-232.

King, A. & Soffe, G. 1994. The Iron Age and Roman Temple on Hayling Island, Hampshire. In A.P. Fitzpatrick & E. Morris (eds.) The Iron Age in Wessex: Recent Work, Salisbury, Association Francaise D'Etude de L'Age du Fer/Trust for Wessex Archaeology, pp114-116.

Kossack, G. 1954. Studien zur Symbolgut der Urnefelder-und Hallstattzeit. Berlin, De Gruyter, Romisch-Germanische Forschungen 24.

Kramer, C. (ed.), 1979. Ethnoarchaeology: Implications of ethnography for archaeology. New York, Columbia University Press.

Kramer, C. 1982. Village Ethnoarchaeology: Rural Iran in archaeological perspective. London, The Academic Press.

Lambrick, G. 1984. Pitfalls and possibilities in Iron Age pottery studies- experiences in the Upper Thames Valley. In BW. Cunliffe & D. Miles (eds.), Aspects of the Iron Age in Central Southern Britain. Oxford, Oxford University Committee for Archaeology Monograph 2, pp162-177.

Last, J. 1992. Domestic refuse as Structured deposition: A new look at LBK settlements. Paper presented at TAG, Southampton, 1992.

Lawrence, D. & Low, S. 1990. The built environment and spatial form. Annual Review of Anthropology 19:453-505.

Lawrence, E. 1990. Rodeo horses: the wild and the tame. In R. Willis (ed.), 1990 Signifying Animals: Human Meaning in the natural world. London, Unwin Hyman, One World Archaeology 16, pp222-235.

Lawson, A. 1994. Potterne, Wiltshire. In A.P. Fitzpatrick & E. Morris (eds.) The Iron Age in Wessex: Recent Work, Salisbury, Association Francaise D'Etude de L'Age du Fer/Trust for Wessex Archaeology, pp42-46.

Leach, E. 1964. Anthropological aspects of language: Animal categories and verbal abuse. In E. Lenneberg (ed.), New Directions in the Study of Language. Boston, MIT Press, pp23-63.

Leach, E. 1968. Ritual. In International Encyclopedia of the Social Sciences. London, Macmillan & The Free Press,, pp520-526.

Leach, E. 1976. Culture and Communication: The logic by which symbols are connected. Cambridge, The University Press.

Legge, A. 1981. Aspects of cattle husbandry. In R. Mercer (ed.), Farming Practice in British Prehistory. Edinburgh, The University Press.

Legge, A. 1991a. The animal remains from six sites at Down Farm, Woodcutts. In J. Barrett, R. Bradley & M. Hall (eds.), Papers on the Prehistoric Archaeology of Cranborne Chase. Oxford, Oxbow Books, Oxbow Monographs 11, pp54-100.

Legge, A. 1991b. Animal bones. In I. Stead, Iron Age Cemeteries in Yorkshire, London, English Heritage, Archaeological Reports 22, pp140-147.

Levi-Strauss, C. 1963. Totemism. Boston, Beacon.

Levi-Strauss, C. 1966. The Savage Mind. Chicago, The University Press

Levi-Strauss, C. 1970. The Raw and the Cooked. London, Cape.

Levitan, B. 1982. Excavations at West Hill Uley: 1979. The sieving and sampling programme. Western Archaeological Trust, Occasional Papers 10.

Levy, J. 1982. Social and Religious Organisation in Bronze Age Demark: An analysis of ritual hoard finds. Oxford, British Archaological Reports (International Series 124).

Lewis, G. 1980. Day of Shining Red: An Essay on the Understanding of Ritual. Cambridge, The University Press.

Lewis, K. 1976. Camden: A Frontier Town. Columbia, University of South Dakota (Anthropological Studies 2).

Liddell, DM. 1933. Excavations at Meon Hill. Proceedings of the Hampshire Field Club 12, pp127-162.

Liddell, DM. 1935. Report on the Hampshire Field Club's excavation at Meon Hill. Proceedings of the Hampshire Field Club 13, pp7-54.

Lock, G. 1987. Aspects of quantification. In B. Cunliffe, Hengistbury Head, Dorset: Vol 1 The Prehistoric and Roman Settlement, 3500BC-AD500. Oxford, Oxford University Committee for Archaeology, pp282-289.

Lock, G. 1989. Comments on an alternative Danebury. Scottish Archaeological Review 6, pp3-5.

Lock, G. 1991. Quantifying problems. In B. Cunliffe & C. Poole (eds.), Danebury: An Iron Age Hillfort in Hampshire vol 5. London, Council for British Archaeology, pp278-284.

Maltby, M. 1979. The Animal Bones from Exeter, 1971-1975. Sheffield, Department of Prehistory and Archaeology, The University.

Maltby, M. 1981. The animal bones. In S. Davies, The excavations at Old Down Farm, Andover. Part 2 Prehistoric and Roman. Proceedings of the Hampshire Field Club 37, pp81-163.

Maltby, M. 1985a. Patterns in faunal assemblage variability. In G. Barker & C. Gamble (eds.), Beyond Domestication in Prehistoric Europe. pp33-74.

Maltby, M. 1985b. The animal bones. In P. Fasham, The Prehistoric Settlement at Winnall Down, Winchester. Winchester, pp97-112.

Maltby, M. 1989. The animal bones. In P.Fasham, D. Farwell,. & R. Whinney, 1989. The Archaeological Site at Easton Lane, Winchester. Winchester, Hampshire Field Club Monograph No. 6, pp122-131.

Maltby, M. 1994. Animal exploitation in Iron Age Wessex. In A.P. Fitzpatrick & E. Morris (eds.) The Iron Age in Wessex: Recent Work, Salisbury, Association Francaise D'Etude de L'Age du Fer/Trust for Wessex Archaeology, pp9-11.

Maltby, M. nd 1. The animal bones from Owslebury, Hampshire. Unpublished Ancient Monuments Laboratory Report.

Maltby, M. nd 2. The animal bones from 1973 excavations at Balksbury Camp, Andover, Hampshire. Unpublished Ancient Monuments Laboratory Report.

Maltby, M. nd 3. The animal bones from 1981 excavations at Balksbury Camp, Andover, Hampshire. Unpublished Ancient Monuments Laboratory Report.

Marchant, T. 1989. The evidence for textile production in the Iron Age. Scottish Archaeological Review 6, pp5-12.

Maltby, M. & Coy, J. 1991. The animal bone analyses on the M3 project - a review. In P. Fasham & R. Whinney, Archaeology and the M3, Winchester, Hampshire Field Club Monograph 7, pp97-1-4.

Marx, K. 1964. Pre-Capitalist Economic Formations. (trans. J.Cohen),London, Lawrence & Wishart.

Mauss, M. 1967. The Gift. London, Routledge, Kegan & Paul.

McGlade 1990. The Emergence of Structure: Modelling Social Transformation in later Prehistoric Wessex. Unpublished PhD thesis, Department of Archaeology, University of Cambridge.

McOmish, DS. 1989. Non-hillfort settlement and its implications. In M. Bowden, D. Mackay & P. Topping (ed.), From Cornwall to Caithness: Some aspects of British Field Archaeology. Oxford, British Archaeological Reports (British Series 209), pp 99-110.

Megaw, J, & Simpson, D. 1979. Introduction to British Prehistory, Leicester, The University Press.

Meillassoux, C. 1972. From reproduction to production. Economy and Society 1. pp93-105.

Merrifield, R. 1987. The Archaeology of Ritual and Magic. London, Guild Publishing.

Merriman, N. 1987. Value and motivation in Prehistory: The evidence for 'Celtic' spirit. In I. Hooder (ed.), The Archaeology of Contextual Meanings. Cambridge, The University Press, pp111-116.

Mewett, P. 1986. Boundaries and discourse in a Lewis crofting community. In A. Cohen (ed.), Symbolizing Boundaries: Identity and diversity in British culture. Manchester, The University Press, pp71-87.

Middleton, A. 1987. Technological investigations of the coatings of some 'Haematite coated' pottery from Southern England. Archaeometry 29, pp250-261.

Miksicek, C. 1987. Formation processes of the archaeobotanical record. Advances in Archaeological Method and Theory 10, pp211-247.

Miller, D. 1985. Artefacts as Categories: A study of ceramic variability. Cambridge, The University Press.

Millett, M. 1980. Aspects of Romano-British pottery in West Sussex. Sussex Archaeological Collections 118, pp57-68.

Millett, M. 1987. An early Roman burial tradition in Central Southern England. Oxford Journal of Archaeology 6, pp63-68.

Millett, M. 1990. The Romanization of Britain: an essay in archaeological interpretation. Cambridge, The University Press.

Millett, M. & James, S. 1983. Excavations at Cowdery's Down, Basingstoke, Hampshire, 1977-1981. Archaeological Journal 140, pp151-279.

Millett, M. & Russell, D. 1982. An Iron Age burial from Viables Farm, Basingstoke. Archaeological Journal 139, pp69-90.

Millett, M. & Russell, D. 1984. An Iron Age and Romano-British Site at Viables Farm, Basingstoke. Proceedings of the Hampshire Field Club 40, pp 49-60.

Millgate, M. 1989. Unreal estate: Reflections on Wessex and Yoknapatawpha. The Thomas Hardy Journal 5, pp32-49.

Mills. B. 1989. Integrating functional analyses of vessels and sherds through models of ceramic assemblage formation. World Archaeology 21, pp133-147.

Monk. M. 1985. The plant economy. In In P. Fasham, The Prehistoric Settlement at Winnall Down, Winchester. Winchester, pp112-117.

Monk, M. & Fasham, P. 1980. Carbonised plant remains from two Iron Age sites in Central Hampshire. Proceedings of the Prehistoric Society 46, pp321-344.

Monk, M. with Murphy, P. 1987. The plant economy. In P. Fasham, A Banjo Enclosure in Micheldever Wood, Hampshire. Winchester, Hampshire Field Club Monograph No. 5, pp54-58.

Moore, H. 1981. Bone refuse - possibilities for the future. In A. Sheridan & G. Bailey (ed.), Economic Archaeology. Oxford, British Archaeogical Reports (International Series 96), pp87-94.

Moore, H. 1982. The interpretation of spatial patterning in settlement residues. In I. Hodder (ed.), Symbolic and Structural Archaeology. Cambridge, The University Press, pp74-79.

Moore, H. 1986. Space, Gender and Text. Cambridge, The University Press.

Moore, J. & Keene, A. 1983. Archaeological Hammers and Theories. New York, Academic Press.

Moore, S.F. & Meyerhoff, B.G. 1977. Secular Ritual. Assen, Van Gorcum.

Morant, G. & Goodman, C. 1943. The human bones. In REM. Wheeler, Maiden Castle, Dorset, London, Report of the Research Committee of the Society of Antiquarians No. 12, pp337-360.

Morris, E. 1981. Pottery and socio-economic change in British prehistory. In H. Howard & E. Morris (eds.), Production and Distribution: A Ceramic Viewpoint. Oxford, British Archaeological Reports (International Series 120), pp67-81.

Morris, E. 1985. Prehistoric salt distribution: Two case studies from Western Britain. Bulletin of the Board of Celtic Studies 33, pp336-379.

Morris, E. 1992. The pottery (from Lains Farm). In P. Bellamy, The investigation of the prehistoric landscape along the route of the A303 improvement between Andover and Amesbury, Wiltshires, 1984-7. Proceedings of the Hampshire Field Club 47, p17-28.

Morris, E. 1984a. The organisation of pottery production and distribution in Iron Age Wessex. In A.P. Fitzpatrick & E. Morris (eds.) The Iron Age in Wessex: Recent Work, Salisbury, Association Francaise D'Etude de L'Age du Fer/Trust for Wessex Archaeology, pp26-29.

Morris, E. 1994b. The organisation of salt production and distribution in Iron Age Wessex. In A.P. Fitzpatrick & E. Morris (eds.) The Iron Age in Wessex: Recent Work, Salisbury, Association Francaise D'Etude de L'Age du Fer/Trust for Wessex Archaeology, pp9-10.

Morris, E. Forthcoming. Pottery production and resource locations: An examination of the Danebury collection.

Mountenay, G. 1981. Faunal attrition and subsistence reconstruction at Thwing. In G. Barker (ed.), Prehistoric Communities in Northern Britain. Sheffield, Department of Prehistory and Archaeology, pp73-86.

Murphy, P. 1988. Plant macrofossils. In N. Brown, A Late Brown Age enclosure at Lofts Farm, Essex. Proceedings of the Prehistoric Society 54, pp281-293.

Murray, P. 1980. Discard location: The ethnographic data. American Antiquity 45, pp490-502.

Mytum, H. 1989. The recognition and interpretation of intra-site patterning on sites with small numbers of finds: The example of Walesland Rath. Scottish Archaeological Review 6, pp65-74.

Neal, DS. 1980. Bronze Age, Iron Age and Roman settlement sites at Little Somborne and Ashley, Hampshire. Proceedings of the Hampshire Field Club 36, pp91-143.

Needham, S & Longley, D. 1980. Runnymede Bridge, Egham: A late Bronze Age riverside settlement. In J. Barrett & R. Bradley (eds.), Settlement and Society in the British Later Bronze Age. Oxford, British Archaeological Reports (British Series 83), pp397-436.

Needham, S. & Sørensen, M-L. 1988. Runnymede refuse tip: A consideration of midden deposits and their formation. In J. Barrett & I. Kinnes (eds.), The Archaeology of Context in the Neolithic and Bronze Age: Recent Trends. Sheffield, The University Press, pp113-126.

Northover, P. 1984. Iron Age bronze metalurgy in central southern Britain. In BW. Cunliffe & D. Miles (eds.), Aspects of the Iron Age in Central Southern Britain. Oxford, Oxford University Committee for Archaeology Monograph 2, pp126-145.

Northover, P. 1988. Copper, tin, silver and gold in the Iron Age. In E. Slater & J. Tate (eds.), Science and Archaeology: Glasgow 1987. Oxford, British Archaeological Reports (British Series 196), pp223-234.

Northover, P. 1994. Bronze, silver and gold in Iron Age Wessex. In A.P. Fitzpatrick & E. Morris (eds.) The Iron Age in Wessex: Recent Work, Salisbury, Association Francaise D'Etude de L'Age du Fer/Trust for Wessex Archaeology, pp19-22.

Nowakowski, J. 1991. Trethellan Farm, Newquay: The excavation of a lowland Bronze Age settlement and Iron Age cemetery. Cornish Archaeology 30, pp5-242.

Oliver, M. & Applin, B. 1979. Excavation of an Iron Age and Romano-British settlement at Ructshalls Hill, Basingstoke, Hampshire 1972-75. Proceedings of the Hampshire Field Club 35, pp 41-92.

Orwell, G.1984 (1937). The Road to Wigan Pier. Harmondsworth, Penguin.

Oswald, A. 1991. A Doorway on the Past: Round-house Orientation and its Significance in Iron Age Britain. Unpublished BA. Dissertation submitted to the Department of Archaeology, University of Cambridge.

Olowo Ojoade, J. 1990. Nigerian cultural attitudes to the dog. In R. Willis (ed.), Signifying Animals: Human Meaning in the natural world. London, Unwin Hyman, One World Archaeology 16, pp215-221.

Ohnuli-Tierney, E. 1992. Vitality on the rebound: Ritual's core. Anthropology Today 8(5), pp17-20.

Panoff, S. 1970 Food and faeces: a Melanesian rite. Man 5, 237-252.

Parker, A. 1988. The birds of Roman Britain. Oxford Journal of Archaeology 7, pp197-226.

Parker-Pearson, M. 1982. Mortuary practices. Society and ideology: and ethnoarchaeological study. In I. Hodder(ed.), Symbolic and Strucutral Archaeology. Cambridge, The University Press, pp99-113.

Parker-Pearson, M. 1984. Economic and ideological change: Cyclical growth in the pre-state societies of Jutland. In D. Miller & C. Tilley (eds.), Ideology, Power and Prehistory. Cambridge, The University Press, pp69-92.

Parker-Pearson, M. 1992. Paper on 'Arras' rite burials presented at New Approaches to the British Iron Age II, Edinburgh October 1992.

Parker-Pearson, M. (Forthcoming). Food, fertility and front doors in the first millennium BC. In T. Champion & J. Collis (eds.), Recent Trends in the Archaeology of Iron Age Britain, Sheffield, The Department of Archaeology and Prehistory, The University.

Parker-Pearson, M. and Richards, C. (1994). Architecture and order: spatial representation and archaeology. In Parker-Pearson, M. and Richards, C. (eds.), Architecture and Order: Approaches to Social Space. London, Routledge, pp. 38-72.

Parkes, P. 1987. Livestock symbolism and pastoral ideology among the Kafirs of the Hindu Kush. Man 22, pp637-660.

Parkin, D. 1991. Sacred Void: Spatial images of work and ritual among the Giriama of Kenya. Cambridge, The University Press.

Parkin, D. 1992. Ritual as spatial direction and bodily division. In D. de Coppe (ed.), Understanding Rituals. Routledge, London, pp11-25.

Patrik, L. 1985. Is there an archaeological record? In M.Schiffer (ed.), Advances in Archaeological Method and Theory 2, New York, Academic Press.

Payne, S. 1972. Partial recovery and sample bias. In E. Higgs (ed.), Archaeozoological Studies. Cambridge, The University Press, pp65-81.

Peacock, D. 1969. A contribution to the study of Glastonbury ware in South Western Briain. Antiquaries Journal 49, pp41-61.

Peacock, D. 1984. Amphorae in Iron Age Britain: A reassessment. In S.Macready & F. Thompson (eds.), Cross-Channel Trade between Gaul and Britain in the Pre-Roman Iron Age. London, Society of Antiquaries Occasional Paper (New Series) 4, pp 37-42.

Peacock, D. 1987. Iron Age and Roman quern production at Lodsworth, West Sussex. Antiquaries Journal 67, pp61-85.

Perry, B. 1969. Iron Age enclosures and settlements on the Hampshire Chalklands. Archaeological Journal 126, pp29-43.

Perry, B. 1972. Excavations at Bramdean, Hampshire, 1965-1966, and a discussion of similar sites in Southern England. Proceedings of the Hampshire Field Club 24, pp41-77.

Perry, B. 1982 Excavations at Bramdean, Hampshire 1973 to 1977. Proceedings of the Hampshire Field Club 38, pp57-74.

Pierpoint, S. nd. The Iron Age and Roman Pottery (from Owslebury). Unpublished Report.

Pitt-Rivers, A. 1887. Excavations in Cranborne Chase I. Privately Published.

Pitt-Rivers, A. 1888. Excavations in Cranborne Chase II. Privately Published.

Pitt-Rivers, A. 1892. Excavations in Cranborne Chase III. Privately Published.

Pitt-Rivers, A. 1898. Excavations in Cranborne Chase IV. Privately Published.

Pred, A. 1986. Place, Practice and Structure. Cambridge, Polity Press.

Prehistoric Ceramics Research Group 1991. The Study of Later Prehistoric Pottery: General Policies. Prehiatoric Ceramics Research Group Occasional Paper 1.

Prehistoric Ceramics Research Group 1992. The Study of Later Prehistoric Pottery: Guidelines for Analysis and Publication. Prehiatoric Ceramics Research Group Occasional Paper 2.

Pryor, F. 1988. Eton, near Maxey, Cambridgeshire: A causewayed enclosure on the Fen-edge. In C. Burgess, P. Topping, C. Mordant & M. Maddison (eds.), Enclosures and Defences in the Neolithic of Western Europe. Oxford, British Archaeological Reports (International Series 403), pp107-126.

Rawlings, M. 1991. The pits. In N. Sharples, Maiden Castle: Excavations and Field Survey 1985-6. London, English Heritage Archaeological Reports 19, pp89-94.

Renfrew, AC. 1972, The Emergence of Civilisation. London, Methuen.

Renfrew, AC. 1984. Monuments, mobilisation and social organisation in Neolithic Wessex. In AC. Renfrew, Approches to Social Archaeology. Edinburgh, The University Press, pp225-247.

Renfrew, AC. 1985. The Archaeology of Cult: The sanctuary at Phylakopi. London, Thames & Hudson/British School of Archaeology in Athens.

Renfrew, AC. 1987. Archaeology and Language, London, Cape.

Reynolds, P. 1967. Experiment in Iron Age agriculture. Transactions of the Bristol and Gloucestershire Archaeology Society 86, pp60-73.

Reynolds, P. 1969. Experiment in Iron Age agriculture II. Transactions of the Bristol and Gloucestershire Archaeology Society 86, pp29-33.

Reynolds, P. 1974. Experimental Iron Age Storage Pits: An interim report. Proceedings of the Prehistoric Society 40, pp118-131.

Reynolds, P. 1984. Iron Age Farm. London, British Museum Publications.

Reynolds, P. 1985. Iron Age Agriculture Reviewed. Wessex Lecture 1, Council for British Archaeology group 12.

Rice, P. 1987. Pottery Analysis: A sourcebook. Chicago, The University Press.

Richards, C. & Thomas, J. 1984. Ritual activity and structured deposition in Later Neolithic Wessex. In R. Bradley & J. Gardiner (eds.), Neolithic Studies : a review of some current research. Oxford, British Archaeological Reports (British Series vol. 133), pp 189-218.

Richardson, K.M. 1951. The excavation of Iron Age villages on Boscombe Down West. Wiltshire Archaeological Magazine 54, pp123-168.

Robertson-Mackay, M. 1980. A 'head and hoofs' burial beneath a round barrow. Proceedings of the Prehistoric Society 46, pp123-176.

Rodgers, P. 1987. The ultilisation of computerised site archives: the problem of accessibility for external users. Archaeological Computing Newsletter 11, pp1-5.

Rodgers, P. 1988. Multi-response permutation procedures. In C. Ruggles & S. Rahtz (eds.), Computer and Quantitative Methods in Archaeology 1987. Oxford, British Archaeological Reports (International Series 393), pp45-54.

Rowlands, MJ. 1980. Kinship, alliance and exchange in the European Bronze Age. In J. Barrett & R. Bradley (eds.), Settlement and Society in the British Later Bronze Age. Oxford, British Archaeological Reports (British Series 83), pp15-55.

Salter, C. & Ehrenreich, R. 1984. Iron Age iron metallurgy in Central Southern Britain. In BW. Cunliffe & D. Miles (eds.), Aspects of the Iron Age in Central Southern Britain. Oxford, Oxford University Committee for Archaeology Monograph 2, pp146-161.

Sahlins, M. 1976. Culture and Practical Reason. Chicago, The University Press.

Saxe, A. 1970. Social Dimensions of Mortuary Practices, Michigan, The University Press.

Schiffer, M. 1972. Archaeological context and systematic context. American Antiquity 37, pp156-165.

Schiffer, M. 1976. Behavioral Archaeology. New York, Academic Press.

Schiffer, M. 1983. Towards the identification of formation processes. American Antiquity 48, pp675-706.

Schiffer, M. 1985. Is there a 'Pempeii Premise' in archaeology? Journal of Anthropological Research 41, pp18-41.

Schiffer, M. 1987. Formation Processes of the Archaeological Record. Albuquerque, Universty of New Mexico Press.

Schiffer, M. & Skribo, J. 1989. A provisional theory of ceramic abrasion. American Anthropology 91, pp105-115.

Sellwood, L. 1984a. Tribal boundaries viewed from the perspective of numistic evidence. In BW. Cunliffe & D. Miles (eds.), Aspects of the Iron Age in Central Southern Britain. Oxford, Oxford University Committee for Archaeology Monograph 2, pp191-204.

Serjeantson, D. 1991a. Bird bone. In B.Cunliffe & C. Poole (eds.), 1991. Danebury: An Iron Age Hillfort in Hampshire. vol 5. London, Council for British Archaeology, pp459-481.

Serjeantson, D. 1991b. 'Rid grasse of bones': A taphonomic study of the bones from midden deposits at the Neolithic and Bronze Age site of Runnymede, Surrey, England. International Journal of Osteoarchaeology 1, pp73-89.

Serjeantson, D. Forthcoming. The Corvid burials. In B.Cunliffe (ed.), Forthcoming. Danebury: An Iron Age Hillfort in Hampshire. vol 5. London, Council for British Archaeology.

Shackley, M. 1976. The Danebury project. An experiment in site sediment recording. In DA. Davidson & ML Shackley (eds.), Geoarchaeology. London, Duckworth, pp9-21.

Shanklin, E 1985. Sustenance and symbol: Anthroplogical studies of domesticated animals. Annual Review of Anthropology 14, pp375-403.

Shanks, M. & Tilley, C. 1982. Ideology, symbolic power and ritual communication: a reinterpretation of Neoltihic mortuary practices. In I. Hodder (ed.), Symbolic and Structural Archaeology. Cambridge, The University Press, pp129-154.

Shanks, M. & Tilley, C. 1987a. Reconstructing Archaeology. Cambridge, The University Press.

Shanks, M. & Tilley, C. 1987b. Social Theory and Archaeology. Cambridge, Polity Press.

Sharples, N. 1985. Individual and community: The changing role of megaliths in Orcadian Neolithic. Proceedings of the Prehistoric Society 51, pp-59-74.

Sharples, N. 1987. Review of Hengistbury Head, Dorset. Proceedings of the Prehistoric Society 53, pp507-508.

Sharples, N. 1990a. Discussion. In G & G Aitken, Excavations at Whitcombe 1965-1967. Proceedings of the Dorset Natural and Archaeology Society 112, pp 57-94.

Sharples, N. 1990b. Late Iron Age society and continental trade in Dorset. Revue Archéologie Ouest Supplement 3, pp299-304.

Sharples, N. 1991a. Maiden Castle: Excavations and Field Survey 1985-86. London, English Heritage Archaeological Reports 19.

Sharples, N. 1991b. Maiden Castle. London, Batsford/English Heritage.

Sharples, N. 1991c. Warfare in the Iron Age of Wessex. Scottish Archaeological Review 8, pp79-89.

Shennan, S. 1988. Quantifying Archaeology, Edinburgh, The University Press.

Sheperd, I. & Sheperd, A. 1989. A grain storage pit of the pre-improvement period at Inchkeil, Duffus, Moray. Proceedings of the Society of Antiquaries of Scotland 119, pp345-351.

Sigaut, F. 1989. A method for identifying grain storage techniques and its application for European agricultural history. Tools and Tillage 6, pp3-32.

Skorupski, J. 1976. Symbol and Theory. Cambridge, The University Press.

Smith, K. 1977. The excavation of Winklebury Camp, Basingstoke, Hampshire. Proceedings of the Prehistoric Society 43, pp31-130.

Smith, N. 1984. Uneven Development. Oxford, Blackwell.

Smith, S. 1984. An Iron Age site at Maddison Street, Southampton. Proceedings of the Hampshire Field Club 40, pp35-47.

Soja, E. 1989. Postmodern Geographies. London, Verso.

Spencer, P. 1988. The Maasai of Matapato: A study of rituals of rebellion. Manchester, The University of Press.

Spratling, M. 1979. The debris of metalworking. In G. Wainwright, Gussage All Saints: An Iron Age Settlement in Dorset. London, DOE Archaeological Reports 10, pp125-149.

Stead, I. 1968. Excavations in Blagdon Copse, Hurstbourne Tarrant, Hampshire 1961. Proceedings of the Hampshire Field Club 23, pp81-89.

Stead, I. 1991. Iron Age Cemeteries in East Yorkshire. London, English Heritage, Archaeological Reports 22.

Stead, I. & Rigby, V. 1989. Verulamium: The King Harry Lane Site. London, English Heritage Archaeological Reports 12.

Stone, S. 1857. Account of certain (supposed) British and Saxon remains recently discovered at Standlake, in the county of Oxford. Proceedings of the Society of Antiquaries 1st Series 4, pp92-100.

Stone, S. 1858. Communication on "recent explorations at Standlake, Yelford and Stanton Harcourt". Proceedings of the Society of Antiquaries 1st Series 4, pp213-219.

Stopford, J. 1987. Danebury: An alternative view. Scottish Archaeological Review 4, pp70-75.

Strathern, A. 1981. Death as exchange: two Melanesian cases. In Humphreys, S.C. & King, H. (eds.), Mortality and Immortality: The Anthropology and Archaeology of Death. London, Academic Press, pp 205-224.

Strathern, M. 1980. No nature, no culture: The Hagen case. In C. MacCormack and M. Strathern (eds.), Nature, Culture and Gender. Cambridge, The University Press, pp174-222.

Sunter, N. & Woodward, PJ. 1987. Romano-British Industries in Purbeck. Dorchester, Dorset Natural History and Archaeological Society Monograph 6.

Sørensen, MLS. 1987. Material order and cultural classification: The role of bronze objects in the transition from Bronze Age to Iron Age in Scandinavia. In I. Hodder (ed.), The Archaeology of Contextual Meanings, Cambridge, The University Press, pp90-101.

Taylor, R. 1993. Hoards of the Bronze Age in Southern Britain: Analysis and interpretation. Oxford, British Archaeological Reports (British Series 228).

Taylor, T. 1991. Celtic Art. Scottish Archaeological Review 8, pp129-132.

Tannenbaum, N. 1992. Households and villages: The political-ritual structures of Thai communities. Ethnology 31, pp259-276.

Tambiah, S. 1969. Animals are good to think with and good to prohibit. Ethnology 8, pp423-459.

Therkorn, L. 1987. The inter-relationships of materials and meanings: Some suggestions on housing concerns in the Iron Age of Noord-Holland. In I. Hodder (ed.), The Archaeology of Contextual Meanings. Cambridge, The University Press, pp102-110.

Thomas, J. 1989. The technologies of the self and the constitution of the subject. Archaeological Review from Cambridge 8:2, pp101-107.

Thomas, J. 1990a. Same, Other, Analogue: Writing the Past. In F. Baker & J. Thomas (eds.), Writing the Past in the Present. Lampeter, St David's University College, pp18-23.

Thomas, J. 1990b. Archaeology and the notion of ideology. In F. Baker & J. Thomas (eds.), Writing the Past in the Present. Lampeter, St David's University College, pp63-68.

Thomas, J. 1991. Rethinking The Neolithic. Cambridge, the University Press.

Thomas, J. & Whittle, A. 1986. The anatomy of a tomb: West Kennet revisited. Oxford Journal Archaeology 5, pp129-156.

Thomas, R. 1989. The bronze-iron transition in southern England. in MLS. Sørensen & R. Thomas (eds.), The Bronze Age-Iron Age Transition in Europe. Oxford, British Archaeological Reports (International Series 483), pp263-286.

Thornton, R. 1980. Space, Time, and Culture among the Iraqw of Tanzania. London, Macmillan.

Tilley, C. 1991. Materialism and an archaeology of dissonance. Scottish Archaeological Review 8, pp14-22.

Todd, M. 1987. The Northern Barbarians 100BC-AD300. Oxford, Blackwell (revised edition).

Traube, E. 1984. Cosmology and Social Life: Ritual Exchange among the Mambai of East Timor, Chicago, The University Press.

Turner, J. 1992. Ritual, habitus and hierarchy in Fiji. Ethnology 31, pp291-302.

Turner, T. 1977. Transformation, heirarchy, and transcendence: a reformulation of Van Gennep's model of the structure of rites de passage. In S. Moore & B. Meyerhoff (eds.), Secular Ritual. Assen, Van Gorcum.

Turner, V. 1967. The Forest of Symbols: Aspects of Ndembu Ritual, London, Routledge Kegan & Paul.

Turner, V. 1969. The Ritual Process: Structure and Anti-Structure , London, Routledge Kegan & Paul.

Van Gennep, A. 1960. The Rites of Passage, London, Routledge Kegan & Paul.

Valeri, V. 1985. Kingship and Sacrifice: Ritual and Society in Ancient Hawaii. Chicago, The University Press.

Wainwright, G. 1968. The Excavation of a Doutrigan farmstead near Tollard Royal in Cranborne, Southern England. Proceedings of the Prehistoric Society 34, pp102-147.

Wainwright, G. 1969. The excavation of Balksbury Camp, Andover, Hampshire. Proceedings of the Hampshire Field Club 26, pp21-56.

Wainwright, G. 1979. Gussage All Saints: An Iron Age Settlement in Dorset. London, HMSO, DOE Archaeological Reports 10, London.

Wainwright, G. & Davies, S. 1994. Balksbury Camp, Andover, Hampshire. In A.P. Fitzpatrick & E. Morris (eds.) The Iron Age in Wessex: Recent Work, Salisbury, Association Francaise D'Etude de L'Age du Fer/Trust for Wessex Archaeology, pp52-56.

Wainwright, G. & Longworth. I. 1971. Durrington Walls: Excavations 1966-68. London, Society of Antiquaries.

Wait, G. 1985. Ritual and Religion in Iron Age Britian, Oxford, British Archaeological Reports (British Series 149).

Walker, L. 1984. The deposition of the human remains. In Cunliffe, B., Danebury: An Iron Age Hillfort in Hampshire. vol 2. London, Council for British Archaeology, pp 442-463.

Watson, J. 1972. Fragmentation analysis of animal bones samples from archaeological sites. Archaeometry 14, pp221-282.

Welbourne, A. 1984. Endo ceramics and power strategies. In D. Miller & C. Tilley (eds.), Ideology, Power and Prehistory. Cambridge, The University Press, pp17-24.

Wheeler, REM. 1943. Maiden Castle, Dorset, London, Report of the Research Committee of the Society of Antiquarians No. 12.

Whimster, R. 1977. Iron Age burial in southern Britain. Proceedings of the Prehistoric Society 43, pp317-327.

Whimster, R. 1981 Burial Practices in Iron Age Britian. Oxford, British Archaeological Reports (British Series 90).

Whinney, R. 1994. Oram's Arbour: the middle Iron Age enclosure at Winchester, Hampshire. In A.P. Fitzpatrick & E. Morris (eds.) The Iron Age in Wessex: Recent Work, Salisbury, Association Francaise D'Etude de L'Age du Fer/Trust for Wessex Archaeology, pp86-91.

White, D. 1970. Excavation of an Iron Age round barrow near Handley, Dorset. Antiquaries Journal 50, pp26-36.

Whitley, M. 1943. Excavations at Chalbury Camp, Dorset ,1939. Antiquaries Journal 23, pp98-121.

Whittle, A. 1984. The pits. In B. Cunliffe, Danebury: An Iron Age Hillfort in Hampshire. vol 2. London, Council for British Archaeology, pp 128-146.

Whittle, A. 1985. Neolithic Europe: A survey. Cambridge, The University Press.

Wijeyewardene, G. 1968. Address, abuse, and animal categories in Northern Thailand. Man 3, pp76-93.

Willis, R. (ed.), 1990. Signifying Animals: Human meaning in the natural world. London, Unwin Hyman, One World Archaeology 16.

Wilson, B. 1979. The animal bones. In M. Parrington, The excavation of an Iron Age settlement.... at Ashville Trading Estate, Abingdon (Oxfordshire). London, Council for British Archaeology, Research Report 28, pp110-137.

Wilson, B. 1980. Bone and shell report. In J. Hinchliffe and R. Thomas, Archaeological investigations at Appleford. Oxoniesia 15, pp84-89.

Wilson, B. 1985. Degraded bones, feature type and spatial patterning on an Iron Age occupation site in Oxfordshire, England. In N.Fieller, D. Gilbertson & N. Ralph (eds.), Palaeobiological Investigations. Oxford, British Archaeological Reports (International Series 266), pp81-100.

Wilson, B. 1989. Fresh and old table refuse. The recognition and location of domestic activity at archaeological sites in the Upper Thames Valley, England. Archaeozoologia 3(1.2), pp237-262.

Wilson, B. 1992. Considerations for the identification of ritual deposits of animal bones in Iron Age pits. International Journal of Osteoarchaeology 2, pp 341-349.

Wilson, C. 1981. Burials within settlements in Southern Britain during the Pre-Roman Iron Age. Bulletin of the Institute of Archaeology of the University of London 18, pp127-169.

Wolseley, GR. & Smith, R.A. 1924. Discoveries near Cissbury. Antiquaries Journal 4, pp347-359.

Wolseley, G.R., Smith, R.A. & Hawley, W. 1927. Prehistoric settlements on Park Brow. Archaeologia 76, pp1-40.

Woodward, A. 1993. The cult of relics in Prehistoric Britain. In In Search of Cult: Archaeological investigations in honour of Philip Rahtz, The Boydell Press, Woodbridge, pp1-7.

	Pits with Layer Info.	Layers with material	Layers with Pottery	Layers with Bone	Layers with Small Finds	Layers with Human Bone	Layers with Art. Bone Groups
Balksbury	111	580	-	580	-	-	-
Lt. Somborne	28	71	71	-	-	-	-
Micheldever	27	249	213	220	-	-	-
Winklebury	72	224	198	158	22	11	13
Winnall EIA	16	83	57	60	13	4	2
Easton L. 6	4	5	5	-	-	0	0
Easton L. 7	15	48	47	-	-	1	4
Easton L. 8	7	30	28	-	-	1	1
Winnall MIA	78	395	277	330	85	26	24

	Mean Sherd Weight	Number of Pot Sherds	Weight of Pottery	Number of Bone Fragments
Balksbury	-	-	-	21.3±28.7 1-337
Lt Somborne	12.6±8 2.5-180	11.8±14.4 1-95	136±165 5-2740	-
Micheldever	15.1±16.4 1-160.5	18.8-38.5 1-448	273±606 1-4996	26±54 1-533
Winklebury	-	-	118±204 1-1648	11±34 1-414
Winnall EIA	12.2±13.3 2-151	12.6±15 1-77	131±163 1-758	18±30 1-168
Easton L 6	9.3±6.2 4-19	8.6±14.8 1-35	53±68 4-170	-
Easton L 7	11.1±8.6 1-40	28.3±63.8 1-357	407±988 2-6052	-
Easton L 8	16.8±18.9 2.5-84	9.3±14.6 1-5	121±176 3-677	-
Winnall MIA	17.9±17.4 1-136	10.4±12.8 1-83	196±320 1-2703	15±26 1-330

	Layers with Cattle	Layers with Horse	Layers with Sheep	Layers with Pig	Layers with Dog	Layers with Other
Balksbury	418	242	483	209	77	31
Micheldever	142	38	175	96	21	14
Winklebury	90	33	116	42	3	14
Winnall EIA	30	14	39	19	2	1
Winnall MIA	180	93	235	114	52	22

Table 5.1. Summary statistics on the characteristics of pit layers at Balksbury, Little Somborne, Micheldever Wood, Easton Lane, Winnall Down and Winklebury.

EIA Winnall

	LOAM	LOAM & CHALK	CHALK	OTHER
Total no. of layers	39	1	29	0
With material	24	0	13	0
With Pottery	13	0	10	0
With Bone	17	0	8	0
With Pot & Bone	9	0	7	0
With Small Finds	8	0	4	0
With Human Bone	3	0	0	0
With Articulated Groups	0	0	1	0
Mean Sherd Weight	16.4±20.3	0	15.6±14.2	0
Bone Number	15±20	0	32±35	0

MIA Winnall

	LOAM	LOAM & CHALK	CHALK	OTHER
Total no. of layers	243	34	177	19
With material	122	12	73	10
With Pottery	94	8	50	6
With Bone	105	10	64	9
With Pot & Bone	80	6	45	6
With Small Finds	27	1	17	6
With Human Bone	8	2	5	1
With Articulated Groups	8	2	6	0
Pot Weight	186±266	72±125	208±266	738±972
Mean Sherd Weight	16.3±17.3	6.8±2.0	20.719.5	25.2±18.0
Bone Number	75±19	20±32	17±43	21±33
Std Dev.+ Pot No.	13	1	3	3
Std Dev.+ MSW	5	0	9	1
Std Dev.+ Bone Number	4	1	2	1

Winklebury

	LOAM	LOAM & CHALK	CHALK	OTHER
Total no. of layers	182	25	124	42
With material	131	11	52	23
With Pottery	119	10	44	18
With Bone	96	6	38	14
With Pot & Bone	90	9	37	11
With Small Finds	12	1	5	2
With Human Bone	8	1	0	3
With Articulated Groups	10	0	1	2
Pot Weight	156±246	40±44	66±102	36±55
Bone Number	15±43	3±5	5±7	8±17
Std Dev.+ Pot Weight	17	1	3	0
Std Dev.+ Bone Number	10	0	1	0

Table 5.2. Tables summarising the characteristics of the finds assemblages recovered from loam, chalk , loam&chalk, and other fills from pits at Winklebury and Winnall.

Micheldever Wood

	Layers with 1 Species	Layers with 2 Species	Layers with 3 Species	Layers with 4 Species	Layers with 5 Species
No of Layers	69	53	65	24	5
	31.9%	21.9%	30.1%	11.1%	2.3%
Sheep	37	47	63	23	5
	21.1%	26.8%	36.0%	13.1%	2.9%
Cattle	17	36	60	24	5
	9.7%	20.6%	34.3%	13.7%	2.8%
Pig	5	14	54	23	5
	4.9%	13.9%	53.5%	22.8%	4.9%
Horse	1	8	12	12	5
	2.6%	21.1%	31.6%	31.6%	13.2%
Dog	1	3	5	10	2
	4.8%	14.3%	23.8%	47.6%	9.5%
Other	1	0	3	5	3
	8.3%		25%	41.7%	25%

Balksbury

	Layers with 1 Species	Layers with 2 Species	Layers with 3 Species	Layers with 4 Species	Layers with 5 Species
No of Layers	145	164	146	101	23
	25.0%	28.3%	25.2%	17.4%	4.0%
Sheep	89	130	141	98	23
	22.8%	33.2%	26.1%	25.1%	5.9%
Cattle	36	125	132	101	23
	8.6%	30.2%	31.7%	24.2%	5.5%
Pig	11	21	63	90	23
	5.2%	10.1%	30.3%	43.3%	11.1%
Horse	6	42	81	29	23
	3.3%	23.2%	44.8%	16.0%	12.7%
Dog	3	5	21	86	23
	2.2%	3.6%	15.2%	62.3%	16.7%

Table 5.3.a. Tables showing the number of different species recovered from each layer, and the distribution of different species across those layers at Balksbury and Micheldever Wood.

EIA Winnall Down

	Layers with 1 Species	Layers with 2 Species	Layers with 3 Species	Layers with 4 Species	Layers with 5 Species
No of Layers	22	8	10	7	1
	45.8%	16.7%	20.8%	14.6%	2.1%
Sheep	13	6	6	7	1
	39.4%	18.2%	18.2%	21.2%	3%
Cattle	6	5	10	7	1
	20.7%	17.2%	34.5%	24.1%	3.4%
Pig	1	3	6	7	1
	5.6%	16.7%	33.3%	38.9%	5.6%
Horse	2	2	4	5	1
	14.3%	14.5%	28.6%	35.7%	7.1%
Dog	0	0	0	1	1
				50%	5.0%
Other	0	0	0	1	0
				100%	

MIA Winnall Down

	Layers with 1 Species	Layers with 2 Species	Layers with 3 Species	Layers with 4 Species	Layers with 5 Species	Layers with 6 Species
No of Layers	102	65	72	41	15	1
	40.5%	21.9%	24.3%	13.8%	5.1%	0.3%
Sheep	60	48	70	41	15	1
	25.5%	20.4%	29.8%	17.4%	6.4%	0.4%
Cattle	23	44	58	40	14	1
	12.8%	24.4%	32.2%	22.2%	7.8%	0.6%
Pig	5	19	40	36	12	1
	4.4%	16.8%	35.4%	31.8%	10.6%	0.9%
Horse	11	11	26	29	15	1
	11.8%	11.8%	27.9%	21.2%	16.1%	1.1%
Dog	1	7	15	16	12	1
	1.9%	13.5%	28.8%	30.8%	23.1%	1.9%
Other	2	2	7	4	6	1
	9.1%	9.1%	31.8%	18.2%	27.3%	4.5%

Table 5.3.b. Tables showing the number of different species recovered from each layer, and the distribution of different species across those layers at Winnall Down.

Winklebury

	Layers with 1 Species	Layers with 2 Species	Layers with 3 Species	Layers with 4 Species	Layers with 5 Species
No of Layers	56	59	26	6	3
	37.3%	39.3%	17.3%	4.0%	2.0%
Sheep	32	49	25	6	3
	27.8%	42.6%	21.7%	5.2%	2.6%
Cattle	16	41	24	6	3
	17.8%	45.6%	26.7%	6.7%	3.3%
Pig	3	14	16	5	3
	7.3%	34.1%	39.0%	12.2%	7.3%
Horse	7	9	10	4	3
	21.2%	27.3%	30.3%	12.1%	9.1%
Dog	0	1	1	0	1
		33.3%	33.3%		33.3%
Other	2	4	0	1	2
	22.2%	44.4%		11.1%	22.2%

Table 5.3.c. Tables showing the number of different species recovered from each layer, and the distribution of different species across those layers at Winklebury.

	Balksbury	Micheldever Wood	Winnall Down EIA	Winnall Down MIA
Sheep & Pig	√	√	√	√
Cattle & Horse	√	–	–	–
Sheep & Cattle	–	–	–	–
Pig & Cattle	√	√	√	√
Horse & Sheep	–	(√)	(√)	–
Pig & Horse	√	–	–	√

√ = Chi Square Relationship significant to probability >0.05

(√) = Chi Square Relationship significant to probability >0.1

Table 5.4. Table showing the statistically significant associations between the presence of the major domestic species in layers in pits at Balksbury, Micheldever Wood and Winnall Down.

	Winklebury	MIA Winnall
Presence of human bone and small finds	prob. 0.0233	prob. 0.0216
Presence of human bone and wild animal/bird bone	prob. 0.0295	prob. 0.0084
Presence of +Std Dev. densities of animal bone and human remains		prob. 0.0084
Presence of +Std Dev. densties of animal bone and small finds		prob. 0.0539
Presence of +Std Dev. densities of animal bone and articulated bone groups	prob. 0.0001	prob. 0.0001
Presence of +Std Dev. densities of pottery and human remains	prob. 0.0095	
Presence of +Std Dev. densties of pottery and small finds	prob. 0.0004	
Presence of +Std Dev. densities of pottery and articulated bone groups	prob. 0.0214	prob. 0.0002
Presence of +Std Dev. densities of pottery and +Std Dev. densities of bone	prob. 0.0001	
Presence of +Std Dev. densities of pottery and +Std Dev. Mean Sherd Weight	-	prob. 0.0003
Presence of +Std Dev. Mean Sherd Weight and small finds	-	prob. 0.0002
Presence of articulated bone groups in a layer and small finds		prob. 0.0001
Presence of articulated bone groups in a layer and wild animal/bird bone	prob. 0.0001	prob. 0.0022

Table 6.1. Summary of the statistically significant relationship between the presence of difference factors within the same third of pit fills at Winklebury and Middle Iron Age Winnall Down.

		Lower	Middle	Upper
MIA BALKSBURY	Complete Skeletons	14	13	5
	Skulls	2	2	4
	Articulated Limbs	19	7	2
	Vertebrae/Ribs	3	7	1
MIA WINNALL DOWN	Complete Skeletons	5	3	2
	Skulls	3	1	2
	Articulated Limbs	5	1	2
	Vertebrae/Ribs	6	2	1
WINKLEBURY	Complete Skeletons	8+	2+	1
	Skulls	1	4	0
	Articulated Limbs	0	0	0
	Vertebrae/Ribs	1	1	1

		Lower	Middle	Upper
MIA BALKSBURY	Sheep	11	13	0
	Cattle	5	4	5
	Horse	6	1	5
	Pig	4	7	3
	Dog	18	5	2
	Bird	2	1	1
MIA WINNALL DOWN	Sheep	4	2	2
	Cattle	3	0	0
	Horse	5	2	1
	Pig	1	1	0
	Dog	5	2	4
	Bird	2	0	0
WINKLEBURY	Sheep	4+	0	1
	Cattle	1	2	0
	Horse	0	4	0
	Pig	2	0	0
	Dog	1	0	0
	Bird	1	0	0
	Deer	1	1	0
	Badger	0	6+	0
	Fox	10+	0	0

Table 6.2.a. The vertical distribution of different types of Articulated/Associated Animal Bone Groups at Balksbury, Winnall and Winklebury.

Table 6.2.b. The vertical distribution of different species of animal bone at Balksbury, Winnall and Winklebury.

(Both show the number of thirds with *ABGs* or different species)

SPECIES	Skeletal Element	Modern Breaks		Fragment. Index	
		Upper Half	Lower Half	Upper Half	Lower Half
CATTLE	Scapula	52.9% n70	41.2% n53	0.379 n33	0.403 n31
	Humerus	32.3% n93	22.7% n44	0.337 n63	0.323 n34
	Radius	17.3% n52	7.4% n27	0.383 n43	0.470 n25
	Ulna	43.3% n30	29.4% n17	0.294 n17	0.396 n12
	Femur	13.9% n43	27.5% n40	0.298 n37	0.379 n29
	Tibia	28.1% n64	19.0% n42	0.298 n46	0.375 n34
	Metapodia	14.4% n90	16.4% n61	0.363 n115	0.576 n51
HORSE	Scapula	63.1% n19	31.8% n22	0.357 n7	0.333 n15
	Humerus	26.3% n19	30.0% n10	0.446 n14	0.393 n7
	Radius	22.2% n9	9.9% n11	0.678 n7	0.563 n8
	Ulna	50.0% n3	0.0% n4	0.500 n3	0.500 n4
	Femur	58.3% n12	27.3% n22	0.500 n5	0.390 n16
	Tibia	25.0% n16	4.8% n21	0.500 n12	0.563 n20
	Metapodia	35.0% n20	20.0% n20	0.710 n13	0.828 n16
SHEEP	Mandible	39.7% n141	27.5% n149	0.356 n85	0.550 n108
	Scapula	31.7% n41	37.1% n62	0.357 n28	0.783 n30
	Humerus	11.5% n53	13.8% n58	0.402 n46	0.650 n50
	Radius	13.3% n120	8.2% n109	0.392 n104	0.545 n100
	Ulna	5.0% n20	35.0% n40	0.303 n19	0.452 n26
	Femur	9.5% n42	16.9% n65	0.382 n38	0.555 n54
	Tibia	21.4% n154	12.1% n141	0.378 n121	0.480 n124
	Metapodia	9.8% n205	7.9% n203	0.404 n185	0.622 n187

Table 6.3. Differences in depth in modern bone breakages and fragmentation of different skeletal elements of cattle, horse and sheep bone at Middle Iron Age Balksbury.

1.Balkbury   CATTLE

Skeletal Element	Upper Half no.	%		Lower Half no.	%
Skull Fragments	102(1)	10.2		104(1)	15.5
Mandible	122(4)	12.2		101(2)	15.1
Loose Teeth	125	12.5		60	8.9
Vertebrae	63(23)	6.3		28	4.3
Scapula	70	7.0		53	7.9
Humerus	93	9.3		44	6.6
Radius&Ulna	82(6)	8.2		44(2)	6.5
Femur	43	4.3		40	6.0
Tibia	64(1)	6.4		42	6.3
Tarsals/Carpals	29	2.9		19	2.8
Metapodia	90	9.0		61(5)	9.1
Phalanges	10	1.0		39(30)	5.8
Other	107(47)	10.7		36(7)	5.2
TOTAL	1000(82)	100		671(47)	100

2.Balksbury   HORSE

Skeletal Element	Upper Half no.	%		Lower Half no.	%
Skull Fragments	12	4.1		26(1)	8.9
Mandible	39	13.2		31(1)	10.6
Loose Teeth	54	18.2		32	11.0
Vertebrae	13	4.4		18(10)	10.3
Scapula	19(1)	6.4		22	7.5
Humerus	19(1)	6.4		10	3.4
Radius&Ulna	15(6)	5.0		15(4)	5.2
Femur	12(1)	4.1		22(3)	7.5
Tibia	16(1)	5.4		21(2)	7.2
Tarsals/Carpals	10(5)	3.4		16(11)	5.5
Metapodia	36(6)	12.2		31(12)	10.6
Phalanges	26(8)	8.8		16(11)	5.5
Other	25(1)	8.4		32(12)	11.0
TOTAL	296(30)	100		292(68)	100

Table 6.4.a. Tables showing the differences in proportions of different skeletal elements of cattle and horse bone with depth in pit fills at Middle Iron Age Balksbury (after Maltby nd2).

Figures in brackets show the number of bones from articulated/associated bone groups.

3.Balksbury   SHEEP

Skeletal Element	Upper Half no.	%		Lower Half no.	%
Skull Fragments	45	4.0		143(14)	8.5
Mandible	141	12.6		149(16)	8.8
Loose Teeth	239	21.4		123	7.3
Vertebrae	12	1.1		294(146)	17.4
Scapula	41	3.7		63(13)	3.7
Humerus	52	4.7		58(14)	3.4
Radius&Ulna	140	12.6		149(35)	8.8
Femur	42	3.8		65(14)	3.8
Tibia	154	13.8		141(16)	8.3
Tarsals/Carpals	6	0.5		30(17)	1.8
Metapodia	6	0.5		30(16)	1.8
Phalanges	8	0.7		53(43)	3.1
Other	30	2.7		211(126)	12.6
TOTAL	1115	100		1691(498)	100

4.Balksbury   PIG

Skeletal Element	Upper Half no.	%		Lower Half no.	%
Skull Fragments					
Mandible					
Loose Teeth					
Vertebrae	30(27)	10.0		108(104)	5.6
Scapula	18(3)	6.0		22(7)	4.4
Humerus	18(5)	6.0		24(9)	4.8
Radius&Ulna	22(9)	7.3		30(22)	6.0
Femur	15(8)	5.0		10(7)	2.0
Tibia	22(9)	7.4		16(9)	3.2
Tarsals/Carpals	7(4)	2.3		27(27)	5.4
Metapodia	39(29)	13.0		46(44)	9.2
Phalanges	4(4)	1.3		46(46)	9.2
Other	35(31)	11.7		93(84)	18.5
TOTAL	299(145)	100		500(372)	100

Table 6.4.b. Tables showing the differences in proportions of different skeletal elements of sheep and pig bone with depth in pit fills at Middle Iron Age Balksbury (after Maltby nd2).

Figures in brackets show the number of bones from articulated/associated bone groups.

5.Balksbury   DOG

Skeletal Element	Upper Half no.	%	Lower Half no.	%
Skull Fragments	9(3)	6.0	26(10)	4.3
Mandible	5(3)	3.3	20(15)	3.3
Loose Teeth	5(3)	3.3	0	0.0
Vertebrae	29(28)	19.3	120(92)	19.9
Scapula	3(2)	2.0	19(18)	3.2
Humerus	4(2)	2.7	26(22)	4.3
Radius&Ulna	10(6)	6.6	51(39)	8.5
Femur	5(3)	3.3	25(18)	4.2
Tibia	5(3)	3.3	33(21)	5.5
Tarsals/Carpals	3(3)	2.1	7(5)	1.1
Metapodia	34(30)	22.7	55(52)	9.2
Phalanges	6(4)	4.0	24(24)	4.0
Other	32(29)	21.3	196(155)	32.5
TOTAL	150(119)	100	602(471)	100

Table 6.4.c. Table showing the differences in proportions of different skeletal elements of dog bone with depth in pit fills at Middle Iron Age Balksbury (after Maltby nd2). Figures in brackets show the number of bones from articulated/associated bone groups.

1.Winnall Down   CATTLE

Skeletal Element	Upper Third no.	%	Middle Third no.	%	Lower Third no.	%
Skull Fragments	34	12.1	26	14.3	14	8.1
Mandible	36	12.8	23	12.6	28	16.2
Loose Teeth	51	18.1	24	13.2	16	9.2
Vertebrae	16	5.7	10	5.5	13	7.5
Scapula	17	6.1	10	5.5	12	6.9
Humerus	15	5.3	13	7.1	6	3.5
Radius&Ulna	28	9.9	15	8.2	13	7.5
Femur	8	2.8	10	5.5	12	6.9
Tibia	20	7.1	14	7.7	8	4.6
Tarsals/Carpals	23	8.2	19	10.4	21	12.1
Metapodia	20	7.1	11	6.0	12	6.9
Phalanges	9	3.2	4	2.2	12	6.9
Other	4	1.4	3	3.5	6	3.5
TOTAL	281	100	182	100	173(27)	100

2.Winnall Down   HORSE

Skeletal Element	Upper Third no.	%	Middle Third no.	%	Lower Third no.	%
Skull Fragments	2	2.7	6 (2)	2.5	7	14.6
Mandible	6	8.0	9	3.8	6	12.5
Loose Teeth	15	20.0	3	1.3	5	10.4
Vertebrae	7	9.3	71(69)	29.8	2	4.2
Scapula	4	5.3	9 (1)	3.8	2	4.2
Humerus	6	8.0	11(1)	4.6	5(1)	10.4
Radius&Ulna	6	8.0	8 (2)	3.4	5(3)	10.4
Femur	4	5.3	5 (1)	2.1	3	6.2
Tibia	4	5.3	5 (4)	2.1	5	10.4
Tarsals/Carpals	3	4.0	21(8)	8.8	2	4.2
Metapodia	8	10.7	17(7)	7.1	4	8.3
Phalanges	7	9.3	5 (5)	2.1	0	0.0
Other	3	4.0	68(59)	28.6	2	4.2
TOTAL	75	100	238(161)	100	48(4)	100

Table 6.5.a. Tables showing the differences in proportions of different skeletal elements of cattle and horse bone with depth in pit fills at Middle Iron Age Winnall Down. Figures in brackets show the number of bones from articulated/associated bone groups.

3.Winnall Down   SHEEP

Skeletal Element	Upper Third no.	%	Middle Third no.	%	Lower Third no.	%
Skull Fragments	37	7.2	34(2)	8.7	28	7.7
Mandible	61	11.9	44(1)	11.3	20	5.5
Loose Teeth	110	21.5	70	18.0	52	14.3
Vertebrae	21	4.1	30(24)	7.7	47(27)	12.9
Scapula	13	2.5	9 (2)	2.3	5	1.4
Humerus	22	4.3	11(1)	2.8	8 (1)	2.2
Radius&Ulna	47	9.2	25(4)	6.4	28(2)	7.7
Femur	25	4.9	23(2)	5.9	13(1)	3.6
Tibia	56	10.9	29(2)	7.5	20(2)	5.5
Tarsals/Carpals	20	3.9	19(4)	4.9	20(6)	5.5
Metapodia	62	12.1	51(2)	13.1	45(8)	12.4
Phalanges	36	7.0	22	5.7	50(36)	13.8
Other	1	0.2	22(3)	5.7	27(24)	7.4
TOTAL	511	100	389(47)	100	363(107)	100

4.Winnall Down   PIG

Skeletal Element	Upper Third no.	%	Middle Third no.	%	Lower Third no.	%
Skull Fragments	28	27.7	15	8.0	12	19.0
Mandible	13	12.9	8	4.3	6	9.5
Loose Teeth	13	12.9	13	6.9	8	12.7
Vertebrae	4	3.9	28(27)	15.0	13(8)	20.6
Scapula	9	8.9	5 (5)	2.7	7	11.1
Humerus	6	5.9	6 (1)	3.2	3	4.8
Radius&Ulna	4	3.9	6 (4)	3.2	3	4.8
Femur	4	3.9	3 (2)	1.6	0	0.0
Tibia	5	4.9	6 (3)	3.2	1	1.6
Tarsals/Carpals	4	3.9	18(15)	9.6	3	4.8
Metapodia	5	4.9	10(10)	5.3	2	3.1
Phalanges	2	1.9	37(35)	19.8	5	7.9
Other	4	3.9	32(32)	17.1	0	0
TOTAL	101	100	181(134)	100	60(8)	100

Table 6.5.b. Tables showing the differences in proportions of different skeletal elements of sheep and pig bone with depth in pit fills at Middle Iron Age Winnall Down. Figures in brackets show the number of bones from articulated/associated bone groups.

5.Winnall Down   DOG

Skeletal Element	Upper Third no.	%	Middle Third no.	%	Lower Third no.	%
Skull Fragments	7 (2)	12.1	4 (1)	3.0	11(10)	2.9
Mandible	5 (2)	8.6	4 (2)	3.0	9 (8)	2.4
Loose Teeth	1	1.7	3	2.3	11(4)	2.9
Vertebrae	1	1.7	29(29)	22.1	82(82)	21.7
Scapula	4 (1)	6.9	3 (2)	2.3	12(11)	3.2
Humerus	4 (1)	6.9	2 (2)	1.5	12(12)	3.2
Radius&Ulna	4	6.9	2 (2)	1.5	11(11)	2.9
Femur	1	1.7	2 (2)	1.5	11(11)	2.9
Tibia	5	8.6	7 (4)	5.3	7 (7)	1.8
Tarsals/Carpals	5 (3)	8.6	22(22)	16.8	19(19)	5.0
Metapodia	10(2)	17.2	4 (4)	3.0	30(29)	8.0
Phalanges	3	5.2	18(18)	13.7	53(53)	14.1
Other	8	13.8	31(29)	23.7	69(69)	18.3
TOTAL	58(11)	100	131(115)	100	377(326)	100

Table 6.5.c. Table showing the differences in proportions of different skeletal elements of dog bone with depth in pit fills at Middle Iron Age Winnall Down.
Figures in brackets show the number of bones from articulated/associated bone groups.

PIT	Depth (m)	Percentage of fill with LIA/ERB pottery	Percentage of fill with IA pottery
8	1.4	10.7	89.3
14	2.15	43.77	56.23
51	0.8	17.12	82.88
98	0.88	100	0
140	0.9	23.81	76.19
146	0.45	64.4	35.6
293	1.03	22.4	77.6
295	0.26	100	0
298	0.94	14.02	85.98
300	1.85	9.41	90.59
309	1.13	0	100
311	1.25	32	68
319	1.05	7.46	92.54
321	0.56	15.36	84.64
409	0.3	0	100
415	1.77	35.17	64.83
417	0.85	31.48	68.52
428	0.98	45.91	54.09
434	1.27	0	100
454	0.65	14.79	85.21
478	1.08	22	78
538	0.85	0	100
608	0.36	0	100
677	0.27	12.9	87.1
701	0.19	66.79	33.21
Mean		27.58±28.72	72.42±28.72

Table 6.6. Micheldever Wood. The proportions of Middle Iron Age pits with Later Iron Age/Early Roman material in their upper fills.

EIA BALKSBURY	LOWER THIRD	MIDDLE THIRD	UPPER THIRD
Total Number of Thirds	19	19	19
Mean Sherd Weight (g)❶	-	-	-
Density of Pottery (g/m3)	-	-	-
Density of Bone (n/m3)	50±69	78±171	43±51
Thirds with Pottery	-	-	-
Thirds with Bone	16	16	17
Thirds with Small Finds❷	-	-	-
Thirds with Human Bone	-	-	-
Thirds with Articulated/ Associated Bone Groups	5	2	3
Total Number of Bone Frags (Number of Articulated Bone)	466(151)	392(42)	464(10)
Percentage of Indentifiable Frags	73.3%	59.2%	57.6%
Percentage of Loose Teeth	3.2%	6.9%	13.1%
Percentage of Articulated/ Associated Bone	32.4%	10.7%	2.2%
Number of Sheep Frags	161(88)	94(21)	144
Number of Cattle Frags	83(13)	64	83(2)
Number of Horse Frags	62(42)	22	15(2)
Number of Pig Frags	10(4)	16	18
Number of Dog Frags	8(2)	21(21)	2
Number of Other Species Frags	2(2)	0	6(6)

❶ No information on Pottery

❷ No information on the position of human remains and small finds

Table 6.7.a. Early Iron Age Balksbury: Summary data on the characteristics of finds assemblages in lower, middle and upper thirds of pits.

MIA BALKSBURY	LOWER THIRD	MIDDLE THIRD	UPPER THIRD
Total Number of Thirds	83	83	83
Mean Sherd Weight (g)❶	-	-	-
Density of Pottery (g/m3)	-	-	-
Density of Bone (n/m3)	64±94	65±99	68±116
Thirds with Pottery	-	-	-
Thirds with Bone	75	72	77
Thirds with Small Finds❷	?	?	?
Thirds with Human Bone	?	?	?
Thirds with Articulated/ Associated Bone Groups	25	14	11
Total Number of Bone Frags (Number of Articulated Bone)	43381(718)	2983(249)	3341(250)
Percentage of Indentifiable Frags	68.2%	66.8%	59.9%
Percentage of Loose Teeth	3.4%	3.8%	8.6%
Percentage of Articulated/ Associated Bone	21.2%	24.9%	7.6%
Number of Sheep Frags	948(205)	826(110)	694
Number of Cattle Frags	509(52)	409(60)	633(24)
Number of Horse Frags	228(41)	101(4)	212(24)
Number of Pig Frags	185(115)	353(272)	222(149)
Number of Dog Frags❸	460(333)	227(211)	41(30)
Number of Other Species Frags❸	14(9)	15(6)	17+12(8+12?)

❶ No information on Pottery

❷ No information on the position of human remains and small finds

❸ 12 Dog bones possibly from Fox in upper third

Table 6.7.b. Middle Iron Age Balksbury: Summary data on the characteristics of finds assemblages in lower, middle and upper thirds of pits.

EASTON LANE eMIA Phases 7 & 7/8 unbracketed MIA Phase 8 bracketed {n}	LOWER THIRD	MIDDLE THIRD	UPPER THIRD
Total Number of Thirds	{ }	{ }	{ }
Mean Sherd Weight (g)	11.8±7.2 {23.7±24.6}	9.5±8.7 {12.4±8.5}	13.0±11.4 {10.6±5.6}
Density of Pottery (g/m3)	1795±4331 {230±518}	429±691 {289±771}	697±965 {185±301}
Density of Bone (n/m3)❶	-	-	-
Thirds with Pottery	9 {5}	8 {5}	10 {4}
Thirds with Bone❶	-	-	-
Thirds with Small Finds❷	-	-	-
Thirds with Human Bone	?	?	?
Thirds with Articulated/ Associated Bone Groups	?	?	?
Total Number of Bone Frags❶ (Number of Articulated Bone)	-	-	-
Percentage of Indentifiable Frags	-	-	-
Percentage of Loose Teeth	-	-	-
Percentage of Articulated/ Associated Bone	-	-	-

❶ No data on the number of animal bone frags.

❷ No data on position of small finds

Table 6.7.c. Early/Middle Iron Age Easton Lane: Summary data on the characteristics of finds assemblages in lower, middle and upper thirds of pits.

LITTLE SOMBORNE	LOWER THIRD	MIDDLE THIRD	UPPER THIRD
Total Number of Thirds	28	28	28
Mean Sherd Weight (g)	11.8±12.3	14.9±9.7	11.5±3.4
Density of Pottery (g/m3)	295±289	487±532	910±1313
Density of Bone (n/m3)❶	-	-	-
Thirds with Pottery	14	18	25
Thirds with Bone❶	-	-	-
Thirds with Small Finds	?	?	?
Thirds with Human Bone	?	?	?
Thirds with Articulated/ Associated Bone Groups	?	?	?
Total Number of Bone Frags❶ (Number of Articulated Bone)	-	-	-
Percentage of Indentifiable Frags	-	-	-
Percentage of Loose Teeth	-	-	-
Percentage of Articulated/ Associated Bone	-	-	-
Number of Layers with;			
+ Std Dev. Mean Sherd Weight	2	4	3
+ Std Dev. Weight of Pottery	2	1	6
+ Std Dev. Number of Bone Frags	-	-	-

❶ No data on the number of animal bone frags.

Table 6.7.d. Little Somborne: Summary data on the characteristics of finds assemblages in lower, middle and upper thirds of pits.

MICHELDEVER WOOD	LOWER THIRD	MIDDLE THIRD	UPPER THIRD
Total Number of Thirds	18	18	18
Mean Sherd Weight (g)	14.8±12.3	11.7±8.3	8.7±4.5
Density of Pottery (g/m3)	616±752	316±210	548±637
Density of Bone (n/m3)	97±99	54±37	86±82
Thirds with Pottery	18	16	17
Thirds with Bone	17	16	16
Thirds with Small Finds❶	-	-	-
Thirds with Human Bone❶	-	-	-
Thirds with Articulated/ Associated Bone Groups❷	-	-	-
Total Number of Bone Frags (Number of Articulated Bone)	1156	1203	2650
Percentage of Indentifiable Frags	44.1%	45.9%	45.2%
Percentage of Loose Teeth	4.1%	4.5%	7.5%
Percentage of Articulated/❷ Associated Bone	-	-	-
Number of Layers with;			
+ Std Dev. Mean Sherd Weight	5	2	1
+ Std Dev. Weight of Pottery	3	3	3
+ Std Dev. Number of Bone Frags	4	4	0
Total Number of Sheep Frags❷	292	284	376
Total Number of Cattle Frags	130	158	401
Total Number of Horse Frags	12	19	268
Total Number of Pig Frags	54	80	142
Total Number of Dog Frags	19	7	9
Total Nmber of Other Species Frags	3	3	3

Table 6.7.e. Micheldever Wood: Summary data on the characteristics of finds assemblages in lower, middle and upper thirds of pits.

❶ No position info. for human bones or small finds
❷ The bone report did not consider the existence of articulated/associated bone groups

EIA WINNALL DOWN	LOWER THIRD	MIDDLE THIRD	UPPER THIRD
Total Number of Thirds	16	16	16
Mean Sherd Weight (g)	11.9±8.5	32.5±52.8	9.8±10.9
Density of Pottery (g/m3)	411±753	481±1113	341±623
Density of Bone (n/m3)	89±161	61±112	50±52
Thirds with Pottery	10	7	11
Thirds with Bone	10	9	15
Thirds with Small Finds	3(n18)	5(n7)	6(n20)
Thirds with Human Bone	0	0	3
Thirds with Articulated/ Associated Bone Groups	2	0	0
Total Number of Bone Frags (Number of Articulated Bone)	500 (55)	200	364
Percentage of Indentifiable Frags	56.6%	65.5%	43.1%
Percentage of Loose Teeth	1.0%	5.0%	4.9%
Percentage of Articulated/ Associated Bone	11.0%	0	0
Number of Layers with;			
+ Std Dev. Mean Sherd Weight	5	2	1
+ Std Dev. Weight of Pottery	1	3	1
+ Std Dev. Number of Bone Frags	2	1	1
Total Number of Sheep Frags	163(41)	101	84
Total Number of Cattle Frags	64	15	42
Total Number of Horse Frags	27	8	10
Total Number of Pig Frags	27(14)	6	19
Total Number of Dog Frags	2	1	0
Total Nmber of Other Species Frags	0	0	2

Table 6.7.f. Early Iron Age Winnall: Summary data on the characteristics of finds assemblages in lower, middle and upper thirds of pits.

MIA WINNALL DOWN	LOWER THIRD	MIDDLE THIRD	UPPER THIRD
Total Number of Thirds	75	75	75
Mean Sherd Weight (g)	18.8±14.3	20.1±15.3	12.5±6.7
Density of Pottery (g/m3)	603±1157	652±1322	625±957
Density of Bone (n/m3)	45±79	35±58	52±76
Thirds with Pottery	47	46	60
Thirds with Bone	48	43	51
Thirds with Small Finds	17(n45)	16(n32)	18(n33)
Thirds with Human Bone	3	9	10
Thirds with Articulated/ Associated Bone Groups	9	6	5
Total Number of Bone Frags (Number of Articulated Bone)	1608 (482)	1437(457)	1839(55)
Percentage of Indentifiable Frags	64.4%	78.4%	58.6%
Percentage of Loose Teeth	5.7%	7.9%	10.4%
Percentage of Articulated/ Associated Bone	30%	31.8%	3%
Number of Layers with;			
+ Std Dev. Mean Sherd Weight	13	14	1
+ Std Dev. Weight of Pottery	6	14	6
+ Std Dev. Number of Bone Frags	11	6	7
Total Number of Sheep Frags	363(107)	389(47)	511
Total Number of Cattle Frags	173(27)	182	281
Total Number of Horse Frags	48(4)	238(161)	75
Total Number of Pig Frags	60(8)	181(134)	101
Total Number of Dog Frags	377(326)	131(115)	58(11)
Total Nmber of Other Species Frags	14(10)	6	52(44)

Table 6.7.g. Middle Iron Age Balksbury: Summary data on the characteristics of finds assemblages in lower, middle and upper thirds of pits.

WINKLEBURY	LOWER THIRD	MIDDLE THIRD	UPPER THIRD
Total Number of Thirds	70	70	70
Mean Sherd Weight (g)❶	-	-	-
Density of Pottery (g/m3)	210±656	96±200	624±1662
Density of Bone (n/m3)	61±374	7±19	23±84
Thirds with Pottery	38	40	54
Thirds with Bone	36	30	37
Thirds with Small Finds	6(n17)	4(n7)	9(n12)
Thirds with Human Bone	3	4	3
Thirds with Articulated/ Associated Bone Groups	6	4	2
Total Number of Bone Frags❷ (Number of Articulated Bone)	1464(633+)	436(198)	580(27)
Percentage of Indentifiable Frags	-	-	-
Percentage of Loose Teeth	-	-	-
Percentage of Articulated/ Associated Bone	45%+	44%	4.6%
Number of Layers with;			
+ Std Dev. Mean Sherd Weight	-	-	-
+ Std Dev. Weight of Pottery	4	5	11
+ Std Dev. Number of Bone Frags	8	1	2
Total Number of Sheep Frags❸	676(220+ 200?	72	255(17)
Total Number of Cattle Frags	398(83)	222(103)	238
Total Number of Horse Frags	28	53(8)	23
Total Number of Pig Frags	75(44)	18	36
Total Number of Dog Frags	73(73)	0	2
Total Nmber of Other Species Frags	214(213)	89(87)	26(10)

Table 6.7.h. Winklebury: Summary data on the characteristics of finds assemblages in lower, middle and upper thirds of pits.

❶ No information on sherd number, so unable to calculate Mean Sherd Weight
❷ Only Number of Identified Bone Fragments given in archive. Information on number of Loose Teeth not recorded
❸ Number of Articulated/Associated Sheep Bone Unclear. At least 200 possible 400+

Site	Pit No.	MSW	Pot Density	Bone Density	Pits with ABG's	Pits with Human Rms	Pits with Small Finds
Danebury cp1-3	532	-	-	-	44	31	84
Danebury cp4-5	142	-	-	-	24	9	42
Danebury cp6	100	-	-	-	21	13	44
Danebury cp7-8	159	-	-	-	57	31	116
Easton Lane	29	12.5±9.0	578±1186	-	5	2	13
Gussage EIA	128	-	-	-	-	1	60
Gussage MIA	69	-	-	-	-	6	40
Gussage LIA	184	-	-	-	-	26	87
Little Somborne	27	14.3±9.4	553±710	-	5	3	7
Old Down Farm 2	3	16.6	1025	216.25	2	1	2
Old Down F. 3 ❶	35	9.0±2.89	778±655	63.2±84.4	7	1	5
Old Down F. 4 ❷	18	15.1±13.4	1170±1210	64.2±83.1	3	2	5
Old Down F. 5 ❸	44	16.7±14.8	1050±977	72.0±138	11	6	17
Micheldever W.	29	12.2±10.6	638±721	65.4±49.7	-	7	16
Winklebury	70	-	476±757	24.2±40.1	11	9	15
Winnall EIA	23	11.3±8.1	1017±2359	64.5±116.6	2	3	10
Winnall MIA	85	14.8±9.0	592±997	42.6±49.4	17	16	30

❶　Information for pottery only available for 12 pits,
❷　Information for pottery only available for 11 pits,
❸　Information for pottery only available for 15 pits,

Table. 7.1 The Overall Contents of Pits: Summary Data

	SHEEP	CATTLE	PIG	HORSE	DOG	WILD
BALKSBURY EIA						
Number Bone Frags	399	230	44	99	31	8
% of Total Identified Bone Frags	49.2%	28.4%	5.4%	12.2%	3.8%	1%
Number of Bone Frags from ABG's	109	15	4	44	2	8
% of Total Bone Frags from all ABG's in phase	59.9%	8.2%	2.2%	24.2%	1.1%	4.3%
% of Bone Frags from each species represented by ABG's	27.3%	6.5%	9.1%	44.4%	6.4%	100%
No. of ABG deposits for each species	7	2	1	10	1	2
% of Total no. of ABG's	30%	8.7%	4.3%	43.5%	4.3%	8.7%
BALKSBURY MIA						
Number Bone Frags	2468	1551	760	351	728	46
% of Total Identified Bone Frags	41.8%	26.3%	12.9%	5.9%	12.3%	0.8%
Number of Bone Frags from ABG's	315	136	536	69	574	23
% of Total Bone Frags from all ABG's in phase	19%	8.2%	32.4%	4.2%	34.8%	1.4%
% of Bone Frags from each species represented by ABG's	12.8%	8.8%	70.5%	19.7%	78.8%	50%
No. of ABG deposits for each species	24	11	21	11	23	4
% of Total no. of ABG's	25.5%	11.7%	22.3%	11.7%	24.5%	4%

Table. 7.2.a **Balksbury**: Summary Data of the total identified bone fragments and total bone fragments from Articulated/Associated Bone Groups for different species.

	SHEEP	CATTLE	PIG	HORSE	DOG	WILD
WINKLEBURY						
Number Bone Frags	1003	858	129	104	75	329
% of Total Identified Bone Frags	40.2%	43.4%	5.2%	4.2%	3%	13.2%
Number of Bone Frags from ABG's	437+	86	44	8	73	310
% of Total Bone Frags from all ABG's in phase	45.6%+	9.0+	4.6%	0.8%	7.6%	32.4%
% of Bone Frags from each species represented by ABG's	43.6%+	10%	34%	&.6%	97.3%	94.2%
No. of ABG deposits for each species	4+	4	2	4	1	17+
% of Total no. of ABG's	12.5%	12.5%	6.25%	12.5%	3.125%	53.125%
WINNALL DOWN MIA						
Number Bone Frags	1148	586	413	348	555	72
% of Total Identified Bone Frags	37%	18.9%	13.3%	11.2%	17.2%	2.3%
Number of Bone Frags from ABG's	106	21	194	155	395	54
% of Total Bone Frags from all ABG's in phase	11.5%	2.3%	21%	16.8%	42.8%	5.8%
% of Bone Frags from each species represented by ABG's	9.2%	3.6%	47%	16.8%	71.2%	75%
No. of ABG deposits for each species	8	3	2	8	12+	3
% of Total no. of ABG's	22.2%	8.3%	5.6%	22.2%	33.3%	8.3%

Table. 7.2.b **Middle Iron Age Winklebury and Winnall** Summary Data of the total identified bone fragments and total bone fragments from Articulated/Associated Bone Groups for different species.

	SHEEP	CATTLE	PIG	HORSE	DOG	WILD
DANEBURY cp1-3						
Number Bone Frags	6053	2534	1648	128	129	400
% of Total Identified Bone Frags	56%	23%	15%	1%	1%	3%
No. of ABG deposits for each species	14	10	14	15	1	(5bird) (2animal)
% of Total no. of ABG's	25.9%	18.5%	25.9%	27.8%	1.8%	
DANEBURY cp4-5						
Number Bone Frags	3485	980	1136	142	261	132
% of Total Identified Bone Frags	57%	16%	19%	2%	4%	2%
No. of ABG deposits for each species	3	4	17	11	5	(2bird)
% of Total no. of ABG's	7.5%	10%	42.5%	22.5%	12.5%	
DANEBURY cp6						
Number Bone Frags	14206	4241	1444	367	703	160
% of Total Identified Bone Frags	67%	20%	7%	2%	3%	1%
No. of ABG deposits for each species	5	3	10	6	5	(2bird) (1animal)
% of Total no. of ABG's	14.3%	10.7%	35.7%	21.4%	17.8%	
DANEBURY c7-8						
Number Bone Frags	27186	8782	5031	1254	1343	207
% of Total Identified Bone Frags	61%	20%	11%	3%	3%	1%
No. of ABG deposits for each species	15	20	40	18	7	(6bird) (1animal)
% of Total no. of ABG's	15%	20%	40%	18%	7%	

Table. 7.2.c **Danebury**: Summary Data of the total identified bone fragments and total bone fragments from Articulated/Associated Bone Groups for different species.

	Cattle				Horse				Sheep				Pig				Dog			
	A	B	C	D	A	B	C	D	A	B	C	D	A	B	C	D	A	B	C	D
Balksbury EIA			1			1	9		3	1	3				1				1	
Balksbury MIA	1	2	5	3		1	8	2	6	4	10	4	12	1	8	2	14		9	
Danebury cp1-3	7	8	3			9	1		4	7			3	12				1		
Danebury cp4-5	1	2			2	1	1		4	9	4		9	2			3	2		
Danebury cp6	2	2	1		1		2		2	7	1		3	3			4	1		
Danebury cp7-8	1	14			1	12	7		10	29	2		13	14			4	3		
Old Down Farm	1	1	1	1		3	4		17+			3					8	1	3	
Poundbury	1	1	1			3			9											
Winklebury	1			3		4			3+	1		1					1			
Winnall EIA									6+	2	1		1	1						
Winnall MIA		2			1	1	4	2	1	2	2	4	1			1	7+	1	2	2

Table. 7.3. The numbers of different types of *ABG's* for each species from six sites.

	Human	Cattle	Horse	Sheep	Pig	Dog
No. of Pits	31	11	14	36	14	6
No. of pits also with Small Finds	18	9	13	30	13	6
Quern Frags	–	(√)	√	–	–	–
Worked Stone	–	√	√	–	–	–
Clay	√	–	√	–	√	–
Worked Antler	√	–	–	–	–	√
Worked Bone	√	–	(√)	–	–	–
Iron	√	–	–	–	–	–
Bronze	–	–	√	–	√	–
Loom Weights	–	–	–	–	√	√
Spindle Whorls	√	–	√	–	–	√
Human Remains		4	6	9	5	3
		e.2.15	e.2.73	e.7.02	e2.73	e.1.17
Type (not Frags)		A,C,	A,A,C,C,	B,D,	B,C,	C

Table. 7.4. **Danebury**: The statistically significant associations between the presence of *ABG's* and different types of Small Finds and Human Remains in cp7-8.

√ = Chi Square probabilities >0.05   (√) = Chi Square probablities 0.1-0.05

No. of Small Finds per Pit	Cp1-3			Cp4-5			Cp6			Cp7-8		
	No. of Pits	Pits with ABG's	Pits with Human Bone	No. of Pits	Pits with ABG's	Pits with Human Bone	No. of Pits	Pits with ABG's	Pits with Human Bone	No. of Pits	Pits with ABG's	Pits with Human Bone
1	57	11	5	27	0	3	29	3	7	35	11	6
2	14	3	3	7	0	1	6	1	2	25	7	4
3	3	0	1	3	0	0	4	1	2	11	3	3
4	2	0	0	1	0	0	1	0	0	14	6	6
5	3	1	1	-	-	-	3	1	1	9	5	5
6	3	2	1	1	0	1	-	-	-	5	1	1
7	1	0	0	1	0	0	-	-	-	3	1	1
8	-	-	-	1	0	0	1	1	0	-	-	-
9	-	-	-	1	0	1	-	-	-	3	3	2
10	-	-	-	-	-	-	-	-	-	-	-	-
11	-	-	-	-	-	-	-	-	-	4	3	2
12	-	-	-	-	-	-	-	-	-	-	-	-
13	1	1	0	-	-	-	-	-	-	-	-	-
14	-	-	-	-	-	-	-	-	-	1	1	1
15	-	-	-	-	-	-	-	-	-	1	0	0
16	-	-	-	-	-	-	-	-	-	2	2	1
17	-	-	-	-	-	-	-	-	-	-	-	-
18	-	-	-	-	-	-	-	-	-	-	-	-
19	-	-	-	-	-	-	-	-	-	1	1	1
20	-	-	-	-	-	-	-	-	-	-	-	-
21	-	-	-	-	-	-	-	-	-	-	-	-
22	-	-	-	-	-	-	-	-	-	-	-	-
23	-	-	-	-	-	-	-	-	-	-	-	-
24	-	-	-	-	-	-	-	-	-	-	-	-
25	-	-	-	-	-	-	-	-	-	1	1	1
26	-	-	-	-	-	-	-	-	-	-	-	-
27	-	-	-	-	-	-	-	-	-	1	1	0

Table. 7.5. **Danebury**: The number of Small Finds recovered from pits compared with the presence of *ABG's* and Human Remains.

Small Finds	Loom Weights	Spindle Whorls	Iron Objects	Querns	Bronze Objects	Bone & Antler Objects	Other Finds
	n17	n3	n7	n18	n3	n8	n4
Mean Sherd Weight	18.9±11.0	18.2±19.5	17.2±10.5	17.6±10.4	31.6±6.5	12.2±4.7	32.8±5.7
Pottery Density	649±936	401±327	862±1047	774±914	2007±1818	398±290	2642±1626
Bone Density	54.2±39.8	48.2±46.9	48.2±42.1	63.3±69.5	61.3±58.1	65.1±36.9	116.1±25.7
Pits with Human Rms	4	1	4	8	3	3	2
Pits with ABG's	4	2	4	8	2	0	2
Pits with							
Sheep bone	16	3	11	16	3	6	3
Cattle bone	16	3	10	18	3	4	3
Pig bone	13	2	10	16	3	3	3
Horse bone	10	3	8	15	3	3	3
Dog bone	11	2	9	8	2	2	3
Wild species bone	8	3	6	6	3	4	2
	3bird	1hare	2bird	3bird	2bird	2bird	2bird
	1hare		1hare	1hare	1hare		

ABG's Species	Sheep	Cattle	Pig	Horse	Dog	Bird	Hare
	n7	n3	n2	n6	n8	n2	n1
Mean Sherd Weight	11.9±5.1	11.7±1.0	32.8±8.0	10.2±3.9	16.7±12.3	19.7±10.4	3.5
Pottery Density	239±268	259±276	1918±1462	170±195	960±1312	1703±1766	118
Bone Density	47.1±37.2	64.8±51.4	130.9±40.4	52.3±38.1	125.2±66.2	116.4±21.6	86.1

ABG's Type	Complete/Partial Carcasses	Skulls	Articulated Limbs	Articulated Vertebrae
	n6	n5	n8	n9
Mean Sherd Weight	15.6±11.9	10.1±4.0	10.9±5.3	14.6±10.2
Pottery Density	523±421	252±197	288±245	1008±1471
Bone Density	135.6±74.8	55.4±42.1	60.7±40.3	82.7±36.3

Table. 7.6.a **Middle Iron Age Winnall:** Summary statistics showing differences in *MSW*, Density of Pottery, Density of Bone and the presence of bone from different species in pits with different types of Small Finds and *ABG's*.

Human Remains	Fragments	Artic. Limb	Partial Adult Skeleton	Complete Adult Skeleton	Infant Burials	All Human Bone
	n15	n2	n1	n5	n4	n.16
Mean Sherd Weight	16.5±9.8	11.5±0.1	40.3	14.0±8.0	15.9±11.5	15.6±9.5
Pottery Density	845±1198	409±507	718	866±1214	1183±1946	796±1129
Bone Density	62.5±43.9	153±187.3	14.4	62.4±58.7	58.0±41.8	74.1±70.3
Percentage of Decorated Pottery	4.5±11.4	2.5±3.5	0	11.3±17.7	0.5±1.0	4.4±10.6
Pits with Small Finds	9	1	1	2	1	9
Pits with ABG's	5	1	0	2	2	10
Pits with						
Sheep bone	14	2	1	4	4	16
Cattle bone	13	2	1	4	4	15
Pig bone	13	2	1	4	4	14
Horse bone	13	2	1	2	3	13
Dog bone	6	1	0	3	3	9
Wild species bone	6	0	1	2	2	6
	5bird	-	hare	2bird	2bird	5bird 1hare

Table. 7.6.b **Middle Iron Age Winnall:** Summary statistics showing differences in *MSW*, Density of Pottery, Density of Bone and the presence of bone from different species in pits with different types of Human Remains.

MIA Winnall Down	Straight Sided Cylindrical	Straight Sided Sub-rectangular	Beehive	Other
No. of Pits	3	27	45	10
Mean Volume (m3)	3.6	1.4	2.5	0.6
Mean Depth (m)	1.8	1.5	1.5	1.1
MSW (g)	8.6±7.3	13.6±8.2	15.9±9.7	14.9±8.5
Pot Density (g/m3)	304±520	410±579	572±966	1264±1750
Bone Density (n./m3)	68.2±61.2	28.9±35.9	51.1±54.4	33.1±49.8
Pits with Small Finds	1	4	25	1
Pits with ABG's	1	2	13	1
Pits with Human Remains	1	3	12	0
Type of Human Remains	Adult Inhum. Frag	Infant Inhum. 3xFrags	5xAdult Inhum. 3x Infant Inhum. 11xFrags	
Pits with Saucepan Pots	0	9	20	0
Pits with Jars	1	2	16	2
Pits with both	0	2	2	0

Winklebury	Straight Sided	Beehive	Other	Conical Clay Pits
No. of Pits	19	25	13	5
Mean Volume (m3)	4.9	4.7	0.7	0.3
Mean Depth (m)	1.5	1.4	0.4	0.5
Pot Density (g/m3)	221±233	602±878	1673±3683	1102±1117
Bone Density (n/m3)	21.8±26.8	28.3±48.2	30.9±82.9	15±30
Pits with Small Finds	5	9	1	0
Pits with ABG's	4	4	2	0
Pits with Human Remains	0	9	0	0
Pits with Saucepan Pots	5	11	1	1
Pits with Jars	6	9	1	0

Table. 7.7 Winklebury and Winnall: The characteristics of finds recovered from different shaped pits.

Winnall Down MIA	Pits with Decorated Pottery	Pits without Decorated Pottery
Number of Pits	16 (18.8%)	69 (80.2%)
Excavated Volume m3	33.4 (30.8%)	75 (69.2%)
Total Pottery gms	21,807	33,439
Density of Pottery g/m3	653	446
Total Bone Frgs	2,135	3,011
Density of Bone n/m3	63.9	40.1
No. of Sheep Bone	548	680
No. of Cattle Bone	258	348
No. of Pig Bone	263	161
No. of Horse Bone	57	296
No. of Dog Bone	339	199
No. of Other Bone	9	64
No. of Pits with Small Finds	14	21
Total no. of Small Finds	37	59
Average Small Finds per Pit	2.31	0.86
No. of Pits with Human Remains	6 (4 Adult Inhumations)	10 (3 Infant 2 Adult Inhumations)
No. of Pits with ABG's	6	11
No. of Jars	38	29
No. of Saucepans	33	61

Winklebury MIA	Pits with Decorated Pottery	Pits without Decorated Pottery
Number of Pits	13 (17.7%)	53 (80.3%)
Excavated Volume m3	30.3 (27.4%)	80.3 (72.6%)
Total Pottery gms	11,930	11,856
Density of Pottery g/m3	394	224
Total Bone Frgs	777	1,197
Density of Bone n/m3	25.6	14.9
No. of Sheep Bone	304	264
No. of Cattle Bone	210	626
No. of Pig Bone	32	49
No. of Horse Bone	44	41
No. of Dog Bone	0	75
No. of Other Bone	198	131
No. of Pits with Small Finds	7	7
Total no. of Small Finds	20	15
Average Small Finds per Pit	1.54	0.28
No. of Pits with Human Remains	6 (3 skeletons 2 skulls)	3 (1 skeleton)
No. of Pits with ABG's	3	7
No. of Jars	12	17
No. of Saucepans	16	13

Table. 7.8 **Winklebury and Winnall:** The characteristics of finds recovered from pits with and without decorated pottery.

Winnall Down MIA

	Pits with Human Remains &/or ABG's	Pits without Human Remains &/or ABG's
Number of Pits	26 (30.6%)	59 (69.4%)
Excavated Volume m3	59.8 (55.1%)	48.8 (44.9%)
Total Pottery gms	35,032	20,214
Density of Pottery g/m3	586	414
Total Bone Frgs	3,725	1,421
Density of Bone n/m3	62.3	29.1
No. of Sheep Bone	876	352
No. of Cattle Bone	478	128
No. of Pig Bone	332	92
No. of Horse Bone	314	39
No. of Dog Bone	511	27
No. of Other Bone	64	6
No. of Pits with Small Finds	20	17
Total no. of Small Finds	54	46
Average Small Finds per Pit	2.08	0.78
No. of Pits with Decorated Pot	9	7
No. of Pits with Burnished Pot	20	25
No. of Jars	55	12
No. of Saucepans	72	22

Winklebury MIA

	Pits with Human Remains &/or ABG's	Pits without Human Remains &/or ABG's
Number of Pits	16 (24.2%)	50 (75.8%)
Excavated Volume m3	51.1 (46.2%)	59.5 (53.8%)
Total Pottery gms	10,198	13,588
Density of Pottery g/m3	200	228
Total Bone Frgs	1,321	652
Density of Bone n/m3	25.8	10.9
No. of Sheep Bone	341	227
No. of Cattle Bone	482	354
No. of Pig Bone	74	35
No. of Horse Bone	61	24
No. of Dog Bone	74	1
No. of Other Bone	327	2
No. of Pits with Small Finds	8	6
Total no. of Small Finds	23	12
Average Small Finds per Pit	1.44	0.24
No. of Pits with Decorated Pot	7	6
No. of Jars	12	17
No. of Saucepans	17	12

Table. 7.9 **Winklebury and Winnall:** The characteristics of finds recovered from pits with or without Human Remains and/or *ABG's.*

Danebury cp1-3

Iron & Worked Bone	χ2 prob .0022
Bone & Bronze	χ2 prob .0018
Bone & Amber/Coral/Glass	χ2 prob .0001
Bone & Worked Stone	χ2 prob .0001
Worked Stone & Amber/Coral/Glass	χ2 prob .0001
Worked Stone & Clay	χ2 prob .0001

Danebury cp4-5

Querns & Clay	χ2 prob .0374
Querns & Worked Stone	χ2 prob .0003
Worked Bone & Worked Stone	χ2 prob .0218

Danebury cp6

Querns & Loom Weights	χ2 prob .0072
Querns & Clay Objects	χ2 prob .0026
Bronze & Worked Stone	χ2 prob .0007
Bronze & Loom Weights	χ2 prob .0032

Danebury cp7-8

Querns & Worked Stone	χ2 prob .0105
Iron & Querns	χ2 prob .0205
Iron & Worked Stone	χ2 prob .0023
Iron & Clay	χ2 prob .0008
Iron & Bronze	χ2 prob .0082
Iron & Worked Bone	χ2 prob .0162
Iron & Worked Antler	χ2 prob .0034
Worked Bone & Bronze	χ2 prob .0027
Worked Bone & Worked Antler	χ2 prob .0084
Worked Antler & Clay	χ2 prob .0026
Clay & Worked Stone	χ2 prob .0364

EIA Gussage

Querns & Spindlewhorls	χ2 prob .0003
Querns & Glass	χ2 prob .0041
Querns & Worked Bone	χ2 prob .0001
Querns & Worked Bone/Antler	χ2 prob .0005
Querns & Iron	χ2 prob .0001
Iron & Shale	χ2 prob .0001
Iron & Glass	χ2 prob .0001
Iron & Worked Bone	χ2 prob .0024
Worked Bone & Glass	χ2 prob .0201
Worked Bone/Antler & Bronze	χ2 prob .0001
Bronze Objects & Shale	χ2 prob .0014
Shale Objects & Glass	χ2 prob .0038

MIA Gussage

Querns & Worked Bone/Antler	χ2 prob .0110
Iron & Worked Bone/Antler	χ2 prob .0512
Worked Bone/Antler & Worked Stone	χ2 prob .0310
Loom Weights & Spindlewhorls	χ2 prob .0027

LIA Gussage

Querns & Spindlewhorls	χ2 prob .0067
Querns & Iron	χ2 prob .0011
Iron & Spindlewhorls	χ2 prob .0509
Worked Bone & Spindlewhorls	χ2 prob .0001
Worked Bone & Worked Stone	χ2 prob .0016
Worked Bone & Loom Weights	χ2 prob .0466
Imported Pottery & Iron	χ2 prob .0002
Imported Pottery & Bronze	χ2 prob .0267

MIA Winnall Down

Querns & Loom Weights	χ2 prob .0012
Iron & Querns	χ2 prob .0003
Iron & Spindlewhorls	χ2 prob .0045
Iron & Loom Weights	χ2 prob .0001
Loom Weights & Spindlewhorls	χ2 prob .0433

Table. 7.10 **Danebury, Gussage and Winnall: The Chi Square probability scores for the statistically significant correlations between the presence of different types of Small Finds.**

	Decorated Sherds	Burnished Sherds
Cattle bone	-	(χ2 prob .0031)
Horse bone	-	(χ2 prob .0226)
Sheep bone	- (χ2 prob .0104)[1]	-
Pig bone	- (χ2 prob .0227)[1]	-
Dog bone	- (χ2 prob .0116)[1]	(χ2 prob .0254)
Bird bone	-	(χ2 prob .0087)
+Std Dev Densities of pot	(χ2 prob .0353)	-
+Std Dev Densities of bone	(χ2 prob .0353)	-
ABG's	-	-
Small Finds	-	(χ2 prob .0003)
Human Remains	(χ2 prob .0547) (χ2 prob .0450)[2]	(χ2 prob .0016)

1= +std dev density of that species bone

2= +std dev % of dec pot

Table. 7.11 **Winnall Down:** The Chi Square probability scores for the statistically significant correlations between the presence of decorated or burnished pottery and other finds in the same pits.

Total Layers 530 164 Layers Unassigned	Inner n193 52.7%	Outer n173 47.3%
Layers with Finds	63	38
Layers with Pottery	41	29
Layers with Bone	37	38
Layers with Fineware	15	12
Layers withHuman Bone	6	6
Layers with Small Finds	9	2
Layers with Cattle Bone	33	18
Layers with Horse Bone	13	6
Layers with Sheep Bone	17	9
Layers with Pig Bone	10	2
Layers with Dog Bone	2	1
Mean Sherd Weight	9.5±6.8	14.9±17.3

Table 8.1. Early Iron Age Winnall Down: Differences in the distribution of finds between ditch fills originating inside and outside the enclosure.

No. of Species	1 n48	2 n25	3 n13	4 n8	5 n2
Sheep	7	14	11	8	2
Cattle	37	24	11	8	2
Pig	0	8	8	8	2
Horse	0	8	8	7	2
Dog	1	0	0	1	2

Table 8.2. Early Iron Age Winnall Down: The number of different species recovered from each layer in the enclosure ditch fills, and the distribution of different species across those layers.

	Upper	Middle	Lower
Thirds with Pottery	23	17	12
Thirds with Bone	24	20	12
Thirds with Fineware	14	12	5
Thirds with Human Bone	8	4	4
Thirds with Small Finds	9	3	2
Thirds with +Std D. MSW	1	1	2
Thirds with +Std D. Fineware MSW	1	2	2
Thirds with +Std D. Pot Density	5	4	1
Thirds with +Std D. % Fineware	2	5	4
Thirds with +Std D. Fineware Density	0	1	2
Thirds with +Std D. Cattle Density	2	4	2
Thirds with +Std D. Horse Density	1	3	1
Thirds with +Std D. Sheep Density	6	1	3
Thirds with +Std D. Pig Density	7	3	3
MSW	10.3±10.5	11.0±6.1	13.8±11.5
Fineware MSW	9.5±6.0	13.3±10.2	17.9±14.9
Pot Density	94±100	67±105	51±98
Bone Density	15.6±16.0	9.5±12.1	6.6±12.1

Table 8.3. Early Iron Age Winnall Down: The characteristics of finds assemblages from the lower, middle and upper thirds of the fills of the enclosure ditch.

South (A)

	Pot No/Wt	MSW	Pot Dens.	% Fineware	Bone No.	Bone Dens.	Cattle	Horse	Sheep	Human Bone	Small Finds
Upper	5/65g	13g	28.7g	0%	41	18.1	5	-	7	Yes	-
Middle	4/56g	14g	37.1g	86%	31	20.5	19	3	5	Yes	-
Lower	2/22g	11g	33.9g	100%	23	35.4	11	7	-	Yes	3Sw 1Lw (Horse Skull)

North (B)

	Pot No/Wt	MSW	Pot Dens.	% Fineware	Bone No.	Bone Dens.	Cattle	Horse	Sheep	Human Bone	Small Finds
Upper	9/156g	17g	61.9g	48%	23	9.1	10	-	5	-	1Lw
Middle	1/14g	14g	7.9g	100%	2	1.1	2	-	-	-	-
Lower	5/203g	41g	134.4g	100%	5	3.3	4	-	1	Yes	-

Table8.4. Early Iron Age Winnall Down: Differences in the deposits made in the southern and northern ditch terminals at the entrance to the enclosure.